JOANNE H. LIM

CHINA

AND THE

WORLD TRADE ORGANIZATION

A LEGAL PERSPECTIVE

CHINA

AND THE

WORLD TRADE ORGANIZATION

A LEGAL PERSPECTIVE

Kong Qingjiang

National University of Singapore

World Scientific
New Jersey • London • Singapore • Hong Kong

Published by

World Scientific Publishing Co. Pte. Ltd.

P O Box 128, Farrer Road, Singapore 912805

USA office: Suite 1B, 1060 Main Street, River Edge, NJ 07661

UK office: 57 Shelton Street, Covent Garden, London WC2H 9HE

British Library Cataloguing-in-Publication Data
A catalogue record for this book is available from the British Library.

ISBN 981-238-039-6

Printed in Singapore by World Scientific Printers (S) Pte Ltd

Foreword

After 15 years' negotiation to "resume the status of contracting party in the GATT" and then "join the WTO," "dark hair has turned to be gray." This long-haul process was finalized on 11 November 2001 in Dora, Qatar, as the Ministerial Conference ratified the Protocol of Accession that set forth the terms for China's accession to the WTO. As a result, China became the 143rd Member of the world trading body on 11 December 2001. The accession to the WTO was a watershed for China comparable to the allying with the United Sates in 1972 and the subsequent establishment of Sino-US diplomatic relations in 1979. It evidenced strong commitment by China's leaders to integrate China into the global rules-based trading system.

However, as Long Yongtu, China's chief negotiator for the WTO accession, pointed out, this development marked "only the end of a beginning," and signified the beginning of sweeping reforms in China. The Chinese government expects the WTO accession to lend support to advance China's reform and development, improve the quality and reduce the cost of goods and services, spur investment and the creation of new jobs, and promote the rule of law.

Foreign companies aspire to reap benefits from China's accession to the WTO, which they had most keenly anticipated over the past two decades and which they expect would foster a more transparent and predictable business environment and dramatically expand market access for foreign goods, services. For the existing WTO Members, however, not only are they concerned about whether their companies would reap real benefits from China's WTO membership, but, at the very least, they would also want to avoid the worst possible scenario from that membership: weakening the framework of what, by many accounts, has been the most successful of international organisations. The WTO operates on the basis of consensus among its Members, and in theory one Member could disrupt the consensus decision-making process.

Also, tempering this positive outlook is that the substantial structural changes, which Chinese institutions must undergo to meet WTO standards, is not easy to implement, despite the government's strong commitment to take the difficult steps necessary to further reform China's economic and legal systems. Given the breadth and depth of the commitments made by China during the negotiation process, full compliance will not be easy and cannot be achieved overnight. Over the course of relatively brief transition periods (i.e., zero to six years, depending on the specific issue), thousands of obsolete laws and regulations at the national and local levels must be amended to become WTO-consistent, and many new laws and regulations must be promulgated to support the development of various industries previously closed to foreign participation. In addition, millions of officials, legislators, and judges—trained over the past 50 years to manage a closed, centrally-planned economy dominated by state-owned enterprises—must be "re-tooled" to regulate a market economy open to foreign participation and committed to the principles of transparency and nondiscrimination against foreign goods and services. All of this must be accomplished in the face of strong opposition from powerful interest groups in the old system.

In this context, foreseeable is that many WTO-compliance issues will arise in China during the next few years, and that much hard work on all sides will be required to resolve them. WTO Members have a vested interest—at various levels—in China's successful integration into the global rules-based trading system. Moreover, they are uniquely positioned to identify gaps between China's obligations and performance, to suggest priorities when deciding which problems to tackle first, and to recommend constructive solutions. It is believed that foreign efforts will generally be most fruitful if foreign countries lend assistance and cooperate with the Chinese government to find solutions to problems, rather than simply point fingers when compliance falls short of expectations.

Bearing these in mind, the author examines and evaluates, from the legal perspective, China's accession process, its commitments relating to the accession, the implications of such commitments on its trade and legal system, its efforts towards WTO compliance, and finally attempts to examine the issue of the capacity of evolving Chinese legal system to ensure the WTO compliance. The book particularly probes into the trade and legal systems at the turn of the WTO accession. Due to the time limitation, the author finds it impossible to cover all the legal issues relating to the accession of China to the WTO. Therefore, the book is intended only to provide the author's evaluations of some selected trade and legal issues, including intellectual property, foreign investment law, government procurement, Internet regulation, judicial system and the settlement of trade disputes.

It should be pointed out that some of the chapters in this book are based on the author's published articles in law journals or China studies journals. The author wishes to acknowledge the kind permissions from the following publishers for the corresponding articles:

Oxford University Press (Journal of International Economic Law): China's WTO Accession: Commitments and Implications,
Kluwer Law International (Journal of World Trade): Enforcement of WTO Agreements: Reality or Illusion?
Institute of International Relations (Issues & Studies): Old Bottle for New Wine: Copyright Legislation in the Digital Context; China's Telecom Regulatory Regime on the Eve of WTO Accession
Werner Publishing Company Ltd. (Journal of World Intellectual Property): Judicial Enforcement of Intellectual Property Rights on the Eve of WTO Accession

The author also wishes to thank Professor K.K. Phua, Dr. Zheng Yongnian, Mr. David Loo King Boon, Ms. Janet Cooper and Mr. Lye Liang Fook for their kind efforts in the publication of this book. Lastly, he wishes to thank the Hangzhou University of Commerce and the East Asian Institute, National University of Singapore for the necessary support, without which the book would not have been completed.

February 2002, Singapore

Contents

Foreword   v
Abbreviations   xi

Part I   China and the WTO Law
Chapter 1   China's WTO Accession: History, Concerns and
             Issues   3
Chapter 2   China's WTO Accession: Commitments and
             Implications   27
Chapter 3   Preparing China's Trade and Legal Systems for
             WTO Compliance   61

Part II   China and the WTO Dispute Settlement Mechanism
Chapter 4   Is China's Judiciary Ready for WTO Entry?   97
Chapter 5   Can The WTO Dispute Settlement Mechanism
             Resolve Trade Disputes Between China And
             Taiwan?   117
Chapter 6   Will China Behave in the WTO Dispute Settlement
             Mechanism?   132

Part III   Towards WTO Compliance: China's Trade Regime
Chapter 7   New Dimension Of China's Foreign Investment
             Regime On the Eve Of WTO Accession   157

Chapter 8   Chinese Law and Practice On Government
              Procurement In the Context Of WTO Accession   183
Chapter 9   China's Online Copyright Protection On the Eve
              Of WTO Accession   207
Chapter 10   China's Telecom Regulatory Regime On the Eve
              Of WTO Accession   230
Chapter 11   Where Will China's Internet Regulation Go
              After WTO Accession?   251
Chapter 12   Judicial Protection of Intellectual Property Rights
              in China: On the Eve Of WTO Accession   269

Part IV   Conclusion

Chapter 13   Enforcement of WTO Agreements in China:
              Reality or Illusion?   295
Appendix   China's WTO Accession: Chronicles   344

Index   347

Abbreviations

Treaties and international agreements

Accession Protocol	Protocol on the Accession of the People's Republic of China
ABTS	Agreement on Basic Telecommunications Services
AGP	Agreement on Government Procurement
DSU	Understanding on Rules and Procedures Governing the Settlement of Disputes
GATT	General Agreement on Tariffs and Trade
MOU	Memorandum of Understanding
TRIMS	Agreement on Trade-related Aspects of Investment Measures
TRIPS	Agreement on Trade-related Aspects of Intellectual Property Rights
WCT	WIPO Copyright Treaty
WPPT	WIPO Performances and Phonograms Treaty
WTO	World Trade Organization

Terms

BOPs	Balance-of-payment measures
CJV	Contractual joint venture
EJV	Equity joint venture

FDI   Foreign direct investment
FIE   Foreign-invested enterprise
forex   Foreign exchange
IPRs   Intellectual property rights
ISP   Internet Service Providers
MFN   Most-favoured-nation treatment
SEZs   Special Economic Zones
SOE   State-owned enterprise
SPS   Sanitary and phytosanitary measures
WFIE   Wholly Foreign-invested Enterprise

Institutions

AB   Appellate Body
APEC   Asia-Pacific Economic Co-operation
AQSIQ   State General Administration for Quality
                Supervision and Inspection and Quarantine
CIQ-SA   China State Administration for Entry-Exit
                Inspection and Quarantine
CSBTS   China State Bureau of Technical Supervision
DSB   Dispute Settlement Body
GCAC   General Customs Administration of China
IMF   International Monetary Fund
MII   Ministry of Information Industry
MOF   Ministry of Finance
MOFTEC   Ministry of Foreign Trade and Economic
                Cooperation
MPC   Ministry of Public Security
NCAC   National Copyright Administration of China
NPC   National People's Congress
NPC   Standing Committee Standing Committee of the
                National People's Congress
SAIC   State Administration of Industry and Commerce

SDPC	State Development and Planning Commission
SERC	State Economic Restructuring Commission
SETC	State Economic and Trade Commission
SIPO	State Intellectual Property Office
SPC	Supreme People's Court
WIPO	World Intellectual Property Organization

Chinese Laws and Regulations

APL	Administrative Procedure Law
CJV	Chinese-foreign Contractual Joint Venture
CJV Law	Chinese-foreign Contractual Joint Venture Law
CPL	Civil Procedure Law
EJV	Chinese-foreign Equity Joint Venture
EJV Law	Chinese-foreign Equity Joint Venture Law
EJV	Regulations Implementing Regulations of the Chinese-foreign Equity Joint Venture Law
GPCL	General Principles of Civil Law
GPL	Government Procurement Law
WFIE Law	Wholly Foreign-invested Enterprise Law
WFIE Rules	Detailed Rules for the Implementation of the Wholly Foreign-invested Enterprise Law

Part I
China and the WTO Law

1

China's WTO Accession: History, Concerns and Issues

1. Introduction

In 1899, John Hay, United States Secretary of State announced the Open Door policy for the Imperial China.[1] The old Open Door policy set a pattern for China and the West in dealing with each other in the 20th century. However, when the People's Republic of China (PRC) was founded in 1949, the old Open Door policy that had been forced upon China by the West experienced a backlash, inaugurating an era of self-isolation and poverty. When the orthodox communism that prevailed in the three decades following the establishment of the new China failed, the realist-minded Chinese leadership with Deng Xiaoping as its core, felt the pressure to re-introduce the Open Door policy.[2] The new Open Door policy was not just a repetition of the old one. It differed from the old one in that this time the Chinese government was no longer forced by western powers to open its doors, but by its anxiety for prosperity. The new Open Door policy set the tone for the past twenty years. China's decision to join the General Agreement on Tariffs and Trade (GATT), and later the World Trade Organization (WTO), was a result of this policy.[3]

More than a hundred years after its adoption, China's Open Door policy is now bearing fruit: at the end of 2001, the first year of the twenty-first century, China formerly became a member of the world trading community.

2. Road Towards a WTO Membership

2.1. China and the GATT

Joining the WTO is a historical event for China. However, China was one of the original Signatories of the GATT, predecessor of the WTO. On 10 April 1947, the Nationalist Government of the then Republic of China attended the Preparatory Meeting of International Trade and Employment Conference in Geneva, Switzerland, which was sponsored by the United Nations Economic and Social Council. As a result of the Conference, the General Agreement on Tariffs and Trade was formulated. On 21 April, the Chinese Representative signed the Protocol on Provisional Application of the General Agreement on Tariffs and Trade. The then Nationalist Government participated in GATT's first two rounds of negotiation.[4]

On 1 October 1949, the People's Republic of China (China) was founded. The United States government assessed that since the Communist Party of China (CPC) took over the whole Chinese mainland, it would be impossible for the Nationalist Government, which had withdrawn from the mainland to Taiwan after its defeat by the CPC, to perform its GATT obligations across the whole Chinese territory, and therefore informed the Nationalist Government on Taiwan that it would submit to the Fourth Contracting Parties' Meeting of the GATT, which was scheduled in February 1950, a proposal suspending the implementation of the preferential tariff rates applied to Taiwan. The Nationalist Government on Taiwan, knowing that export of Taiwan origin only accounted for a very small proportion of all the Chinese exports that were entitled preferential treatment under the GATT, decided to withdraw China's contracting party in the GATT to prevent the communist government on the mainland from reaping the benefits of China's status as a GATT contracting party. The withdrawal was made in the name of the Republic of China on 5 May 1950.[5] Thereinafter, the Contracting Parties that had concluded negotiations on tariff concession with China withdrew their tariff concession to China.

As the Nationalist Government on Taiwan withdrew from the GATT, the government of the PRC, which claimed to be the sole legitimate representative of Chinese people, did not attempt to resume its status as a GATT contracting party. Since then, China had lost contact with the multilateral trading body for 30 years.[6]

In 1981, China attended, as a non-voting delegate, the third Multi-Fibre Agreement (MFA) negotiation under the auspices of the Textile Committee under the GATT. In May 1981, China became an observer of the Textile Committee. In the following year, the then Ministry of Foreign Trade submitted a report to the State Council, suggesting that China should join the GATT, and on 31 December 1982 the report was approved.[7] In fact, before the approval, i.e. in November 1982, China attended, for the first time, as an observer, the 38th Contracting Parties' Meeting of the GATT, during which the Chinese representative affirmed China was an original signatory of the GATT, and expressed China's interest in "exploring the possibility of developing further relations with the GATT." China also exchanged views with the GATT Secretariat about the legal problems concerning China's pursuit to resume its status as a GATT contracting party. In 1984 China became a member of the Multi-fibre Agreement, which was unique in the GATT-administered trade agreements and allowed membership to non-GATT members. In November 1984, as an observer, China was allowed to attend the GATT Council and the meetings of its subordinate institutions.[8] China has since then attended the GATT Contracting Parties' annual meeting. In April 1985, China became a member of the Informal Consultation Group of Developing Countries within the GATT.

In July 1986 China filed its application to join the GATT or, in Chinese terms, to resume its status as a contracting party.[9] China argued that the withdrawal of the Nationalist Government on Taiwan from the GATT was null and void because the Nationalist Regime had ceased to be the legitimate government of China upon the founding of the PRC and the government of PRC has never consented to the withdrawal.[10] Immediately after submitting the request, China participated in the 8th round of negotiation, or the Uruguay Round Negotiation, that the GATT launched in September 1986. In March 1987, the Working Party on China's Status as a Contracting Party (Working Party) was set up, with Ambassador Pierre-Louis Girard (Switzerland) as its Chairman. Its responsibilities were to examine the request of China for resumption of its status as a GATT contracting party, and to submit to the Council recommendations which may include a Draft Protocol on the Status of China.[11]

In fact, the process to the GATT roughly consisted of two phases, i.e. trade regime examination and market access negotiations. The process of trade regime examination was one of fact finding, designed to give CONTRACTING PARTIES an understanding of the applicant country or territory, its economy and, in particular, its trade regime.[12] The Working Party spent an unusually long period of six years reviewing the trade regime of China, because, unfortunately, the Tiananmen incident in 1989 substantially deferred the process.[13] It was until 1992 during his southern tour, the late patriarch leader Deng Xiaoping called on embracing market economy wholeheartedly. The 14th CPC Congress formally adopted the "socialist market economy" policy goal and that the process was given a spur. At the 14th meeting of the Working Party in 1992, Girard announced the concluding of the first phase of accession process, i.e. trade regime examination, and the commencement of the second phase, i.e. market access negotiations. However, as a result of the Uruguay Round, the negotiation which initially had concerned only China's trade regime for goods, was broadened, in its scope, to include trade in services, new rules on non-tariff measures and rules relating to intellectual property rights. Moreover, at this time, the bargaining requirements set out by the GATT's contracting parties had been substantially raised. Therefore, although China took part in the ensuing negotiations and three Ministerial Meetings, and submitted schedules of concessions on agriculture, non-agricultural goods, trade in services and intellectual property, China had been unsuccessful in its effort to resume its status as a GATT contracting party before the GATT was replaced by the WTO.[14]

2.2. WTO Accession Process

Having failed to join the GATT before 1 January 1995 when the WTO replaced the GATT, China renewed its application under the WTO.[15]

The process of accession to the WTO basically follows that of GATT. Submission of an application proceeds the establishment of a Working Party by the General Council.[16] In the case of China, the Working Party on accession to the WTO was merely the successor of the Working Party on China's Status as a Contracting Party.

The next phases in the process are trade regime examination and market access negotiation. In the case of China, since the Working Party had concluded the phase of trade regime in the GATT era, the WTO accession process primarily focused on the market access negotiation.

Because the Working Party makes decisions by consensus, all WTO members and the country seeking membership must be in agreement that their individual concerns have been met and that all outstanding issues have been resolved in the course of their deliberations. At the bilateral level, however, negotiations have been primarily conducted between China and the US, the EU, Japan, and Canada, with the Sino-US relationship dominating the accession negotiations. Since 1986, many questions have been raised as to when China could accede to the WTO and whether it would accede as a developing or developed country. The conclusion of the agreements between China and the US and the EU in November 1999 and May 2000 signified a major breakthrough in the process.[17] On 13 September 2001, China finished negotiation with all of the 37 Working Party members that expressed interest in negotiation of bilateral market access agreements.

Multilateral negotiation took place under the auspices of the Working Party, which met 18 times from 1995 to 2001. On 17 September 2001, the 18th meeting of the Working Party finalized the Draft Protocol on the Accession of the People's Republic of China (Accession Protocol), which incorporated all the bilateral agreements China had concluded with 37 WTO Members and laid down the terms and conditions for China's entry into the organization. On 10 November 2001, the Ministerial Meeting of WTO Members in Qatar approved this Accession Protocol. The next day, China submitted to the WTO the ratification by the National People's Congress (NPC) Standing Committee. Thirty days later, China formerly joined the WTO on 11 December 2001.

3. Context of China's WTO Accession

3.1. Open door policy and economic integration

China's move towards the GATT and the WTO clearly reflects the open-up and reform process. In retrospect, it can be seen clearly that the Open Door policy involved two dimensions. The first dimension was domestic.

With the opening drive, the Chinese government set up special economic zones, coastal open cities, coastal open areas, and key cities along borders, rivers, and in inland areas with a view to bringing into play the influencing and driving role of the open areas. In conjunction with the deepening of internal economic reform, the government is continuing to accelerate the development and opening of areas along major transport lines, encouraging the mid-western areas to expand, opening both externally and internally. It is no exaggeration that the Chinese government has formed an all-directional, multi-layered and varied opening pattern.

As to the international dimension, China's opening drive has been oriented mainly towards the developed world, which consists of the major WTO members, to tap the trade and investment benefits.[18] In this regard, it is worth noting that the Chinese government attaches great importance to the multilateral co-operation with international economic and trade establishments, particularly, the organisations of the United Nations (UN) development system.

International co-operation and international competition is forging an open economy and forcing the domestic economy to integrate with the world economy. The Chinese economy, consequently, has become increasingly dependant on economic co-operation with the rest of the world.

3.2. Economic integration and institution building

It is observed that economic integration has played an unprecedented role in guiding the remoulding of legal systems.[19] The need to integrate into the world economy requires adapting to international economic and trade norms in the course of establishing an operating mechanism that will satisfy globally prevalent economic rules and lend impetus to domestic economic and legal reforms. A good example is the institutional implications of China's joining the international establishments.

Almost immediately after China inaugurated its Open Door policy, China took specific measures to join international institutions.[20] International institutions are key channels through which economic co-operation at the multilateral level is conducted. Such economic co-operation then facilitates the further integration of the Chinese economy into the world economy and increases interdependency with the rest of the world.

As a matter of fact, China's membership in international institutions not only served an economic purpose, but also brought changes to the Chinese legal system. International trade and economic co-operation require legal protection. When there was hardly a legal system to speak of with respect to trade and investment, nothing could convince the international community of China's willingness to integrate more than its effort to join the international organisations. And this in turn called for economic legislation.

There is empirical evidence that economic legislation and institutional changes have always followed international economic exchange. A typical example is the gradual improvement of the intellectual property rights regime. It is no exaggeration that the regime, which in letter is more or less compatible with that of the major WTO members, in terms of the standard for protection of foreign intellectual property, is a result of China's embracing the World Intellectual Property Organisation (WIPO).[21]

As a matter of fact, not only did international institutions like the World Bank and the International Monetary Fund (IMF), of which China has become a member, have a positive impact on institution building, but also the rules and principles of the GATT/WTO, to which China has not been admitted, served as a model for Chinese institution building through the whole negotiation process over the past fourteen years. The relaxation of price controls,[22] the continuous reduction of tariffs, the gradual phasing out of non-tariff barriers, and the promulgation of the Foreign Trade Law,[23] which has made the foreign trade regime more transparent and more liberal, all are evidence of the influence of the GATT/WTO rules.

4. China's Perspective on WTO Accession

4.1. Political concerns

China is the world's most populous country and one of the five permanent members of the Security Council of the United Nations. After two decades of the Open Door policy, China has emerged indisputably as a regional power and even a potential world power.[24] During the same period it has joined virtually all the major international organisations except the WTO.[25] The WTO has mandates ranging from trade to investment and is a rule-making body and therefore is conceived of as one of the three pillars of the international community.[26] China felt that, as one of the initial signatories to the GATT, it could not afford, from political point of view, being excluded from the world's trading body. It has been trying to convince WTO members that the WTO, without China, is not a completely global trade organisation. It is eager to enjoy the international prestige, which WTO membership assures.

The right to participate in future multinational trade negotiations is also expected by the Chinese government. Like other developing countries, China has, from time to time, demonstrated its dissatisfaction with the existing international order, in which the major countries play a crucial role, by joining the developing world in calling for the reconstruction of a new and fairer international economic order. This reflects the fact that as China emerges on the international scene, it must strive for international influence. As a major developing country, China's position in this regard cannot be neglected. However, China's dissatisfaction cannot be interpreted as an indication that it will become a prospective outlaw. As a country that has long remained outside the GATT/WTO, and that is eager to reap economic benefits from WTO membership, China knows that it has no other alternative but to accept the existing rules. From the perspective of real-politik it is understandable that China aims at the right to participate in rule-making by preparing its WTO membership.

Another political concern that has been almost entirely neglected is the Taiwan issue, which remains a top priority of the Chinese government. The Chinese government realised that there is a possibility to address the Taiwan issue within the WTO framework. It has done all that it can to undermine the foundation for the independence of the island, which it views as a renegade province. The strategy of the Chinese government in the short run is to induce or compel Taiwan to lift its ban to direct communications with China, which would make Taiwan more dependent on China. In accordance with an understanding between China and the General Agreement on Tariffs and Trade, Taiwan acceded to the WTO as a separate customs territory after China's accession.[27] Taiwan did not invoke the clause of exclusion against China.[28] Consequently, Taiwan has acted to relinquish its long-held policy regarding prohibitions of direct communications with China.

4.2. Economic concerns

It goes without saying that WTO accession is not merely a matter of political concern for China. China is keenly interested in accessing a broader international market resulting inevitably from WTO membership. In other words, China sees WTO accession as an opportunity to address the economic issues that confront it and that have not been, from the Chinese perspective, dealt with properly, with a view to gaining such tangible benefits as most-favoured-nation (MFN) treatment from its trading partners and access to the WTO mechanism for settling trade disputes.

4.2.1. Fair anti-dumping treatment

The United States is China's No. 2 trade partner. However, many US practices adversely affect the growth of China' s exports to the United States and thus remain offensive to China. The most problematic aspect of US practice is its anti-dumping regulations.[29] The United States uses a surrogate country approach to determine the existence of dumping and dumping margin on the assumption that China is still "a non-market economy."[30] China insists that the United States fails to acknowledge China's reality as a socialist market economy after 20 years of reform and opening-up. It obviously hopes that after its WTO accession the United States will abandon the "outdated concept and practice" as soon as possible and "render fair treatment to Chinese enterprises and products." Recently, Australia, New Zealand and the EU have made some adjustments in their practices. The Chinese government hopes that the United States will follow this trend and remove the unfair elements in its anti-dumping policy, so as to ensure the smooth development of Sino-US trade relations.

4.2.2. Free from unilateral measures

China has been complaining it suffers under the unilateral protectionist measures of WTO Members. For example, on 14 December 2001, under the pretext of the so-called illegal trans-shipment of textile products made by Chinese mainland enterprises, the US government decided to unilaterally reduce China's textile quotas by 300 percent which are worth approximately US$28 million. From the Chinese perspective, the unilateral action without support of solid evidence, is in blatant violation of the Sino-US bilateral agreement on textiles.[31]

Now that China has joined the WTO, it is justified in assuming that it will not continue to be a victim of "blatant violation[s] of bilateral agreements" by the governments of WTO Members, and the dispute settlement mechanism should provide assurance to this end.[32]

4.2.3. Permanent normal trade relation with the United States

In July 1979, China and the United States signed the Agreement on Trade Relations between the two countries, which enabled the two sides to give each other MFN treatment (termed "permanent normal trade relations" or PNTR since 1998). MFN is by nature a mutually beneficial trade arrangement between the two countries. Though, pursuant to the U. S. Trade Act of 1974 (i.e., the Jackson-Vanik amendments), the United States cannot grant non-discriminatory treatment to products of a communist country that denies its citizens the right to emigrate, or imposes conditions on emigration.[33] The mutual granting of MFN had never become a problem—the same legislation authorises the President to waive these requirements, subject to congressional review—until the Tiananmen Square incident in June 1989, which made the MFN a contentious issue in Sino-U.S. relations. Some members of the US Congress submitted various bills each year demanding the removal of the MFN for China, or conditioning its extension. Although the U.S. Government announced the de-linking of the annual MFN review and China's human rights record in May 1994, the Chinese government failed to secure exemption from annual review for two decades. It has been noted that there seems to be an inherent risk for China where the anti-dumping provisions and the Jackson-Vanik amendments interact: treating China as a non-market economy where situations arise within the anti-dumping provisions would fulfill a condition for justification of non-extension of normal trade relations to China. Therefore, China requested that the US commit itself in the Sino-US agreement to grant China the PNTR status as a condition for China's signing the agreement. The US House of Representatives approved the permanent extension of normal trade relations status to China on 25 May 2000.[34]

4.3. Methodological concern: Bilateral approach versus multilateral approach

Indeed, since the adoption of the open-up policy, China had been negotiating bilateral trade and economic cooperation agreements. With the rapid expansion of trade between China and the contracting parties of the GATT, China felt the bilateral agreements could not meet the demands of such expanded trade relations. In order to develop further trade relations with other countries, China needed to be part of the multilateral trading system, the GATT. In the early 1980s, China's reform was basically carried out in rural areas, its long-standing centrally planned economic structure, i.e. its trading system and state-owned enterprises (SOEs), were barely touched upon. This is why China took a gradual and prudent approach towards the GATT. Only when China started the reform on SOEs and trading practice,[35] and when it began to gain first-hand knowledge of the GATT via an observership in the GATT and had benefited from its membership in one of the committees of the GATT, i.e. the Textile Committee,[36] did China feel comfortable to procure its status as a GATT contracting party.

5. Major WTO Members' Perspective of China's WTO Accession

The re-introduction of China's Open Door policy immediately caused positive reactions from the international community, which had targeted the enormous market potential of China. But soon their expectations were, if not wholly, partially frustrated. Thousands of years of imperial traditions and decades of communist rule had made China a country culturally unique but somewhat impenetrable to the international community. Those international businessmen that came earliest to do business in China were disappointed to find that up to the early 1990's the actual Chinese market only existed in their fantasy. To make things worse, they were also daunted by the disorder of the market. For example, before 1992 almost every businessman had experienced a broad range of arbitrary administrative interference, unfair trade practices, trade barriers, discriminatory regulatory processes, lack of transparency, and other policies, which limited their participation in the Chinese market or unfairly affected their trade. Although it was indisputable that China was moving to a open society, any pressure for fast-track reform met with the in-born Chinese obsession for self-governing (*dulizizhu*). This mentality, from time to time, caused some disharmonious noise in the policy-making process, of which opening-up has been the tone. It is not difficult to note that on numerous occasions China insisted that it should be the one—not the outsider, even speaking on behalf of GATT—that decided if and how the Open Door policy should be implemented. This random and inconsistent practice inevitably caused a dilemma among WTO Members: while they welcomed China's Open Door policy, they became more and more impatient with the slow progress.

When China began its effort to join the GATT and then the WTO, western countries realised that it represented an opportunity for them to address the broad range of unfair trade practices, trade barriers, discriminatory regulatory processes, lack of transparency, and other policies, which limited their participation in the Chinese market or unfairly affected their trade. Furthermore, they knew that China's further opening of its market was perhaps, only possible after its accession to the world trade body.

For current WTO members, China's membership in the world trading body not only concerns economic issues, but also concerns the issue of global integration. The admission of China into the rule-based organisation and more open trade between China and the rest of the world will not only benefit the business community but will also be conducive to subjecting China to outside influence.[37] The WTO rules would oblige China to behave according to the western-style rules of law and to expand its Open Door policy, thus exposing more of China to western ideas. In this regard, WTO members welcome China's accession. They have, from time to time, echoed the Chinese government that a WTO in which China plays no part is a contradiction in terms, and that the international norms that the WTO represents will not be fully accepted until the institution embraces all nations,[38] and they have engaged themselves in serious negotiations with China. This perception was heightened when China's role in promoting regional prosperity and stability became evident in the Asian financial crisis.[39]

On the other hand, given their concerns about the capacity of China's exports to disrupt the international market and China's inability to implement the rules, current WTO members are reluctant to admit China except on "a commercially meaning term."[40] China's major trading partners observe that China is already a formidable export competitor, particularly in low-value manufactured goods such as toys and textiles, and is rapidly moving up the technology ladder in electronics. With the help of WTO membership, China will become an even more formidable competitor. While the Chinese government insists that China should accede to the WTO as a developing country, the western countries feel that developing country status would lead Chinese exports to disrupt their domestic markets. Moreover, China's continued refusal to accept commercially meaningful terms not only suggested that it preferred the status quo, in which it enjoyed wide access to overseas markets on a bilateral basis without being subject to the trade body's rules, but it also led them to doubt China's political will to abide by the trade rules. In this context, they have tried to block China's decade-long accession process. Consequently, trade disputes have arisen. To make matters worse, the trade disputes are accompanied by disputes over other issues, particularly human rights issues. Given the prospect that China will emerge as an economic super power in terms of economic size, western countries are even more concerned about whether China will be a responsible partner.

Obviously, the expectation that the interests of the international community will be enhanced with the admission of China to the WTO is conditional on China's compliance with the WTO rules. However, it is also certain that including China in the WTO is better than leaving China outside the world trade body, since after its accession China will be bound by the WTO rules rather than remain at large. In the past, foreign business interests chafed at restrictions on foreign participation in many areas of the Chinese economy, the non-transparent and sometimes arbitrary legal and regulatory regime, and the denial of equal treatment to many foreign goods and services. But if China finally adopts the rules, enforceable in the WTO, the number of such complaints may be substantially reduced.

In this regard, it is more important for the international business community to see the prospect of China being bound by a formal dispute-settlement mechanism, which is deemed a crucial aspect of an efficient and effective multilateral trade system, rather than being subject to the whims of local politicians and import-substituting industrialists.

6. Some Prominent Issues in the Accession Process

On 17 June 1998, at the critical moment of negotiation, President of China, Jiang Zeming, pointed out three principles on which China should pursue its WTO membership: First, since WTO is supposed to be a global trade organization, it would be an incomplete one without the participation of China, the largest developing country in the world; secondly, China would only accede to the WTO as a developing country; and thirdly, China would accede to the WTO with a balanced agreement. China never elaborated, in the process of negotiation on its accession to the WTO, what the exactly the three principles mean. Nevertheless, the three principles highlighted the issues facing the negotiators of China and the WTO Members.

6.1. A WTO with halfhearted China v. An incomplete WTO without China

It is generally agreed that with China's membership, the WTO will take a major step towards becoming a truly world organization.[41] Indeed, on the one hand, the WTO Members aspired to know whether they would reap bonus from China's WTO membership; on the other, they at least wanted to avoid the possible worst from that membership: weakening the framework of what, by many accounts, has been the most successful of international organizations. The WTO operates on the basis of consensus among its Members, and in theory one Member could disrupt the consensus decision-making process.

In this context, making China accept the rules-based system became a crucially important objective, which is as important as, if not more important than, securing China's commitment on market access. This explained why the primitive legal system of China became the concerns of the Working Party Members and why they unusually conditioned China's admission to the WTO on its commitment to improve the legal system. Even after the conclusion of the substantial market access agreements, the Working Party insisted China make specific commitments in this regard. Although China was initially reluctant to engage in negotiations in this respect, the legal status of the Working Party Members facilitate the realization of their purpose. The agreement on non-discriminatory treatment and judicial review reached on 23 May 1997 under the auspices of the Working Party signified the major concession China made in this regard.

As a result of bargaining, China was "forced" to enter a series of important commitments on legal reform, which covers uniform application of law, judicial review.

6.2. Developed country v. Developing country

China stated that although important achievements have been made in its economic development, China was still a developing country and therefore should have the right to enjoy all the differential and more favourable treatment accorded to developing country Members pursuant to the WTO Agreement. In order to gain the benefits reserved for developing members, China had long argued that it was a developing country and insisted acceding to the WTO as a developing country.

The GATT, through the Generalised System of Preferences (GSP), provided developing contracting parties with superior non-reciprocal tariff benefits for certain exports extended by developed contracting parties. Although the WTO approaches the developing countries issue differently from the GATT, it still tries to help developing members adjust to global competition by allowing them to adhere to less demanding standards and to take a longer time to implement trade liberalisation than developed members. For example, in agriculture, developed members must cut the value of their export subsidies by 36 percent and the volume of their subsidised exports by 21 percent over six years, while developing members are required to cut the value of their export subsidies by 24 percent and the volume of their subsidised exports by only 14 percent over ten years. Another example is that developed members must implement the Agreement on Trade-Related Aspects of Intellectual Property Rights (TRIPS Agreement) within one year and the Agreement on Trade-Related Aspects of Investment Measures (TRIMS) within two years, whereas developing members may take up to four years and five years, respectively, to implement the provisions.

Some existing WTO Members indicated that because of the significant size, rapid growth and transitional nature of the Chinese economy, a pragmatic approach should be taken in determining China's need for recourse to transitional periods and other special provisions in the WTO Agreements available to developing country WTO Members. Each agreement and China's situation should be carefully considered and specifically addressed. In this regard it was stressed that this pragmatic approach would be tailored to fit the specific cases of China's accession in a few areas, which were reflected in the relevant provisions set forth in the Accession Protocol and Working Party Report. In other words, the firm standing of these existing WTO Members is that China must take the "pragmatic approach" in a few areas, as a result of which its treatment in the WTO would be different from and less favourable that the treatment for developing countries embodied in the WTO Agreements.

In response, China agreed that it would undertake bilateral market access negotiations with respect to industrial and agricultural products, and initial commitments in services. It clearly shows that, on the part of China, a realistic assessment has replaced the vain debate whether China is a developing or developed country[42] and the long-term interests have been put above short-term political expediency. On the part of the rest of the world, a consensus has emerged: China will not be destined to be an outcast in the international business community and integrating China successfully will strengthen the WTO's mandate, whereas keeping China out would extract certain institutional costs in terms of the WTO's legitimacy as an organisation representing the world's trading states.

6.3. Commercially meaningful package v. Balanced solution

All the debates on the above two issues finally boil down to this issue of commercially meaningful versus balanced solution.

Any country or customs territory may accede to the WTO upon the consent of current members. Despite the well-established pattern of accession to the WTO, which is based on the procedures set out in a note by the WTO Secretariat on 24 March 1995,[43] the WTO (Article XII), like the GATT 1947 (Article XXXIII), places no limits on the terms of accession, which were to be developed through negotiation with current Members.[44] While it is generally agreed that the terms should guarantee a balance of rights and obligations, current Members arguably insist that the accession of new governments should strengthen the system, not weaken it and that acceding governments must therefore demonstrate their willingness to comply fully with the WTO rules upon accession. A number of different criteria were suggested for judging market-access commitments, the most frequently cited being that these should be, "commercially viable," "meaningful in trade terms," "meaningful," "fair," or "appropriate to the level of economic development of the applicant." Both the Singapore 1996 and Geneva 1998 Ministerial Declarations call for "meaningful market-access commitments."[45]

In the bilateral negotiation on China's accession to the WTO, particularly with the United States, China's accession was made conditioned on a commercially meaningful package, which was defined as including a commitment by China that "opens China's goods, services and agricultural markets to our goods, services and agricultural providers," "requires enforceable market-access commitments, transparency, non-discriminatory regulatory systems, and effective national treatment at the border and within China's economy," and "requires addressing [the United States'] bilateral trade concerns," and "requires agreement on all WTO rules."[46]

In retrospective, as a result of the negotiation, the terms for China's accession to the WTO, as initially set forth in the bilateral agreements (primarily in the China-US agreement and the Sino-EU agreement), and later confirmed in the Accession Protocol, reflect that China made unprecedented substantial commitments. Arguably, therefore, the accession process in fact took the "commercially meaningful" approach.

Notes

1. The Open Door (*menhu kaifang*) was a trade policy designed to persuade or coax China to open its market to the rest of the world while calling on the European powers and Japan to accept "perfect equality of treatment for navigation and commerce" for all countries trading with China. For an elaboration of the formulation of the Open Door Policy, see, for example, Warren I. Cohen, *America's Response to China*, New York: John Wiley & Sons, Inc., 1971, pp. 46-52.

2. The new Open Door (duiwai kaifang) was first proposed by Deng Xiaoping in his talk with a press delegation from the Federal Republic of Germany on 10 October 1978 and was formally adopted as the state policy in the Third Plenary Session of the Eleventh Central Committee of the Chinese Communist Party in December 1978. In the eyes of Deng Xiaoping, "Open Door policy" is a means to the objective of modernization, which is impossible to achieve without international cooperation.

3. Some observers hold that China's decision to accede to the WTO is as important as its move to receive the late President of the United States Nixon in 1972. According to the WTO Director-General Mike Moore, joining the WTO is the biggest decision for China since 1949. See Xinhua, China's WTO entry good for all, *China Daily*, 15 February 2000, available at <http://www.chinadaily.com.cn/cndydb/2000/02/d3-4wto.215.html>.

4. During the sessions, negotiations were held on tariff concessions. This was the first round of multilateral negotiation on tariff concession in the history of the GATT. On 8 April 1949, the second round of negotiation was held in France.

5. The withdrawal was first made to the Secretary General of the United Nations on 6 March 1950. The following day, the UN Secretary General addressed the Executive Secretary of the GATT and replied to the Taiwan Foreign Minister to the effect that the withdrawal would take effect on 5 May 1950. The Contracting Parties were also informed of the withdrawal. No Contracting Parties but Czechoslovakia challenged the legal force of the withdrawal.

6. In October 1971, the United Nations General Assembly passed Resolution 2758, which authorized the resumption of the People's Republic of China's membership in the United Nations. Later on, China became a member of the International Trade Centre affiliated to the United Nations on Trade and Development and the GATT. After that, China resumed contact with the GATT. China had little knowledge of the WTO, presuming that it was the club for rich countries. As China aspired to be the spokesman of the developing world, then it did not apply for the resumption of its status as a Contracting Party of the GATT.

7. See Xinhua News Agency, 11 November 2001.

8. The Chinese representative admitted that by attending the activities of the GATT, China learned more about the GATT, and this would eventually facilitate the Chinese government to make a decision on the resumption of the status of a contracting party in the GATT.

9. In fact, prior to the submission of the application, China had expressed the intention. On 10 January 1986, the then Chinese leader discussed this with the visiting Secretary-General of the GATT, Dunkel. On 10 July 1986, China

informed Director-General of the GATT, formally submitting a request for the resumption of China's status as a GATT signatory. The Request Note recalled that China was an original signatory of the GATT and hence it decided to request for the resumption of its status as a contracting party in the GATT. It elaborated that China's on-going economic restructuring helped expand China's economic and trade links with other GATT Contracting Parties, and China's participation in the GATT activities as a signatory would facilitate the realization of the GATT's goal.

10. See, generally, Chung-chou Li, Resumption of China's GATT Membership, 21 *Journal of World Trade* 4 (1987), pp.25-48.

11. The Working Party on China's Status as a Contracting Party met on 20 occasions between 1987 and 1995.

12. The applicant is required to submit a Memorandum for circulation to all WTO Members. The Memorandum shall describe in detail the applicant country or territory's foreign trade regime and providing relevant statistical data, annex copies of legislation, and contain data on applied duty rates, on agricultural domestic support and export subsidies and on services. The applicant shall also address the questions that members of the Working Party may raise in this process.

13. In fact, there had been no negotiation between China and any Western country on China's resumption of its status as a GATT contracting party until February 1992.

14. Indeed, on 15 April 1994, when the Uruguay Round Negotiations concluded with the publication of the Marrakech Ministerial Statement in Morocco, China initialed the Final Results of the Uruguay Round, which meant that the agreements of the final result of the Uruguay Round would apply to China if it became a member of the to-be WTO. China failed to become an original WTO Member.

15. On 7 December 1995, China applied for accession to the Agreement Establishing the World Trade Organization pursuant to Article XII of this Agreement; the existing Working Party on China's Status as a GATT 1947 Contracting Party was transformed into a WTO Accession Working Party.

16. The Working Party is open to all interested WTO Members. Its responsibilities are set with standard terms of reference, which read as follows:

    "to examine the application of the Government of [name of country concerned] to accede to the World Trade Organization under Article XII and to submit to the General Council/Ministerial Conference recommendations which may include a draft Protocol of Accession."

17. As a matter of fact, there were ensuing negotiations after the conclusion of the Sino-US and Sino-EU agreements. As a result, China and the US reached consensus on agricultural subsidies, and China and the EU on insurance.

18. For the role of foreign trade and investment in the Chinese economic reform, see Nicholas R. Lardy, "The Role of Foreign Trade and Investment in China's Economic Transformation," 144 *The China Quarterly* (1995), pp. 1065-1082.

19. See, generally, Thomas Yunlong Man, National legal restructuring in accordance with international norms, 4 *Indiana Journal of Global Legal Studies* 1 (1996), pp. 471-507; Guiguo Wang, Economic Integration in Quest of Law: The Chinese Experience, 29 *Journal of World Trade* 2 (1995), pp.5-28; Harold K. Jacobson *et. al, China's Participation in the IMF, World Bank, and GATT*, 1990, p. 146.

20. In this regard, it may be fair to mention the role of China being admitted into the United Nations in 1971, i.e., among others, establishment of the legal entity in the international community.

21. See, generally, Qingjiang Kong, Protection of Intellectual Property Rights in China—The perspective of A Chinese Lawyer, 58 *Heidelberg Journal of International Law* 1 (1998), pp. 181-204.

22. Pricing reform was among the priority reforms that were set into motion in the early 1980's. By the mid-1990s prices had been largely set by the market.

23. The Foreign Trade Law was adopted at the 5th Session of the Standing Committee of the 8th National People's Congress and became effective on 1 July 1994.

24. China is now the world's third largest economy, behind only the United States and Japan. Figures for 1998 show China as the world's 7th largest trader. The value of China's foreign trade in 2000 was US$474.3 billion. See the Expedite Statistics Report on Import and Export (*in Chinese*), December 2000, available at <http://www.moftec.gov.cn/moftec_cn/tjsj/jcktj/200012_1.html>.

25. Among the international organisations to which China is a member are Asian-Pacific Economic Co-operation forum (APEC), Asian Development Bank (AsDB), Bank of International Settlement (BIS), Customs Co-operation Council (CCC), Economic and Social Commission for Asia and Pacific (ESCAP), Food and Agriculture Organisation (FAO), G-77, International Atomic Energy Agency (IAEA), International Bank for Reconstruction and Development (IBRD), International Civil Aviation Organisation (ICAO), International Fund for Agricultural Development (IFAD), International Labor Organisation (ILO), International Monetary Fund (IMF), International IMO, Interpol, International Olympic Committee (IOC), International Standard Organisation (ISO), International Telecommunication Union (ITU), Patent Co-operation Agency (PCA), United Nations (UN), UN Security Council, United Nations Conference on Trade and Development (UNCTAD), United Nations Educational, Scientific and Cultural Organisation (UNESCO), United Nations Higher Commissioner for Refugees (UNHCR), United Nations Industrial Development Organisation (UNIDO), Universal Postal Union (UPU), World Health Organisation (WHO),

World Intellectual Property Organisation (WIPO), World Meteorological Organisation (WMO). See CIA-The World Factbook, 2001, Country Listing-China, available at < http://www.cia.gov/cia/publications/factbook/index.html>.

26. The other two pillars are the United Nations and the International Monetary Fund.

27. In early 1965 Taiwan requested and was granted observer status at sessions of the General Agreement on Tariffs and Trade (GATT 1947). In 1971, this status was removed, following a decision by the UN General Assembly that recognised the People's Republic of China as the only legitimate government of China. At its September 1992 meeting, the GATT's Council of Representatives decided to establish a separate working party to examine the request for accession of the Separate Customs Territory of Taiwan, Penghu, Kinmen and Matsu ("Chinese Taipei"). The Chairman said he had carried out extensive consultations on the subject of establishing a working party. He noted that all contracting parties had acknowledged the view that there was only one China, as expressed in the United Nations General Assembly Resolution 2758 of 25 October 1971. Many contracting parties, therefore, had agreed with the view of the People's Republic of China (PRC) that Chinese Taipei, as a separate customs territory, should not accede to the GATT before the PRC itself. Some contracting parties had not shared this view. There had been, however, a general desire to establish a working party for Chinese Taipei. He concluded there was a consensus among contracting parties on the following terms: First, the Working Party on China's status as a contracting party should continue its work expeditiously, taking account of the pace of China's economic reforms, and report to the Council as soon as possible. Second, a Working Party on Chinese Taipei should be established at the present meeting, and should report to the Council expeditiously. Mr. Martin R. Morland (United Kingdom) still serves as Chairman of the Chinese Taipei working party. Third, the Council should give full consideration to all views expressed, in particular that the Council should examine the report of the Working Party on China and adopt the Protocol for the PRC's accession before examining the report and adopting the Protocol for Chinese Taipei, while noting that the working party reports should be examined independently.

28. In theory, Taiwan could have invoked Article XIII of the Agreement Establishing the World Trade Organization before the Ministerial Conference approves the Protocol on the Accession of Taiwan to exclude the application of the WTO agreements as between it and China. However, in fact, such an invoking was unlikely since China, which would join the WTO before Taiwan, might take advantage of the opportunity to try blocking Taiwan's accession and other WTO members would doubt Taiwan's seriousness in becoming a

full and responsible WTO member. For a further analysis, see Ying-jeou Ma, The ROC (Taiwan)'s Entry into the WTO: Progress, Problems and Prospects, 15 *Chinese Yearbook of International Law and Affairs* (1996–1997), pp. 48-55.

29. Up to 31 December 2001, the United States had lodged 78 anti-dumping cases against Chinese products and became one of the countries which most frequently resort to anti-dumping measures against Chinese exports. Figures available at the website of the On-line Anti-dumping Library maintained by the State Economic and Trade Commission <http://www.cacs.gov.cn/infor/lszl/lszl4.htm>.

30. The term "non-market economy country," as in the Trade Act of 1974 is a term of art that is synonymous with "communist country." See, Daniel F. Wilhelm, *Most-Favored-Nation Certification and Human Rights: A Case Study of China and the United States* (1996), p. 52, quoted from Sylvia A. Rhodes and John H. Jackson, United States Law and China's WTO Accession Process, 2 *JIEL* 3 (1999), p.501.

31. See remarks by the Ministry of Foreign Trade and Economic Co-operation (MOFTEC) Spokeswoman on 14 December 2001, available at <http://202.96.57.185:7777/Detail.wct?RecID=38&SelectID=1&ChannelID=8085&Page=2>.

32. Ironically, the textile-specific safeguard provided for in the Sino-US bilateral textile agreement of 1994 will remain valid until 2008 and therefore, in the field of textiles, the WTO's built-in dispute settlement mechanism will not function.

33. Section 402 of the Trade Act 1974.

34. The US House of Representatives has passed the PNTR bill (i.e., H R 4444 bill), extending the PNTR treatment to China, but authorising the establishment of a congressional-executive commission to monitor, among other things, human rights development in China. The Senate later passed the PNTR bill as well.

35. In 1984, the CPC launched a reform to invigorate the ill-performed SOEs.

36. China's export in textiles, for instance, surged from US$ 6.6 billion in 1984 to US$ 17.8 billion in 1991.

37. For instance, as a result of China's accession to the WTO, China should open its telecommunications market, including to Internet and satellite services and its people will be more exposed to information, ideas, and debate from around the world.

38. For example, the European Union claims to be "a consistent and vocal supporter of China's entry into the WTO." It "believes the WTO is not truly a 'World' Trade Organisation without China." See <http://www.europa.eu.int/comm/trade/faqs/china_wto.htm>.

39. When the Asian financial crisis started in 1997, China insisted on non-de-valuating its currency albeit under tremendous pressure, consequently alleviating the pressure on its neighbours to further devaluate their currencies.

40. According to the United States Trade Representative Office (USTR), "commercially meaningful" or "commercially viable" has four meanings: First, the accession agreement must be comprehensive. It will cover agriculture, industrial goods, and services. It will deal with unfair trade practices including tariffs, quotas, other non-tariff measures, non-scientific agricultural standards, discriminatory regulatory processes, lack of transparency, export subsidies, and other barriers to trade. It will address the tariffs and other barriers China applies at the border; the limits China places on sales, customer service and maintenance within the domestic market; China's unwarranted sanitary and phytosanitary standards; and limits on the rights of service providers to set up businesses in China. Second, the agreement shall grant China no special favours. It will require China to reduce its trade barriers to levels comparable to those of major trade partners, including industrial countries. Third, it must be enforceable. The commitments China makes in all areas will be specific, measurable, and will be fully enforceable. Fourth, it delivers market-based reforms fast. Immediately upon accession, China will make substantial cuts in agricultural and industrial tariffs; begin opening sectors from insurance to telecommunications to professional services to foreign service providers. The phase-in of further broad concessions in all these areas will be limited to five years in the vast majority of cases and in many cases between one and three years. See, USTR press release, 8 April 1999, available at <http://www.ustr.gov/releases/1999/04/99-34.html>.

41. See Mike, Moore, Director-General of the WTO, said this at the conclusion of the meeting of the Working Party on China's Accession.

42. Chinese President Jiang Zemin made clear in his talks with US President Clinton in Seattle in 1993 that China insisted on joining the GATT on three conditions, one of which is that China is a developing country and it makes commitments comparable to that status. See Chronicles of China's GATT/WTO Accession, People's Daily On-line, available at <http://www.peopledaily.com.cn/GB/channel3/topic216/3.html>.

43. See WT/ACC/1, The procedures for WTO accession in the note were modeled on those followed by the CONTRACTING PARTIES to GATT 1947.

44. Since the inauguration of the WTO, the WTO Members had been further involved in a discussion on the process of accession to the WTO, particularly on the terms and conditions of accession. The discussion particularly took place at the Ministerial Conferences in Singapore (1996) and Geneva

(1998) as well as the meeting of the WTO General Council in December 1998. It was only on 1 November 2001, the WTO Secretariat formulated a Technical Note on the Accession Process, which summarized such discussions.

45. See, respectively, Singapore Ministerial Declaration, adopted on 13 December 1996 (WT/MIN(96)/DEC), part 8, and the WTO Ministerial Declaration, adopted on 20 May 1998, part 7, available at <http://www.wto.org/french/news_f/pres96_f/wtodec.htm>, and <http://www.wto.org/english/thewto_e/minist_e/min98_e/mindec_e.htm>.

46. Barshefsky's 30 March 1999 Remarks on China WTO Accession Talks, available at <http://usinfo.state.gov/regional/ea/uschina/barshf30.htm>.

2

China's WTO Accession: Commitments and Implications*

1. Introduction

China became a Member of the WTO at the end of 2001. For this accession to the WTO, China has made remarkable commitments, particularly in relation to its current trade practice. The long process of China's GATT/WTO accession has drawn considerable scholarly attention.[1] However, there is little detailed analysis publicly available about the commitments and implications of China's WTO accession. The thrust of this chapter is to examine China's commitments and gauge the implications of the WTO membership on China. It starts by measuring the gap between China's commitments for WTO membership and its current practice, and moves further with an assessment of the implications: Can China be trusted with international agreements of this magnitude?

The analysis allows the tentative conclusion that the internal drive for openness evidenced in recent practice, and the external monitoring assisted with persuasion will outweigh the negative historical context.

* This chapter is based on an article, first published in the *Journal of International Law*, 2000 (pp. 665-690), and reproduced by the permission of the publisher.

2. The Cost of China's WTO Accession

China acceded to the WTO on the terms and conditions set out in the Accession Protocol.[2] As a necessary cost of the WTO accession, China has made, in the Protocol, remarkable commitments particularly in relation to its current trade practices. The cost of China's Accession is the gap between China's commitments and its present trade practices.[3] The following sections provide an overview of China's commitments as contained in the Accession Protocol, and its trade-related practice with a view to measuring these costs.

The first look centres around China's specific market access commitments with regard to tariffs and taxes, service industries, removal of non-tariff trade barriers, following which an examination of investment rules, transparency, intellectual property rights (IPRs), non-discrimination, trading rights and other restrictions is made.

2.1. Market Access

2.1.1. Tariffs and taxes
Until the mid-1990s, China's tariffs were often high enough to preclude most imports. As a result of bilateral negotiations and its bid to join the WTO, the tariff rate was reduced considerably. Up until 1 October 1997 the average import tariff had been lowered to 22.1 percent. Despite gradual tariff reductions—with the latest round of cuts effective 1 January 2001[4]—since the conclusion of the 1999 Sino-US Agreement on WTO accession, the average import tariff is still 15.3 percent.[5] In accordance with the Protocol, China has committed itself to cut duties from an overall average of 22.1 percent to 17 percent in three years and to an average of 9.4 percent by 2005. In relation to agricultural commodities, the overall average will be 17.5 percent and for some products 14 percent (down from 31 percent) by January 2004. With respect to industrial products, tariffs will be cut from an average of 24.6 percent to an average of 9.4 percent overall and 7.1 percent on some products. China will further reduce import duties on over 150 products, such as machinery, ceramics and glass, textiles, clothing, footwear and leather goods, cosmetics, and spirits. Agreed levels are generally around 8–10 per cent.

Tariff cuts will evidently be a significant step that China is obliged to take. It has so far conformed to the commitments that were first specified in the Sino-US agreement and finally reflected in the Protocol. However, more difficult for China to deal with will be the levelling of the application of the uniform tariff rate. In respect to the current tariff-related trade barriers, unpredictable application of those rates creates difficulties for companies trying to export to, or import into, the Chinese market. Tariffs may vary for the same product, depending on whether the product is eligible for an exemption from the published NTR tariff. Tariffs may also vary depending on the geographical point of entry. Also, local tariffs may be applied to imports even after the importer paid the national tariff at the port. High-technology items whose purchase is incorporated into state plans, for instance, have been imported at tariff rates significantly lower than the published NTR rate. China implemented a new import tariff-exemption plan for some goods under revised investment guidelines on 1 January 1998. The plan is designed to increase investment in high-tech manufacturing by domestic and foreign firms. China's Customs has also granted preferential tariff rates through special exemptions or more informal means.[6]

Customs valuation is an issue closely related to tariffs. Foreign businesses selling goods in China used to complain about the lack of uniformity in customs valuation practices. Different ports of entry might charge significantly different duty rates on the same products. Because there was flexibility at the local level in deciding whether to charge the official rate, actual customs duties, like many taxes, were often the result of negotiation between business persons and Chinese Customs officers.[7] On the accession day, China began to apply fully the Customs Valuation Agreement, including the customs valuation methodologies set forth in Articles 1 through 8 of the Agreement. In addition, China would apply the provisions of the Decision on the Treatment of Interest Charges in Customs Value of Imported Goods, and the Decision on the Valuation of Carrier Media Bearing Software for Data Processing Equipment, adopted by the WTO Committee on Customs Valuation, as soon as practicable, but in any event no later than two years from the date of accession.

In addition to tariffs, imports may also be subject to value-added and other taxes. Foreign industries have complained that the current value-added taxing system (VAT) amounts to an added surcharge on both imported goods and domestic products and discourages consumers by raising prices. China's VAT is usually 13 or 17 percent, and China levies that VAT after first imposing the import tariff and applicable consumption tax and incorporating those amounts into the base on which the VAT is applied. Thus, a product subject to a 17 percent import tariff, a 17 percent VAT, and a consumption tax would be taxed ultimately at a rate in excess of 34 percent. Since some domestic and foreign firms are able to avoid the VAT through negotiation, foreign firms that "play by the rules" are at a competitive disadvantage.

2.1.2. Service industries: specific market access commitments

China has made commitments to phase out most restrictions in a broad range of service sectors, including distribution, banking, insurance, telecommunications, professional services, such as accountancy and legal consulting, business and computer related services, motion pictures, and video and sound recording services.

With regard to distribution, China has agreed to liberalise wholesale and retail services for most products, including imported goods, throughout China in three years. In addition, China has agreed to open up the logistical chain of related services such as maintenance and repair, storage and warehousing, packaging, advertising, trucking and air express services, marketing, and customer support in three to four years. China has also committed itself to lifting the specific joint venture restriction on large department stores and for virtually all chain stores, as well as lifting the 20,000 m^2 size limit for foreign-owned stores.

With respect to telecommunication, China will gradually open its market for paging and value-added services, domestic and international services, and mobile telephone services. China will permit 50 percent foreign equity share for value-added and paging services two years after accession; for domestic and international services it will open up its leasing market in three years, allowing foreign operators to rent capacity from Chinese operators and resell it, and 25 percent foreign equity share three years after accession, 35 percent after five years, and 49 percent six years after accession; it will allow for 25 percent foreign equity share for mobile services as of accession, 35 percent one year after accession, 49 percent three years after accession.[8] China also committed to phasing out all geographic restrictions by allowing foreign operations between Chinese cities and not restricting them to activity within each city. Moreover, China has agreed to implement the regulatory principles of interconnection rights and independent regulatory authority embodied in the Agreement on Basic Telecommunications Services and will allow foreign suppliers to use any technology (e.g., cable, wireless, satellites) they choose to provide telecommunications services.

With respect to the banking industry, China has committed itself to full market access in five years for foreign banks. Foreign banks will be able to conduct local currency business with Chinese enterprises starting two years after accession. They will be able to conduct local currency business with Chinese individuals beginning five years after accession. Foreign banks will have the same rights (national treatment) as Chinese banks within designated geographic areas. Both geographic and customer restrictions will be removed in five years. Non-bank financial companies can offer auto financing upon accession.

Relating to the insurance industry, China agreed to award licenses solely on the basis of prudential criteria, with no economic-needs test[9] or quantitative limits on the number of licenses issued. China will progressively eliminate all geographic limitations within three years. Internal branching will be permitted consistent with the elimination of these restrictions. China will expand the scope of activities for foreign insurers to include group, health and pension lines of insurance, phased in over three years.[10] Foreign property and casualty firms will be able to insure large-scale commercial risks nationwide immediately upon accession. Effective management control has been negotiated for foreign participants in life insurance joint ventures, through choice of partner, and a legal guarantee of freedom from any regulatory interference in private contracts on a 50-50 equity basis for life insurance. For non-life, China will allow branching or 51 percent ownership on accession and wholly owned subsidiaries in two years. Reinsurance is completely open upon accession. Foreign brokers will be able to operate in China, free of any joint-venture requirement, five years after accession.

In relation to securities, beginning on the 11 December 2001, foreign service suppliers are now permitted to establish joint ventures with foreign investment up to 33 per cent to conduct domestic securities investment fund management business. Three years after accession, foreign ownership of these joint ventures will be allowed to rise to 49 percent. As the scope of business expands for Chinese firms, foreign joint venture securities companies will enjoy the same expansion in scope of business. In addition, 33 percent foreign-owned joint ventures will be allowed to underwrite domestic equity issues and underwrite and trade in international equity and all corporate and government debt issues.

With respect to professional services, China has made strong commitments, including the areas of law, accounting, management consulting, tax consulting, architecture, engineering, urban planning, medical and dental services, and computer and related services. For example, for accounting, auditing, and bookkeeping services, China has agreed to market access and national treatment. Foreign accounting firms will be permitted to affiliate with Chinese firms and enter into contractual agreements with their affiliated firms in other WTO Members; for management consulting and taxation services, foreign firms can be established as a profit-making representative office,[11] or as a joint venture with a majority equity share upon China's accession to the WTO, and a wholly owned subsidiary five years after accession. For legal services, foreign law firms will be able to provide legal services in the form of a profit-making representative office[12]; and for architectural, engineering, and urban planning services, foreign firms will be able to establish majority owned joint ventures, or provide cross-border services in co-operation with Chinese professional organisations. China's commitments will lead to greater market access opportunities and increased certainty for foreign services companies doing business in China.

2.1.3. Removal of non-tariff barriers

Non-tariff barriers to trade are distinctive characteristics of a non-market economy. Prior to the mid-1980's, the Chinese government employed numerous non-tariff barriers to gain absolute control over foreign trade. At the heart of the non-tariff barriers designed to control imports was the mandatory import plan and canalisation of imports. Since then, and particularly since the Sino-US Memorandum of Understanding on Market Access (Market Access MOU) was signed in 1992, China has made remarkable progress in the reduction of non-tariff barriers. Not only has the importance of the import plan diminished, the other non-tariff barriers have also been substantially removed. For example, on the date China formerly became a WTO Member, it phased 47 product items previously subject to import license only. The remaining non-tariff barriers exist at both national and sub-national levels. At the national level, non-tariff barriers are administered by the State Economic and Trade Commission (SETC), the State Planning Commission (SPC), and the MOFTEC. Non-tariff barriers at sub-national levels are basically a result of the decentralised interpretation and enforcement of national policies relating to non-tariff barriers, which lead to distortion and complicate trade in the concerned commodities.[13]

The prevailing non-tariff barriers include import and export licenses, import quotas, and the covert import substitute policy. With respect to import licensing, in 1999, China applied import licensing restrictions to 35 product categories.[14] China confirmed that the list of all entities responsible for the authorization or approval of imports would be updated and republished in the official journal, the MOFTEC Gazette, within one month of any change thereto.

Among the non-tariff barriers, the import substitution, which has been a longstanding Chinese trade policy, attracts considerable criticism from the international business community. As a result of foreign pressure, early in the 1992 MOU, China promised that it would not subject any products to import substitution measures in the future while stating that it had eliminated all import substitution regulations, guidance, and policies.[15] Despite this commitment, in late 1998 the Ministry of Information Industries (MII) issued a circular instructing telecom companies to buy components and equipment from domestic sources. Another example was China's 1994 automotive industrial policy that included import substitution requirements. This policy, designed to foster development of a modern automobile industry in China, explicitly called for production of domestic automobiles and automobile parts as substitutes for imports, and established local content requirements, which would force the use of domestic products, whether comparable or not in quality or price. China's industrial ministries can have considerable impact on foreign firms through import substitution policies.

As a result of the negotiation on China's accession to the WTO, China listed, in Annex 3 of the Protocol, all of the products subject to quotas, licenses and such tendering requirements in China. It confirmed that after China's accession, no non-tariff measures would be implemented unless justified under the WTO Agreements, and that all non-tariff measures, whether or not referred to in Annex 3, would be allocated and otherwise administered in strict conformity with the provisions of the WTO Agreement, including Article XIII of the GATT 1994 and the Agreement on Import Licensing Procedures, including notification requirements.[16] China further committed itself to implementing the growth rates for quotas as indicated in Annex 3 during the relevant phase-out period, and not imposing upon quota holders any commercial terms of trade, including product specifications, product mix, pricing, and packaging.[17] In the process of negotiation, China confirmed that it would not introduce, re-introduce or apply non-tariff measures other than listed in Annex 3 of the Protocol unless justified under the WTO Agreement. Since the conclusion of the Sino-US Agreement, China had refrained from introducing new non-tariff barriers, or increasing the coverage of existing non-tariff barriers. However, existing non-tariff barriers had largely remained untouched before the WTO accession.[18]

According to the Protocol, China will cease to apply a number of measures, including export performance and local content requirements, and industrial export subsidies. China's government procurement system will be transparent, and will not discriminate between foreign bidders. China will abolish preferences to domestic producers in the fields of pharmaceuticals, chemicals, after-sales services, cigarettes, and spirits.

2.2. Transparency

Due to its political tradition, the Chinese government has been used to governing the state in a non-transparent manner. Foreign companies noted the difficulty in finding and obtaining copies of regulations and other measures undertaken by various ministries as well as those taken by provincial and other local authorities. Transparency of regulations and other measures, particularly of sub-national authorities, was essential since these authorities often provided the details on how the more general laws, regulations and other measures of the central government would be implemented and often differed among various jurisdictions. However, over the years, particularly after China signed the market access agreement with the United States in 1992, significant progress has been made in this regard, including the publication of a central repository for all central government trade regulations and publication in the provinces of all trade and investment-related trade regulations.[19] The MOFTEC gazette was established to carry official texts of trade-related laws and regulations at the national level. While the gazette has contributed significantly towards transparency, there are still many internal documents that are not circulated or not easily accessible. Moreover, it does not feature regulations from other departments and local agencies, which may have a significant impact on foreign firms. The opaque nature of customs and other government procedures, however, still compromises the important steps taken towards improving transparency in the import approval process, especially for industrial goods.

China undertakes that only those laws, regulations and other measures pertaining to or affecting trade in goods, services, TRIPS or the control of foreign exchange that are published and readily available to other WTO Members, individuals and enterprises, shall be enforced. In addition, China shall make available to WTO Members, upon request, all laws, regulations and other measures pertaining to or affecting trade in goods, services, TRIPS or the control of foreign exchange before such measures are implemented or enforced. In emergency situations, laws, regulations and other measures shall be made available at the latest when they are implemented or enforced.

2.3. Investment rules

In relation to investment, there used to be a huge gap between the Chinese practice and the WTO investment rules. China's industrial policies, which include performance requirements and forced technology transfer, serve as examples. Industry policies were formulated to protect China's infant industries. For example, China forbided foreign investment in some industries and requires local partnership in others.[20] These provisions are in clear violation of WTO's National Treatment principle. By placing performance requirements on foreign investment, such as minimum local content requirements,[21] and requiring minimum export commitments,[22] China apparently jeopardized the TRIMS Agreement. Similarly, requiring the transfer of patented technology as a precondition for approving foreign investment[23] was against the letter and spirit of the TRIPS Agreement.[24] China's examining and approval practice could also be used to prevent foreign investment from entering the protected industries.

In accordance with the Accession Protocol, China has agreed to implement the TRIMS Agreement, beginning the accession day, to cease enforcing trade and foreign exchange balancing requirements, as well as local content requirements, and contracts imposing these requirements, and to impose or enforce laws or other provisions relating to the transfer of technology or other know-how only if they are in accordance with the WTO Agreements on protection of IPRs and trade-related investment measures. China particularly agrees to remove the special restriction on types of vehicles that the automotive makers build and the joint-venture restriction for engine production upon accession. The Accession Protocol also raises the approval thresholds of provincial authorities from US$30 million to US$150 million, thus simplifying the examining and approval procedure.[25]

These provisions will also help protect foreign companies against forced technology transfers. Beginning the accession day, China does not condition investment approvals, import licenses, or any other import approval process on performance requirements of any kind, including local content requirements, offsets, transfer of technology, or requirements to conduct research and development in China.

2.4. Intellectual property rights

Inadequate protection of foreign IPRs in China is one of the issues that causes the most complaints from the international community and once constituted one of the biggest obstacles to China's accession to GATT/WTO. As a result of US pressure,[26] China has established a comprehensive and high-standard regime for protecting IPRs. Moreover, China has started implementing the TRIPS Agreement since accession—with no transition period. The commitment to abide by the TRIPS Agreement, which requires a WTO Member to make available enforcement measures and sanctions able to deter further infringing activity, is expected to strengthen the protection of IPRs.

2.5. Non-discriminatory treatment

For China, the challenge arising from the non-discriminatory treatment principle lies primarily in dealing with inefficient SOEs. China has confirmed the applicability of WTO rules to SOEs and extended those rules to state-invested enterprises, e.g., companies in which the government has an equity interest. Under these commitments, China has agreed to stop the practice of subsidizing SOEs. China's state-owned and state-invested enterprises are required to buy and sell based on commercial considerations, such as quality and price. Although purchases and sales of goods and services by SOEs, for commercial resale, or for use in the production of goods for commercial sale, are not considered government procurement and are subject to WTO rules, the other WTO Members can determine whether government benefits, such as equity infusions or soft loans, have been provided to an industry using market-based criteria rather than Chinese government benchmarks. Specifically, where government benefits are provided to an industry sector and SOEs are the predominant recipients or receive a disproportionate share of those benefits, the other WTO Members, e.g. the United States, could take action under their unfair trade laws.

2.6. Trading rights and other restrictions

Perhaps the most fundamental aspect of the Chinese economy before the Open Door policy was state ownership of the means of production. As an integral part of the economy, foreign trade was placed under direct control of the central government. China restricted the types and numbers of entities that had the legal right to engage in international trade. As a matter of fact, foreign trade is still the exclusive domain of those having the right to conduct foreign trade (*waimao jingyingquan*). Moreover, most of the companies entitled to foreign trade are state-owned trading companies, although numerous non-state entities have been granted the right to conduct foreign trade. For example, in a statement of basic foreign trade policies, the MOFTEC declared that joint state companies[27] shall be established to exercise unified and joint transaction over a few especially important commodities that concern the national economy or people's livelihood, while other import and export goods shall be liberalised for transaction by companies with foreign trade rights.

Foreign companies trading with China are forced to go through, in most cases, state trading companies that have the right to import goods into China[28] or to export goods abroad,[29] rather than to deal directly with customers or producers. Given that these commodities are of great commercial value to both China and its trading partners, this practice often gives rise to complaints. To make matters worse, in some cases specific government agencies impose informal market access barriers for imports that fall under their jurisdiction. Some agencies allow import by only a certain group of companies, and end users are sometimes required to obtain purchase certificates before they are allowed to import. Also, China's restrictive approach to licensing the scope of a business's operations (defining and limiting the types of goods in which a company may deal and operations in which a company may engage in China) has a negative impact on foreign companies.

In the context of its WTO accession negotiations, China has pledged to liberalise the availability of trading rights, i.e., the right to import, export and have access to China's distribution system, over a three-year period. At the end of that transition period all foreign and domestic enterprises will have trading rights. China will also have to ensure that liberalisation of trading rights is meaningful to the private sectors. For example, the Accession Protocol requires that China open the crude and processed oil sectors, as well as NPK fertiliser, to private traders through a process of gradual liberalisation.[30] Given that the SOEs account for a substantial part of those having the right to foreign trade, China is required to give extra protection to the actual rights of non-state companies in the transitional period.[31]

It is clear from the above comparison between the commitments it has already made and its current practice that the challenges facing China in the implementation of its commitments are formidable as a WTO Member.

3. Implementation of China's Commitments

3.1. An examination of the laws regarding implementation of international agreements

3.1.1. Legal status of international agreements in China

Needless to say, as China joins the WTO its commitments in the WTO accession agreements and the WTO Agreements themselves become international agreements to which China is a party. In this regard it is useful to examine the legal status or the force of law of an international agreement under Chinese law.

According to the Chinese Constitution, the State Council is responsible for "conducting foreign affairs and conclud[ing] treaties and agreements with foreign states."[32] The power to ratify international agreements rests with the NPC Standing Committee of.[33] Since the Constitution does not require the publication of an international agreement as a precondition of its validity, it may be assumed that an international agreement signed by the State Council becomes effective upon its ratification by the NPC Standing Committee.

For the international community, it remains to be clarified whether an international agreement signed by the State Council would be ratified by the NPC Standing Committee. The de facto supremacy of the Communist Party Central Committee and particularly its Politburo over all the state organs ensures the conclusion and ratification of treaties in conformity with party line. In practice, there has been no case yet in which the NPC Standing Committee refused to ratify an international treaty submitted to it by the State Council for ratification. It can be reasonably assumed that the trade treaties signed by the State Council will be ratified by the NPC Standing Committee and thus become effective in China.

A further question arises as to the legal status of an international agreement: in the case of a conflict between the Chinese laws and an international agreement, which shall prevail? Although the Constitution is non-committal on this point, numerous laws provide that the international agreement shall prevail. For example, the General Principles of Civil Law (GPCL) stipulate: "If any international treaty concluded or acceded to by the People's Republic of China contains provisions differing from those in the civil laws of the People's Republic of China, the provisions of the international treaty shall apply, unless the provisions are ones on which the People's Republic of China has announced reservations."[34] In view of this, it can be held that in case of disagreement between an international agreement and relevant Chinese laws and regulations, the international agreement shall apply. As a huge gap exists between present Chinese trade-related laws and the WTO rules, this is particularly crucial to the implementation of its commitments.

3.1.2. Application of international agreements in China

An international agreement concluded and ratified in due course has the force of law in China, but in theory it is not necessarily directly applicable since there is a distinction between "self-executing" and "non-self-executing" treaties. According to conventional usage of the terms, a "self-executing" international treaty can be applied directly, while a non-self-executing agreement cannot be directly applied, but must be implemented by legislative or other measures. From the international law perspective, it is an issue to be decided by the constitution of the Parties concerned. The Chinese constitution again remains silent on this issue.

One might argue that, where the direct application of international agreements is not specifically authorised by the constitution, the implementation of those agreements may be facilitated by direct incorporation of the international commitments into binding domestic rules. Unfortunately, the Chinese practice in this regard is not consistent. When the United Nations Convention on Contracts for the International Sale of Goods was ratified and became effective, the Supreme People's Court (SPC) promulgated, for the purpose of implementing the Convention, an internal directive, which ordered the courts at different levels to apply the convention directly in relevant cases.[35] When China joined the international copyright conventions in accordance with its commitments under the Memorandum of Understanding between China and the United States on the Protection of Intellectual Property (IPRs MOU) in 1992, the State Council promulgated regulations to implement the agreement.[36] When China joined the Patent Co-operation Treaty in 1993, it took a similar measure to implement the agreement.[37]

In this regard, it is interesting to note that the State Council and the SPR, rather than the NPC or its Standing Committee, which may incorporate the international agreements into laws, adopted the administrative regulations or judicial directives for the purpose of implementing the international agreements. Thus a legal loophole remains: Due to the hierarchy of the law of NPC, the administrative regulations of the State Council and the judicial directives of the SPC, the administrative regulations or the judicial directives concerning the implementation of the agreements will not ensure the implementation of the agreements in case of conflicts between the international agreements and existing laws of the NPC.[38] It is proposed that in relation to international agreements to which China is a party, the NPC Standing Committee should adopt laws in the same way that the State Council adopts administrative regulations for the purpose of the implementation of the agreements.[39]

3.1.3. A brief view of China's behaviour in the World Bank and IMF

China's likely behaviour in the WTO is also predictable based on its record in the World Bank and the IMF. Here, the record is unambiguous.

The World Bank's experience with China is extensive. Since joining the Bank in 1980, the Bank has supported 220 projects covering most of the provinces for a total of more than US$30 billion.[40] China has acquired long-term funding, technical assistance, and strategic advice on reforming its economy. The Bank has become China's largest single source of long-term foreign capital, and China has been one of the Bank's largest clients since Fiscal Year 1993.

The World Bank often cites China as a model member. The quality of the Bank's project portfolio in China is one of its best. China projects are well implemented, within budget, and on time, and China has grown from a quiet presence to a mature partner.[41]

China's profile has been lower in the IMF. China has borrowed minimally and repaid immediately. More importantly, China has been active in absorbing the IMF expertise and advice.[42]

China is not perceived as a disruptive force in either of these institutions. Far from resenting these foreign institutions, China highly values the role of the World Bank and the IMF.[43] It benefits not only from the influx of capital, but also from the expertise and technical assistance of these organisations. The World Bank and IMF have served as a kind of airlock between the Western financial world and China, providing Chinese reformers with a training ground and a cushion until they could bring their personnel and expertise up to speed. Chinese reformers have often benefited from China's participation in them. In domestic debates in particular, Chinese officials were able to use World Bank and IMF standards in conjunction with China's desire to be an accepted member of global organisations as an impetus for economic liberalisation.

It was even observed that in relation to its role in the United Nations, China has become a "system maintainer" rather than a "system transformer."[44]

3.2. Domestic constraints on the implementation of the WTO rules

For the Chinese government, the incorporation of the WTO rules and its commitments in laws and policies is the easier part; it is the non-market factors and domestic legal restraints that pose a greater challenge to the implementation of the WTO rules.

3.2.1. Non-market factors

China has been on the way to market-oriented reform for two decades. The Chinese government has recognised that economic reform and market opening are cornerstones of sustainable economic growth. Nonetheless, these reforms have been difficult for certain constituencies, particularly in the ageing industrial sector and the heavily protected agricultural sector. Thus, while the market-oriented reform begun 20 years ago has contributed a great deal to the institution of a more open and competitive economy, very substantial barriers remain. As a result of the decentralisation that has stemed from the reform, governments at the provincial and local levels have assumed more control over measures that were previously exercised by the central government. It has been found that localities are trying to protect emerging industries and non-competitive sectors from external competition.[45] Resistance at the provincial and local levels not only fragments the market as a whole, but also substantially restricts the central government's ability to implement trade reforms.[46]

It may be too early to predict if WTO membership will sway local governments to continue operating in their own interests and against the policy directives from the centre. However, it is fair to argue that China's accession agreement per se is evidence of the central government formally committing itself to further pro-market-reforms as required by the WTO. In return, China's WTO accession will deepen and entrench market reforms— and strengthen the central leadership who want their country to move further and faster toward economic freedom and away from local protectionism, thus ensuring the faithful implementation of WTO commitments.

3.2.2. Legal restraints

Legal restraints might well be the biggest obstacle to China's implementation of the WTO rules.

"Rule of Law" or "Rule through law." It is widely observed that China has no tradition of the rule of law. Rather the rulers at different times have demonstrated their preference for a rule of man (*ren zhi*). In China, there is a bureaucratic tendency that once a law is passed, the problem that the law is supposed to address is assumed to have been addressed. The distinguishing feature of the rule of man can be described as "law being conceived of as an instrument of the ruler." This conception of rule of man fully resonated with the Marxist dogma and thus was strengthened when the People's Republic of China was founded. The practice of the rule of man culminated in the Cultural Revolution.

In the wake of the chaos and accompanying poverty, people became aware of the devastating force of the rule of man and began to study the institutional shortcomings. Accordingly, *fa zhi* (legality) was proposed as a substitute for *ren zhi* (the rule of man). Since 1979, when China set of the goal of legalism, China has made remarkable progress in the development of its legal system. China's significant and ever-growing body of legislation is clear evidence of the achievement. However, the over-arching principle is still legal instrumentalism. It is fair to argue that the feature of this legalism is the use of liberal language, rhetoric, and the ritual of law to pursue distinctly illiberal political and social objectives; it is the rule through law rather than the rule of law.

Ambivalence of law. The lack of a clear and consistent framework of laws and regulations is an effective barrier to the participation of foreign firms in the domestic market. A comprehensive legal framework, coupled with adequate prior notice of proposed changes to laws and regulations, and an opportunity to comment on those changes, greatly enhances business conditions, promotes commerce, and reduces opportunities for corruption. In China, laws are promulgated by a host of different ministries and governments at the provincial and local levels, as well as by the NPC, and the implementation of law, to a large degree, depends on the bureaucracy. As a result, laws and regulations are frequently at odds with each other and they often leave room for discretionary application—either through honest misunderstanding or through selective application—or they are ignored outright. Moreover, they are not uniformly implemented because the implementing authority is either capricious or interest-driven. For example, while governments in some localities lack incentive to implement law or policy that will not bring benefits to the locality concerned, they are insatiable in the random collection of fees from, among others, foreign companies. Also, some ministries who see their interests threatened may be reluctant to enforce the laws concerned.[47]

Credibility of dispute resolution mechanisms. The highly personalised nature of business in China often makes arbitration or other legal remedies impractical. Even when they have strong cases, people often decide against using legal means to resolve disputes out of concern over permanently alienating critical business associates or government authorities.

Scepticism about the independence and professionalism of China's court system and the enforceability of court judgements and awards remains high in the international community.[48] This has often caused both foreign and domestic companies to avoid enforcement actions through the Chinese courts. The Chinese government is moving to establish consistent and reliable mechanisms for dispute resolution through the adoption of improved codes of ethics for lawyers and judges and increased emphasis on the consistent and predictable application of laws.

3.2.3. The Chinese attitude towards international law

The Chinese attitude towards international law is the other face on the "rule of law" coin. Mao-era China, too weak and too isolated to pose any threat to international law and order, was perceived by some critical Western observers as an outlaw vis-à-vis international society. Evidence of this negative attitude towards Western-style international law can be found in an observation of Huan Xiang, the former Chairperson of the China International Law Society and senior diplomat: "Principles and rules of international law since Hugo Grotius's time, [in general] reflected the interests and demands of the bourgeoisie, the colonialists and in particular of the imperialists. The big and strong powers have long been bullying the small and weak nations, sometimes even resorting to armed aggression. International law has often been used by the imperialists and hegemonists as a means to carry out aggression, oppression and exploitation and to further their reactionary foreign policies. Apologies for aggression and oppression can often be found in the writings on international law."[49] His viewpoint seemed to be an absolute negation of international law.[50] However, China's international behaviour in the post-Mao-era has demonstrated a noteworthy change in its attitudes towards international law.

The current Chinese attitude towards international law can be fairly described in this way: while tending to underestimate the importance of customary international law, it recognises the existence of international law and its universal applicability, with emphasis on the principle of absolute sovereignty.[51] In this regard, it should be noted that the Chinese perspective on sovereignty is different from that of Western countries. Notwithstanding this, the recognition of a body of international norms is a positive phenomenon. It is justified to assert that it is a result of the introduction of the Open Door policy and engagement with the international community.

It should be pointed out that unfortunately the doctrine of legal instrumentality also finds another expression in the current attitude of China towards international law. As interpreted by Chinese diplomats, international law serves the foreign policy goal of China. Among the factors that influence China's attitude towards international law and international behaviour are China's perceived national interests, the current international situation, domestic concerns and policy, and China's historical experience with international law.

China suggests that it has acknowledged that its interests lie in trade with the rest of the world by declaring that the Open Door policy is a cornerstone of its policy (*guo ce*). It also knows that expanding trade is only possible by adapting itself to, rather than by changing, the existing multilateral trading system. In the meantime, its self-identification also has an impact on its international legal behaviours. It views itself as a weak developing country vis-à-vis developed countries and a responsible and trustworthy agent of the developing countries. In view of this, China reiterates "supporting any effort to build up a fair, safe and non-discriminatory multilateral trade system,"[52] in which the special interests of the developing country should be adequately addressed. Under such circumstances, it may play the role of "one of the multi-poles." Consequently it has shown strong interest in participating in rule-making. It may be argued that China's desire to play a role in international rule-making, if properly nurtured, would be conducive to enhancing China's willingness and capability to abide by international law.

3.3. External monitoring of the implementation of China's commitments

3.3.1. Enforcement mechanism of the WTO

It is widely agreed that the dispute settlement machine is the backbone of the enforcement mechanism of the WTO.[53] The WTO dispute settlement mechanism not only facilitates the settlement of trade disputes among the WTO members, but also serves as a means for the enforcement of the WTO rules and the commitments of the WTO members. As a matter of fact, the machinery has been widely used since the establishment of the WTO.[54]

Needless to say, the WTO enforcement mechanism is crucial to the implementation of China's commitments under the accession agreements. China's commitments will be enforceable through the WTO dispute settlement for the first time. In no previous trade agreement has China agreed to subject its decisions to impartial review, and ultimately to the imposition of sanctions if necessary. China will not be able to block panel decisions. If China loses a dispute, it will have to change the offending practice, provide compensation, or be subject to denial of access to the foreign market in an amount proportional to the harm it causes. The possibility of the participation of private parties, which claim to be victims of a certain Chinese trade measure, and which have secured the authorisation from their own governments to participate in the DSB fora, provides a further effective monitoring force.

The safeguard provision in the WTO Agreements can act as a deterrent that discourages China from breaching its commitments.

The WTO embodies the Trade Policy Review Mechanism (TPRM), which is intended to enable "the regular collective appreciation and evaluation of the full range of individual Members' trade policies and practices and their impact on the functioning of the multilateral trading system."[55] Each Member is subject to review. Although the purpose of the TPRM reviews is "to help improve adherence by all Members to rules, disciplines and commitments made " under the WTO Agreements, the unique system can actually serve to monitor the implementation of the obligations by each Member. In the case of China, the TPRM will also act to monitor China's implementation of its commitments.

In addition, the Protocol designed a special trade policy review system for China. According to this design, those subsidiary bodies[56] of the WTO shall, within one year after accession, review, as appropriate to their mandate, the implementation of the WTO Agreement and of the related provisions of the Accession Protocol by China. Each subsidiary body shall report the results of such review promptly to the relevant Council established by paragraph 5 of Article IV of the WTO Agreement, if applicable, which shall in turn report promptly to the General Council. The General Council shall, within one year after accession, review the implementation by China of the WTO Agreement and the provisions of this Protocol in the light of the results of any reviews by any subsidiary body. China shall provide relevant information to each subsidiary body in advance of the review. The General Council may make recommendations to China. After accession such reviews will take place each year for eight years. Thereafter there will be a final review in year 10 or at an earlier date decided by the General Council.

3.3.2. Extra-WTO mechanism for monitoring China's enforcement of its commitments

No agreement on WTO accession has ever contained stronger measures to bolster guarantees of fair trade than that governing China's accession. For example, under the Accession Protocol, WTO Members may maintain all prohibitions, quantitative restrictions and other measures, as listed in Annex 7, against imports from China in a manner inconsistent with the WTO Agreement. For example, the United States maintains the right to use the full range of American trade laws, namely Special 301, Section 301, Section 201, and the US antidumping laws.[57] Though, the mechanism embodied in all these laws are used to advance U.S. interests, they are to serve as useful and effective extra-WTO mechanism for monitoring China's enforcement of its commitments in a WTO-consistent manner.

Product-specific safeguard. Considering China's potentially enormous export capacity, the Protocol incorporated the product-specific safeguard mechanism, which provides a means to address Chinese exports that cause or threaten to cause "market disruption." In cases where products of Chinese origin are being imported into the territory of any WTO Member in such increased quantities or under such conditions as to cause or threaten to cause market disruption to the domestic producers of like or directly competitive products, the WTO Member so affected may request consultations with China with a view to seeking a mutually satisfactory solution, including pursuit of the application of a measure under the Agreement on Safeguards. If, in the course of these bilateral consultations, it is agreed that imports of Chinese origin are such a cause and that action is necessary, China shall take such action as to prevent or remedy the market disruption. If consultations do not lead to an agreement between China and the WTO Member concerned within 60 days of the receipt of a request for consultations, the WTO Member affected shall be free, in respect of such products, to withdraw concessions or otherwise to limit imports only to the extent necessary to prevent or remedy such market disruption. Noteworthy is that the product-specific safeguard differs from traditional safeguard measures. This mechanism re-introduces bilaterally agreed-on voluntary export restraints, which are not permitted under the WTO Safeguards Agreement, and more importantly, WTO Members are able to apply restraints unilaterally based on legal standards that differ from those in the WTO Agreement on Safeguards.[58] Moreover, China cannot retaliate in response to the use of the product-specific safeguards by WTO Members. The product-specific safeguard provision is a result of political compromise. It sets up a special mechanism that permits WTO Members to take measures such as import restrictions to address imports solely from China (rather than from the whole world)[59] that are a significant cause of material injury.

The product-specific safeguard, which will remain in force for 12 years after China accedes to the WTO, is a distinctive characteristic of a "commercially viable agreement" for WTO Members.

The extra-WTO mechanism guarantees the United States and other WTO members new leverage to ensure fair trade and protect their domestic industries from import surges, unfair pricing, and abusive investment practices and also gives the international business community a mandate to monitor China's enforcement of its commitments.

Antidumping and subsidies methodology. The agreed protocol provisions ensure that industries of concern to WTO Members will have strong protection against unfair trade practices, including dumping and subsidies. For example, the U.S. and China have agreed that the U.S. will be able to maintain its current antidumping methodology (treating China as a non-market economy) in future anti-dumping cases.[60] Moreover, when the U.S. applies its countervailing duty law to China it will be able to take the special characteristics of China's economy into account when it identifies and measures any subsidy benefit that may exist. This provision will remain in force for fifteen years after China's accession to the WTO.

Besides the unilateral measures guaranteed by the Accession Protocol, the other WTO Members can take numerous initiatives to monitor and enforce China's WTO compliance. The US Department of Commerce, for example, proposed a five-point plan to monitor and enforce trade agreement.[61] The European Union also proposed to provide technical assistance to facilitate the implementation of China's commitments.[62]

4. Concluding Remarks

With respect to the prospect of China's implementation of its commitments, the author disputes two prevailing but different viewpoints: the over-optimistic and the over-pessimistic ones. To over-optimists who are eager to reap the bounty of embracing China, the author would say China's WTO accession is only the starting point of a long process of integration. It is true that membership in the WTO is a testament to China's determination to integrate with the world economy. However, for China's trading partners, the effort to integrate China into the wider world is far from complete. Formal and informal trade barriers remain high. Moreover, internal restraints add to the difficulty China will have implementing WTO rules. In this context, it will not be surprising to see China adjust its practices as readily as the accession agreements require. Given that trade growth resulting from the WTO membership is understandably accompanied by an increase of trade disputes, the author would suggest that the WTO and its major members be fully prepared to accept a China slowly but steadily moving into conformity with WTO standards. Those who are aware of the effect of their stance on Chinese domestic policymaking should seek to develop a strategy that allows China to continue with domestic reforms and give it time to learn to comply with the WTO rules, rather than merely pressing China into compliance overnight.

As for the over-pessimists, the author would first agree with them that the substantial costs China will have to bear for WTO membership, as well as the institutional shortcomings and the history of the PRC in dealing with the international community, do not suggest that China will surely become a full-fledged member; The quick institutional transition also poses difficulties for predicting the likelihood of China's honouring its commitments. However, the author would remind them that the past is no reliable indicator of what would happen in the future. The past few years have already witnessed the good record of China's behaviour in international economic organisations and its earnestness in implementing the bilateral trade agreements with the United States. Moreover, the moves of the Chinese government since the conclusion of the Sino-US agreement have been promising signs in terms of implementation of its WTO commitments. These moves did not necessarily suggest that before WTO accession China was fully prepared for the implementation of all the relevant WTO obligations, but they do demonstrate that China is serious about its commitments. With the fledging out of its market-oriented reform and the proper functioning of institutional rule-based mechanisms, the world will see a co-operative China in the international community. One has more reason to assure the effectiveness of the dispute settlement mechanism within the multilateral trading system and other external monitoring mechanisms. China can be shepherded into the role of a responsible world power.

Notes

1. The following articles, found from a vast pool of literature, deal with important aspects of the process of China's GATT/WTO accession: Guiguo Wang, China's Return to GATT, 28 *Journal of World Trade* 3 (1994), at: 51; James V. Feinerman, Chinese Participation in the International Legal Order: Rogue Elephant or Team Player?, 141 *The China Quarterly* (March 1995), at: 186; Thomas Yunlong Man, National legal restructuring in accordance with international norms, *Indiana Journal of Global Legal Studies*, 4 (1996) 1, at 471; A. Neil Tait and Kui-Wai Li, Trade Regimes and China's Accession to the World Trade Organization, 31 *Journal of World Trade* 6 (1997) at: 93; Zhao Wei, China's WTO accession—Commitments and prospects, 32 *Journal of World Trade* 2 (1998), at: 51; Willem van der Geest, Bringing China into the Concert of Nations: An Analysis of its Accession to the WTO, 32 *Journal of World Trade* 3 (1998), at: 99; David M Blumenthal, Applying GATT to marketizing economies, 2 *JIEL* 1 (1999), at: 113; Sylvia A. Rhodes, John H. Jackson, United States Law and China's WTO accession Process, 2 *JIEL* 3 (1999), at: 497.

2. According to the Protocol, China is bound not only by "the WTO Agreement as rectified, amended or otherwise modified by such legal instruments as may have entered into force before the date of accession," but also by the this Protocol, which shall include China's commitments referred to in paragraph 342 of the Working Party Report.2 The "WTO Agreement" here refers to Agreement Establishing the World Trade Organization, the agreements and associated legal instruments included in Annexes 1, 2 and 3 (i.e. Multilateral Trade Agreements). In other words, China's obligations after its WTO accession are under various legal instruments, which shall be an integral part of the WTO Agreements.

3. Theories of international trade seem to have paid insufficient attention to the cost of adjustment a country must incur as it moves from a closed economy to an open economy. The theories emphasise the gains from trade. It is true for the industries enjoying a comparative advantage; however, it does not hold for the industries that do not enjoy a comparative advantage where the country is opened to trade. The latter has difficulty adjusting to the new environment. As a matter of fact, the Chinese government's bid for WTO accession caused concerns about the impact of a WTO membership on nearly all walks of life in China. One concern is about the soaring unemployment that entry into the WTO would lead to. According to an estimate, within seven years of China joining the WTO, 14.5 percent of jobs in the automobile industry, or 500,000 positions, will be lost and 3.6 percent of agricultural jobs, or 10 million positions, will disappear. But the same study also predicted a leap of 52.3 percent of jobs in the clothing industry and a 23.6 percent increase in positions in the textile industry as foreign quotas on imports of the industries' products are removed. See, *Beijing Youth Daily*, 16 November 1999, p. 2. In order to appease these concerns, the government has to defend that "[n]ot one of 134 member countries saw its economy collapse because of entry into the WTO." Xinhua News Agency, 2 January 2000.

4. See Hong Kong Trade Development Council, "China Announces New Round of Tariff Cut," *SME News Flash*, 7 March 2001.

5. In contrast, the ratio of duties collected to imports ranged from 2.5 percent for the US (excluding imports from NAFTA partners), over 2.3 percent in Japan and to 1.7 percent for the EU (excluding intra-EU imports) in 1999.

6. For example, while the automotive part duties ranged as high as 50 percent on parts from MFN trading partners, in notices issued on 10 July 1997, China Customs granted 20 percent import duty rates to two Chinese automobile manufacturers for their imports of certain automobile parts. The Notices cited domestic content exceeding 80 percent in sedans manufactured by the two automobile manufacturers as the basis for granting preferential import duties on parts imported by the two manufacturers.

7. In August 1998, Customs launched an ambitious program to standardise regulatory enforcement as part of an anti-smuggling campaign. Early reports indicate that the program has reduced the flexibility of local customs offices to "negotiate" duties but it is too early to measure the permanent effects of the program on customs enforcement.

8. According to Protocol, China committed itself to open its mobile telephony market in five yeas. The EU successfully negotiated with China to allow foreign participation two years ahead of schedule in the Sino-EU agreement. It may be interesting to note that EU has secured from its agreement with China a satisfactory settlement concerning the mobile investments of EU

telecommunication companies (France Telecom, Siemens/Deutsche Telekom and Telecom Italia) in the second Chinese operator, China Unicom.

9. Economic needs test means, to a degree, that the examining and approving authorities may act on their discretion to decide whether the proposed foreign investment is needed by the national economy.

10. Insurance business will be opened to foreign companies five years after accession according to Sino-US agreement, but the Sino-EU agreement places the schedule two years sooner than foreseen in the Sino-US agreement. The European Union secured from its agreement an extra Chinese commitment, i.e., seven new licences to European insurers that are to be issued immediately after conclusion of the agreement.

11. According to the current Interim Provisions on the Administration of Resident Representative Offices of Foreign Enterprise (30 October 1980), no representative offices of foreign firms are allowed to engage in profit-making business.

12. Ibid.

13. Although China clarified that only the central government could issue regulations on non-tariff measures and that these measures would be implemented or enforced only by the central government or sub-national authorities with authorization from the central government, sub-national authorities have been observed to impose, *de facto*, many non-tariff measures on a non-transparent, discretionary and discriminatory basis.

14. Products covered were (1) Processed oil; (2) Wool; (3) Polyester fibre; (4) Acrylic fibres; (5) Polyester fillet; (6) Natural rubber; (7) Vehicles tyres; (8) Sodium cyanide; (9) Sugar; (10) Fertilizer; (11) Tobacco and its products; (12) Acetate tow; (13) Cotton; (14) Motor vehicles and their key parts; (15) Motorcycles and their engines and chassises; (16) Colour television sets and TV kinescope; (17) Radios, tape recorders and their main parts; (18) Refrigerators and their compressor; (19) Washing machines; (20) Recording equipment and its key parts; (21) Cameras and their bodies (without lenses); (22) Watches; (23) Air conditioners and their compressor; (24) Audio and video tape duplication equipment; (25) Crane lorries and their chassises; (26) Electronic microscopes; (27) Open-end spinning machines; (28) Electronic colour scanners; (29) Grain; (30) Vegetable oil; (31) Wine; (32) Colour sensitive material; (33) Chemical under supervision and control that were used for chemical weapon; (34) Chemicals used to produce narcotics; and (35) Laser disc production facilities.

15. This included a commitment, for example, that a Chinese Government agency would no longer deny permission to import a foreign product because a domestic alternative exists.

16. One exception is that only the machinery and electronic products listed in Annex 3 were subject to specific tendering requirements and that these requirements would be administered pursuant to Chinese regulation, that is, Chapter III of the Interim Measures for Import Administration of Machinery and Electronics Products (approved by the State Council on 22 September 1993 and promulgated in Order No. 1 by the State Economic and Trade Commission and Ministry of Foreign Trade and Economic Cooperation on 7 October 1993).

17. China confirmed that these commercial terms of trade would be at the sole discretion of the quota holder, so long as the products are within the relevant quota category.

18. Nicholas Lardy, a leading China economy observer from Brookings Institution, estimates that the number of products subject to quotas and licenses was 261 tariff lines in 1999 (1,247 in 1992). While comparable estimates of the trade coverage of non-tariff barriers over time are not available, the number of tariff lines subject to quotas and licenses were 261 in 1999 (384 in 1997).

19. For instance, the MOFTEC has been authorised by the State Council to publish irregularly the foreign trade- and foreign investment-related policies, laws and regulations and invitations to bid for quotas and the results in International Business (Guoji Shangbao), the official newspaper of MOFTEC.

20. The Interim Provisions on Guidance for Foreign Investment and the Catalogue for the Guidance of Foreign Investment Industries are the regulations to this end. The Interim Provisions classify projects involving foreign investment into four categories: projects in which foreign investment shall be encouraged, permitted, restricted or prohibited. They provide, for example, that broadcasting and television stations are closed to foreign investment, and broadcast and television transmitting systems are only partially open to foreign participation. For the latter, majority Chinese participation is a must.

21. In this respect, the practice often differs from the law. For example, Article 37 of the Detailed Rules for the Implementation of the Law of the People's Republic of China on Chinese-Foreign Co-operative Joint Ventures provides: a co-operative joint venture may decide, on its own, to purchase either within the territory of China or from foreign countries machines and equipment, raw materials, fuels, parts and components, accessories, transportation tools and office articles, etc. But in practice the partners are "encouraged" by the local government to make a commitment on the local content rate. Failure to set a local content may sometimes result in disapproval of the contract.

22. Article 12 (8) of the above-cited Detailed Rules is a similar provision in relation to the minimum export rate which reads: "[The contract of a co-operative joint venture shall bear the following items:] Arrangement for sales of products in and outside China." A minimum export rate of the sales is not referred

to directly but has the same effect. Article 38 further confirms that "The State encourages co-operative joint ventures to sell their products on international markets."

23. Article 46 (4) of the Implementing Regulations of the Chinese-Foreign Equity Joint Venture Law provides: "[A]fter the expiration of the licence agreement, the importing party is entitled to further use of the licensed technology."

24. Article 28 (1), (2) of TRIPS Agreement.

25. It has been a practice that the authorities at the provincial level have a say over the proposed foreign investment that falls within the geographical scope of the province, but within the approving scope of the central government. Moreover, the central authority is normally stricter than the local authorities in screening proposed foreign investment since the latter is always eager to reap the direct benefits that the proposed foreign investment project might result in, while the central authority might be so concerned with the overall economic equilibrium as to dismiss the investment proposal at a particular locality.

26. For instance, under extraordinary US pressure, China in 1994 signed an agreement with the United States, committing itself to establish a regime for IPRs, which is comparable to the regime embodied in the current international treaties. The agreement establishes the model for China to follow in its legislation on IPRs.

27. To establish joint trade companies is part of China's efforts to invigorate the SOEs, including the state trading companies. However, while the reform aims to shape the ill-performing state trading companies into genuine "operating entities which are autonomous in their operations, responsible for their own profits or losses, self-developing and self-restraining," it employs administrative measures, thus making it difficult to evaluate the impact of the reform.

28. The commodities that are imported principally through state trading enterprises include grains, cotton, vegetable oils, petroleum and certain related products.

29. Until now all foreign purchases of Chinese raw silk—accounting for 70 percent of the world total production—had to go through state export channels.

30. The oil and fertiliser sectors are the most significant domains where a state import monopoly has been in place.

31. To open industries that are under exclusive control of SOEs to foreign investors provides an additional stimulus for the government to open the industries concerned to domestic private companies. For instance, in the Chinese People's Political Consultative Conference (CPPCC) conference, an initiative to open the telecommunication industry that used to be monopolised by the SOEs and that was to be opened to foreign participation under the Accession Protocol to domestic private enterprises gained much support. Also, in the

Accession Protocol, China has committed itself to establishing large and increasing tariff-rate quotas for wheat, corn, rice and cotton with a substantial share reserved for private trade.

32. Article 89 (9) of the Constitution (as amended in 1998).

33. Article 67 (14) of the Constitution provides that the Standing Committee of the National People's Congress has the power to "decide on the ratification or abrogation of treaties and important agreements concluded with foreign states." The provision suggests the agreements that are not "important" are not subject to approval by the NPC Standing Committee.

34. Article 142 of the GPCL. Also, see Article 238 of the Civil Procedure Law (CPL), which reads, "Where the provisions of international treaties which China has concluded or to which China is party are different from those of this law, the former shall apply, except those clauses to which China has made reservation."

35. Similarly, on 10 April 1987, the SPR issued the Notice on the Implementation of the Convention on the Recognition and Enforcement of Foreign Arbitral Awards to Which China Has Acceded. The Notice, which serves as internal directive within the judiciary, requires the courts which receive an application or are requested for judicial assistance to conscientiously handle the matter strictly in conformity with the provisions of the treaties which China has concluded or acceded to.

36. Provisions on the Implementation of the International Copyright Treaties (30 September 1992).

37. The Provisions on the Implementation of Patent Co-operation Treaty in China (23 November 1993).

38. According to the Legislation Law, laws are enacted by the NPC or its Standing Committee while the State Council is responsible for adopting administrative regulations in accordance with the constitution and the laws. See Article 7 and Article 56 respectively. Presumably laws shall prevail in case of conflicts between laws and administrative regulations. According to the Law for the Organisation of the People's Courts, the SPR have the power to issue, to the people's courts at all levels, judicial interpretations regarding the application of the laws and the decrees. See Article 33. Presumably, the judicial interpretations shall not contravene with the laws.

39. Li Peng, Chairman of the NPC Standing Committee, was reported to hold that the NPC should make feasibility studies on incorporating international agreements into national laws whose enactment falls exclusively within the scope of the NPC or its Standing Commitment. See *Legal Daily*, 29 April 2000, available at <http://www.legaldaily.com.cn/20000430/200004300102.html>. Like in other countries, the State Council (executive branch of the Chinese govern-

ment) assumes more and more powers that formerly belonged to the legislature (the NPC and its Standing Committee). Li's proposal might result from a consideration that the legislature should secure more power from the State Council. But, it would result in a positive effect on the implementation of the international agreements if it became a reality.

40. See The World Bank Beijing Office Press release, 8 July 1999, available at: <http://www.worldbank.org.cn/english/news/press/99fyresult.htm>.

41. See, for instance, Jemal-ud-din Kassum, the World Bank Vice President for the East Asia and Pacific Region, who, in his visit to China in March 2000, expressed satisfaction with the strong and fruitful collaboration that the Bank has developed with China over the past two decades and reaffirmed the bank's strong commitment to China. See The World Bank Beijing Office Press release, 17 March 2000, available at <http://www.worldbank.org.cn/english/news/press/kassum1.htm>.

42. An example is that the IMF and the People's Bank of China established a medium-term joint training program, targeted at Chinese officials involved in the formulation and implementation of macroeconomic and financial policies, as well as the compilation and analysis of statistics. See *The International Monetary Fund News Brief*, No. 00/11, 21 February 2000.

43. For example, Xiao Gang, Deputy Governor of the People's Bank of China, in his statement at the International Monetary and Financial Committee meeting on 16 April 2000, reiterated that the role of the IMF is "irreplaceable." The statement is available at <http://www.imf.org/external/spring/2000/imfc/CHN.HTM>.

44. Quoted from Margaret M. Pearson, China's Track Record and the Global Economy, *The China Business Review*, January-February 2000, also available at <http://www.uschina.org/public/wto/uscbc/pearson.html>.

45. Take the protection for local automobile industry as an example. In order to create more market shares for local automobile industries before foreign auto giants are allowed to compete in the domestic market after the WTO accession, the provinces and municipalities, where large automobile companies are located, have begun to remove the restraints on auto sales, such as reducing plate charges which might be as much as half of the sale price of auto levels. However, some localities apparently have gone this far against the policy of the central government. For example Hubei Province, which hosts a Chinese-French automotive joint venture and the No. 2 Auto Factory, one of the largest Chinese auto makers, adopted a policy which pegss the plate charges for autos manufactured outside the province at prices three times higher than those for local-made autos. See *Economic Daily* (Jiji Ribao), 20 June 2000, available at <http://WWW.peopledaily.com.cn/GB/channel3/25/20000620/110620.html>.

46. For a review of the centre-locality relations, see James V. Feinerman, The Give and Take of Central-Local relations, 25 *China Business Review* 1 (1998), pp. 16-25.

47. Notably the Ministry of Information Industry, which oversees telecoms and the Internet, is particularly unwilling to open the telecommunication service market to foreign participation. According to a report, before the conclusion of the Sino-EU agreement, Minister Wu Jichuan, albeit liberal in rhetoric, moved to cancel foreign equity stakes in China Unicom and in Chinese Internet content providers. See Susan V. Lawrence et al, Deal of the Century, *Far Eastern Economic Review*, 25 November 1999, available at <http://www.feer.com/9911_25/p80trade.html>.

48. In contrast, the China International Economic and Trade Arbitration Commission (CIETAC) has become a relatively effective forum for the arbitration of trade disputes. CIETAC's policies that approve foreign professionals to act as arbitrators, and streamline procedural requirements to allow for timely resolution of disputes have been well received by the foreign business community. The business community continues to press, however, for improvements in CIETAC rules, including increased flexibility in choosing arbitrators, and enhanced procedural rules to ensure orderly and fair management of cases.

49. See Huan Xiang, Strive to Build up New China's Science of International Law, in Selected Articles from *Chinese Yearbook of International Law*, Beijing: China Translation & Publ. Corp. 1983, p. 3.

50. Understandably, this negative viewpoint of international law is closely linked to the unhappy historical experience with international law.

51. It has been a practice that China promotes its theory of Five Principles of Peaceful Existence on almost every international forum. The Five Principles, which are based on the notion of absolute sovereignty, include: mutual-respect sovereignty and territorial integrity, mutual non-aggression, mutual non-interference with internal affairs, equality and mutual benefits, and peaceful co-existence.

52. For instance, see The WTO needs China more and China needs the WTO (in Chinese), *Jingji Ribao* (Economic Daily), 20 January 2000, available at <http://www.xinhua.org/ssjj/cnwto_08/files/201414081.htm>.

53. As a matter of fact, it is perceived by the drafters of the Dispute Settlement Understanding that "The dispute settlement system of the WTO is a central element in providing security and predictability to the multilateral trading system." See Article 3.2 of the Dispute Settlement Understanding.

54. For example, the U.S. has been the most frequent user of the WTO dispute settlement mechanism, obtaining favourable results so far on 23 of the 25 complaints that it has initiated and that have been acted upon.

55. Annex 3, part A (i).

56. Council for Trade in Goods, Council for Trade-Related Aspects of Intellectual Property Rights, Council for Trade in Services, Committees on Balance-of-Payments Restrictions, Market Access (covering also ITA), Agriculture, Sanitary and Phytosanitary Measures, Technical Barriers to Trade, Subsidies and Countervailing Measures, Anti-Dumping Measures, Customs Valuation, Rules of Origin, Import Licensing, Trade-Related Investment Measures, Safeguards, Trade in Financial Services.

57. It is surprising that China agreed to the U.S. unilateral invoking of Special 301, Section 301 trade legislations, to which China had been strongly opposed. Presumably, the WTO's ruling on the legality of the provision against the European Union in relation to the WTO rules was the reason behind the agreement in this regard. With respect to the treatment of China as a non-market economy in the application of antidumping rules, Australia and European Union have agreed to drop such treatment after China's entry into the WTO.

58. The Agreement on Safeguard provides that "...a Member may apply a safeguard measure to a product only if that Member has determined that such product is being imported into its territory in such increased quantities, absolute or relative to domestic production, and under such conditions as to cause or threaten to cause serious injury to the domestic industry that produces like or directly competitive product." Here, "serious injury" means a significant overall impairment in the position of a domestic industry. In determining whether increased imports have caused, or are threatening to cause, serious injury to domestic industry, the authorities should evaluate "all" relevant factors of an objective and quantifiable nature having a bearing on the situation of that industry, including inevitably the rate and amount of the increased product from the whole world. For an analysis of the Agreement on Safeguards, see, for instance, Y.S. Lee et al., Reflections on the Agreement on Safeguards in the WTO, 21 *World Competition* 6 (1997/1998), pp. 25-49.

59. According to the WTO Agreement on Safeguards, safeguard measures, in principle, have to be applied irrespective of source. However, it would be possible for the importing country to depart from this approach if it could demonstrate, in consultations under the auspices of the Safeguards Committee, that imports from certain contracting parties had increased disproportionately in relation to the total increase and that such a departure would be justified and equitable to all suppliers.

60. Chinese industries will continue to carry the burden of proving that market economy conditions prevail in their industry to avoid application of the non-market economy methodology. However, China also continues to have the opportunity to establish that market conditions prevail in a particular sector

or the economy as a whole and that the U.S. non-market economy methodology should not apply. Commerce is charged with evaluating any such claims.

61. The plan includes the following: 1) establishing a new Deputy Assistant Secretary for China devoted to monitor and enforcing trade agreement; 2) assembling a rapid response team of 12 compliance and trade specialists based both in Washington, DC and China; 3) dispatching immediately a team member to China to assess compliance needs and priorities of the U.S. business community; 4) establishing a China-specific subsidy enforcement team to ensure that China abides by its WTO commitments; 5) launching a new website containing detailed information on China's accession commitments, contact names, and up-to-date information on China's laws and regulations; etc. Available at the White House's China Trading Relations Working Group's website, <http://www.chinapntr.gov/factsheets/cinitiative.htm>.

62. See <http://europa.eu.int/comm/trade/bilateral/china/imp.htm>.

3

Preparing China's Trade and Legal Systems for WTO Compliance

1. Introduction

As a rule-based multilateral trading body, the WTO requires its mem bers to conform to WTO Agreements, which are in essence the product of the well-established market economies.[1] As a WTO Member, China has to follow suit.[2] To align with the WTO requirements, China has to bridge the gap between its trade-related regime and the WTO Agreements. That is to say, current laws and regulations pertaining to or affecting trade in goods, services, IPRs or the control of foreign exchange (forex), investment, business operations, and electronic commerce, etc., need to be drastically changed, revised or enacted.

More profoundly, China's WTO entry has introduced a new dimension to its on-going legal reform. In fact, the legal instrument that sets out the terms and conditions for China's accession to the WTO, i.e. the Accession Protocol, established a comprehensive framework for China's ongoing reforms and for further development of healthy commercial relations between China and the other WTO Members. Among other things, China's administrative and legal environment needs to be further developed to make it more complete, consistent, transparent, and enforceable. In other words, China has to create a "rule of law" environment consistent with WTO Agreements.

It is safe to say that, while generating certain immediate improvements in the trade and investment environment, China's WTO accession set the goal for the legal reform in China. However, it is fair to argue that with or without WTO membership, there is no turning back for China's progress into a market-oriented economy and rule-based society. While WTO accession will not change China overnight legally as well as economically, it will provide an impetus for the country to push forward the many much-needed reforms.

2. Benchmark for Furthering China's Market-oriented Economic Reform

Since 1979, China had been progressively reforming its economic system, with the objective of establishing and improving the socialist market economy. The reform, which covered the banking, finance, taxation, investment, forex and foreign trade sectors, had brought about major breakthroughs in China's socialist market economy. To name a few: SOEs had been reformed by a clear definition of property rights and responsibilities, a separation of government from enterprise, and an establishment of the modern enterprise system. Consequently, the state-owned sector is getting on the track of growth through independent operation, responsible for its own profits and losses. China is aiming at a nation-wide unified and open market system, an improved macroeconomic regulatory system that allows market forces to play a central role in economic management and the allocation of resources, and an effective tax and financial system. The central bank severed its commercial arm and focused on financial regulation and supervision. The exchange rate of the Chinese currency RMB had been unified and remained stable. The RMB had been made convertible on current account. As a result of continuous liberalization of pricing policy, the majority of consumer and producer products are subject to market prices only.

However, due to the inheritance of various characteristics of the centrally-planned economy, market economy is far from established in China. Fortunately, the WTO Agreements act as a valuable reference for China's market economy. The WTO multilateral trade system is based on the market economy. Among the members of WTO, more than 120 are countries of market economy, and another 10 are transitional countries from the East Europe or former Soviet Union. The tenet of the WTO is to reduce trade barriers, advance trade freedom through implementation of non-discrimination principle, and to allow for the optimal use of resources in accordance with the objective of sustainable development. In the process of negotiation on China's accession to the WTO, China was urged to put in place a fair and equitable market system, which embodies the benchmarks for China to restructure its economic system. The following is an elaboration of these benchmarks:

Non-discrimination: in respect of the procurement of inputs and goods and services necessary for production of goods and the conditions under which their goods were produced, marketed or sold, in the domestic market and for export, and in respect of the prices and availability of goods and services supplied by national and sub-national authorities and public or state enterprises, in areas including transportation, energy, basic telecommunications, other utilities and factors of production, contrary to the long-held practice of discriminating between Chinese and foreign individuals and enterprises and between different foreign individuals and enterprises, China entered a commitment to provide the same treatment to Chinese enterprises including foreign-invested enterprises (FIEs), and foreign enterprises and individuals in China, and eliminate dual pricing practices as well as differences in treatment accorded to goods produced for sale in China in comparison to those produced for export. It would also provide non-discriminatory treatment to all WTO Members, including Members of the WTO that were separate customs territories.

Fiscal and monetary policy: With respect to fiscal and monetary policy, China committed to further improving its taxation system and the efficiency of fiscal expenditure through implementing reform measures such as sectoral budget, centralized payment by the national treasury and zero base budget, as well as improving management of fiscal expenditure. It will also continue to pursue a prudent monetary policy, maintain the stability of RMB, promote interest rate liberalization, and establish a modern commercial banking system.

Foreign exchange and payments: China would implement its obligations with respect to forex matters in accordance with the provisions of the

WTO Agreements and related declarations and decisions of the WTO that concerned the IMF. In accordance with these obligations, and unless otherwise provided for in the IMF's Articles of Agreement, China would not resort to any laws, regulations or other measures, including any requirements with respect to contractual terms, that would restrict the availability to any individual or enterprise of forex for current international transactions within its customs territory to an amount related to the forex inflows attributable to that individual or enterprise.

Balance-of-payments measures: China would fully comply with the provisions of the GATT 1994 concerning balance-of-payment measures (BOPs) and the Understanding on the Balance-of-Payments Provisions of the GATT 1994. Further to such compliance, China would give preference to application of price-based measures as set forth in the BOPs Understanding. It confirmed that measures taken for BOPs reasons would only be applied to control the general level of imports and not to protect specific sectors, industries or products.

Investment regime: China had a long practice of guiding investment to targeted areas and sectors. In the Accession Protocol, China confirmed that these investment guidelines and their implementation would be revised to be in full conformity with the WTO Agreements.

State-owned and state-invested enterprises: State-owned and state-invested enterprises had played a leading role in China's economy and the government had continuously created such enterprises through investment. In the process of negotiation, China entered a commitment not to influence, directly or indirectly, commercial decisions on the part of state-owned or state-invested enterprises, including those on the quantity, value or country of origin of any goods purchased or sold, except in a manner consistent with the WTO Agreements.

In addition, China also committed to reform its **pricing policies** and **competition policy**, two important aspects of China's economic system.

3. Criteria for Updating the Trade Regime in Line with the Accession Protocol

There were huge gaps between China's trade regimes and the Accession Protocol before China acceded to the WTO. In view of this, the Accession Protocol set forth the criteria for a WTO-consistent trade regime in China. The criteria primarily concern three aspects: policies affecting trade in goods, trade-related investment measures, and IPRs.

3.1. Policies affecting trade in goods

Policies affecting trade in goods concern trading rights, importation regulation, export regulation, internal policies affecting trade in goods.

3.1.1. Trading rights

Trading rights is the historical issue of China's trade regime. As a legacy of the centrally planned economy, only companies with the necessary right, i.e. trading right, are allowed to conduct foreign trade. Most of these companies are state-owned trading enterprises, although numerous non-state entities have also been granted the right to conduct foreign trade; more importantly, the conditions for obtaining trading rights for both private enterprises and SOEs converged on 1 January 2001.[3] However, a few commodities critical to the national economy and the people's livelihood are still monopolized by joint state companies.[4] Private companies and companies with trading rights are barred from transacting in these commodities.[5] In addition, FIEs had the right to trade, although this was restricted to the importation for production purposes and exportation, according to the enterprises' scope of business. Such restrictions were inconsistent with WTO requirements, including Articles XI and III of GATT 1994. China has committed to progressively liberalize the availability and scope of the right to trade so that within three years after accession all enterprises would have the right to import and export all goods (except for the share of products listed in Annex 2A to the Accession Protocol reserved for importation and exportation by state trading enterprises) throughout the customs territory of China.

3.1.2. Import regulation

Import regulation covers regulation of tariff and non-tariff measures.[6] The latter includes rules of origin, fees and charges for services rendered, application of internal taxes to imports, tariff exemptions, tariff rate quotas, quantitative import restrictions, import licensing, customs valuation, preshipment inspection, anti-dumping, countervailing duties and safeguards. The following is to examine the major import regulation.

Tariffs: Tariffs are regulated by the Customs Law, the Import and Export Tariff Regulations, and the Customs Import and Export Tariff Schedule, and administered by the General Administration of Customs directly under the State Council. This legal framework makes tariff regulation in China exceptionally transparent as compared to other aspects of trade regime. Moreover, China had up to the accession conformed to the tariff reduction commitments that were first specified in the Sino-US agreement and reflected in the Accession Protocol,[7] although its average tariff level was still high in comparison with the WTO's developed country Members and most developing Members.

Non-tariff measures: As a result of the negotiation on China's accession to the WTO, China listed, in Annex 3 of the Accession Protocol, all of the products subject to quotas, licenses and such tendering requirements in China. It confirmed that after China's accession, no non-tariff measures would be implemented unless justified under the WTO Agreements, and that all non-tariff measures, whether or not referred to in Annex 3, would be allocated and otherwise administered in strict conformity with the provisions of the WTO Agreements, including Article XIII of the GATT 1994 and the Agreement on Import Licensing Procedures, including notification requirements.[8] China further committed to implementing the growth rates for quotas as indicated in Annex 3 during the relevant phase-out period, and not imposing upon quota holders any commercial terms of trade, including product specifications, product mix, pricing, and packaging.[9] In the process of negotiation, China confirmed that it would not introduce, re-introduce or apply non-tariff measures other than listed in Annex 3 of the Accession Protocol, unless justified under the WTO Agreements.

Rules of origin: China committed to establishing in China's legal framework by the date of accession a mechanism that meets the requirements of the WTO Agreement on Rules of Origin, which required provision upon request of an assessment of the origin of an import or an export and outlined the terms under which it would be provided. In contrast with the widespread transhipment practice, e.g. by exporters in textile, China promised not to use the rules of origin as an instrument to pursue trade objectives directly or indirectly.

Import Licensing: in 1999, China applied import licensing restrictions to 35 product categories.[10] China confirmed that the list of all entities responsible for the authorization or approval of imports would be updated and republished in the official journal, the MOFTEC Gazette, within one month of any change thereto. China also would bring its automatic licensing system into conformity with Article 2 of the Agreement on Import Licensing Procedures upon accession.

Customs valuation: In respect of customs valuation, China confirmed that, upon accession, China would apply fully the Customs Valuation Agreement, including the customs valuation methodologies set forth in Articles 1 through 8 of the Agreement. In addition, China would apply the provisions of the Decision on the Treatment of Interest Charges in Customs Value of Imported Goods, and the Decision on the Valuation of Carrier Media Bearing Software for Data Processing Equipment, adopted by the WTO Committee on Customs Valuation, as soon as practicable, but in any event no later than two years from the date of accession.

Anti-dumping: Anti-dumping is another prominent issue that reveals a gap between the WTO Agreements and the Chinese trade regime. Like their counterparts in other countries, Chinese industries have increasingly invoked regulatory barriers to curb the impact of cheap imports.[11] According to foreign traders, serious deficiencies are present in China's Regulations on Anti-dumping and Anti-subsidies of 1997 in the light of the Anti-dumping Agreement in the WTO. In certain cases, the basis for calculating dumping margins for a preliminary affirmative determination was not disclosed to interested parties. Furthermore, the determination of injury and causation did not appear to have been made on an objective examination of sufficient evidence-all inconsistent with the WTO Anti-dumping Agreement. Against this backdrop, China committed to revising its current regulations and procedures prior to its accession in order to fully implement China's obligations under the aforesaid WTO Agreement, including instituting judicial review.[12]

Safeguards: In the Accession Protocol, China promised to adopt and implement a new regulation that would be fully consistent with the WTO Agreement on Safeguards.

3.1.3. Export regulation

Export regulation concerns such issues as customs tariffs, fees and charges for services rendered, application of internal taxes to exports, export licensing and export restrictions, and export subsidies. In this regard, China's export licensing and restrictions are most controversial.

China applied its export license system to certain agricultural products, resource products and chemicals. In contrast, export prohibitions, restrictions and non-automatic licensing could only temporarily be applied under Article XI of the GATT 1994 to prevent or relieve critical shortages of foodstuffs or other products essential to an exporting WTO Member. Despite the steady reduction in the number of products subject to export licensing in China, the remaining number of such restrictions was still high, covering about ten per cent of export trade. China committed to abiding by WTO rules in respect of non-automatic export licensing and export restrictions. The Foreign Trade Law, from which the export licensing and restrictions result, would also be brought into conformity with GATT requirements. Moreover, export restrictions and licensing would only be applied, after the date of accession, in those cases where this was justified by GATT provisions.

3.1.4 Internal policies affecting foreign trade in goods

Internal policies affecting foreign trade in goods cover a variety of policy issues, including taxes and charges levied on imports and exports, industrial policy, technical barriers to trade, sanitary and phytosanitary measures (SPS), trade-related investment measures, state trading entities, special economic areas, transit, and agricultural policies. In the following, China's commitments relating to technical barriers to trade, SPS measures will be visited.

Technical barriers to trade: As a result of China's efforts in the past 20 years, the use of international standards as the basis for technical regulations had increased from 12 per cent to 40 per cent. The rest are so-called national, local and sectoral standards, the adoption of which is often without prior public consultation and comment. In the Accession Protocol, China made a commitment that upon accession, it would have in place minimum timeframes for allowing public comment on proposed technical regulations, standards and conformity assessment procedures as set out in the TBT Agreement and relevant decisions and recommendations adopted by the TBT Committee, and that notices of adopted and proposed technical regulations, standards and conformity assessment procedures would be published. Given various government standardizing bodies at various levels, China had, prior to the accession, merged the China State Administration for Entry-Exit Inspection and Quarantine (CIQ-SA) and the China State Bureau of Technical Supervision (CSBTS)[13] into the State General Administration for Quality Supervision and Inspection and Quarantine (AQSIQ); China entered a commitment that it would, upon accession, provide a list of relevant local governmental and non-governmental bodies, and, not later than four months after accession, notify acceptance of the Code of Good Practice. In addition, it would speed up its process of revising the current voluntary national, local and sectoral standards so as to harmonize them with international standards.

Sanitary and phytosanitary measures: China would not apply SPS measures in a manner which would act as a disguised restriction on trade. In accordance with the SPS Agreement, China would ensure that SPS measures would not be maintained without sufficient scientific evidence. China would fully comply with the SPS Agreement and would ensure the conformity with the SPS Agreement of all of its laws, regulations, decrees, requirements and procedures relating to SPS measures from the date of accession.

3.2. Trade-related IPRs regime

In the process of negotiating the Accession Protocol, China entered commitments to expand its IPRs regime to cover all the main areas of IPRs so that protection of geographical indications and layout designs of integrated circuits would be available,[14] to raise the substantive standards of protection, including procedures for the acquisition and maintenance of IPRs, to take further measures to control abuse of IPRs, and to fortify enforcement. For example, in relation to IPRs enforcement, China committed to amending civil judicial procedures and remedies, making available provisional measures,[15] strengthening administrative sanctions against IPRs infringement, improving special border measures for IPRs protection, and lowering the threshold for initiating criminal procedures to ensure full compliance with the TRIPS Agreement.

3.3. Policies affecting trade in services

Among the policies affecting trade in services are licensing, choice of partner, modification of the equity interest, and minority shareholder rights.

Licensing: upon accession China would ensure that China's licensing procedures and conditions would not act as barriers to market access and would not be more trade restrictive than necessary.

Choice of partner: Pre-accession Chinese practice that imposed conditions on Chinese companies allowed to partner with foreign service suppliers could amount to *de facto* quotas, as the number of potential partners meeting those conditions might be limited. In a move which contrasted starkly with the old practice, China confirmed that a foreign service supplier would be able to partner with any Chinese entity of its choice, including outside the sector of operation of the joint venture, as long as the Chinese partner was legally established in China.

Modification of the equity interest: Foreign partners in joint ventures often find it difficult to modify the equity interest to meet the needs, as they have to procure the consent of the Chinese partners and the approval of the Chinese authorities. In the Accession Protocol, China confirmed that the Chinese and foreign partners in an established joint venture would be able to discuss the modification of their respective equity participation levels in the joint venture, and more importantly, that that such an agreement would be approved if consistent with the relevant equity commitments in China's Schedule of Specific Commitments.

Minority shareholder rights: In the Accession Protocol, China confirmed that, while China had limited its market access commitments in some sectors to permit foreigners to hold only a minority equity interest, a minority shareholder could enforce rights in the investment under China's laws, regulations and measures. Moreover, WTO Members would have recourse to WTO dispute settlement to ensure implementation of all commitments in China's schedule under the GATS.

In this regard, it should be pointed out that in the Schedule of Specific Commitments, reproduced in Annex 9 to the Accession Protocol, China made specific market access commitments in respect of services.

4. WTO Accession Sets Goal for Reforming China's Legal Systems

Since 1978, establishing a regulatory regime to sustain a market economy has been brought to the forefront of the market-oriented reform in China. The country has made enormous strides in constructing the framework and necessary institutions. The NPC and its Standing Committee have promulgated 406 laws; the State Council has adopted over 889 pieces of administrative regulations; and local people's congresses and local people's governments have made more than 8,000 local regulations and rules.[16] These laws, administrative regulations, and local regulations and rules constitute the country's basic legal framework. However, China is still far from having in place highly sophisticated and efficient legal and administrative systems. The rule of law has not progressed in tandem with market reform, which has been accompanied by a high degree of decentralization. Increasingly, more power is devolved to regional and local bureaucrats; as a result, administrative and legal mandates from the central authority are often ignored at local levels, though to a lesser degree in major cities, e.g. Beijing and Shanghai.[17] Consequently the uniform implementation of law became even more difficult to achieve. Moreover, the basic legal framework still falls short of the standards required for proper functioning in a market economy. One example is the independence of the industry regulator. In China, no clear-cut mandatory division between regulator and operator exists. Although the Anti-unfair Competition Law (1993) prohibits price-fixing, prevents predatory pricing, etc., it did not have any substantive or proper procedures in place to prevent anti-competitive behavior by the dominant state operators.[18]

The WTO Agreements contain minimum standards of due process, which are in line with highly sophisticated and efficient legal and administrative systems found in market economies. These include theoretical provisions for notice of hearings; the right to appear with a counsel in court; publication of the rationale behind new commercial and investment regulations; introduction of standards of evidence; and an obligation for prompt legal and administrative decisions, accompanied by a discussion of the reasons behind the action. In other words, member states are to have in place a credible and equitable system of commercial and administrative law. These laws, regulations and rules of general application are to be published or made accessible and be implemented uniformly.

In the Accession Protocol, China declared that, by accession, it would repeal and cease to apply all such existing laws, regulations, measures, rules and notices, or any other form of stipulations or guidelines whose effect was inconsistent with WTO principles on national treatment.[19] China confirmed that administrative regulations, ministerial rules and other central government measures would be promulgated in a timely manner so that China's commitments would be fully implemented within the relevant time frames. If administrative regulations, ministerial rules or other measures were not in place within such time frames, the authorities would still honour China's obligations under the WTO Agreements and the Accession Protocol. China further confirmed that the central government would undertake in a timely manner to revise or annul administrative regulations, ministerial rules, local regulations, government rules and other local measures if they were inconsistent with China's obligations under the WTO Agreements and Accession Protocol. China further confirmed that the central government would ensure that China's laws, regulations and other measures, including those of local governments at the sub-national level, conformed to China's obligations undertaken in the WTO Agreements and the Accession Protocol. It further confirmed that the provisions of the WTO Agreements, including the Accession Protocol, would be applied uniformly throughout its customs territory, including in SEZs and other areas where special regimes for tariffs, taxes and regulations were established, and at all levels of government. In order to address the concerns of foreign traders over the lack of transparency regarding the laws, regulations and other measures that applied to matters covered in the WTO Agreements and the Accession Protocol and the difficulty in finding and obtaining copies of regulations and other measures undertaken by various ministries as well as those taken by provincial and other local authorities, China entered a commitment, among other things, to apply those laws, regulations, rules and other measures that have been made public in designated official publications.

In reply to the concerns about whether China's central government would be sufficiently informed about non-uniform practices and would take necessary enforcement actions, China committed to establishing, upon accession, a mechanism by which any concerned person could bring to the attention of the central government cases of non-uniform application of the trade regime and receive prompt and effective action to address situations in which non-uniform application was established. Therefore, all individuals and entities could bring to the attention of central government authorities cases of non-uniform application of China's trade regime, including its commitments under the WTO Agreements and the Accession Protocol. Such cases would be referred promptly to the responsible government agency, and when non-uniform application was established, the authorities would act promptly to address the situation utilizing the remedies available under China's laws, taking into consideration China's international obligations and the need to provide a meaningful remedy.

As for judicial review that had not been firmly established in China, the Accession Protocol dictated that China revise its relevant laws and regulations in accordance with the requirements of the WTO Agreements and the Accession Protocol on procedures for judicial review of administrative actions.

It is not difficult to find that the commitments or obligations, as specified in the Accession Protocol, are substantial in any sense because they basically concern all the major important dimensions of a legal system, align laws and regulations adopted by authorities at various levels, uniform administration of laws and regulations, transparency and institutionalising of judicial review.

In fact, these commitments are the goals for the legal reform in China. It is safe to say that, to fully perform its international obligations, China needs to engage in an unprecedented project to systematically revise and update its relevant domestic laws. This is the first time in the history of the PRC that the legal system is remolded in a substantial scale merely to keep in line with international treaties.[20] In other words, fulfilling the commitments in the Accession Protocol is tantamount to embrace a sweeping legal reform, including reforming the power structure.[21]

5. On-going Institutional Reform towards WTO Compliance

5.1. An overview of the efforts towards WTO compliance

China's efforts to prepare for WTO accession have so far involved state organs with legislative powers, administrative organs and the judiciary. What appears to be of top priority is the legislative constituent, with the focus on amending laws and regulations governing trade-related regimes.

5.1.1. Legislative efforts

To satisfy the WTO requirements, new laws and regulations are adopted, many existing ones revised, and conflicting laws and regulations removed. Therefore, various authorities with legislative powers—the NPC and its Standing Committee, the State Council, ministries, and local People's congresses and local governments, have been busy doing so to provide legislative assurance for the new situation after the WTO entry. As part of the efforts, after the conclusion of the Sino-US agreement on China's accession to the WTO in November 1999,[22] the State Council established a WTO Leadership Team, a ministerial-level coordination body reporting directly to the State Council Legislative Office. The Team has the mandate to, among others, guide the work of "cleansing and revising laws and regulations." The Legislative Office even sent a delegation to India, a similarly populous developing country, to learn how India adjusted its laws to meet the requirements of the WTO.[23] In this regard, the MOFTEC set up another working group (i.e. the Leadership Team for WTO-related Legal Work) soon after the signing of the Sino-US agreement in December 1999 to study similar issues. The MOFTEC team was also tasked by the State Council to review and revise all the trade-related laws and regulations as well as the rules of other ministries. It worked closely with ministries to review and revise certain trade-related rules these ministries had adopted. All non-trade-related laws and regulations would fall within the purview of the State Council Legislative Office under the guidance of the WTO Leadership Team.

In 2000–2001, the aforesaid body launched a second round of comprehensive review of the administrative regulations. The compliance of the WTO requirements was used as the express criteria for the new round of review. As a result, the State Council promulgated the Decision on Termination and Repealing of Certain Administrative Regulations Promulgated before the End of 2000 on 6 October 2001.[24] According to Shi Guangsheng, Minister of Foreign Trade and Economic Cooperation, the State Council alone had, up to August 2001, revised or repealed 2,300 regulations and legal instruments.[25] After completing the amendments to most national laws and regulations, China has started streamlining local regulations and rules.

The following illustrates the major results of the legislative efforts towards WTO compliance.

In the recent two years, the NPC and its Standing Committee enacted or revised 10 laws pertaining to or affecting foreign trade and investment. They are the Contract Law, the Customs Law,[26] the Drug Administration Law, the Wholly Foreign-invested Enterprise Law (WFIE Law), the Chinese-Foreign Contractual Joint Venture Law (CJV Law), the Chinese-Foreign Equity Joint Venture Law (EJVL), the Patent Law, the Trademark Law and the Copyright Law. The NPC Standing Committee is currently preparing to revise or enact the Law on Foreign-invested Enterprise Income Tax, the Partnership Law, the Foreign Trade Law, the Law on Import and Export Commodity Inspection, the Government Procurement Law, the Quarantine Law, the Insurance Law, the Anti-monopoly Law, the Telecommunications Law. It is also drafting the Law on Compulsory Administrative Measures (*xingzheng qiangzhi cuoshi fa*), the Administrative License Law (*xingzheng xüke fa*), the Administrative Billing Law (*xingzheng shoufei fa*), and the Administrative Process Law (*xingzheng chengxu fa*).[27] It has been reported that the NPC annual meeting in March 2002 will focus on these legislations.[28] China is reportedly preparing to update the Unfair Competition Law.

On the part of the State Council, it has carried out most of the burdensome work for adopting, revising and abrogating laws and regulations. For example, it promulgated the Anti-dumping Regulations and the Anti-subsidies Regulations to replace the Anti-dumping and Anti-subsidy Regulations. Also, the Safeguard Regulations, the Regulations on Goods Import and Export, the Regulations on Technology Import and Export, the Regulations on Foreign Investment in Telecommunications Enterprises, the Regulations on International Maritime Transportation, the Regulations on Foreign-Invested Insurance Companies, the Regulations on Cinema, and the Regulations on Representative Offices of Foreign Law Firms in China were adopted.[29] The Regulations on Travel Agencies and the Regulations on Foreign-invested Financial Institutions were amended.[30]

Ministries and commissions, which adopt various ministerial rules, have also mobilized to this end. For example, the State Development Planning Commission (SDPC) has, among a total of 341 regulations and instruments released before the end of 2000, dumped 124 price regulations and will further revamp another 51 price regulations in order to fit its price laws into the framework of the WTO.[31] The State Economic and Trade Commission (SETC) repealed 13 pieces of its ministerial rules released before the end of 2000.[32] Also, the People's Bank of China, the country's central bank, abrogated 9 legal instruments that had been adopted from 1 January 1999 to 30 June 2001. The Ministry of Agriculture also annulled 11 pieces of ministerial rules partially inconsistent with the WTO Agreements and would further repeal 15 pieces.[33]

In addition, local people's congresses and local people's governments have acted to streamline the local regulations and rules in line with the WTO Agreements. Not only have the developed coastal regions spared no efforts in this regard, but the economically backward regions are also doing so. For example, while Shanghai has planned to spend two years cutting red tape to ensure it is in full compliance with the WTO, Ganshu Province, declared that 41 pieces of WTO-inconsistent local regulations or rules had been repealed before the accession.[34]

5.1.2. *Administrative efforts*

Administrative measures taken for the WTO accession include setting up an enforcement task force and specialized agencies for WTO affairs, reforming governmental functions, launching pilot projects for foreign participation, and training trade and law-enforcing officials. Accustomed to using special task force to attain its policy goal, the Chinese have, for example, established a new National Anti-counterfeiting Coordination Committee to bring IPRs enforcement into WTO compliance. The task force is chaired by Vice-Premier Wu Bangguo. Numerous provinces and municipalities have also set up their own anti-counterfeiting teams. Specifically, on 1 November 2001, the MOFTEC set up, within the Ministry, the Department of WTO Affairs (*shijie maoyi zuzhi si*), the China-WTO Notification Enquiry Center (*zhongguo zhengfu shijie maoyi zuzhi tongbao zixun ju*) and the Fair Trade Bureau for Import and Export (*jinchukou gongping maoyi ju*). The SETC set up the Office for the Investigation of Injuries to Domestic Industries (*guonei chanye shunhai diaocha ju*) within the Commission. The State Administration of Industry and Commerce set up the Registration Office for Foreign-invested Enterprises (*waishang touzi qiye zhuce ju*) within the Administration. The Department of WTO Affairs is responsible for regular negotiation within the WTO framework, and China's relations with the WTO; the China-WTO Notification Enquiry Center is in charge of China's regular notification and enquiry as well as the deliberation over trade policies; the Fair Trade Bureau for Import and Export works on anti-dumping, anti-subsidy and safeguard measures, and coordinate China's response to foreign anti-dumping suits against Chinese exports.[35] The Investigation Office for Injuries to Domestic Industries is fully responsible for investigating the injuries suffered by the Chinese domestic industries as a result of foreign import surge. The Registration Office for Foreign-invested Enterprises administers the registration of FIEs and issuance of their business licenses.[36] In addition, prior to the accession, China had, pursuant to the WTO Agreement on Technical Barriers to Trade and Agreement on the Application of Sanitary and Phytosanitary Measures, set up a TBT notification authority and two enquiry points regarding technical barriers to trade, and an SPS notification authority and an SPS enquiry point. The establishment of the specialized agencies provides institutional safeguard for implementing China's WTO obligations.

Various governmental agencies have shifted their functioning focus from administering economic activities to serving the public. A typical example is the substantial slash of the licensed items. The SETC has cancelled 30 of 122 items of economic activities that needed licensing before operation. According to the drafter of the Administrative License Law, more than 1,000 items of licenses will be further cancelled.[37]

The Chinese authority has launched several pilot projects to experiment with allowing foreign investment in previously restricted sectors, including telecommunication services and fund management.[38] The Ministry of Information Industry (MII) and the State Development Planning Commission have also recommended special policies to lure initial foreign investment to China's northwest regions where telecom infrastructure and services are underdeveloped.

To familiarize its officials with WTO, the Chinese government has launched WTO training programs since 1999 at the central and provincial levels. Training programmes are not only prepared for high-ranking officials,[39] but also planned for all the civil servants across the country.[40] In addition, public lectures are also held from time to time to enhance the WTO-awareness.[41] The government has even acquired the cooperation and support from its major trading partners. The EU is spending 25 million euros (US$23 million) to train up Chinese officials on WTO rules and concepts, especially in translating them to domestic legislation. A consortium comprising the Washington-based International Law Institute, the University of Toronto and the Australian National University has set up a WTO training centre in Beijing to bring international experts to teach courses for Chinese administrators and lawyers on China's commitments.[42]

At local levels, governments have also taken measures to familiarize themselves with the WTO. Early in September 2000, the Shanghai Municipal Government adopted a "Shanghai Action Agenda: China's WTO Entry."[43] The Agenda provides guiding principles for the governmental agencies to prepare for the WTO accession. In addition, Shanghai initiated a WTO-awareness training project for 50 to 100 senior professionals.[44]

In addition to the government-sponsored training programmes, other training courses mushroomed after China's WTO entry.

5.1.3. Judicial efforts

Efforts of the judiciary to keep in line with the WTO Agreements must understandably coincide with those made by the legislature and administrative bodies. The Supreme People's Court (SPC) formally established a Leading Group of Judicial Preparation for the WTO Accession (*rushi sifa zhunbei gongzuo lingdao xiaozu*) in August 2001.

Judicial efforts include streamlining judicial interpretation, moving for more judicial independence, and promoting the professionalism of judges.

Judicial interpretations by the SPC play a special role in the Chinese legal system. These interpretations fall under the category "rules of general application" and are binding on the courts nationwide. The judiciary has realized that judicial interpretations and laws and regulations that are inconsistent with WTO Agreements must be sorted out and amended. The SPC adopted the Work Arrangement for Cleansing Judicial Interpretations Relating to the WTO (*guanyu qingli yu WTO youguan de sifa jieshi gongzuo anpai*).[45] It pledged to step up the drafting of judicial interpretations to clear the way for the judges. These judicial interpretations concern copyright cases, trademark cases, electronic commerce cases and administrative cases in association with the WTO.[46] According to the Press Conference held by the Court on 9 November 2001, the SPC had sorted 1,200 pieces of judicial interpretations for repealing or revising, which spanned from 1951.[47] In fact, up to 24 December 2001 it had published, in four batches, a list of repealed judicial interpretations adopted.

To reduce local interference, the SPC has already taken measures to reform the leading structure, switching gradually from two-fold leadership to vertical leadership. This means the higher court will have more say in the selection and appointment of ranking judicial staff of a lower court, which used to be reserved for the local party committee. The judiciary is also empowering judges to decide on cases. A scheme, "Judge in charge" (*zhusheng faguan*), is being carried out on a pilot basis. In the scheme, selected judges have the autonomy to adjudicate cases under their charge.

However, the "judges-be-responsible-for-wrongly-adjudicated-cases" (*faguan cuoan jiuzezhi*) movement counteracts the "judge in charge" effort. To address this, the professionalism of judges need to be raised. Chinese courts, particularly those in major cities, are working hard to improve the professional standard of judges. Some courts recruit law professors as judges,[48] some send their staff for further study in overseas universities.[49] The SPC has plans for systematic training of the presidents of High People's Courts and major Intermediate People's Courts. The National Judges College (affiliated to the SPC) has started to provide WTO-awareness training courses for 800 to 1,000 selected judges.

5.2. An evaluation of selected aspects of the institutional changes

5.2.1. Institutional change in trade system

Import and Export: China has spared no effort to align its trading regime in line with the WTO Agreements and the Accession Protocol. It has substantially changed its policies affecting trade in goods and services. The number of Chinese and foreign-invested companies with trading rights has increased with the removal of the elimination of export performance, trade balancing, forex balancing and prior experience requirements, such as in importing and exporting, as criteria for obtaining or maintaining the right to import and export upon accession. Its restrictive regulatory regime for import has been further liberalized by constant slashes of high tariffs, a standstill and gradual phase out of non-tariff barriers centred on import licensing and quotas,[50] and an amelioration of transparency of its administration of trade.[51] Particularly noteworthy is the change in anti-dumping regulation. The anti-dumping procedures of the new Anti-dumping Regulations differ substantially from old procedures, as the new Anti-dumping Regulations provide for administrative, arbitral, or judicial review, and require that such reviews be independent or effective.

China's export regulatory regime has also experienced major change, as China has, *inter alia*, streamlined its regulation on export licensing and restrictions, and standardized its application of internal taxes to export in line with its obligations under the Accession Protocol and the WTO Agreements. In addition, China has substantially reformed its internal policies affecting trade in goods by, for example, liberalizing its industrial policies, streamlining its technical regulation and sanitary and phytosanitary measures in accordance with the WTO Agreements.[52]

With respect to trade in services, China has also, *inter alia*, amended its regulations on licensing, deregulated choice of partners, and taken measures to protect minority shareholder rights, in addition to opening the sectors to foreign investment as specified in the Schedule of Specific Commitments.[53]

Trade-related investment measures: With regard to investment, numerous laws and regulations, including the CJV Law, the WFIE Law, the EJV Law, the Detailed Rules for the Implementation of the Wholly Foreign-invested Enterprise Law (WFIE Rules) and the Implementing Regulations of the Chinese-Foreign Equity Joint Venture Law (EJV Regulations), were revised to keep in line with the WTO Agreements. Limitations on foreign investors in terms of forex balance, priority of material purchasing in China, and sale of products to overseas markets were removed. New measures have been formulated covering such areas as the establishment of investment companies by FIEs and foreign companies engaged in contracting projects, and the setting up of research and development institutions by multinational corporations. China is also reviewing and revising its policies regarding taxation and forex transactions of FIEs in bank accounts opened in different localities. Efforts have also been made to attract more foreign capital to the reorganisation and reform of SOEs. For example, the Investment Fund Law is being drafted to this end.

However, some provisions in the amended foreign investment laws and regulations may still be controversial. For example, the previous provision allowing wholly foreign-invested enterprises to either export all or most of their products, or to use high-tech and advanced equipment has been re-phrased as "the State encourages the establishment in China of foreign-funded ventures whose products are export-oriented or with high technologies." The problem lies with terms such as "encourage" which leave room for manipulation by the relevant approving authorities.

Intellectual property rights: China had made the protection of IPRs an essential component of its reform and opening-up policy. The formulation of laws and regulations in this field could be traced back to the late

1970s. Since then, China had joined relevant international conventions and had actively participated in the activities sponsored by relevant international organizations.[54] As a result, notwithstanding the initial stage of its development, China's IPRs protection system is aimed at achieving world dimension and world standards. IPRs is one of the first areas which China undertook to align with the WTO Agreements, primarily due to the conclusion of Sino-US MOUs in 1992 and 1885. Immediately after the Sino-US IPRs MOU in 1995, the Intellectual Property Working Meeting under the State Council was set up in 1996 to overhaul China's IPRs legislations to bring them fully in line with the TRIPS Agreement. This had been taken before the conclusion of historical agreement between China and the United States on China's accession to the WTO in 1999. China committed, in the Sino-US Agreement, to bring the IPRs regime in full compliance with the TRIPS and reiterated this later in the Accession Protocol. China had conducted an intensive work programme to examine and revise the IPRs laws, administrative regulations and ministerial rules relating to the implementation of the WTO Agreements and China's accession commitments.

China committed itself to implement the TRIPS Agreement immediately upon accession—with no transition period. Therefore, the Patent Law, the Trademark Law and the Copyright Law had been revised and entered into force before the accession. Similarly, the Regulations for the Implementation of the Patent Law[55] had also been amended and came into effect before China's accession. The Regulations on the Protection of Computer Software were promulgated on 20 December 2001 and took effect on 1 January 2002. The Provisions on the Implementation of the International Copyright Treaty, the Regulations on Customs' Protection of Intellectual Property Rights, the Regulations on the Protection of New Varieties of Plants, the Regulations on the Implementation of the Integrated Circuit Layout Design are to be revised to conform to the TRIPS Agreement. In addition, upon accession China abrogated the ministerial rules regarding IPRs that were inconsistent with the TRIPS Agreement, i.e. the Interim Rules on the Administration of Patents in Agriculture, Animal Husbandry and Fisheries, the Notice on the Interim Regulation on the Protection of Copyright of Books and Magazines, the Detailed Rules of the Interim Regulations on the

Protection of Copyright of Books and Magazines, and the Regulations on the Administration of Audiovisual Products. All the newly amended or enacted laws and regulations, together with other applicable administrative regulations[56] and various ministerial rules[57] constitute a TRIPS-compatible IPRs regime.

Realizing that inadequate protection of foreign IPRs in China had been one of the main complaints from the international community, the drafters of the newly amended IPRs laws strengthened the enforcement mechanisms. For example, with respect to the protection of copyright and neighbouring rights, amendments to the Copyright Law in 2001 clarify the payment system by broadcasting organizations that use the recording products. The following provisions were also added to broaden the scope of copyrightable items: rental rights in respect of computer programs and movies, mechanical performance rights, rights of communication to the public and related protection measures, protection of database compilations. Moreover, provisional measures are specified, and the legitimate compensation amount increased to strengthen protection of copyrights. Similarly, modifications of the Trademark Law were mainly made to the following aspects: to include the trademark registration of three-dimensional symbols, combinations of colours, alphabets and figures; to add the content of collective trademark and certification trademark (including geographical indications); to introduce official symbol protection; to protect well-known trademarks; to include priority rights; to modify the existing trademark right confirmation system and offer interested parties the opportunity for judicial review concerning the confirmation of trademark rights; to crack down on all serious infringements; and to improve the system for providing damages for trademark infringement.

In addition, the latest revisions emphasize enforcement by including specifying detailed procedures for litigation, granting more power to local officials to investigate cases of infringement, and offering more compensation for infringement. With this TRIPS-compatible IPRs regime, the infringing activities could be curbed in a timely and effective manner and the legitimate rights of the right-holders could be protected.

5.2.2. Institutional change in legal system

Transparency: The legal system has to contend with long-held traditions of imperial China now inherited by the communist leadership, where law is subordinated to policy and used as a means to achieve the goals of the state. Hence, there have been cases of officials denying the public access to certain "normative documents" (*guifanxing wenjian*)—administrative directives that control government actions—which in fact belong to the public domain. In some cases, even judicial interpretations are held back from the public.[58] All these are against the WTO transparency discipline.[59] China undertakes that only those laws, regulations and other measures pertaining to or affecting trade in goods, services, IPRs or the control of forex that are published and readily available to other WTO Members, individuals and enterprises, shall be enforced. In addition, China shall make available to WTO Members, upon request, all laws, regulations and other measures pertaining to or affecting trade in goods, services, IPRs or the forex control before such measures are implemented or enforced. In emergency situations, laws, regulations and other measures shall be made available at the latest when they are implemented or enforced. Moreover, China would make available to WTO Members translations into one or more of the official WTO languages, of all laws, regulations and other measures pertaining to or affecting trade in goods, services, IPRs or the forex control, and to the maximum extent possible would make these laws, regulations and other measures available before they are implemented or enforced, but in no case later than 90 days after they are implemented or enforced. The State Council promulgated the Regulations on the Procedures for Enacting Administrative Regulations and the Regulations on the Procedures for Enacting Ministerial Rules On 26 November 2001, and the Regulations for Filing Regulations for Record on 21 December 2001, which became effective on 1 January 2002. These regulations not only provide the procedures for the State Council to adopt administrative regulations and for the ministries to adopt ministerial rules, but also, for the first time in the legislation history, require government to hold hearings before hammering out administrative regulations and ministerial rules and to release drafts of administrative regulations and ministerial rules that impact the interests of individual citizens, legal persons and other organizations to the public. Moreover, while previously, most administrative regulations and ministerial rules were effected the day they were promulgated. These regulations provide for a time between the date of promulgation and date of entry into force for the public to make comments on the regulations to be implemented.[60] These regulations would improve the transparency regarding administrative regulations and ministerial rules.

Despite this progress, access to information is still a problem. Chinese ministries routinely implement policies based on "guidance" or "opinions" that are not available to foreign firms and have not always been willing to consult with Chinese and foreign industry representatives before new regulations are implemented. Experimental or informal policies and draft regulations are regarded as internal matters and access to them is tightly controlled. It can be extremely difficult to obtain copies of draft regulations, even when they have a direct effect on foreign traders and investors. The opaque nature of customs and other government procedures also compromise the ability of businesses to take full advantage of commercial opportunities in China.

Law enforcement: Any discussion on legal reform in China is incomplete without reference to law enforcement in the country. In fact, the gap between the Chinese legal regime and the WTO requirements is most pronounced when it comes to enforcement of China's obligations under the Accession Protocol and the WTO Agreements. So far, attempts by Chinese authorities to improve law enforcement have been centred around administrative and judicial measures. Much work is still needed to ensure that agreements are not only honoured but also implemented. Recent years have seen attempts by the Chinese government to strengthen its hand administratively in the field of law enforcement.[61] Legal reform has strengthened the power of higher-level administration, enabling it to execute its orders more easily. In addition, it is able to ward off local protection with regard to trademark infringement and unfair-competition conduct.[62] In an effort to enhance fairness, openness and independence of its judicial process, on 20 February 1999, the SPC formally unveiled a comprehensive and ambitious five-year (1999–2003) court reform plan.[63] Among the announced principles for the reform are upholding the independent exercise of judicial power, upholding the unity of the legal system, and absorbing and contextualizing overseas experience in court and personnel management. Lawyers play an indispensable part in law enforcement in most advanced societies. In the Chinese context, the role of lawyers in law enforcement is far from what is due. Chinese lawyers are not only deficient in numbers,[64] but also generally not well trained.[65] Moreover, most Chinese law firms are small and suffer from a lack of specialization. All these cast doubts as to whether Chinese lawyers are able to meet the challenges posed by the WTO accession.

Yet, another interference in the proper functioning of the legal system in China has not been addressed, that is the culture of shared responsibility—by the legislature, the executive and the judiciary—that eschews the separation of power. Thus, while institutional change is occurring, Chinese courts interpreting and applying laws and procedures, for example, often defer to other entities (such as Party committees and governmental departments) at the cost of judicial independence, a necessary requirement dictated by the WTO Agreements.[66]

Notes

1. Before China acceded to the WTO, the world trading body had 142 Members, most of which are market economies or transitional economies.
2. For example, Premier Zhu Rongji assured US trade representative Barshefsky that China "will not renege on its promise and prove to be a responsible country" after its entry into the WTO when President Clinton sent her to China two days after he signed into law the bill on permanent normal trade relations (PNTR). See Zhu Rongji, "China to fulfill WTO Entry Promises," *China Daily*, 13 October 2000.
3. Currently, over 1,000 private enterprises (foreign investment enterprises excluded) have acquired their trade rights. See CCH's *China Law Update*, February 2001, p.13.
4. In 1999, there were 13 commodity categories which were imported by the foreign trade companies designated by MOFTEC. These categories were as follows: (1) Processed oil; (2) Fertilizer; (3) Tobacco; (4) Vegetable oil; (5) Grain; (6) Natural rubber; (7) Wool; (8) Acrylic fibers; (9) Sugar; (10) Cotton; (11) Crude oil; (12) Steel; and (13) Plywood. The designated trading accounted for 11 and 7 percent respectively of total imports in 1996. See World Bank *China Engaged: Integration with the World Economy*, 1997.

5. The MOFTEC declared this in a statement of basic foreign trade policies. See http://www.MOFTEC.gov.cn/moftec/business/questions_answers.html (last visited in May 2001).
6. Non-tariff measures refer to technical, bureaucratic or legal issues that may involve hindrances to trade. The WTO Secretariat lists the following as non-tariff trade barriers: technical regulations and standards, import licensing, rules for the valuation of goods at customs, preshipment inspection (further checks on imports), rules of origin and investment measures. See WTO Secretariat, Trading Into The Future: The Introduction to the WTO, available at http://www.wto.org/english/thewto_e/whatis_e/tif_e/agrm8_e.htm.

   Nicholas Lardy, a leading China economy observer from Brookings Institution, estimates that the number of products subject to quotas and licenses was 261 tariff lines in 1999 (1,247 in 1992). While comparable estimates of the trade coverage of non-tariff barriers over time are not available, the number of tariff lines subject to quotas and licenses was 261 in 1999 (384 in 1997).
7. For instance, on 1 January 2002, China further reduced its average tariff rate from 15.3 percent to 12 percent in accordance with the schedule set forth in the Accession Protocol.
8. One exception is that only the machinery and electronic products listed in Annex 3 were subject to specific tendering requirements and that these requirements would be administered pursuant to Chinese regulation, that is, Chapter III of the Interim Measures for Import Administration of Machinery and Electronics Products (approved by the State Council on 22 September 1993 and promulgated in Order No. 1 by the State Economic and Trade Commission and Ministry of Foreign Trade and Economic Cooperation on 7 October 1993).
9. China confirmed that these commercial terms of trade would be at the sole discretion of the quota holder, so long as the products are within the relevant quota category.
10. Products covered were (1) Processed oil; (2) Wool; (3) Polyester fibre; (4) Acrylic fibres; (5) Polyester fillet; (6) Natural rubber; (7) Vehicles tyres; (8) Sodium cyanide; (9) Sugar; (10) Fertilizer; (11) Tobacco and its products; (12) Acetate tow; (13) Cotton; (14) Motor vehicles and their key parts; (15) Motorcycles and their engines and chassises; (16) Colour television sets and TV kinescope; (17) Radios, tape recorders and their main parts; (18) Refrigerators and their compressor; (19) Washing machines; (20) Recording equipment and its key parts; (21) Cameras and their bodies (without lenses); (22) Watches; (23) Air conditioners and their compressor; (24) Audio and video tape duplication equipment; (25) Crane lorries and their chassises; (26) Electronic microscopes; (27) Open-end spinning machines; (28) Electronic colour scan-

ners; (29) Grain; (30) Vegetable oil; (31) Wine; (32) Colour sensitive material; (33) Chemical under supervision and control that were used for chemical weapon; (34) Chemicals used to produce narcotics; and (35) Laser disc production facilities.

11. Since the promulgation of the Anti-dumping and Anti-Subsidy Regulations in 1997, 12 investigations had been conducted as of 7 December 2001. Final determinations have so far been made in seven investigations. See the anti-dumping website maintained by the SETC: http://www.cacs.gov.cn/infor/lszl/lszl17.htm.

12. Interestingly, China has secured consent from the Working Party members that determinations made by China during investigations initiated pursuant to applications made before accession should be free from challenge under the Anti-Dumping Agreement by the Members of the WTO.

13. The CSBTS was responsible for adopting, administering and implementing technical regulation, standards and conformity assessment procedures for domestic products, and the CIQ-SA for imports.

14. Although the relevant rules of the SAIC and the State General Administration of the People's Republic of China for Quality Supervision and Inspection and Quarantine partly provided protection for geographical indications, including appellations of origin, the pre-amendment Trademark Law did not have a specific provision on the protection of geographical indications. Similarly, although China was one of the first countries to sign the Treaty on Intellectual Property in Respect of Integrated Circuits in 1989, it had not promulgated the specific Regulations on the Protection of Layout Designs of Integrated Circuits until April 2001. The Regulations came into effect on 1 October 2001.

15. Although in China's CPL there were provisions on property preservation, no explicit stipulations had been provided to authorize the people's court to take measures for the prevention of infringements prior to formal institution of a lawsuit by a party involved before the revisions of the IPRs laws and regulations.

16. Li Peng, The Work Report of the Standing Committee of the National People's Congress, *Gazette of the Standing Committee of the National People's Congress*, 2001, p. 243.

17. Prime Minister Zhu Rongji has often lamented that "resistance to the principles, policies and measures of the central authorities" is strong and unrelenting.

18. Take as example the Ministry of Information Industries (MII). While the MII and its provincial branches are the primary regulators and policymakers for the telecommunications sector, the same entities have remained as the dominant service providers in the sector. This is a clear violation of the principle

embodied in the WTO Basic Telecommunication Agreements to which China has agreed to subscribe.

19. However, in the cases of pharmaceuticals, spirits and chemicals, China would reserve the right to use a transitional period of one year from the date of accession in order to amend or repeal the relevant legislation.

20. In contrast, the bilateral agreements between China and the United States in 1992 and 1995 prompted China to reform its IPRs regime only.

21. In the negotiation, China clearly stated that sub-national governments had no autonomous authority over issues of trade policy to the extent that they were related to the WTO Agreements and the Accession Protocol.

22. China's preparation for the WTO accession began even earlier. Early in 1994, in an effort, in part, to become an original WTO Member, the State Council undertook a comprehensive review of its administrative regulations.

23. See Agence France-Presse (AFP) news, 12 November 2000.

24. This review repealed or declared ineffective pieces of administrative regulations, many of which pertain to foreign trade and foreign investment in China.

25. *Lianhe zaobao*, 18 August 2001.

26. The new Customs Law laid down the provisions concerning customs protection of IPRs and of origin and replaced the WTO-inconsistent rules of customs valuation in the old Law.

27. Li Peng, Chairman of the NPC Standing Committee, revealed this in his speech at the 4th Session of the 9th National People's Congress on 9 March 2001.

28. *Ming Pao News*, 12 December 2001.

29. On 31 October 2001, the State Council adopted the Anti-dumping Regulations, the Anti-subsidies Regulations, the Safeguard Regulations, the Regulations on Goods Import and Export and the Regulations on Technology Import and Export, which took effect on 1 January 2002. On 5 December 2001, the State Council adopted the Regulations on Foreign Investment in Telecommunications Enterprises, the Regulations on International Maritime Transportation, and the Regulations on Foreign-Invested Insurance Companies. The former two took effect on 1 January 2002 and the third on 1 February 2002. The Regulations on Cinema were adopted on 12 December 2001 and took effect on 1 February 2002; the Regulations on Representative Offices of Foreign Law Firms in China were adopted on 19 December 2001 and took effect on 1 January 2002.

30. The State Council amended the Regulations on Travel Agencies and the Regulations on Foreign-invested Financial Institutions on 5 December 2001 and 12 December 2001. The former took effect on 1 January 2002 and the latter on 1 February 2002.

31. Xinhua News Agency, 23 November 2001.

32. Xinhua News Agency, 10 December 2001.
33. *Economic Daily*, 14 December 2001.
34. *Legal Daily*, 11 December 2001.
35. The MOFTEC, News Release, 1 November 2001, available at http://www.moftec.gov.cn:7777/Detail.wct?RecID=20&SelectID=1& ChannelID=1951&Page=1.
36. *Ming Pao News*, 26 November 2001.
37. See Luo Xuhui and Zou Xinyu, One Thousand Licenses will be cancelled, *China Youth Daily*, 15 November 2001.
38. On 13 June 2000, Vodafone and China Unicom signed an agreement to cooperate in roaming services (http://www.vodafone.com/media/press_releases/ 9222.htm, last visited in July 2001). Lucent Technologies has secured a CDMA project with China Unicom to provide mobile telecommunication service (http://www.lucent.com.cn/, last visited in July 2001). Singapore Telecom is reported to have obtained permission to participate in the Internet services with the establishment of its alliance with China Netcom. Paris Asset Management and International Financial Corporation and China Shenying-International Securities, the leading Chinese financial services company, agreed to set up a joint venture fund management company "when time is ripe."
39. For instance, in November 2001, training courses kicked off in Beijing to train ministerial level officials. Many key personnel in ministries or provinces have attended the training course on the WTO that cover WTO-related issues, including the background on the WTO, information on WTO Agreements, and the impact of China's WTO accession on key industries. Courses for the highest-ranking officials have even covered the actual terms contained in China's bilateral agreements.
40. Zhang Xuezhong, Minister of Personnel, released this plan in a national conference on 4 January 2002. See Xinhua News Agency, 4 January 2002.
41. For instance, on 23 November 2001, some 3,500 Party and government officials and army officers in Beijing attended a lecture on China's accession into the WTO given by Shi Guangsheng, minister of Foreign Trade and Economic Cooperation.
42. Dan Biers, On Second Thought..., *Far East Economic Review*, Issue coverdated 22 February 2001.
43. Xu Kuangdi, Mayor of Shanghai, released the information in his speech at the 13th International Business Leaders Advisory Council for the Mayor of Shanghai on 4 November 2001.
44. Shangahi launch the three-year-long plan, aimed at training 100 senior professionals from 50 governmental agencies, large-scale SOEs, professional services and industrial associations. See Xinhua News Agency, 2 October 2001.

45. Li Guoguang, Vice-President of the Supreme People's Court released the information in his article "Prepare for the WTO Accession and Meet the Challenge" (in Chinese), available at the website of the People's Court Daily: <http://www.rmfyb.com.cn/public/detail.asp?id=30315&keyword=>.
46. *China Intellectual Property News*, 19 November 2001.
47. *People's Court Daily*, November 2001
48. For instance, the SPR has two former law professors as its Vice-Presidents. High People's Courts or Intermediate People's Courts of Shanghai, Beijing, Nanjing and Wuhan, etc. also have former law faculty staff as ranking judges.
49. The SPC, the High People's Courts of Beijing, Shanghai and Guangdong have dispatched 186 judges overseas for WTO awareness. The SPC planned to send overseas 70 more judges from selected High People's Courts and major Intermediate People's Courts for further studies.
50. Since the conclusion of the Sino-US Agreement, China had refrained from introducing new non-tariff barriers, or increasing the coverage of existing non-tariff barriers. In order to fulfil its commitment to bring its automatic licensing system into conformity with Article 2 of the Agreement on Import Licensing Procedures upon accession, it, *among other things*, promulgated the Measures for the Administration of Important Industrial Products Subject to Automatic Licensing on 15 January 2002, which entered into force on 1 February 2002.
51. China made public the list of import products subject to tariff rate quotas (TRQs), the List of Goods Specifically Reserved for Importation by State Trading Enterprises, the List of Goods Specifically Reserved for Exportation by State Trading Enterprises, the List of Importing State Trading enterprises, the List of Exporting State Trading Enterprises, the List of Goods Reserved for Importation by Designated Trading Enterprises, the List of Goods Reserved for Exportation by Designated Trading Enterprises, the List of Designated Importing Enterprises, the List of Designated Exporting Enterprises on 11 December 2001, and the Interim Measures for Tariff Rate Quotas of Chemical Fertilizers on 18 January 2002. However, the TRQs for agriculture products have not been official published, although the Draft Interim Measures for Tariff Rate Quotas of Agriculture Products have been made public for comment.
52. On 7 December 2001 a National Compulsory Product Certification System and a Catalogue of the First Products Subject to Compulsory Certification were announced to be established, effective on 1 May 2002.
53. For instance, China's insurance regulator approved plans by New York Life Insurance Co., Metropolitan Life Insurance Co. and other foreign insurance companies to set up life insurance operations on the day China became a WTO Member.

54. China became a member of the World Intellectual Property Organization in 1980. In 1985, China became a member of the Paris Convention for the Protection of Industrial Property. China was one of the first countries that signed the Treaty on Intellectual Property in Respect of Integrated Circuits, the negotiation of which was concluded in 1989. In 1989, China became a member of the Madrid Agreement Concerning the International Registration of Marks and in 1992, China became a member of the Berne Convention for the Protection of Literary and Artistic Works. In 1993, China became a member of the Convention for the Protection of Producers of Phonograms Against Unauthorized Duplication of Their Phonograms. In 1994, China became a member of the Patent Cooperation Treaty and a member of the Nice Agreement Concerning the International Classification of Goods and Services for the Purposes of the Registration of Marks. In 1995, China became a member of the Budapest Treaty on the International Recognition of the Deposit of Micro-organisms for the Purposes of Patent Procedure and applied for membership in the Protocols of the Madrid Agreement Concerning the International Registration of Marks. In 1996, China became a member of the Locarno Agreement on Establishing an International Classification for Industrial Designs; and in 1997, China became a member of the Strasbourg Agreement Concerning the International Patent Classification. Besides the above efforts, China participated in the TRIPS negotiations during the Uruguay Round and initialled the Final Act.

55. Adopted by the State Council on 15 June 2001 and entered into force on 1 July 2001.

56. The Provisions on the Implementation of the International Copyright Treaty

57. In the process of negotiation, China listed 35 pieces of ministerial rules related to IPRs that were currently in force.

58. Ironically, up to the date when China signed the Accession Protocol, all the bilateral agreements and multilateral instruments had not been made public. While the English version of the Accession Protocol was released via the Internet on 11 December 2001, the day China formally joined the WTO, the Chinese translation had not been made public until 26 December 2001.

59. Broadly defined, transparency would include: allowing business and other interested parties to comment on draft laws and regulations before they are finalized; making public all laws and regulations in full detail; and making public the reasoning used in later interpreting these laws and regulations. In China, making public all laws and regulations alone is a problem. Although the Legislation Law of 2000 requires laws, administrative regulations, local regulations, regulations for Self-government in minority autonomous regions, ministerial rules, and local government rules should be made public, this Law

does not authorize unified publication, thus cannot solve the problem of inaccessibility of the rules.

60. All the administrative regulations and ministerial rules, except for those concerning national security, forex policy and monetary policy and those which necessitate implementation on the day of promulgation, shall enter into force thirty days after their promulgation: *China Daily*, 28 November 2001.

61. In April 1998, the Patent Administration Office was transformed into the State Intellectual Property Office, a move some observers believe is the first step towards unifying the regulators in the field of IPRs. In December 1999, the Administration of Industry and Commerce was restructured to the effect that a lower Administration of Industry and Commerce is directly responsible to the Administration of Industry and Commerce above, rather than to the local government.

62. Take the example of law enforcement in the field of IPRs. Enforcement campaigns in the past years by the administrative organs have been so effective that production of pirated compact discs in China was almost wiped out overnight, so much so that the United States in April 1997 removed China from its "priority watch list" under the special 301 trade legislation that authorizes the United States to impose trade sanctions on countries not meeting its standards. China is on a lower level watch list, which still requires it to show "continuous improvements" in IPRs enforcement.

63. The SPC, Outline of Five-year Reform of the People's Courts, 20 October 1999.

64. China has only 101,220 lawyers as of 31 December 1998, accounting for 0.01 percent of the whole population.

65. Even according to the Lawyers Law that the NPC Standing Committee amended on 29 December 2001 to raise the benchmark for entry into the law profession, the following persons are eligible to become lawyers: those who hold (1) an undergraduate degree in law from an institution of higher education; (2) an undergraduate degree or higher qualification in another discipline or area of specialization from an institution of higher education, and who pass the examination for qualification as a juridical worker. Of all the lawyers, only 23,767 hold first law degrees, and 4,055 hold either a master's or doctor's degree or two bachelor degrees. See *China Judicial Administration Yearbook* (in Chinese), *1999*, Beijing: Law Press, 1999, p. 579.

66. Article X (3) of the GATT, Article VI of the GATS and Article 41 of the TRIPS Agreement all spell out the obligations for the WTO Members to ensure the independence of the administrative body or judiciary.

Part II

China and the WTO
Dispute Settlement Mechanism

4

Is China's Judiciary
Ready for WTO Entry?*

1. Introduction

Now that China has become a WTO Member, its foreign trade is ex
pected to increases. As a result, the number of disputes is also likely
to increase. It is expected that the WTO dispute settlement mechanism will
be able to resolve trade disputes between the Chinese government and
other WTO Members. Disputes between Chinese and foreign companies,
however, must rely largely on China's domestic judicial system for resolution. Moreover, the WTO dispute settlement mechanism needs the
cooperation of the Chinese domestic judiciary to enforce its rulings. Foreign
companies in China also need the domestic judiciary to enforce their rights
under the WTO Agreements in any dispute brought against the Chinese
government.

Given the perceivably huge gap between Chinese judicial system and
the requirements of WTO Agreements, China's entry into the WTO imposes the biggest ever challenge to its judicial system, which is crucial to
enforcing WTO-administered agreements within its territory.

---

* An earlier version of this article appeared in the *Harvard Asian Quarterly*. Autumn 2001.

This chapter examines the attempts of the Chinese judiciary to prepare for the WTO entry and align itself with the requirements of the WTO Agreements. Although any conclusive findings must await the availability of more empirical information, it is concluded that while the present unprecedented momentous efforts will help China conform to the WTO Agreements, there will still need to be further concerted measures to address the fundamental structural defects of its judicial system.

2. Relation between the WTO Agreements and the Judiciary of a WTO Member

2.1. WTO requirements for Members' judicial systems

2.1.1. Establish proper judicial procedures

The WTO Agreements lay down rules for instituting proper judicial procedures that provide prompt review of, and where justified, appropriate remedies for, administrative decisions. Article X (3) (b) of the GATT provides that each contracting party shall maintain, or institute as soon as practicable, judicial, arbitral or administrative tribunals or procedures for the purpose, *inter alia*, of the prompt review and correction of administrative action relating to customs matters. Article VI (2) (a) of the GATS provides that each Member shall maintain or institute as soon as practicable judicial, arbitral or administrative tribunals or procedures which provide, at the request of an affected service supplier, for the prompt review of, and where justified, appropriate remedies for, administrative decisions affecting trade in services. Article 41 (1) of the TRIPS Agreement also sets out the obligations of member governments to provide procedures and remedies under their domestic law to ensure that IPRs can be effectively enforced, by foreign right holders as well as by their own nationals. The purpose of these provisions is, *inter alia*, to put in place proper judicial procedures, which are the basic components of any judicial system.

It is true that the WTO Agreements do not require the institution of such tribunals or procedures inconsistent with its constitutional structure or the nature of its legal system.[1] However, for some Members, the provisions regarding the judicial system are presented in a surprisingly detailed way and amount to an obligation to revise their judicial systems substantially, particularly their judicial review system.[2]

2.1.2. Transparency of judicial proceedings

Article X:1 of the GATT provides that "[l]aws and regulations, and judicial decisions and administrative rulings of general application, made effective by any contracting party…shall be published promptly in such a manner as to enable governments and traders to become acquainted with them." Article 63 of the TRIPS Agreement provides that "[l]aws and regulations, and final judicial decisions and administrative rulings of general application, made effective by a Member pertaining to the subject matter of this Agreement…shall be published, or where such publication is not practicable made publicly available, in a national language, in such a manner as to enable governments and right holders to become acquainted with them." Here, the WTO Agreements actually require all the rules that judiciary apply, irrespective of the form they take, to be made accessible to the public.

2.1.3. High demands on adjudicators

The WTO Agreements implicitly set forth high demands for its Members' judiciary and other law enforcers. In addition to rules, the WTO Agreements provide for many standards, which are not specific enough to be directly applied.[3] An example is Article XX of the GATT, which requires further interpretation in order to be applicable.[4] The judiciary of its Members by implication has to draw or deduce from the disciplines the rules that are to be applied.

2.2. Uniform application of the WTO Agreements dependent on the judiciary

The *Agreement Establishing the World Trade Organization* provides that "(e)ach Member shall ensure the conformity of its laws, regulations and administrative procedures with its obligations as provided in the annexed Agreements."[5] Article X:3.a of the GATT further sets an obligation for the WTO Members to "administer in a uniform, impartial and reasonable manner all its laws, regulations, decisions and rulings." Article XXIV:12 of GATT also provides that WTO Members "shall take such reasonable measures as may be available to it to ensure observance of the provisions of this Agreement by the regional and local governments and authorities within its territories." The judiciary is viewed as the final arbitrator in relation to law enforcement and therefore is crucial to the uniform application of domestic laws and regulations. The judiciary will play an irreplaceable role in ensuring the uniform application of laws and regulations as required by the WTO Agreements and other obligations of the Member under the WTO Agreements.

2.3. Enforcement of private rights under the WTO Agreements

While most treaties are designed to create rights and obligations between the contracting parties, the WTO Agreements leave room for private parties to enforce their rights under the agreements. The TRIPS Agreement is an example. It requires Members to provide private entities with legal remedies under domestic law, thus making available enforcement to private parties.

It should be noted that private enforcement of WTO Agreements, theoretically, encompasses two situations: enforcement by a private party against its own state and enforcement by a private party against another WTO Member, either in the jurisdiction of that country or in an international forum.

2.4. Enforcement of WTO Panel rulings

A further relevant issue is related to the WTO dispute settlement mechanism. WTO Panel and Appellate Body Reports are binding in the domestic law of a WTO Member. Therefore, presumably, a foreign private party attempting to defend its interests vis-à-vis that Member's trade measures which the Panel finds to be not in conformity with the WTO Agreements, can enforce the findings in a WTO Member.

3. Defects of the Chinese Judiciary

3.1. Lack of independence

Although the Chinese authority has always insisted that judicial process in China is fair and open and that the judiciary is independent of all other state authorities, judicial fairness, openness, transparency and independence are goals rather than the reality. The unique Chinese political environment is unfavourable to judicial independence.

3.1.1. Preempting political task of the judiciary

It is well known that the judiciary is still used by the Party as an instrument to attain changing political goals.[6] There is an intrinsic conflict between the judiciary's assigned political function and its natural function as a neutral arbitrator. Courts dedicated to promoting that ideal of impartiality cannot be instruments of the Party that uses them to promote changing political tasks.

3.1.2. Highly politicized personnel management of the judiciary

According to the practice of cadre administration, judges, who fall within the category of cadres, are selected and appointed by either the Party Committee within the court or the local Party Committee.[7] Although the *Organizational Law of People's Courts* and the *Judges Law* provide that court presidents, vice presidents, chief judges of court divisions and judges are appointed by the standing committees of local People's Congresses at corresponding levels,[8] these personnel are in practice recommended by the local Party committee for the people's congress for approval.[9] Moreover, courts are regarded as state/Party organs and judges, particularly the presidents, vice presidents, may be former Party/government officials. The interaction between judges and other officials is highly probable. Therefore, courts are constrained by the local Party Committee and local people's congress at the personnel level. In this regard, it is fair to argue that judicial independence will never be fully realized without the clear-cut separation of powers among legislatures, executive and judicial branches. In view of this, President Jiang Zemin's recent speech denouncing the principle of separation of powers is a blow to the judicial independence.[10]

3.1.3. Budget allocation constraint

In addition, at the level of budget administration, courts are treated the same as other Party/state organs in that their budget is appropriated by the local people's government through the financial department, whose budget plan is subject to the approval of the local people's congress. That is to say, courts are dependent on the local financial authorities.

3.1.4. Supremacy of the Party's political-legal committee

According to the institutional arrangement, the local Party political-legal committee, which is a leadership organ within the Party for political and legal work, orders that the important and difficult cases be referred to it for "discussion." Consequently, local interference is commonplace.

3.1.5. The hierarchical structure of the judiciary

Judicial independence also means that judges handling a given case should be free from interference from other judges. However, the hierarchical structure of the Chinese judiciary hampers judges from independently adjudicating cases. In the Chinese context, judges are not equal. Instead, they are fixed into a hierarchical bureaucracy. Every judge is made responsible for the head of a division that he belongs to, and the division is responsible to the Judicial Committee (*shenpan weiyuanhui*) that is headed by the President of the court.[11] In most, if not all, cases, it is the division head or the president or the Judicial Committee, rather than the judges that handle the given cases, who render judgements. As regards important cases, the rendering of judgments is exclusively within the province of the Judicial Committee.

3.1.6. Non-institutional center-locality relationship

The non-institutional center-locality relationship harbours local protectionism. China is a vast, multi-ethnic, centralized country. In theory, all local powers stem from the centre. Even regions with ethnic minorities where a certain degree of self-government is instituted do not possess similar powers to those of sub-federal entities in federal nations. With the introduction and development of reform that aims at economic mobility, the localities have been given more powers and thus more resources to administer the economy in the localities. Driven by local interests, local leaders have become less obedient to the centre. As a result, the laws and regulations promulgated by the centre are unevenly implemented at the local levels.[12] The disobedience of sub-central government authorities often take the form of interfering with local judicial process, particularly in the enforcement of judgements unfavourable to local interests.

3.2. Lack of professionalism

Judges are not regarded as professionals who require systematic and profound training. The 1995 *Judges Law* requires judges to be graduates of tertiary educational institutions in law or in other subjects who have acquired specialized legal knowledge.[13] However, the *Judges Law* permits judges appointed before the coming into effect of this law, who do not meet such standards, to retain their posts by undergoing necessary training. Most judges are not university graduates. Many are former PLA officers. They learn law on the job and through such court-sponsored training programs as the "Spare Time Universities" (*yeyu daxue*) affiliated with High People's Courts or Intermediate People's Courts. Moreover, the presidents or vice presidents and other ranking court officials are normally transferred from military, Party or government posts. The professional level of the judiciary does not measure up to those in other jurisdictions.

Moreover, Chinese judges are not creative in the interpretation and application of laws and procedures. They tend to rely on existing rules for adjudicating cases since they do not have the power to make rules by adjudicating cases. Moreover, they rely heavily on their superior courts for interpretations or directives. Due to this dependence and the average low capacity of the judiciary, the judiciary lacks judicial initiatives.

3.3. Susceptible to corruption

Corruption is widespread in China and the judiciary is no exception.[14] Bribery among Chinese judges and Party or governmental officials seems to indicate public disrespect for the law. Various reasons have been offered for this anti-social behaviour.[15] Although the *Judges 'Law* prohibits judges to meet privately with litigants and their agents, approaching judges and discussing litigated matters with them outside the courtroom, a practice illegal in nearly every country with an established legal system, is a common sight in China.[16] Making matters worse, such advocacy often occurs over meals or in a karaoke lounge. Moreover, the conduct of litigation, e.g. providing funds to judges collecting evidence and seeking favoritism, nurtures the corruption in the judiciary.[17]

3.4. Unreliable enforcement practice

Enforcement proceedings represent an area in which foreign and domestic litigants often encounter difficulties and enforcement has become an increasingly large problem. A particular problem is the backlog of non-enforced judgments. A typical example is that local courts and their enforcement personnel are coaxed by local companies or are placed under pressure from local government to delay or avoid enforcing court judgments.[18] Although the Supreme People's Court (SPR) occasionally launches an enforcement campaign, enforcement of judgments remains a recurring problem. Xiao Yang, President of the SPR, admitted this in his Work Report of the SPR at the 4th Session of the 9th National People's Congress on 10 March 2001.[19]

3.5. Lack of transparency

3.5.1. Judicial interpretations are not accessible to the general public
In the Chinese sources of law that the courts must observe, judicial interpretations of the SPR belong to the category of rules of general application. Courts may interpret laws and regulations only when adjudicating cases. Nevertheless, the judicial interpretations of the SPRs play a special role in the Chinese legal system. The Constitution does not specify whether they have legal force. However, for the uniform application of laws, the NPC Standing Committee authorizes the SPR to interpret laws and decrees relating to their specific application at trial.[20] Moreover, the SPR has asserted that it has the authority to give courts at different levels directives, in the form of judicial interpretations, concerning the application of laws and regu-

lations in relevant cases.[21] In fact, its directives are binding on the courts across the country, thus assuming the same legal effect as laws and regulations.

3.5.2. The proceedings are not transparent

Due to the practice of advocacy outside the courtroom, the existence of the real decision-making body of the Judicial Committee in the courts and the overriding political-legal committees of the Party, the judicial proceedings may vary from case to case, despite the provisions of the procedural laws. Therefore, the proceedings are not transparent. Also the judgments are generally not made public, although selected cases have been publicized for various purposes.[22] This lack of accessibility is disastrous when it comes to the judgments of the SPR because the precedents of the SPR are perceived to be able to serve as reference where courts adjudicating cases are to identify the applicable law, though it is unclear how binding they are.

3.6. Unique judicial mentality

The Chinese have a traditional aversion to litigation. The preference for non-adversary resolution has also affected the mentality of the Chinese judiciary. The Civil Procedure Law (CPL) authorises the tribunal or judges to sponsor non-adversarial processes even during the proceedings.[23]

Due to the underdevelopment of law, the Chinese judiciary used to adjudicate cases on the principle of "equality and mutual benefit." The stress on this abstract principle may affect the manner in which judges approach the task of resolving disputes and deter the Chinese judiciary from centering on the rights and obligations as provided for by the laws and regulations.

4. On-going Judicial Reform

Despite the many defects, the judicial scene is being changed through reforms, which started from 1996, and is best exemplified by the promulgation of the revised *Criminal Procedure Law* that year. Since then, pressures to reform China's civil and economic trial procedures have begun to emerge within and outside the judiciary. It is fair to say that the fundamentally flawed judicial process has been put on the legislative and judicial reform agenda.

On 20 February 1999, the SPR formally unveiled its comprehensive and ambitious Outline of Five-year (1999–2003) Reform of the People's Courts (*Outline*). Among the plans announced for the reform are moves towards the independent exercise of judicial power, upholding the unity of the legal system and the absorption of overseas experience in court and personnel management while paying attention to China's own circumstances.

In order to alleviate local interference, the SPR has already taken measures to reform the leading structure, switching gradually from two-fold leadership (*shuangchong lingdao*) to vertical leadership (*chuizhi lingdao*). That means that the supervising court will have more input into the selection and appointment of ranking judicial staff of a lower court, which have hitherto been the exclusive domain of the local Party Committee.

Also, as part of the efforts to achieve greater judicial independence, reform is being carried out to award judges more power to decide cases. The principle of "judge in charge (*zhusheng faguan*)" is being implemented on a pilot basis to allow these selected judges to have greater autonomy in adjudicating the cases in hand. However, the "judges-be-responsible-for-wrongfully-adjudicated-cases" (*faguan cuoan jiuzezhi*) movement counteracts the "judge in charge" effort.

Since the promulgation of the *Outline*, the efforts to promote the professionalism of judges have been quite steady. Chinese courts, particularly those in major cities, are working hard to improve the professional standard of judges. Some courts have recruited judges from among law professors.[24] Others send their staff to study in universities. The SPR has formulated a plan for systematically training presidents of High People's Courts and of major Intermediate People's Courts. The National Judges College, affiliated to the SPR has started to provide selected judges with a series of training courses, among which is a series of WTO-related training courses.[25] Some courts in major cities have also engaged in their own training programs for judges. It has been observed that the judicial reforms could substantially improve the work of the judiciary as well as the judiciary itself.[26]

In addition, particularly noteworthy is that on 1 January 2002, not long after China's formal accession to the WTO, the SPR launched a comprehensive website for the nation's judicial work involving foreign elements and maritime adjudication. Among other things, it exhibits the notice of hearings of courts and publishes laws and regulations, judicial interpretations, and judgments and awards.[27] This new development is expected to further improve judicial practice involving foreign elements.

5. China's Commitments Relating to the Judicial System

5.1. A separate tribunal to ensure the administrative compliance of WTO Agreements?

In the process of negotiation on China's WTO accession, some members of the Working Party pointed out that China should designate, among others, independent tribunals for the prompt review of all administrative actions relating to the implementation of laws, regulations, judicial decisions and administrative rulings of general application referred to in Article X:1 of the GATT 1994, including administrative actions relating to import or export licences, non-tariff measures and tariff-rate quota administration, conformity assessment procedures and other measures. Designating tribunals, embodied in the proposal, is tantamount to setting up separate tribunals for the purpose of implementing the WTO Agreements.

Indeed, in the Chinese judicial system, there are already established special court or tribunals for various purposes. Examples are the Courts of Railway Transportation, Maritime Courts across the country and Adjudicating Tribunals for Intellectual Property Cases in major courts at various levels.

Noteworthy is that China did not respond directly to the proposal; instead, it confirmed that China would revise its relevant laws and regulations so that its relevant domestic laws and regulations would be consistent with the requirements of the WTO Agreements and the Accession Protocol on procedures for judicial review of administrative actions. In response to questions from certain members of the Working Party concerning judicial independence, China further stated that the tribunals responsible for such reviews would be impartial and independent of the agency entrusted with administrative enforcement, and would not have any substantial interest in the outcome of the matter.

5.2. Institutionalising judicial review for WTO Compliance?

In the process of negotiations on China's WTO accession, many members of the Working Party sought explicit confirmation that certain types of measures, such as decisions relating to standards and chemical registration, would be subject to judicial review. Some members of the Working Party also demanded that the administrative actions subject to review include any actions required to be reviewed under the relevant provisions of the TRIPS Agreement and the GATS. These members demanded that such tribunals be independent of the agencies entrusted with administrative enforcement of the matter and should not have any substantial interest in the outcome of the matter, and that such review procedures should include the opportunity for appeal, without penalty, by individuals or enterprises affected by any administrative action subject to review. If an initial right of appeal were to an administrative body, there should be an opportunity to choose to make a further appeal to a judicial body. Any decision by any appellate body and the reasons therefore would be communicated in writing to the appellant, together with notification of any right to further appeal.

In response, China confirmed that it would revise its relevant laws and regulations so that its relevant domestic laws and regulations would be consistent with the requirements of the WTO Agreement and the Accession Protocol on procedures for judicial review of administrative actions. China confirmed that administrative actions related to the implementation of laws, regulations, judicial decisions and administrative rulings of general application referred to in Article X:1 of the GATT 1994, Article VI of the GATS and the relevant provisions of the TRIPS Agreement included those relating to the implementation of national treatment, conformity assessment, the regulation, control, supply or promotion of a service, including the grant or denial of a licence to provide a service and other matters, and that such administrative actions would be subject to the procedures established for prompt review under Section 2(D)(2) of the Accession Protocol, and information on such procedures would be available through the enquiry point that China would establish upon accession.

6. What Needs to Be Done to Align the Judiciary with the WTO Requirements?

The NPC Standing Committee and the State Council have been taking measures to identify and revise laws and regulations inconsistent with the WTO Agreements. In order to align with the WTO Agreements, the effort of the judiciary must coincide with the endeavors of the legislature and administrative bodies. By and large, the judiciary needs to take the following measures:

6.1. Re-examination of judicial interpretations

The judiciary has realized that judicial interpretations that are inconsistent with the WTO Agreements or those laws and regulations required by the WTO Agreements must be identified and amended. In fact, up to 24 December 2001 it had published, in four batches, a list of repealed judicial interpretations adopted before the end of 2000. The SPR has also pledged to accelerate the drafting of judicial interpretations to ease the work of judges.[28]

6.2. Refuting domestic rules limiting due judicial powers

The *Administrative Procedure Law* (APL) provides that an individual, Chinese or foreign, may bring administrative proceedings against any government agency whose "specific administrative act" causes damages to the individual.[29] The same law commands courts to reject litigations against "specific administrative acts that shall, as provided by law, be finally decided by an administrative organ" and against administrative orders with general binding nature.[30] In this connection, a private party may take administrative actions against the Chinese government for damages incurred as a result of non-compliance if it constitutes a "specific administrative act" that does not belong to the province of statutory administrative power: Where the Chinese government infringes the interests of private parties in implementing laws and regulations that contravene the WTO Agreements, the private parties do not have access to judicial remedy.

In other words, the provisions limit the judicial review of abstract administrative acts and final administrative decisions. The judicial power to review abstract administrative acts is related to private enforcement of rights under WTO Agreements that are not asserted by administrative rules or procedures. It is therefore questionable whether a private party can bring an administrative proceeding against the Chinese government for damages incurred as a result of non-compliance with the WTO Agreements by the government.

It might be desirable for the judiciary to note that these provisions are not in conformity with China's international obligations under treaties to which China is a party. Article VI of the GATS, as cited above, has laid down the obligation of the WTO Member to allow, at the request of an affected service supplier, judicial review of administrative decisions affecting trade in services. Article 41 (4) of the TRIPS Agreement, as cited before, also requires the WTO Member to permit judicial review of the administrative acts that are final under the domestic laws and regulations.

This means that the Chinese judiciary has the obligation to recognize the right of foreign private parties to enforce their rights under WTO Agreements, however the domestic provisions may hold.

The SPR has, in its practice, begun asserting the power of the judiciary to review the administrative decisions, despite the statutory provisions upholding the final administrative decisions. A typical example is the TMT trademark case.[31]

6.3. Securing judicial independence

Although much has been done to shield the judicial process from outside interference, nothing has been done to overcome the fundamental obstacle to judicial independence: judicial interference from the Party. To achieve a really independent judiciary, politically sensitive reform must be instituted to separate the judiciary from the Party and from other authorities. As an intermediate solution, reforms aimed at cutting the financial and personnel linkages between courts and local Party Committees and other authorities should be launched.

6.4. Establishment of the precedence of WTO Agreements over domestic laws

It is impossible to put in place immediately all the domestic laws and regulations required by the WTO Agreements. Judges need to understand that WTO Agreements may be directly applied and in cases of conflict between domestic law and WTO Agreements, the WTO Agreements should be given priority. If the prevalence of the WTO Agreements is established in the judicial practice, the role of inconsistent domestic laws and regulations would be minimized. For example, the WTO Agreements require that all the administrative decisions be subject to judicial review while Chinese law establishes numerous cases of final administrative decisions.[32] Under such circumstance, if the court applied the WTO rules to accept the administrative litigation, the different domestic provisions would not hinder the instituting of judicial review.

6.5. Strengthening legal training and further promoting the judiciary's professionalism

Given their lack of training, judges in China need to become acquainted with the disciplines and rules embodied in the WTO Agreements. Since many of the WTO disciplines are not specific enough to be applied directly, Chinese judges need to be taught to deduce, as their counterparts in the West, the applicable rules from the WTO disciplines.

In this regard, temporary training will not solve the problem. One drastic way to reform the judiciary is by replacing the incompetent judges with well-trained academic or practicing lawyers.

7. Concluding Remarks

The impending WTO entry sets out demanding requirements for the Chinese judiciary and offers new incentives and impetus for institution-building in the judicial system. However, it will not necessarily create a thoroughly independent judiciary. The judicial system's inherent defects, in parallel with the political system, suggest that the Chinese judiciary may have difficulty ensuring the implementation of the WTO Agreements. To conform to the WTO Agreements, further judicial reform needs to be carried out to address the structural defects. Concerted efforts on the part of the Party, legislature and administrative bodies are needed for the judiciary to play its expected role in enforcing the WTO Agreements.

Notes

1. See Article VI:2.b of the GATS. The GATT has a similar provision. Article X:3.c of the GATT does not "require the elimination or substitution of procedures in force in the territory of a contracting party on the date of this Agreement which in fact provide for an objective and impartial review of administrative action even though such procedures are not fully or formally independent of the agencies entrusted with administrative enforcement." In the words of the TRIPS Agreement, there is no obligation to put in place a judicial system distinct from that for the enforcement of laws in general (Article 42 (1)(5))

2. For instance, in addition to providing for the general obligation of instituting a judicial system, Part III of the TRIPS Agreement specifically lays down the requirements for procedures, evidence, injunctions and other remedies.

3. Professor Zhao Weitian, a renowned Chinese expert on the WTO law, argued that "rules" refer to those foreseen *extante* and specifically laid down in the WTO Agreements while "standards" are those whose gap with the "rules" requires to be filled *ex post* through interpretation when they are being applied. See Zhao Weitian, *WTO and International Law* (in Chinese), available at <http://www.chinalawinfo.com>.

4. The article provides, among others, that "...nothing in this Agreement shall be construed to prevent the adoption or enforcement by any contracting party of measures:
   (a) necessary to protect public morals;
   (b) necessary to protect human, animal or plant life or health;..."

5. Article XVI (4) of the *Agreement Establishing the World Trade Organization*.

6. For instance, whenever the Party decides to launch a campaign, be it "strike hard crimes" or "fight the Falun Gong cult," the SPR responds by calling all the "judicial cadres and policemen" (*sifa gan jing*, an often used term referring to all the staff within the court system) to carry out the task.

7. It is well known that cadre administration or personnel affairs are within the exclusive purview of the Party. A cadre is appointed, recommended for office,

"administered" and removed by a corresponding Party committee according to his rank.

8. Article 35 of the *Organizational Law of People's Courts* and Article 11 of the *Judges Law*.

9. At each level (the central level and various local levels), there is a *nomenklatura*, upon which the positions of court presidents and vice-presidents are listed. The positions listed in the *nomenklatura* are controlled by the Party Organization Department at the corresponding level.

10. On 1 July 2001, in his speech commemorating the 80th anniversary of the Communist Party of China, Jiang vowed that "[w]e must resolutely resist the impact of Western political models such as the multi-party system or separation of powers among the executive, legislative and judicial branches." For the text of this speech, see <http//www1.chinadaily.com.cn/highlights/doc/01-07-2001/17461.html>.

11. The Judicial Committee is an institution unique to the Chinese courts. Article 11 of the *Organizational Law of the People's Courts* states that a judicial committee is responsible for "summarizing judicial experience, discussing important and difficult cases and other questions relevant to judicial work."

12. For an analysis of the decentralising process in China, see Li Donglu, The Trend of Economic Decentralizing and its Impact on Foreign Policies (in Chinese), *Strategy and Management (Zhanlue yu guanli)*, vol. 6, 1996, pp. 44-49.

13. Article 9 of the *Judges Law*.

14. While Xiao Yang, President of the SPR, admitted that 1,292 judges were punished in 2000 for "violation of Party and administrative rules' and 46 for "violation of law," Han Zhubin, President of the Supreme People's Prosecutorate, raised the figure of indictment of "law enforcement officials" in 2000 to 4,626. See *Gazette of the Supreme People's Court*, 2001 (2), p. 43. Communique of Supreme People's Prosecutorate, 2001 (2), p. 6. A high-profile case is that of ex-President of the Jiangxian County People's Court of Sanxi Province, who had served on that post for years before he was found collecting money by using his influence and raping women. He was even found heading a local triad.

15. According to a study, the following elements are responsible for corruption in China: the legal system is unable to keep pace with economic change; the change from a centrally planned to a socialist market economy has created difficulties; officials are underpaid; poor supervision; lack of a code of conduct for officials; ineffective law enforcement; the nexus between the Party and government; nepotism; poorly drafted laws. See H. Chu "Perfecting China's Legal System to Fight Crimes of Bribery," in Guiguo Wang et al. (eds), *Legal developments in China: Market Economy and Law*, Sweet & Maxwell, 1996, pp. 325, 327-328.

16. It is hoped that that practice would be discouraged with the promulgation of the Basic Rules on Professional Ethics of Judges on 18 October 2001 by the SPR. The Basic Rules provide that during the trial process, the judges shall not separately and privately meet either party or his attorney and that before pronouncing the sentence of a case, the judges shall not reveal his own opinions and attitude on the sentence by his words, expressions and acts.

17. In addition to parties, judges in China may also collect evidence. See Article 64 of *CPL*.

18. The following bizarre case illustrates how difficult enforcing a judgment can be. China Pencil Co. Ltd (Benbu Branch) lost in a lawsuit and was ordered by the Fengyang County People's Court of Anhui Province to pay 170,000 *yuan*. The company refused to perform the obligations. Upon request by the awardee, the court tried to seize the property of the company, but in vain. Anhui Legal News, a local newspaper, published an article by using the information provided by the court, criticizing the company and its director (a powerful figure in the area) and arguing that the director should honor the judgment. The director was annoyed by the report and sued before the Benbu City Intermediate People's Court the Fengyang court as well as the newspaper publisher for defamation. Rather than rejecting the request, the Intermediate People's Court accepted the lawsuit. For the case report, see the website of the People's Court Daily: <http://www.rmfyb.com.cn>.

19. See *Gazette of the Supreme People's Court*, 2001 (2), p. 44.

20. Resolution regarding the Strengthening of Legal Interpretation Work, promulgated by the 19th Session of the Standing Committee of the 5th National People's Congress on 10 June 1981.

21. See the SPR, Several Provisions concerning Judicial Interpretations (23 June 1997).

22. From time to time, the SPR publishes selected cases in print and on the website of the People's Court Daily (<http://www.rmfyb.com.cn/>).

23. Article 85 of the *CPL*.

24. For example, the SPR has two former law professors, serving as its Vice-Presidents. High People's Courts or Intermediate People's Courts of Shanghai, Beijing, Nanjing and Wuhan, etc., also have former law faculty staff as ranking judges.

25. Cao Jianming, Vice-President of the SPR released the information in a seminar in February 2001. For a report of the seminar, see Shao Zongwei, Supreme court gets ready for WTO entry, *China Daily*, 22 February 2001.

26. See Jianfu Chen, Judicial Reform in China, CCH's *China Law Update*, May 2000, p.7.

27. http://www.ccmt.org.cn.

28. Same as note 26.
29. Foreign citizens share the same rights as Chinese on the basis of reciprocity. Articles 67 of the *APL* provides that "[a] citizen, a legal person or any other organizations who suffers from damages because of infringement upon his or its lawful rights and interests by a specific administrative act of an administrative organ or the personnel of an administrative organ, shall have the right to claim compensation." Article 71 provides that "(f)oreign nationals, stateless persons and foreign organizations that are engaged in administrative suits in the People's Republic of China shall have the same litigation rights and obligations as citizens and organizations of the People's Republic of China."
30. Private party cannot challenge the non-conforming laws and regulations per se. See Article 12 (2) of the APL.
31. Trademarks TMT, TMC and TMT were designed and first used and registered abroad by TMT Company, a Hong Kong-based firm. In 1979, TMT Company authorized Guangdong Light Industry Products Imp. & Exp. Company to produce articles bearing the trademarks. All these articles were exported for sale by TMT Company. In 1980, as a foreign firm, TMT Company failed to register the trademarks in China under the trademark regulations then, and authorized Guangdong Light Industry to register the trademarks with the Trademark Bureau of China in its own name. In 1997, the long-standing cooperation between the two firms broke up and TMT renamed another Chinese firm to replace Guangdong Light Industry. Guangdong Light Industry submitted an application to the Customs, in the name of the owner of the trademarks, for an injunction on the exports bearing the trademarks and claimed royalty for use of the trademarks from TMT Company. Subsequently, TMT Company brought a suit before the High People's Court of Guangdong Province for termination of the agency between the two firms and claimed damages. The High Court rendered a judgment in favour of TMT Company. Guangdong Light Industry appealed to the SPR. Guangdong Light Industry pleaded, among others, that the High People's Court did not have jurisdiction over this case because it was about the propriety of trademarks. Regardless of the statutory provisions asserting the decisions of the Trademark Bureau of China are final concerning the propriety of trademarks, the SPR seized the jurisdiction and pronounced a judgement by holding that disputes over propriety of trademarks belong to disputes over civil rights. See SPR, *Min shi pan jue shu, fa gong bu* (2000), No. 25, available at <http://www.rmfyb.com.cn/>.
32. Article 12 of the APL provides that courts shall not accept any suits against "specific administrative acts that shall, as provided by law, be finally decided by an administrative organ." Both the former *Patent Law*, prior to 1 July 2001 and the former *Trademark Law*, prior to 27 October 2001, had provisions

supporting final decisions by administrative organs. All these statutory provisions are inconsistent with TRIPS Agreement allowing judicial review. See Articles 43 and 49 of the *Patent Law*, Articles 21, 22, 29 and 35 of the *Trademark Law*, and Article 41 (4) of the TRIPS Agreement.

5

Can The WTO Dispute Settlement Mechanism Resolve Trade Disputes Between China And Taiwan?

1. Introduction

Both China and Taiwan[1] have become WTO Members.[2] Not only are the WTO accessions important to both China and Taiwan, but they have also an important impact on the economic and trade relations between them. While many observers are optimistic about the prospect that the entries of Beijing and Taipei into the WTO are to help accelerate economic and trade ties and thus reduce the likelihood of confrontation across the Taiwan Straits, they fail to heed adequate attention to the possibility that the WTO framework may be helpless to the political issues that had plagued the cross-straits economic and trade ties before the accessions; moreover, the cross-straits economic and trade relations may tarnish the credibility of the WTO's built-in dispute settlement mechanism.

The article aims to assess the interaction between the WTO dispute settlement mechanism and the economic and trade relations across the Taiwan Straits.

2. Cross-straits Economic and Trade Relations at the Turn of WTO Entries

There is so far no bilateral legal or political framework governing the cross-straits economic and trade relations, which are regulated by either side through unilateral means.

On the Chinese side, since Taiwan is viewed as part of China and Taiwanese as Chinese nationals, all the laws and regulations theoretically ought to govern the trading and investment activities by Taiwanese businesses. In practice, however, many special policies and sometimes laws and regulations have been adopted specifically to govern cross-straits economic and trade relations. A typical example is the "Law on the Protection of Investment of Taiwan Compatriots."[3]

In this regard, it is noted that many local governments have adopted their own policies and regulations to govern trade and investment between Taiwan and the localities concerned.[4] Moreover, where there is no specific law, regulations or policies that can be invoked, laws and regulations governing foreign trade and investment in general can be applied as reference to Taiwan. An example is the Detailed Rules for the Implementation of Wholly Foreign-invested Enterprise Law of the People's Republic of China.[5]

A look into these various sources of policies, laws and regulations governing China's trade ties with Taiwan will reveal that all these policies, laws and regulations have one thing in common, that is, fostering cross-straits trade relations. In general, Taiwanese traders and investors are welcomed like their counterparts from any third country or region. Put in other way, Taiwanese are given no less favourable treatment than traders and investors from foreign countries. As a matter of fact, foreign businesses in China often find their Taiwanese counterparts having freer access to business opportunities in many ways and in many regions as governments at various levels spare no effort to attract Taiwanese investment. In short, the Chinese legal framework does not constitute legal barriers to cross-straits economic and trade ties.

On the Taiwan side, however, there exist substantial barriers in the legal framework governing economic and trade relations with China. The Regulations on the Cross-straits Relations of the Republic of China is the overriding framework governing cross-straits relations. Derived from these Regulations, the Regulations Governing Permission of Trade between Taiwan Area and Mainland Area lays down the legal framework for trade between Taiwan and China. The derivative Regulations specifically prohibit direct trade between Taiwan and mainland China.[6] This explains why the cross-straits trade ties are by large "indirect." A term has long been coined to describe the state of no direct cross-straits relations: "No Three Links"(links in mail, transportation and trading).[7] The only exception to the "No Three Links" is the so-called "Mini Three Links." The Provisional Implementation of "Mini Three Links" between the Offshore Islands of Kinmen and Matsu and Mainland China, adopted at the end of 2000, authorize small-time trade between the offshore islands of Kinmen and Matsu and the Chinese coast. The launch of the Mini Three Links "aims to improve the cross-straits relationship through positive and constructive exchanges between the two sides."[8] However, the implications of the legal instrument are very limited. While it is officially hailed in Taiwan as "a small but encouraging step,"[9] it is downplayed as a gesture on the Chinese side and viewed as "a dismal failure" by Taiwanese press.[10]

Indeed, with or without the WTO accession, Taipei will finally have to allow for direct trade. At present, however, it is not prepared to do so, notwithstanding the WTO accession.[11] According to Taipei's blueprint, the "Three Links" will only come into being at a time when both sides sign peace treaty and terminate hostility.[12]

Parallel with the "No Three Links" trade policy is the "*No haste, be patient*" (*jiejiyongren*) policy which had been in place for years for Taiwan's investment in China,[13] by which the Taiwan authorities banned local businesses from realizing investment plans worth more than US$50 million in mainland China and imposed strict restrictions on local investment in mainland's hi-tech and infrastructure projects.[14] The government even proposed to levy a "national security tax" on Taiwanese investors in mainland China.[15]

Despite the legal barriers to cross-straits economic and trade relations, trade and investment flows have increased remarkably. According to the Board of Foreign Trade of Taiwan, the gross value of the cross-straits trade in 2000 exceeded US$30 billion, among which, Taiwan harvested a huge indirect trade surplus of approximately US$20 billion from the mainland.[16] China has become Taiwan fourth trade partner, given the cross-straits trade from January to October 2001.[17] The Mainland Affairs Council (MAC) of Taiwan estimated that Taiwan's trade with China accounted for 25 percent of its total trade in 1999.[18]

In relation to Taiwanese investment in China, as no other country has imposed restrictions on investing in China, many Taiwanese companies managed to make investments in China through a third country. While the Ministry of Economic Affairs (MOEA) recorded a total sum of US$19.6 billion of approved Taiwanese investment in China as of November 2001,[19] the total Taiwanese investment in China was estimated to be US$60 billion by the end of 2001,[20] ranking Taiwan the third largest source of foreign investment in China. The robust trade and investment ties across the Straits shows that the "No Three Links' and "no haste, be patient" policies are more of a symbolic moral exhortation than a legal restriction. In fact, many Taiwanese companies are planning to invest in China while pushing for a policy adjustment.[21]

While its policy towards cross-straits trade remains basically unchanged, the Taiwanese authorities had acted to substantially lift restrictions on Taiwanese investment in China, due to, in part, the pressure from the businesses. When the Economic Development Advisory Conference (EDAC) of Taiwan proposed to scrap the "no hast, be patient" policy, Taipei endorsed an "active opening and effective management" policy on 7 November 2001 by promulgating the "Executive Plan for the 'Implementation of Investment in the Mainland, Active Opening, and Effective Management.'" The new policy was put into effect on 1 January 2002.

The main contents of the present adjustment to cross-straits investment policy are:

- Opening direct investment, there is no need for enterprises to set up a subsidiary company in a third place.

- Abolishing the regulation on the ceiling of accumulative total investment amount of US$50 million for individual case.

- Relaxing the ceiling of accumulative total investment made in the mainland by individuals and small and medium-sized enterprises, with 60 million new Taiwan dollars being adjusted to 80 million.

- Simplifying the classification of industries for investment in the mainland, the current "prohibition category," "permission category" and "category for special case check" were to be simplified into "prohibition category" and "general category." Those not under the "prohibition category" can invest in the mainland so long as they go through the procedures for individual case check.

- Relaxing control on the use of funds of listing and counter companies.

- Allowing branches of international banking businesses to conduct direct banking business contacts with the mainland financial institutions and their overseas branches, with the mainland legal persons, organizations and other institutions.

However, this policy still contains various restrictions and uncertain factors affecting Taiwanese investment in China. For example, high-tech industries and infrastructure construction enterprises intending to invest in the mainland are still placed under strict control; the current regulations on the ceiling of accumulative total or proportion of investment made in the mainland by individuals and enterprises are still retained; an investment trend regulatory mechanism is still there, whereby the competent department will regularly or, when necessary, invite relevant organizations to examine and deliberate various factors, so as to decide where or not to readjust the standard for the accumulative total investment amount made by individual enterprises, etc.

3. Post-Accession Cross-Straits Trade Policies Harbour Trade Disputes between China and Taiwan

In the post-accession era, both China and Taiwan must review and adjust its existing trade regime to meet WTO requirements. It should be first pointed out that Article XIII of the Agreement Establishing the World Trade Organization shall not be interpreted as the WTO being able to force its Members to establish direct trade link, although this provision suggests that WTO Members shall apply the multilateral trade agreements between themselves if they do not invoke to exclude such application between themselves. Since either China or Taiwan did not invoke, before acceding to the WTO, the provision to exclude application of multilateral trade agreements between themselves, the MFN treatment embodied in the WTO obliges both China and Taiwan not to grant less favourable treatment to each other if they decide to maintain any trade tie. In this connection, any efforts to adjust their respective trade regime to align with the WTO Agreement shall include their respective policy and measures related to cross-straits economic and trade relations.

As a matter of fact, both sides have started to adjust their respective policy and measures related to cross-straits economic and trade ties. On the Taiwan side, it has declared its cross-straits trade policy in a report on WTO accession entitled "An Elaboration of Policies relating to the Accession of Our Country to the WTO." So far, the Taiwan side has only acted to ease travel restrictions on mainland Chinese professionals residing in a third country and relax curbs on fund flows. Clear is that Taiwan is not eager to change its policy towards cross-straits trade relations soon. Nevertheless, Taiwan has shown its interest in pushing up the trade relations through the WTO framework.[22]

On the part of China, although it has not officially made pubic systematically its policy towards cross-straits trade and investment in the post-WTO era, the announcements and press interviews sporadically released, as well as its practice around the WTO accession, have given a hint of the dimension of China's policy. In response to the formal acceptance of Taiwan into the WTO on 11 November 2001, the State Council's Taiwan Affairs Office and the MOFTEC issued a joint statement, welcoming "Chinese Taipei" into the WTO, and saying that this will be helpful for the development of cross-straits trade. Nevertheless, the statement said that after both sides accede to the WTO, cross-straits trade relations would continue as between "China proper and its separate customs territory." In a concrete effort, China announced that had granted permits to Taiwanese banks to open offices in mainland China before the end of 2001,[23] and opened its airspace around the southern island of Hainan to civilian flights and had given several Taiwan airlines approval to fly over the area.[24]

However, a close look shows that the dimension of both sides' proposed cross-straits economic and trade policies will be a deviation from their respective WTO obligations.

On the part of China, it will further facilitate cross-straits economic and trade relations by liberalizing the trade regime in general on the one hand; on the other, as Tang Shubei, former Executive vice-president of the Association for Relations Across the Taiwan Straits, pointed out at a seminar, WTO and Cross-straits Economic and Trade Ties, China strongly opposes any attempt to discuss cross-straits economic and trade affairs under the WTO framework. Moreover, as Zhang Mingqing, spokesman for the Taiwan Affairs Office of the State Council made clear, China does not intend to resort to the dispute settlement mechanism to resolve the trade disputes between mainland China and Taiwan.[25]

On the Taiwan side, it will implement a cross-straits economic and trade policy that differs from its trade policies towards other WTO Members. Taiwan will put its security concerns above its economic and trade policy towards China. It will only adjust its economic and trade ties with mainland China to comply with WTO rules only when it perceives the adjustment does not jeopardize Taiwan's security.

Such deviations suggest ample possibility of trade disputes between China and Taiwan in the future.

4. WTO Dispute Settlement Mechanism

The WTO Agreement distinguishes WTO Members into countries (sovereign state) and separate customs territories. Article XII of the WTO Agreement clearly states that "[a]ny State or separate customs territory possessing full autonomy in the conduct of its external commercial relations and of the other matters provided for in this Agreement and the Multilateral Trade Agreements may accede to this Agreement, on terms to be agreed between it and the WTO." Each WTO Member, irrespective of whether it is a sovereign state or a separate customs territory, has the right of accessing to the dispute settlement mechanism, and that each WTO Member involved in the dispute settlement procedures, is treated equally. That is to say, given a dispute between a sovereign state and a separate customs territory, the separate customs territory is not to be given less favourable treatment in the dispute settlement mechanism. Although, as the DSU clearly states, the use of the dispute settlement mechanism should not be intended or considered as contentious acts,[26] the possibility that a WTO Member may use the WTO framework, particularly, the dispute settlement mechanism, to attain the political goal under hidden agenda cannot be ruled out. For example, a separate customs territory may use it in association with a dispute with a state Member to convey the message that it is on par with the latter.

It is known that Taiwan acceded to the WTO as a separate customs territory, of which China, Taiwan and other WTO Members may have different interpretations. For China, Taiwan's WTO membership is that of a "separate customs territory" of China, though Taiwan itself and other Members may see it differently. Nevertheless, it should be noted that Taiwan's rights and obligations in the WTO would be affected notwithstanding its perceived identity, because every WTO Member, be it a sovereign state or a separate customs territory, is treated equally.[27] In the event a dispute occurs between China and Taiwan and the dispute settlement procedures are initiated, Taiwan will be treated the same way as China; moreover, such procedures may be used to back Taiwan's contention that it is on par with China.

The WTO dispute settlement mechanism was designed as "a central element in providing security and predictability to the multilateral trading system."[28] The mechanism is presided over by DSU, which is an integral part of the single undertaking package of the WTO. A new organ-the Dispute Settlement Body (DSB), which is in fact an alter ego of the Council, has been created and has compulsory jurisdiction to resolve disputes initiated by WTO Members. The DSB has its own rules and presidency, and its functions are, *inter alia*, to establish panels at the request of a complaining party, to adopt panel reports, to monitor the implementation of its decisions, and to authorize compensatory measures when appropriate. According to the procedure called "negative consensus," both the adoption of the panel and the Appellate Body reports are decisions to be taken automatically, unless the DSB decides by consensus not to adopt the report.

It should not be forgotten that the dispute settlement mechanism basically promotes negotiation, although the susceptibility of such a negotiation must respect the mandatory principle that underlines the many possible outcomes.[29] As a matter of fact, the dispute settlement procedure begins with a formal request for consultation.[30] Only if the requested Member does not respond within 10 days after the date of receipt of the consultation request, or does not enter into consultation within a period of no more than 30 days, or a period otherwise mutually agreed, after the date of receipt of the request,[31] or if such consultations fail to resolve the dispute within 60 days after the date of receipt of the request for consultations,[32] then the Member that requested the holding of consultations may proceed directly to request the establishment of a panel.

Establishment of a panel is also quasi-automatic since the rule of negative consensus is applicable.[33] Once the panel is established, it must be consistent with the terms of reference as defined by the parties, and "make an objective assessment of the matter before it, including an objective assessment of the facts of the case and the applicability of and conformity with the relevant covered agreements, and make such other findings as will assist the DSB in making the recommendations or in giving the rulings provided for in the covered agreements."[34] The panel report will be adopted by negative consensus, unless one or both parties to the dispute appeal its legal findings and conclusions before the Appellate Body (AB), a standing organ of the WTO with jurisdiction "limited to issues of law covered in the panel report and legal interpretations developed by the panel."[35] After examining the case, "the AB may uphold, modify or reverse the legal findings and conclusions of the panel,"[36] and its report shall be adopted by the DSB by negative consensus.

In the post-panel phase the DSB supervises the proper implementation of its recommendations. The losing party has a reasonable period of time to bring the disputed measure into conformity with the WTO Agreement concerned. The failure to implement the recommendations of an adopted report may lead to compensation or suspension of concessions, subject to the authorization by the DSB.

5. Different Approaches to the WTO Dispute Settlement Mechanism

Although the possibility that either China or Taiwan will use the WTO card to trump the other side into political negotiation as it has in mind cannot be excluded, China and Taiwan hold different approaches to the WTO dispute settlement mechanism.

Undoubtedly, accession to the WTO is a key step for Taiwan's government to return to the international stage in its own name, and a major breakthrough for pragmatic diplomacy.[37] As the WTO is the only international organization of which Taiwan is a full member, it is expected that Taiwan will not spare this unprecedented opportunity to use the WTO as a forum to boost its image as a political entity that is different from and, on par with, China.

For Taiwan, the built-in dispute settlement mechanism (including procedures on consultation) within the WTO provides a golden opportunity to promote its political ambition. Taipei will do all that it can to take advantage of the built-in dispute settlement mechanism, among other things, to counter China's diplomatic efforts. Taipei can take the initiative to bring China to the DSB whenever China is viewed as breaching its WTO obligations vis-à-vis Taiwan: Even the possibility cannot be ruled out that Taipei will also induce China to sue Taiwan before the DSB by a deliberate failure to enforce its WTO obligations vis-à-vis China.

Also foreseeable is that in the post-accession era Beijing will be steadfast in opposing any attempt to discuss in the international arena the Taiwan issue which China views as an internal affair within the context of one country.[38] China has made clear that it will not try to resolve cross-straits trade disputes. When Zhang Mingqing, spokesman for the Taiwan Affairs Office of the State Council made clear China's intention, he pointed out that China would follow an approach to cross-straits trade disputes on a case-by-case. A reasonable interpretation would be that China would at least try to refrain from using the WTO dispute settlement mechanism.[39]

Nevertheless, it is unclear whether China will not be willing to enter into consultation with Taiwan when a trade dispute occurs between them. China might refrain from seeking consultation with Taiwan over such a dispute;

however, it is difficult to turn down the request for consultation by Taiwan over such a dispute.

The use of the WTO dispute settlement mechanism, being initiated by China or Taiwan, will result in a dilemma for China. On the one hand, the use of the mechanism may lead to the resolution of trade disputes between the two sides and thus facilitate cross-straits economic and trade ties; on the other, use of the dispute settlement mechanism will help Taipei boost its image as a political entity on par with China.

Given that China will presumably not be happy to see that, it will refrain from using the dispute settlement mechanism to solve trade disputes in the cross-straits relations. Since each Member is obligated to "accord sympathetic consideration to and afford adequate opportunity for consultation regarding any representations made by another Member concerning measures affecting the operation of any covered agreement taken within the territory of the former," China will find it difficult to turn down consultation requests by Taiwan; even if China does not respond to the request or enters into consultation within the specified periods, Taiwan may proceed directly to request the establishment of a panel. Given the mandatory jurisdiction of the DSB over trade disputes between WTO Members, however, China will not be in a position to prevent Taiwan from initialising the dispute settlement procedures.

6. Concluding Remarks

The above analysis allows the following conclusion:

The cohabitation of China and Taiwan in the same international organisation on the one hand provides chances for both China and Taiwan to deal with each other, and on the other hosts friction if either side is overwhelmed by non-trade-related concerns. Unless two sides ignore the possible trade disputes at the cost of trade benefits, they will have to find an approach to the dispute settlement mechanism acceptable to both sides. However, if China cannot compromise its goals of pursuing trade interests and forcing a recognition of "One China" principle, or if Taiwan aspires to take advantage of the dispute settlement mechanism to promote its international stance, the mechanism will not be able to play its expected role of settling disputes between China and Taiwan; moreover, the credibility of the mechanism itself will be jeopardized by their conducts. In this context, it is advisable for the other WTO Members that are least interested in seeing a politicised dispute settlement mechanism[40] to help both China and Taiwan foster a common approach to the mechanism. Otherwise, there will be a risk that political concerns on the China and Taiwan sides will interrupt the trade body's agenda.

Notes

1. While Taiwan strives to maintain its identity as an international legal person, China views Taiwan as a renegade province. It has done all that it can to undermine the foundation of the island's independence. China does not establish diplomatic relationship with any country that maintains relationships with Taiwan; it even severs existing political and trade relationship with a country when the country develops political relationship with Taiwan. As a matter of fact, the question of Taiwan may be used as an excuse for punishment both for small countries or those that are insignificant to China and for powers like the United States. For instance, whenever the United States develops a closer relationship with Taiwan, China may reward the less unfriendly European Union or Japan by treating them with trade favours.

2. In July 1986 China filed its application to join the then GATT or, in Chinese terms, to resume its status as a contracting party. In 1990 Taiwan applied to join the GATT as the Separate Customs Territory of Taiwan, Penghu, Kinmen and Matsu. In 1992, China and the GATT reached an understanding concerning Taiwan's status in the GATT. The Chairman of the GATT's Council of Representatives said there was a consensus that "the Council should examine the report of the Working Party on China and adopt the Protocol for the People's Republic of China's accession before examining the report and adopting the Protocol for Chinese Taipei, while noting that the working party reports should be examined independently." Consequently, Taiwan acceded to the WTO, the successor of the GATT, after China's accession: China and Taiwan joined the WTO on 11 December 2001 and 1 January 2002 respectively.

3. Adopted at the 6th Meeting of the Standing Committee of the 8th National People's Congress on 5 March 1994, and effective as of the date of promulgation

4. For instance, Zhejiang Province promulgated the Regulation of Encouraging Investment by Taiwan Compatriots in Zhejiang Province in 1992.

5. Article 82 of the Detailed Rules.

6. Article 5 of the Regulations Governing Permission of Trade between Taiwan Area and Mainland Area provides that "trading activities between Taiwan Area and Mainland Area shall be executed in an indirect manner, whereby the buyers or the sellers shall be the traders in third territories outside the Mainland Area and permitted to do direct trade with traders in Taiwan Area, and the goods/articles involved in such transactions shall be transhipped via third territories."

7. Taiwan has banned direct trade, transport and postal links with mainland China since the end of the civil war in 1949. "Three Links" were first proposed by China on 1 January 1979 by Ye Jianying, then Chairman of the NPC Standing Committee of China, in the name of the NPC Standing Committee. Taiwan merely ignored the proposal then.

8. MAC, Overview of the Provisional Implementation of "Mini-three-links" between the Offshore Islands of Kinmen & Matsu and Mainland China, 18 December 2000.

9. *The China Post* (Taiwan), 4 January 2001.

10. According to a headline article of Taipei Times of 18 October 2001, the "mini three links" were "doomed to failure' from the very beginning and "have achieved almost nothing other than de-criminalizing small-time trade between the offshore islands and the Chinese coast."

11. Taipei argues that it is not yet a ripe timing to launch direct link in transportation so far since such direct link in transportation involves extremely complicated issues.

12. MAC, "Three Links": Across the Taiwan Straits, October 1999.

13. The "no haste, be patient" policy was put forward by former President Lee Teng-hui at the Taiwan "Administrators Meeting" in September 1996 for security consideration.

14. For instance, domestic computer companies are banned from investing in the production of low-end notebook computers in mainland China

15. *The Taipei Times*, 19 May 2000.

16. Quoted from *People's Daily*, 28 February 2001.

17. http://cus.trade.gov.tw/cgi-bin/pbisa60.dll/customs/uo_o_roc/of_o_ fsr11_report.

18. http://www.mac.gov.tw/english/CSExchan/tmtrade.gif.

19. MOEA, Approved Investment on Mainland, available at http://www. moea.gov.tw/~meco/stat/four/e-7.htm

20. *The Economist*, 5 January 2000, p. 27.

21. It has been reported, for example, that Formosa Plastics Group, Taiwan's largest petrochemical firm, has a plan to pour US$13 billion into building a large naphtha-cracking complex in Ningpo, China. Its Chairman Y.C. Wang has been outspoken in criticizing the "no haste, be patient" policy.

22. Premier Chang Chun-hsiung of Taiwan stated that in the post-accession era the two sides would "be able to work within the same international organization and under the same set of rules to develop relations in an orderly and more positive fashion." Commercial Times, November 13, 2001.

23. *The Taiwan Economic News*, 22 October 2001.

24. *China Times*, 1 November 2001.

25. "There are some issues which do not need to be resolved under the framework of the WTO," *The China Post*, 1 November 2001

26. Article 3.10. of DSU.

27. The Agreement Establishing the World Trade Organization, in its "Explanatory Notes," explains:

    "The terms "country" or "countries" as used in this Agreement and the Multilateral Trade Agreements are to be understood to include any separate customs territory Member of the WTO. "In the case of a separate customs territory Member of the WTO. where an expression in this Agreement and the Multilateral Trade Agreements is qualified by the term "national," such expression shall be read as pertaining to that customs territory. unless otherwise specified."

28. Article 3.2 of DSU.

29. Article 3.7 of DSU: "A solution mutually acceptable to the parties to a dispute and consistent with the covered agreements is clearly to be preferred."

30. Article 4 of DSU, and Article XXII of GATT.

31. Article 4.3 of DSU.

32. Article 4.7 of DSU.

33. Article 6 of DSU.

34. Article 11 of DSU.

35. Article 17.6 of DSU.

36. Article 17.13 of DSU.

37. Taipei has been accused by China of using "money diplomacy" and "transit diplomacy' to strive for wider international recognition. A MAC official was quoted as admitting that it used to take tremendous efforts for us to open even one door to international exchanges. But [the] WTO entry now helps us open 143 doors to international changes at the same time." Taipei risks 'crisis' over use of WTO for own ends, *China Daily*, 9 January 2002, p. 1.

38. Beijing even opposes any ties between the government of Taiwan and foreign investment firms also wishing to do business on the mainland. Chinese imposition of punishment on Crédit Suisse First Boston for its contacts with senior Taiwan officials is an example. The Chinese government cancelled two lucrative agreements between Credit Suisse and state-owned China Unicom after discovering that the bank had hosted Taiwanese finance officials on a promotional tour of Europe earlier 2001. The official standing of the Chinese

government is referred to as it does not object to "unofficial commercial activities" by international financial institutions on Taiwan. September 12, 2001, available at http://www.latimes.com/news/nationworld/world/la-000073530sep12.story?coll=la-headlines-world

39. In his words, "[a]s for what exactly constitutes a dispute, we will have to analyse the situation on a case-by-case basis." *China Post*, 1 November 2001.

40. The United States and other WTO Members have made clear that the WTO will not be used as a political forum for both China and Taiwan to discuss the policy issues of "One-China" or Taiwan's independence.

6

Will China Behave in the WTO Dispute Settlement Mechanism?

The law and practice of the Chinese approach to trade disputes

1. Disputes Expected between China and other Trade Partners after China's Entry

In laborious negotiations with WTO members, particularly with the United States and the European Union, China agreed to make vast market-opening changes to its hybrid economy.[1] However, it is increasingly clear that trade between China and the rest of the world (the United States in particular) may grow contentious as China gains marketing and manufacturing prowess, and particularly after it enters the WTO.

Firstly, the conflict of interests between China and other WTO Members is the source of trade disputes between them. As China's cheap products pour into the developed countries after the WTO entry, the industries of the same or like products in these countries will most likely be affected. Similarly, relatively cheap Chinese products will stiff the competition between China and those developing countries with similar economic and export structure. All these will hence produce political pressures on the governments to restrict the Chinese exports. Take China-US trade as example, the trade imbalance,[2] antidumping,[3] intellectual property rights protection,[4] the

US export control,[5] trade in textile[6] and prison product export[7] are the main areas where trade dispute are likely to occur between the two countries.

Secondly, China is woefully unprepared to do so much work in so little time. Given the magnitude of preparatory work necessary to implement the WTO Agreements fully, it is not surprising to see that the details of many implementing measures have not been worked out beforehand.[8] In this context, trade friction is expected to arise from China's inability to meet all of the many concessions it has made to get into the WTO.

Thirdly, although China has a generally satisfactory history of adhering to international treaties,[9] there are sure to be lingering struggles between China and its trade partners about the exact nature of some of China's commitments.[10] China may be reluctant to yield to the claims of its trade partners; on the other hand, China is a good fighter for its presumed legitimate interests[11] and will predictably begin using the WTO rules to protect its perceived interests.[12]

In fact, trade disputes have come to the attention of interested trade and legal circles within and outside China. Two days after China became a WTO Member, China accused the United States of unilaterally deducting textile quota worth of US$28 million and breaching the bilateral textile agreement between the two countries.[13] Six weeks after China's accession to the WTO, Assistant US Trade Representative Joseph Papovich accused China of making little progress in ending rampant copyright piracy.[14] Almost in the meantime, another dispute occurred between China and the European Union on the import ban of Chinese animal products.[15] Although neither China or its trade partner has not threaten to file a complaint in the WTO Dispute Settlement Body (DSB), these events highlight the need to study how will China approach to trade disputes, particularly within the WTO dispute settlement mechanism.

2. Understanding the Chinese Practice of Dealing with Trade Dispute with Its Trade Partners

2.1. Statutory provisions concerning dealing with trade disputes

Until the promulgation of the Foreign Trade Law,[16] there had been no legal grounds for China engaging in trade disputes with other countries. The Foreign Trade Law lays down a provision for dealing with trade disputes with other countries. Article 7 of the Law provides that "[I]n the event that any country or region applies discriminatory prohibition, restriction or other similar measures against the People's Republic of China in respect of trade, the People's Republic of China may, as the case may be, take counter-measures against the country or region in question."

The Anti-Dumping and Anti-Subsidy Regulations,[17] which were adopted in accordance with this provision of the Foreign Trade Law, further provide that "[b]ased upon actual circumstances, the People's Republic of China may adopt corresponding measures against any country or region adopting discriminatory anti-dumping or anti-subsidy measures against its exports." (Article 40)

The statutory provisions give China leeway to restrict foreign imports for indefinite periods in engaging trade disputes.

2.2. Case studies

As China's trade surges,[18] China has scuffled with its major trade partners. The United States, European Union, South Korea and Japan have all encountered disputes with China.

A look at how China approached these disputes would not only shed light on the Chinese practice in trade dispute settlement, but also help predict how China will behave regarding the WTO dispute settlement mechanism after its WTO accession.

2.2.1. China-US dispute of textile transhipment

This is a case where the dispute was settled with China making concessions.

China is the second largest supplier of imported textile and apparel products in the United States.[19] Textile exports account for 10 percent of the overall Chinese exports to the US. Because of the importance of the textile industry to the Chinese economy and of the trade in textiles to Sino-US trade relations, textile export to the United States has been a major source of disputes in China's trade relations with the United States. Alleged transshipment, which involves Chinese companies labeling textiles made in

China as having originated elsewhere (usually Hong Kong or Macau) to avoid quota limits, is a conspicuous example.[20]

In February 1997, China and the United States concluded a new agreement on textile trade.[21] Under this four-year agreement, the United States promised to extend quota arrangement for Chinese textile imports under the previous agreement (1994 agreement)[22] in exchange for Chinese promises to reduce tariffs and non-tariff barriers to US textile imports[23] and to crack down on transhipments. The new agreement maintained strong enforcement measures including the ability to "triple charge" quotas for repeated violations of the agreement, i.e. cutbacks in those areas where investigations have discovered illegally shipped products. Also, the agreement incorporates arrangements to implement an "electronic visa" information system to more effectively track textile and apparel shipments. In addition, a number of procedural measures were provided to improve the bilateral consultation process, which states consultation shall be held within 30 days after either party has requested so, and shall be concluded within 120 days. However, the agreement authorized the United States to impose the aforesaid "triple charge" measures on proved transhipments if the parties cannot reach an agreement of settlement.

On 5 May 1998, the United States announced it would impose punitive charges of US$5 million on China for exporting textiles to the United States via third countries to circumvent quotas. China initially responded by accusing the United States of "wantonly" violating the bilateral agreement with the unilateral deduction of the quotas. China was not happy because it had not been consulted. Interestingly, despite the vehement rhetoric, the Chinese did not resort to retaliation. Instead, given the widespread transhipment, it tightened the enforcement of the rule against transhipments.

2.2.2. China-EU dispute on interpretation of trade agreement
This is a case where the dispute ended in an agreed solution based on China's concession.

The Agreement on Trade and Economic Co-operation between the European Economic Community and the People's Republic of China (1985) is the guiding agreement on trade relationship between China and the EU. However, the Agreement does not contain a provision for resolution of disputes and therefore, no reference can be made to this Agreement to solve the trade disputes between the two parties.

As a result of the conclusion of Memorandum of Understanding on the Protection of Intellectual Property between the United States and China in January 1992, China adopted the Regulations on the Administrative Protection of Agrochemical Products on 26 December 1992 and the Regulations on the Administrative Protection of Phamaceuticals on 19 December 1992. The Regulations grant administrative protection to phamaceuticals and agrochemical products patented in other countries.[24] In 1994, China and the EU reached the agreement on administrative production for phamaceuticals and agrochemical product inventions. At the concluding of the agreement, the EU consisted of 12 Member States. When later other three states, i.e. Austria, Finland and Sweden, acceded to the EU, the Chinese authorities which have always previously given a restrictive interpretation and application of the Agreement, denied administrative protection to applicants from these new EU Member States, causing the European industry an estimated loss of €25 million. The EU had since raised the issue of equal treatment to these Member States on several occasions. In June 2000, EU Commissioner Pascal Lamy requested urgent action for equal treatment for all EU Member States from China's Trade Minister Shi Guangsheng. At the subsequent EU-China Joint Committee in October 2000, Minister Shi agreed in principle to an extension. The European Commission Delegation in Beijing and the Chinese Ministry of Foreign Trade and Economic Co-operation finally reached a new agreement in February 2001. The new agreement confirms that administrative protection for pharmaceuticals and agrochemical products in China will extend to applicants from Austria, Finland and Sweden.[25]

2.2.3. China-EU dispute regarding telecommunications investment

China prohibited foreign participation in telecommunications network ownership, operations, and management. However, China Unicom, the second largest telecommunications operator, and its incorporators devised a model—the *"Zhong-Zhong-wai"* (Chinese-Chinese-foreign) mode—to circumvent this regulation. In a *"Zhong-Zhong-wai"* arrangement, a foreign investor (Foreign) forms a joint venture with Chinese partners (Chinese) which is either the incorporator of China Unicom or the companies designated by China Unicom (these Chinese partners are not in the field of telecommunications sector). The joint venture will build the network and sign revenue sharing and other network services agreements with China Unicom (Chinese). The foreign investor typically contributes the majority of the funding needed for network buildup and in return shares the revenue allocated to the joint venture from China Unicom. In this way, the foreign investor seemingly could reap "equity-like" returns without breaking Chinese rules. According to one study, during the four years from 1995 to late 1998, nearly fifty "*Zhong-Zhong-wai*" projects were established, involving US$1.4 billion of foreign investment from companies from the United States, Canada, Germany, France, Italy, Japan, South Korea, and Singapore. In September 1998, the Chinese government issued a decree calling for the ban of the "*Zhong-Zhong-wai*" investment model.[26]

The move was apparently a major setback for ambitious EU telecommunications operators who were using this model to circumvent the Chinese government's ban on foreign participation in the telecommunications services industry. The European Commission intervened for the sake of the European telecommunications investors in China Unicom. In the process of bilateral negotiation between China and the EU concerning China's WTO entry, the EU secured from its agreement with China a satisfactory settlement concerning the mobile investments of EU telecommunication companies

2.2.4. China-Korea dispute of garlic export

This is another case where China and the other disputant agreed on a settlement, with the other disputant making more concessions.

China was the third largest trade partner of Korea and Korea the fourth of China in 2000. The total volume of trade between the two countries has exceeded US$300 billion in 2000. Korea enjoyed a trade surplus of US$11.9 billion in 2000.

The year 1999 saw a 30 percent drop in garlic prices in Korea. Korean farmers suffering from such a price drop blamed the cheap foreign imports for their loss. The Korean Finance and Economy Ministry issued its No.

141 order on 31 May 2000 which declares that starting from 1 June 2000 Korea would adopt restrictive measures on garlic imports and a tariff rate as high as 315 percent will be levied on imported garlic. As the major garlic exporter to Korea, China thought that Korea's limitation on garlic import was actually targeted at it. It dismissed the assertion that "the increase of garlic imports has caused a reduction in garlic prices and damaged the garlic industry in Korea" as unjustified. It argued that "[a]ny damage to Korea's garlic industry is caused entirely by the sharp increase of its garlic production at home, instead of the minor increase of its garlic imports."[27] It further asserted that the unilateral measures Korea had adopted without consultation with China not only seriously obstructed China's garlic export and affected the normal development of bilateral trade, from which China had sustained a huge amount of deficits for a long time, but also did not accord with the regulations of the WTO. China announced suspension of the import of Korean mobile telephones (including vehicular mobile sets) and polyethylene on 7 June 2000.

However, on 1 August 2000, in a surprising move, China declared that the two countries had reached an agreement on garlic trade and it would lift its two-month ban on import of mobile phones (including vehicular mobile sets) and polyethylene from the Korea. Under the agreement, Korea would import 32,000 tons of Chinese garlic at low tariffs in 2000, and the amount will grow by 5.25 percent annually within a term of three years.[28]

For the purpose of implementing the agreement on the Chinese part, the MOFTEC promulgated the Provisional Rules on Management of Export of Garlic to South Korea to regulate and rectify the garlic exports to Korea.

2.2.5. *China-Japan dispute of agriculture products*
This is a case where parties involved in the dispute were once at the verge of resorting to the WTO dispute settlement mechanism, but finally settled the dispute through consultations.

Japan is now China's largest trade partner and China Japan's second, with almost no imbalance, importing US$41.7 billion worth of goods from China and exporting US$41.5 billion in 2000.

On 22 December 2000, Japan decided to investigate the imports of three farm products: leeks, shiitake mushrooms and straw, more than 90 percent of which came from China.[29] On 11 April 2001, the Japanese Embassy in Beijing informed the Chinese government that Japan had decided to impose "provisional safeguard measures" on the imports of Chinese leeks, shiitake mushrooms and straw for a period of 200 days starting from 23 April 2001. China protested, arguing that Japan used double standards that were against the principle of fairness. From the Chinese perspective, Japanese decision was politically motivated.

The MOFTEC argued that the Japanese decision ran against the WTO rules in several aspects—selection of products to investigate, basic conditions to impose the safeguard measures, the objectiveness of the decision.[30] While strongly urging Japan to retract the decision, China threatened that a possible retaliation would be imminent if Japan did not suspend the restrictions. Japan had given no regard to China's objection, arguing it had imposed provisional safeguard measures under the WTO rules, which preclude retaliation.[31] On 19 June 2001, an angered China announced it would soon impose "prohibitively high tariffs" of 100 percent on imports of Japanese cars, mobile phones and air-conditioners, with the total value of about US$500 million. Seemingly, this will be the most severe retaliatory measure taken by the Chinese authorities against Japan's "wrong decision and discriminatory actions."

The trade dispute has the following features:

1) On the Japanese side, the disputed items from China make up only a very small portion of Japan's total imports in terms of value.[32] From the Chinese perspective, therefore, the restrictions are politically motivated.[33]

2) On the Chinese side, it had reason to fear that the Japanese import curbs could spread to other Chinese agricultural products and eventually to light and heavy industry products.[34]

3) While Japanese safeguards are limited to Chinese agricultural products, China's retaliatory measures target leading Japanese industrial products.

However, the extra tariffs are not expected to have much influence on Japanese manufacturers since the affected Japanese exports only account for a small portion of Japan's total exports in terms of value;[35] Furthermore, the majority of these brands, except for some cars, are manufactured in China.[36] The Chinese move was believed to be more symbolic than anything else,[37] necessary only to dissuade Japan from spreading its protective and discriminatory measures to other Chinese exports and also to deter other countries from adopting similar measures against China.

Both parties' ensuing behaviours brought a pause rather than an escalation in events. A clear indication is that, although Japan accused China of violating the 1974 Trade Agreement between China and Japan and the WTO rules in the aftermath of China's announcement of retaliation, both China and Japan soon sent to each other conciliatory signals. While playing down the adverse impact of the dispute, China expressed that it might resort to the WTO dispute settlement mechanism for resolution of the disputes after its accession to the WTO.[38] Japan also expressed it would approach the dispute in a flexible manner and in accordance with the WTO rules.[39] In fact, the two parties engaged themselves in talks.[40] All these left room for the trade dispute to be resolved without resorting to a war of retaliation. After four rounds of talks at different levels (including one talk at non-governmental level), the protracted dispute was finally settled at the ministerial talk between China and Japan on 21 December 2001, when the duration for investigation elapsed and the Japanese government had to decide whether to impose formal safeguard measures up to a four-year period (including the duration of the "provisional safeguard measures").[41] According to the Memorandum on the settlement, China decided to cancel the restrictions on the aforesaid Japanese products and Japan agreed not to initiate formal safeguard measures.[42] Moreover, both agreed to set up a "trade cooperation and coordination mechanism" to stabilize trade relations, and engage in consultation when necessary.

A study of the above selected cases shows that China employs different strategies to resolve trade disputes with its trade partners. China clearly depends on the existing agreement and the generally recognized trade and legal norms as part of its bargaining posture. In the China-EU case concerning trade agreement interpretation, China was justified, from the international law perspective, in sticking to narrow interpretation of the relevant agreement and when it conceded to the expansive interpretation of the EU. China's eventual concession was to some extent a reward to the EU for maintaining a good bilateral relation. In the China-US case, China accused the US of breaching its obligations under the textile trade agreement between the two countries. In the China-Japan case, China accused Japan of violating trade liberalism and the principle of fairness. In the China-Korea case, China equated the Korean measures as a violation of the WTO disciplines. In the China-EU case concerning telecommunications investment, China knew that it had gone back on a promise by annulling the previous approval, and it was because of this knowledge that China took a conciliatory stance in the negotiation.

China is also good at utilizing its trade status to strengthen its bargaining posture. In the China-Korea case, the realistic Chinese government succeeded in utilizing the trade deficit issue to force concessions from Korea. However, its trade partners can also use the trade status against China. In the China-US case, Chinese textile export's reliance on the US market and the huge Chinese trade surplus weakened the bargaining power of China in dealing with the dispute.

Political relations with the disputant country as of the time of the dispute are also taken into consideration in formulating a proposed approach to the dispute in question. In the above China-US case, when the US unilaterally deducted the quotas, alleging that China had violated the China-US agreement on textiles, what China opposed to was merely such unilateral measures, hinting it would be willing to accept a bilateral deduction of the quotas. This softened tone was obviously a result of the fear of a deteriorating China-US relation.[43] In the China-Japan case, China seemed to have an understanding of the Japanese government's decision resulting from domestic political pressure and therefore imposed seemingly punitive but *de facto* light measures to warn Japan. This was understandable against the backdrop of the bilateral relations between China and Japan.[44]

Nevertheless, there are common elements among the different approaches to the various trade disputes. Firstly, it is noteworthy that China attached great importance to consultation as a means of trade dispute settlement. A close look at the practice would reveal a link between advance consultation and the tone of China's position. There is no empirical evidence supporting an idea that an imminent trade dispute would be avoided if China were consulted in advance for a trade issue that if improperly dealt with, would lead to a dispute. However, it is obvious that China opposes any unilateral trade measures meted by its trade partners without advance consultation. Unilateral trade measures by its trade partners often give rise to trade disputes. Moreover, China would normally react strongly to such unilateral measures. What is noteworthy is that in the agreements on settlement with both Korea and Japan embody provisions for consultation to handle future disputes.[45]

Secondly, China has showed its inclination to resort to retaliation where its trade partners impose restriction on its exports in a way it deems unfair. In both the China-Korea case and China-Japan cases, China did not hesitate to use retaliation to force or attempt to force concession from the other disputants.

3. Dispute Settlement Mechanism within the WTO Framework

The WTO Agreement set up a new institutional framework for the governance of international trade with a vigorous dispute settlement system.[46] The system is presided over by the Understanding on Rules and Procedures Governing the Settlement of Disputes (DSU), which is an integral part of the single undertaking package of the Organization. The WTO dispute settlement mechanism is the central element in providing security and predictability to the multilateral trading system.[47] It is essential to the enforcement of WTO Agreements.[48]

The WTO established a DSB charged with creating panels, adopting panel and appellate body reports, and monitoring compliance with decisions and recommendations. Only Members can initiate WTO dispute settlement procedures against other Members. Refusal of a WTO Member involved in a dispute dealt with by a WTO panel to take recommended compliance measures, would lead to unilateral retaliation.

The WTO Agreements require its Members to take measures to ensure observance of the WTO Agreements by its regional or local governments and authorities.[49] In fact, according to the DSU, the WTO Dispute Settlement Mechanism could result in sanctions even where it is a provincial or municipal government rather than the central government that is responsible for the breach.[50]

4. Prospect of China's Behaviour Relating to the Dispute Settlement Mechanism

In this regard, it should be first pointed out that the WTO dispute settlement mechanism can only play a role in areas covered by WTO Agreements. Part of the reality is that many dimensions of China's political-economic system are not accounted for by current WTO Agreements.[51] Where such practice culminates in a dispute between a WTO Member and China, the DSB might be frustrated in dealing with it.

As Professor Jackson pointed out, "[a] very important consideration affecting a nation's willingness to accept the WTO dispute procedures is that nation's view of the role that the treaty and its institutions should play in its international economic diplomacy."[52] China has consistently opposed any unilateral measures by its trade partners. However, the multilaterality of the WTO dispute settlement mechanism will not necessarily provide an impetus for China's preference for the multilateral approach. Two factors my account for this:

Firstly, China is more used to the bilateral approach. To some extent, it is part of the Chinese legacy. China has demonstrated its sophisticated skills in dealing with different negotiating partners at the bilateral level. Due to lack of experience, however, China is still clumsy at multilateral forum. It has remained out of the international arena for too long; even becoming a UN member was a matter of 30 years ago. Western specialists on international affairs have no difficulty noticing that though China is a permanent member, it has been "cooperative" on almost every issue referred to the UN Security Council. It reflects how little creative thinking there is in China about managing world affairs. Indeed there is arguably no huge gap between bilateral and multilateral approaches, but it will take time for China to feel comfortable with multilateral forum.

Secondly, due to its culture, China is never shy to express its preference for amicable means of dispute settlement in diplomacy.[53] Furthermore, China has been reluctant to concede itself to any international tribunal. There has never been a dispute involving China that was adjudicated by an international tribunal. The only exception is that China acceded to the Convention on Settlement of Investment Disputes between Nations and Nationals of other Nations, which obliges China to accept the jurisdiction of the International Centre for Settlement of Investment Disputes (ICSID) on the condition that China and the disputant foreign national have reached an agreement on the jurisdiction matter.

Thirdly, even if China is willing to use the dispute settlement mechanism or if other WTO Members "grill" China on the dispute settlement mechanism, the limited capacity of the WTO dispute settlement mechanism to handle disputes[54] may frustrate China and its partners from using the mechanism to resolve disputes involving China.

The amalgam of these factors boils down to this: China may be cautious to use, or even accept, the adjudicating method used by WTO panels for dispute settlement, which is arguably the strength of the WTO dispute settlement mechanism.[55]

Nevertheless, as a WTO Member, China is now bound by the WTO Agreements including the DSU. Even its inclination to resort to retaliation should be restrained. Unlike other international organs for dispute settlement, the jurisdiction of the DSB is compulsory. Whenever China's partner feels Chinese trade measures are violating the WTO Agreements, it can bring China to the DSB without prior procurement of China's consent. China cannot challenge the jurisdiction of the DSB that receives the application of that Member. Needless to say, in cases where a complainant can show that China has violated WTO rules, the WTO dispute settlement system mechanism will be in a position to recommend that China change its behaviour and comply; moreover, if compliance is not forthcoming, the DSU will ensure an automatic right to retaliation by the injured WTO Member.

The adjudication and consultation processes are not mutually exclusive. In fact, they are compatible within the procedures of the WTO dispute settlement mechanism. This provision leaves more room for China to participate.

Furthermore, the WTO dispute settlement mechanism, since the inauguration of the WTO, has had a history of successfully and efficiently settling trade disputes between Members.

Finally, subjecting itself to the dispute settlement mechanism—no matter how unwilling China might be—would result in a desirable side effect per se: it may develop an interest in defending its rights through a generally viable and fair quasi-judicial body.

5. Concluding Remarks

While the Chinese law provides China with teeth to cope with trade disputes with its trade partners, China's peculiar approaches to trade disputes, as exemplified by the Chinese practice of dealing with such disputes, give a murky sign that China will probably accustom itself to the adjudicating procedures of the WTO dispute settlement mechanism, however it will pursue its own interests within the framework. On the other hand, as China wishes to become a key player in the WTO, it has a fundamental interest in both the promotion and the proper regulation of trade at the global level. Based on such grounds, one has no reason to believe that China will become a rogue elephant of the trade rules.

Appendix: What if Japan imposed the restriction or referred the dispute to the DSB after China's accession to the WTO?

A. What if Japan imposed the restriction after China's accession to the WTO?

In the Accession Protocol, China agrees to a 12-year product-specific safeguard, which allows the WTO Members to address rapidly increasing Chinese imports in a targeted fashion, if they are disrupting the market of other WTO Members. This provision, which does not apply to exports to China, requires a less strict standard than the WTO Safeguards Agreement. While WTO Members can act unilaterally to limit imports to the extent necessary to prevent or address the market disruption, China cannot retaliate in response to the use of the product-specific safeguards by WTO Members for 2 years, if measure/restraint based on relative increase in imports; or for 3 years, if measure/restraint based on absolute increase in imports. Moreover, China-specific remedy-restricts imports from China only, rather than requiring restrictions of imports from all WTO members as provided in the Agreement on Safeguards. In case of critical circumstances, provisional relief can be taken immediately based on a preliminary determination of market disruption or threat. Such action may precede bilateral consultations and last for up to 200 days.

Therefore, Japan would be justified to impose the restriction under this Accession Protocol, if Japan imposed the restriction after China's the accession to WTO. It is clear now that in fact Japan rendered itself in a dubious status by imposing the restriction at a wrong time.

B. What if Japan referred the dispute to the DSB after China's accession to the WTO?

Here the answer hinges on whether the Accession Protocol could have retrospective effect in relation to the China-Japan dispute, since the Accession Protocol did not come into effect until China acceded to the WTO on 11 December 2001. However, *US v Korea DRAMS Antidumping case* has indicated,[56] WTO Agreements can be invoked to cover the disputes that occurred before the date of the entry into force of the Agreement concerned, provided the effect of the dispute lingered until after the date. Therefore, China's commitment in the Accession Protocol should be applicable to the China-Japan dispute which occurred before the entry into force of the Accession Protocol.

In short, if the dispute were submitted to the DSB after China's accession to the WTO, the Accession Protocol would be deemed to have retrospective effect. As a consequence, Japan's imposition of the restrictions before the date would very likely be justified by the DSB.

Notes

1. For a description of China's commitments, see, *for instance*, Qingjiang Kong, China's WTO Accession: Commitments and Implications, 3 *Journal of International Economic Law* (2000) 4, pp. 655-690.

2. Despite the difference between the Chinese Customs' statistics and those of the United States, it is a fact China has gained a substantial annual trade surplus over the United States.

3. Anti-dumping has remained a major problem in the trade relations between China and the United States. From 1980 to the end of 1999, the United States had launched 73 anti-dumping investigations against imports from China, thus creating a major barrier for Chinese exports. According to the bilateral agreement between China and the United States on China's WTO accession, the United States will be able to apply the current US anti-dumping acts that treat China as a non-market economy.

4. Inadequate protection of foreign intellectual property rights has been a major concern for US traders and investors in China. Although Chinese intellectual property law is up-to-date and basically compatible with the TRIPS Agreement, enforcement of intellectual property law is still a problem.

5. The US has maintained control over hi-tech export to China and China has been complaining about the practice. The bilateral agreement between China and the United States does not cover US export control, and therefore, the US practice will likely continue.

6. Textile is one of the major products that China exports to the United States. According to the bilateral agreement between China and the United States, the US side will maintain its current quota arrangement for China before 1 January 2009, although the WTO Agreement on Trade in Textiles and Clothing requires an earlier relaxation.

7. Although the bilateral agreement does not cover Chinese export of prison products, the bill that the US Congress passed concerning China's permanent normal trade status required the US administration to monitor the Chinese export of prison products.
8. For example, China has to redraw its rules and regulations to come into compliance with its new responsibilities. Government officials, bureaucrats and judges have to be trained to ensure enforcement. All these constitute a formidable task for China.
9. See Margaret M. Pearson, China's Track Record in the Global Economy, *China Business Review*, January–February, 2000, available at http://www.chinabusinessreview.com/0001/pearson.html.
10. For instance, soon after China and the EU reached the agreement on China's WTO accession in May 2000, the two parties disputed on the number of licenses that should be awarded to allow European insurance companies to operate in China. The EU said China had failed to implement previous agreements on market access for the insurance companies.
11. One may be wondering why China, in the following China-Japan case, has taken a tough approach to Japan on the eve of China's entry in to the WTO. One explanation is that it is never shy to defend its perceived interests. This speculation being true, China's behaviour after the WTO accession would be anticipated.
12. The promulgation of the Anti-Dumping and Anti-Subsidy Regulations of the People's Republic of China is already a good example.
13. MOFTEC Press Release, 14 December 2001.
14. *South China Morning Post*, 23 January 2002.
15. According to a *China Daily* report of 28 January 2002, Chinese foreign trade authorities have said the European Union Commission's ban on animal-based food products from China was "unacceptable" and might seriously affect bilateral trade between the two. China has urged that the problem be solved through negotiations. China was seriously concerned over a decision made by departments of the EU to fully ban animal-based food products from China.
16. Adopted at the Seventh Session of the Standing Committee of the Eighth National People's Congress on 12 May 1994.
17. Promulgated by the State Council, 25 March 1997.
18. According to the WTO, China is the seventh largest exporter and eighth importer in the world in 2000.
19. See Bernard A. Gelb, Textile and Apparel Trade Issues, *Congressional Research Service, Report for Congress, RS20436*, 20 March 2001.
20. According to a US Customs Service study, in 1999 as much as US$10 billion in Chinese textile exports were not officially accounted for—much of this was believed to have gone into the U.S. market, quoted from Greg Mastel, Testi-

mony before The Trade Deficit Review Commission (United States), 24 February 2000.

21. Before this pact, there existed four agreements on textile trade between the United States and China, the first being concluded in 1980 and the recent in 1994. Under the 1994 agreements the USTR imposed sanctions against China's apparel quotas on three occasions, including imposing triple charges for illegally transhipped merchandise in September 1996.

22. The 1994 agreement generally provides that there is an annual increase in quota for Chinese textile export to the US. Ironically, the new agreement reduces quota levels in 14 apparel and fabric product categories where there were repeated violations of the 1994 agreement through transhipment or overshipment.

23. These barriers related to a number of products including high volume, high quality cotton and man-made fibre yarns and fabrics, knit fabrics, printed fabrics; high volume knit apparel such as T-shirts, sweatshirts and underwear; and advanced speciality textiles used in construction of buildings, highways and filtration products.

24. Administrative protection is a system that grants market exclusivity in China to foreign patented pharmaceutical and agrochemical products.

25. The EU and China settle long-running dispute over pharmaceuticals, European Commission Delegation in China, Press Release, Beijing, 6 February 2001.

26. See He Xia, Strategic Selections for Financing China's Telecommunications Industry, in *Regulation and Competition in China: Theories and Practice* (in Chinese), ed. Zhang Xinzhu *et al.*, Beijing: Shehui kexue wenxian chubanshe), 2000, pp. 310-312.

27. Citing the Korean Customs statistics, the MOFTEC pointed out the domestic output of garlic in the Korea increased by 90,000 tons in 1999, while its import only increased by 1,200 tons. It concluded the price drop in Korea's garlic market is mainly due to overproduction in Korea.

28. It was reported that the South Korean government had asked local mobile phone and polyethylene exporters instead to share the cost for importing the remaining 10,000 tons of garlic, worth some 10 billion *won* (US$7.5 million). See *People's Daily*, 17 April 2001.

29. According to the MOFTEC, although the imports of other three farm products, i.e., tomato, green pepper and onion, sharply increased from 1996 to 2000 and the prices of the same products from Japan have been evidently affected by the imports, the Japanese side, which had planned to investigate, finally decided not to make any investigation into the imports of the three products: See *China Daily*, 28 June 2001.

30. According to the Agreement on Safeguards (Article 2.2), safeguard measures shall be applied to a product being imported "respective of its source." The MOFTEC elaborated that the Japanese side selected the three farm products, rather than those surging imports of farm products from some WTO members, for investigation. Such an investigation contravened non-discrimination principle of the WTO.

    The MOFTEC complained that the Japanese side only provided China statistics of the increase of imports and the decline of relevant industries without an objective, just and convincing conclusion of investigation, nor an explanation of the relations between the import increase and the declining of the industries, which according to the MOFTEC, are "a must to impose import curb in accordance with relevant rules of the WTO."

31. The WTO Agreement on Safeguards does not authorize a WTO Member to resort to retaliation in the event of safeguards by another Member. However, the Accession Protocol rules out the possibility of retaliation by China in response to our use of this safeguard for two years, if the measure/restraint is based on relative increase in imports; or for three years, if the measure/restraint is based on absolute increase in imports.

32. According to 2000 statistics of Japanese source, Japan imported 4 billion *yen* worth of leeks, 10 billion *yen* worth of mushrooms and 10 billion *yen* worth of rush from China. The total value of the three imported items, 24 billion *yen*, accounts for only 0.05 percent of Japan's total imports of 40.938 trillion *yen*. See Asahi, 31 August 2001, available at <http://www.asahi.com/english/oped/K2001083100556.html>.

33. First, the ruling Liberal Democratic Party (LDP) had to secure the vote of farmers, which are traditionally the LDP's supporters. Secondly, the government was seemingly trying to divert public attention from such domestic problems as structural reform and bad debts.

34. In fact, Japan decided on 7 June 2001 to temporarily stop the import of Chinese poultry on alleged 'bird flu' fears, while China denied any local outbreak of the virus. It was reported that Japanese necktie makers who have been persuading the Japanese government to take similar protective measure are delaying their own quest for tariff help. See *South China Morning Post*, Editorial: Trading troubles, 21 June 2001.

35. Japan exported 45.2 billion *yen* worth of automobiles, 11.1 billion *yen* worth of mobile phones and 5.6 billion *yen* worth of air conditioners to China for a total of 61.9 billion *yen*, accounting for 0.12 percent of Japan's total exports of 51.654 trillion *yen*. Incidentally, Japan's automobile exports to China make up only 0.65 percent of Japan's total automobile exports, worth 6.93 trillion *yen*. See Asahi, 31 August 2001, available at <http://www.asahi.com/english/oped/K2001083100556.html>.

36. Japanese statistics show that there are almost no mobile phones and air conditioners actually imported from Japan.

37. Xu Changwen, a senior researcher with the Chinese Academy of International Trade and Economic Co-operation under the MOFTEC, holds the view. See Counter-tariffs set to warn Japan, *China Daily*, 20 June 2001.

38. When Japanese Prime Minister Junichiro Koizumi visited China on 8 October 2001, Chinese Premier Zhu Rongji reportedly said the dispute was not something insurmountable. Also, Long Yongtu, Vice-Minister of the MOFTEC, had reportedly said that. See *Lianhe Zaobao*, 23 August 2001.

39. Japanese Economic, Trade and Industry Minister Takeo Hiranuma, was quoted to have said that. See *South China Morning Post*, 26 October 2001.

40. The first talk was held from 3 to 4 July 2001 in Beijing. According to the Chinese side, in this talk Japan only proposed to turn the provisional safeguard measures into formal safeguard measures, and did not intend to negotiate a compensation plan for the loss incurred by the Chinese side due to the safeguard measures of Japan, which is also stipulated in WTO rules. Although it ended in failing to reach a settlement, both parties stressed the importance of the China-Japan trade relations. Japanese Prime Minister Junichiro Koizumi's talks with Chinese Premier Zhurongji during his China visit on 8 October 2001 and with President Jiang Zemin during his attendance of the APEC Summit on 22 October further precipitated a second talk, which started on 1 November 2001 and renewed on 7 November 2001. In the former talk, the leaders cited the importance of an early solution through mutual discussion, and expressed their wish to resolve the trade dispute from a broad perspective through friendly consultation; during the latter talk, the leaders reportedly agreed to the dispute being resolved through negotiation. The talks culminated when the talk at vice-ministerial level failed on 19 December 2001. The two sides immediately launched a new round of talk at a higher level between the trade ministers. See, respectively, Ministry of Foreign Affairs of Japan, Visit to the People's Republic of China by Prime Minister Junichiro Koizumi (Overview and Evaluation), 8 October 2001 (available at http://www.mofa.go.jp/region/asia-paci/china/pmv0110/overview.html), *Lianhe Zaobao*, 22 October 2001, and Xinhua News Agency, 20, 21 December 2001.

41. According to the WTO Agreement on Safeguards, the "provisional safeguard measures" shall not exceed 200 days (Article 6). Moreover, according to the Japanese law, the aforesaid investigation shall conclude within one year.

42. There were observations that although both parties called the agreement a compromise, most of the concessions came from Japan, which touched off

the dispute nine months ago by taking unilateral action. See, for instance, *Asian Wall Street Journal*, 24-25 December 2001.

43. China had just succeeded in forging a closer relation with the United States as a result of the US engagement policy. Among others, Chinese president Jiang Zemin paid the first state visit to the United States since the Tiananmen incident in 1989 and the Sino-US relation had just recovered from the shocking Taiwan Strait missile launch during Taiwan's first presidential election.

44. The relation between China and Japan had been suffering from a series of events, such as the history textbook, pro-independence former Taiwan leader Lee Teng-hui's visit to Japan, and Junichiro Koizumi's visit to the Shrine. China was reluctant to see a further deterioration of the bilateral relation.

45. The agreement ending the garlic export dispute between China and Korea states: "The two countries also agreed to operate regular negotiation channels between the Korean Ministry of Foreign Affairs and Trade and the Chinese Ministry of Foreign Trade and Economic Co-operation in order to prevent trade disputes that may occur as the economic and trade co-operation between the two countries increase. And in case of disputes, the two countries agreed to resolve them as early as possible through close co-operation and mutual negotiations between relevant ministries."

46. See, generally, Ernst-Ulrich Petersmann, *The GATT/WTO Dispute Settlement System: international law, international organizations and dispute settlement*, London: Kluwer Law International, 1997; David Palmeter and Petros Mavroidis, *Dispute Settlement in the World Trade Organization*, The Hague: Kluwer Law International, 1999.

47. Article 3.2. of the DSU.

48. Confidence in the system is borne out by the number of cases brought to the WTO—167 cases by March 1999 compared to some 300 disputes dealt with during the entire life of GATT (1947—94).

49. For instance, Article XXIV(12) of GATT also provides that WTO Members "shall take such reasonable measures as may be available to it to ensure observance of the provisions of this Agreement by the regional and local governments and authorities within its territories."

50. Article 22.9. of DSU provides: "The dispute settlement provisions of the covered agreements may be invoked in respect of measures affecting their observance taken by regional or local governments or authorities within the territory of a Member. When the DSB has ruled that a provision of a covered agreement has not been observed, the responsible Member shall take such reasonable measures as may be available to it to ensure its observance."

51. For instance, the draftsman of the GATT, who designed an article (i.e. Article XVII) to discipline activity by state enterprises, could never have anticipated

that this article and the GATT as a whole would not sufficiently address problems created by the accession of a country as big as China and with such a big role for state enterprises. Even according to the most generous estimates of the extent to which China's market has liberalized, at least thirty-five percent of Chinese gross domestic product is still produced by SOEs. Therefore, questions relating to SOEs are sure to be encountered in China. The risk is that action by SOE has the potential to undermine the fundamental rules of the GATT. For the most part, the GATT assumes that economic decision-making is made by producers and consumers based on price, but SOEs do not always make decisions based on price. It is not difficult to see many SOEs that utilise computer chips make all their computer chips purchases from state-owned chip manufacturers. This would not only contravene the primary requirement of Article XVII, that is, state enterprises shall make purchases or sales "solely in accordance with commercial considerations," but also effectively undermine the GATT's Article III national treatment provision. Similar arguments can be made about how SOEs may engage in behaviour that would undermine the GATT Article I commitment of MFN treatment, the Article II commitment to a schedule of concessions, and the Article XI commitment against maintaining quantitative restrictions. Given that the reason for purchases or sales by state enterprises is not transparent, none of these disciplines could be effective.

52. John H. Jackson, *The World Trade Organization: Constitution and Jurisprudence*, London: The Royal Institute of International Affairs, 1998, pp. 76-78.

53. Probably, the traditional preference for consultation and other amicable means for dispute settlement may find support in a new context. A major power, with attractive market potential, presumably owns more bargaining power in diplomacy-negotiation-oriented processes of dispute settlement.

54. Given its tremendous responsibilities, the WTO has a tiny team of professional staff in its secretariat and a tight budget. The dispute settlement mechanism can handle only about 45 cases annually.

55. The DSU indeed leaves room for Members concerned to engage in consultation to settle their disputes. It, however, only requires parties to mutually "give sympathetic consideration to and afford adequate opportunity for consultation." See Article 4.2. of the DSU.

56. See DSB, United States—Anti-Dumping Duty on Dynamic Ramdom Access Memory Semiconductors (DRAMS) of one Megabit or above from Korea, available at <http://www.wto.org/english/tratop_e/dispu_e/99r.pdf>.

Part III

Towards WTO Compliance: China's Trade Regime

7

New Dimension Of China's Foreign Investment Regime On The Eve Of WTO Accession

1. Introduction

Substantial academic work has been done, showing that foreign investments play an indispensable role in achieving development goal for developing countries.[1] Market size is an important consideration for a foreign investor contemplating a particular foreign investment. However, without a favorable investment regime, foreign investors are either unable or reluctant to enter the market.

The foreign investment regime in China is generally regarded as favourable to foreign investment.[2] It has played a very positive role in attracting foreign investment into China. The annual foreign investment influx has remained the second largest among all the recipient countries in the world since 1992[3] and reached US$46.8 billion in 2001. By the end of 2001, the foreign investment stock was US$395.5 billon.[4]

As a result of its bid to join the WTO, China's foreign investment regime is becoming more market-friendly, although certain heritages of the transitional economy are still perceivable. This chapter aims to evaluate the compatibility of the foreign investment regime of China and the WTO investment rules.

Since the WTO Agreements will not be directly applicable, the laws and regulations China revises and adopts—rather than the text of Accession Protocol or the WTO Agreements—will provide the roadmap that government agencies and courts will use to implement WTO commitments. In this context, such evaluation would be meaningful.

2. An Overview of the WTO Rules on Investment

The inclusion of investment rules in multilateral trade agreements was a major breakthrough of the Uruguay Round as well as an achievement by the multilateral trading system in establishing a global investment protection mechanism. The reason behind was that transnational trade and investment are increasingly interrelated.[5] Nevertheless, the WTO does not contain an investment agreement *per se*. In fact, it does not contain the kind of investment protection provisions[6] commonly found in many of the bilateral investment agreements. Nor does it embody such features as a mechanism allowing private investors direct access to an international dispute settlement mechanism, which is common in bilateral investment agreements.[7] However, as a result of the Uruguay Round negotiations, the WTO began to embody various investment-related rules. The GATS, the TRIPS Agreement, and the Agreement on Trade-related Investment Measures (TRIMS) contain such provisions.[8] Take the GATS as example. As has been noted, the supply of many services to a particular market is difficult or impossible without the physical presence of the service supplier. Article 1:2 of the GATS defines "trade in services" as encompassing four modes of supply, including the supply "by a service supplier of one member, through commercial presence in the territory of any other member." The term "commercial presence" is defined in Article XXVIII (d) as "any type of business or professional establishment, including through (i) the constitution, acquisition or maintenance of a juridical person, or (ii) the creation or maintenance of a branch or a representative office, within the territory of one member for the purpose of supplying a service." As a consequence, the GATS covers forms of establishment which correspond to the notion of foreign investment. All WTO Members have established specific commitments under GATS in relation to the four modes of supply. These commitments bind governments to guarantee conditions of market access in respect of the modes and sectors indicated in schedules of specific commitments. In the absence of specifications to the contrary, Members guarantee both the right of market entry (Article XVI) and the right to national treatment (Article XVII) in scheduled sectors, which, to some extent, establish the foreign investors' right of entry regarding their admission.

The TRIPS Agreement contains a set of rules governing host country's treatment of foreign companies. Although the TRIPS Agreement does not directly address foreign investment, its provisions on minimum standards for the protection of intellectual property, domestic enforcement procedures and international dispute settlement are directly relevant to the legal environment affecting foreign investment. As a matter of fact, the definition of "investment" in many intergovernmental investment agreements expressly includes intellectual property. Under the TRIPS Agreement, each WTO Member is required to accord in its territory the protection required by the TRIPS Agreement to the IPRs of the nationals of other WTO Members.

The TRIMS Agreement aims not only at the progressive liberalization of world trade, but also the facilitation of investment across borders. The TRIMS Agreement has a conspicuous feature: it specifies that certain types of investment measures are inconsistent with the GATT. According to the Illustrative List, annexed to the TRIMS Agreement, these measures essentially concern local content and trade-balancing requirements; they may include mandatory or enforceable measures, or those measures whose compliance is necessary to obtain an advantage. The TRIMS Agreement provides, in connection with local content, export performance requirements and foreign exchange restrictions, that it is a violation of the requirement of national treatment for an investment measure to require the purchase of local products by foreign enterprises to be tied with its exports. Similarly, it is a violation of prohibitions of quantitative restrictions when investment measures require an enterprise to use its own forex reserve to import products. The prohibition of quantitative restriction is similarly violated if export is tied in any way with the local production.

More importantly, all these WTO Agreements containing investment rules put important obligations, based on the fundamental principles, on WTO Member governments with regards to the treatment of foreign nationals or companies within their territories. They include: non-discrimination (MFN treatment and national treatment), freer trade, predictable policies, and encouraging competition.[9] In other words, WTO Members should renounce unreasonable measures that contravene the principles established within the WTO framework, and should promptly announce trade-related investment laws and policies.

An examination of the WTO investment rules would find that these rules fall within two categories: rules disciplining various and often-conflicting investment measures concerning admission of foreign investments, which, in a broad sense, also covers incentives for investment, including tax concessions, tariff concessions, investment subsidies designed to divert foreign investment to targeted sectors and areas of host countries; and rules disciplining national measures concerning operational requirements, including vehicles available to foreign investors to form their invested enterprises. While the investment rules embodied in the GATS are primarily related to admission of foreign investment in host countries' services sectors, those in the TRIPS Agreement concern operation of investment. In contrast, the TRIMS Agreement contains investment rules of both categories.

This is the basis of the effects of WTO accession on China's foreign investment regime.

3. Assessment of China's Prior Foreign Investment Regime

3.1. Features of the Chinese foreign investment framework

3.1.1. Characteristics in form

The formation of a foreign investment in China started from the adoption of the Chinese-foreign Equity Joint Venture Law (EJV Law) by the National People's Congress in 1979. Since then, the foreign investment regime has been fragmented. Although the MOFTEC proposed that the laws on foreign-invested enterprises (FIEs) be codified after China reached the bilateral agreement with the United States on China's accession to the WTO, there remains to be no single foreign investment code. Foreign investment law contains numerous laws and regulations.[10]

The mainstream of these laws and regulations are directly related to foreign investment, which form the basic framework of the Chinese foreign investment regime. The rest of the laws and regulations, such as those on IPRs, foreign trade, are only relevant to the foreign investment environment.

Take as example the laws and regulations that are directly relevant to foreign investment, there are laws by the NPC or its Standing Committee,[11] administrative regulations by the State Council,[12] ministerial administrative rules,[13] and local regulations or government rules[14].

3.1.2. Characteristics in substance

A foreign investment regime shall deal not only with the issues of foreign investment protection and dispute settlement, but also admission of foreign investment and operation of foreign invested projects. It goes without saying that, for foreign investors, being free from expropriation and exchange control is of extreme importance. Fortunately, these concerns have been fully or at least, adequately addressed by Chinese laws, particularly, the bilateral investment treaties between China and other countries.[15] Therefore, in this context, the Chinese foreign investment regime addresses the concerns of foreign investors about whether they can invest in lucrative industries and whether their operation can be free from interference.

Nevertheless, like other countries', China's foreign investment regime attached great importance to the promotion of foreign investment. To this end, various Chinese laws and regulations relating to foreign investment provide incentives for FIEs, particularly those established in targeted areas such as Special Economic Zones (SEZs), the Economic and Technical Development Zones of open coastal cities and the Central and Western China in the newly launched go-west development campaign. As a matter of fact, the Chinese foreign investment regime used to be basically an incentive-based and regional-oriented regime, which affected the admission and operation of foreign investment in China.

3.2. A review of the Chinese foreign investment regime before the conclusion of Sino-US agreement

3.2.1. Admission

Admission of foreign investment is related to China's industrial policies. The EJV Law does not have any provisions regarding sectors prohibited or restricted to foreign investment; Instead, this Law merely provides that the technology and equipment contributed by an equity joint venture's foreign partner as its investment must be really "advanced technology and equipment that suit China's needs."[16] The Implementing Regulations of the Chinese-foreign Equity Joint Venture Law (EJV Regulations), which were promulgated by the State Council on 20 September 1983, list the sectors where foreign investment participation is allowed and provide guidance for allowing such foreign investment participation.[17] Similarly, the WFIE Law and the Detailed Rules for the Implementation of the Wholly Foreign-invested Enterprise Law (WFIE Rules) provide specifically for the sectors that deny or restrict foreign investment admission.[18] In practice, in relation to the restricted sectors, there often lie a percentage of share requirement and other thresholds for foreign participation. In these sectors, foreign investment participation, even in the form of joint venture, is rare.

It is not difficult to find that the EJV Regulations, the WFIE Law and the WFIE Rules established general requirements for foreign investment admission, that is, foreign investment shall be admitted in such a manner as to help the development of China's national economy; and foreign investors shall use advanced technology or market all or most of their products outside China.[19]

Nevertheless, what is notable is that in relation to foreign investment admission, China had not had formal and systematic industrial policies until the promulgation of the Provisional Regulations on Foreign Investment Guidelines (Guidelines) and the Catalogue of Industries for Guiding Foreign Investment (Catalogue) in 1995.[20] Two points need to be emphasized: First, the industrial policies, as embodied in the Guidelines and Catalogue, stressed the hi-tech and export-oriented policies.

Secondly, the comprehensive framework for admission of foreign investment occurred with the Guidelines and Catalogue, representing a new attitude towards foreign investment. The Guidelines lay down the principles of industrial policy for foreign investment. Basically, industries are divided into three categories: industries where foreign investment is encouraged, industries where foreign investment is restricted and industries where foreign investment is prohibited. In general, while China encourages foreign investment in priority infrastructure sectors such as energy production, communications, agriculture, forestry, environmental protection, and transportation, potential foreign investors are barred from investing in sectors, such as telecommunications services, news media, broadcasting and television sectors, which are considered sensitive from a national security perspective; they are restricted in participating in sectors such as services and automotive sector, where there is a desire to protect a domestic industry.[21] In many cases foreign investors must form a joint venture with a Chinese company, and restrict their equity ownership to a minority share, in order to invest in these restricted sectors. Take the services sector as example. At present, foreign service providers are largely restricted to operations under the terms of selective "experimental" licenses. The strict operational limits on forms of establishment for entry, and restrictions on the geographic scope of activities, severely limit the growth and profitability of these operations.[22]

Another area relating to the admission of foreign investment in the Chinese foreign investment regime is the preferential treatment granted to foreign investment and FIEs.[23] This is in contrast with the restrictive industrial policies. In order to attract foreign investment, China implemented a dual-track tax system whereby domestic and FIEs were levied different income taxes.[24] FIEs located in SEZs or the Economic and Technical Development Zones of open coastal cities were entitled to a corporate income tax rate of 15 per cent (the normal income tax was 33 per cent). Profits remitted abroad by foreign investors were exempted from income tax. The preferential income tax rate of 15 per cent is applicable to hi-tech items or projects with foreign investment of over US$30 million, as well as enterprises that operated in the fields of energy, transport and port construction. The income tax concessions extended to FIEs are not granted to domestic enterprises.[25] As for circulation-related taxes, FIEs could enjoy rebates on their tax burden resulting from the replacement of the consolidated industrial and commercial tax and special consumption tax by value-added tax, consumption tax and business tax, which domestic enterprises were not entitled to.[26] With regard to tariffs, foreign enterprises are exempt from tariffs on the import of production equipment, parts and components as well as raw materials, auxiliary materials, components, parts and packaging materials imported for the production of goods for export in accordance with law (this measure was abolished in 1996 but reinstated in 1998).[27] Export-oriented and hi-tech foreign investment projects are entitled to government-assigned land use rights for a given period.[28] SEZs and the Economic and Technical Development Zones of open coastal cities often offer considerable concessions to foreign firms on land use fees. Foreign investment projects on education, culture, science and technology, medical and health care, and public facilities as well as export-oriented and hi-tech projects enjoy even more favourable terms. FIEs have the privilege of recruiting talent from other cities.[29] They are also granted import and export rights, management autonomy, a freer hand in forex management.

In addition, examination and approval procedures are an integral part of the practice for admission of foreign investment. A dominant weakness in China's foreign investment regime lies in the fact that examination and approval procedures are excessively complicated and insufficiently transparent. In fact, they can be used to dissuade unwanted foreign investment projects. For example, it was often discouraging that any foreign investment project with an investment of more than US$30 million must obtain final approval from the State Council, even though they might have gone through approvals by various authorities at various levels.

3.2.2. Operational environment of FIEs

Vehicles for foreign investment: Vehicle options for foreign investment are an important aspect of operational environment. Before 1993, vehicles for foreign investment are limited to three options: Chinese-foreign equity joint venture (EJV), Chinese-foreign contractual joint venture (CJV) and wholly foreign-invested enterprise (WFIE). In fact, EJV, CJV and WFIE are the three major forms of foreign direct investment in China.

Among these, the *EJV* used to be the most dominant form of investment. The rights and obligations of the Chinese and foreign partners to an

EJV are determined in proportion to their respective capital contribution. However, the proportional contributions between Chinese and foreign participants in Chinese-foreign equity joint venture have changed. Before the first amendment of EJV Law in 1990, a foreign majority stake was rare and difficult to obtain. Recently, more and more foreign partners prefer arrangements for foreign controlling stakes. Foreign partners not only design a controlling stake for themselves in newly established Chinese-foreign EJVs, but also do so in relation to the existing Chinese-foreign EJVs.

Regarding the *CJV*, the rights and obligations of the Chinese and foreign partners are determined by contractual arrangement, which may not necessarily be in line with the capital contribution proportion. That is, the legal relationship between Chinese and foreign partners is determined by their bargaining power. However, the CJV Rules limit the contractual autonomy, thus making the vehicle of CJV less appealing. In fact, many existing CJVs have been reshaped into EJVs.

Initially, the *WFIE* was not preferable from the perspective of the government which was concerned with foreign control. However, the WFIE has become the preferred foreign investment vehicle. Not only do new foreign investments take the vehicle, but the existing EJVs have also been reshaped into WFIEs. In 1997, of all FIEs, 45.2 percent were WFIEs; 43.5 percent EJVs and 11.3 percent CJVs. The growing popularity of the WFIE can be attributed to several factors. In the early days of China's opening-up and reform, the majority of foreign investors chose to enter the China market through equity joint ventures. This was partly due to the limited scope of China's opening at the time. On the other hand, it was in the interest of foreign investors to set up joint ventures with Chinese partners because they could capitalise on the latter's market share and access to local distribution channels. As China became more liberalised and foreign investors grew more familiar with the China market, wholly foreign-invested operation increasingly became a preferred option. This trend was driven by the fact that differences in corporate culture and management philosophy between the foreign and Chinese parties to a joint venture have often created difficulties in operation. As a result, some foreign investors switched to wholly foreign-invested operation through injecting more funds or expanding their equity share. Meanwhile, as more MNCs are expanding their research & development (R&D) activities in China, they tend to operate in the form of WFIE in order to protect their technologies. Both EJVs and WFIEs must take the form of limited liability company. CJVs may take the form of either limited liability company or partnership. In fact those CJVs that take the form of limited liability company do not differ from EJVs.

Since 1993 more vehicles had been introduced for FIEs, they are companies limited by share, holding companies, merger and acquisition (M & A), building-operation-transfer (BOT) and venture capital. The Company Law of 1993 provides for the establishment of *companies limited by shares*. However, it does not specifically address the possibility of foreign investment in this type of company. The Promulgation of the Tentative Provisions on Certain Questions on Establishment of Foreign Investment Companies Limited by Shares by MOFTEC in 1995, made it possible for foreign investors to set up foreign investment companies limited by shares. In fact, the existing FIEs can also be reorganized into this type of company.

In 1995 MOFTEC promulgated the Tentative Provisions on Establishment of Companies with an Investment nature by Foreign Investors. With this, foreign investors may set up *holding companies*. However, the Tentative Provisions set forth stringent requirements.[30] It seems that China wants to limit holding companies to multinational corporation investors.

M & A has become o popular vehicle for investment. However, for quite a long time, foreign investment had not been able to take the form of M & A. With the Circular on Examination and Approval of Projects Utilizing Foreign Investment for the Reformation of Existing Enterprises by the State Economic and Trade Commission in 1995, forming an FIE by acquiring a Chinese enterprise as a whole became an option for prospective foreign investor. Foreign investor looking for business opportunity in China are increasingly interested in exploiting the M & A vehicles. A typical example was the "China Strategy" or "*Zhongce*" phenomena. Using about RMB 1 billion *yuan*, the Hong Kong-based China Strategy acquired dozens of ill-performed SOEs in various cities in East China and North China worth of RMB 3 billion *yuan*, the balance being obtained from listing the acquired enterprises in overseas stock market. Sometimes, M & A is the only way to take a share of the Chinese market. By acquiring a 15 percent stake in the

Bank of Communications, China's fifth-largest commercial bank, Citibank became the front-runner in the banking industry

In 1997, *BOT* was formally introduced as a new foreign investment vehicle with the completion of the Laibin B Power Plant in the Guangxi Zhuang Autonomous Region based on the UNIDO (United Nations Industrial Development Organization) BOT model. The issuance of the Provisional Measures on the Administration of International Project Finance by the State Development and Planning Commission (SDPC) further legalized the investment vehicle. It is particularly popular in the infrastructure sector. In a BOT project a foreign investor is given a concession to finance, build and operate a facility that would normally be built and operated by the Chinese government. At the end of the concession period the foreign investor returns the ownership of the project to the government. The concession period is determined primarily by the length of the time needed for the facility's revenue stream to pay off the company's debt and provide a reasonable rate of return for its effort and risk. One of the major differences between BOT and other vehicles is government involvement, government concession or government guarantee. And because of this, all the BOT projects need to be approved by the SDPC.

Monopoly: Monopoly, is another factor pertaining to or affecting the operation of foreign investment, that has not yet been adequately addressed in China. There has so far been no anti-monopoly law. Although in September 1993, China passed an "Anti-Unfair Competition Law" which prohibits price-fixing and prevents predatory pricing, this law was so vague as to make enforcement difficult. For example, the law indeed has sought to prevent telecommunication operators from collecting telecommunications charges in excess of what was stipulated, but the law does not have substantive or predictable procedures in place to prevent anti-competitive behaviour by the dominant operators (China Telecom), let alone challenge the *de facto* or *de jure* monopoly resulting from the government authority. Similarly, the Price Law, the Law on Tendering and Bidding, the Criminal Law, although containing provisions on anti-monopoly and unfair competition, fail to institute a full-fledged mechanism for anti-monopoly. Designation of key state enterprises in many industries, in particular the high technology sector, as the exclusive base for the development of critical technologies, limits the choice of joint venture partners. Such designated partners are sometimes unattractive for various business reasons such as lack of experience, inappropriate staffing levels, or weak finances.

Other operational restrictions: There were other operational restrictions on foreign investments after their entry and establishment. These restrictive measures relating to operation included discriminatory treatment FIEs receive in certain areas, such as local content requirements, forex balancing requirements[31] and export requirements. For example, Article 20 of the pre-amendment CJV Law stipulated that: "A contractual joint venture shall achieve on its own the balance of its forex receipts and expenditures. If a contractual joint venture is unable to achieve the balance of its forex receipts and expenditures on its own, it may, in accordance with State provisions, apply to the relevant authorities for assistance." Article 18 (3) of the previous WFIE Law provided that: "Wholly foreign-invested enterprises shall manage to balance their own forex receipts and payments. If, with the approval of the competent authorities, the enterprises market their products in China and consequently experience an imbalance in forex, the said authorities shall help them correct the imbalance." It is therefore not surprising that foreign investors often complain about unfair and discriminatory treatment.

4. China's Commitments relating to Foreign Investment

In order to join the WTO, China made substantial commitments relating to the admission and operation of foreign investment, which were specified primarily in the bilateral agreements with the United States and the European Union, and later reflected in the Accession Protocol on China's accession to the WTO. With regard to admission, China's commitments cover nearly all major sectors, and within reasonable periods (ranging from immediately upon accession to within five years after accession), it will eliminate most foreign equity restrictions in nearly all sectors. Industries that have been closed to foreign investment, such as telecommunications and securities, will be opened to foreign investment. Some industries where foreign investment has had to be approved on a trial basis, such as banking and retailing, will allow foreign participation in principle. Industries where foreign investment has had to form a joint venture with government-approved Chinese partners, such as accountancy, will be opened for greater foreign participation.[32] Moreover, China made specific commitments regarding amendment to the Industrial Policy for the Automotive Sector to ensure compatibility with WTO rules and principles. It is apparent that China's investment market will be open to multinational corporations (MNCs) in a very short period of time. In this regard, it should be pointed out that commitments can be compromised. For example, China's commitments do not mean foreign banks will have unfettered access to the Chinese market: first, there are still general regulations on both foreign and domestic banks; secondly, some regulations, though permissible in almost every country, are specifically set out for foreign banks. For example, there is a substantial restriction on foreign banks to set up a branch (among others, It has to own assets exceeding US$20 billion). While for domestic banks the establishment of branches needs only to gain the approval from the authorities, it might be difficult to argue that the provision should be terminated for the sake of the WTO Agreement, even though the authorities are preparing to lower the criteria.

With regard to examination and approval procedures, China agreed, in the Accession Protocol, to raise the limit within which investments in motor vehicle manufacturing could be approved at provincial government level only, from the current level of US$30 million, to US$60 million one year after accession, US$90 million two years after accession, and US$150 million four years after accession.

With respect to operational environment of FIEs, China has made commitments to comply fully with the TRIMS Agreement upon accession, without recourse to Article 5 thereof.[33] It would only impose, apply or enforce laws, regulations or measures relating to the transfer of technology, production processes, or other proprietary knowledge to an individual or enterprise in its territory that were not inconsistent with the TRIPS Agreement and the TRIMS Agreement. Accordingly, China promised to eliminate forex balancing and trade balancing requirements, local content requirements and export performance requirements. Moreover, it has made commitments not to enforce the terms of contracts containing such requirements. The allocation, permission or rights for importation and investment would not be conditional upon performance requirements set by national or sub-national authorities, or subject to secondary conditions covering, for example, the conduct of research, the provision of offsets or other forms of industrial compensation including specified types or volumes of business opportunities, the use of local inputs or the transfer of technology. Permission to invest, import licences, quotas and tariff rate quotas would be granted without regard to the existence of competing Chinese domestic suppliers.

In addition, China made commitments regarding other aspects of the operational environment of FIEs. For example, with respect to forex, China committed itself to implementing its obligations in accordance with the provisions of the WTO Agreement and related declarations and decisions of the WTO that concerned the IMF, and, in accordance with these obligations, and unless otherwise provided for in the IMF's Articles of Agreement, not to resort to any laws, regulations or other measures, including any requirements with respect to contractual terms, that would restrict the availability to any individual or enterprise of forex for current international transactions within its customs territory to an amount related to the forex inflows attributable to that individual or enterprise. Another example is price control, which used to cover various services sector. In the Chinese commitments, for instance, foreign legal service providers engaged in activities such as those listed in China's GATS schedule, would be able to determine the appropriate charges and fees, rather than be subject to government pricing or guidance pricing.

China has also committed itself to improving the transparency and law enforcement. In respect to transparency, China undertook that only those laws, regulations and other measures pertaining to or affecting trade in goods, services, TRIPS or the control of foreign exchange that were published and readily available to other WTO Members, individuals and enterprises, should be enforced. In addition, China shall make available to WTO Members, upon request, all laws, regulations and other measures pertaining to or affecting trade in goods, services, TRIPS or the control of foreign exchange before such measures are implemented or enforced. As for law enforcement, China confirmed that the provisions of the WTO Agreements, as well as the Accession Protocol, would be applied uniformly throughout its customs territory, including in SEZs and other areas where special regimes for tariffs, taxes and regulations were established and at all levels of government, and that it would upon accession establish a mechanism under which individuals and enterprises can bring to the attention of the national authorities cases of non-uniform application of the trade regime. China's local regulations, rules and other measures of local governments at the sub-national level shall conform to the obligations undertaken in the WTO Agreement and the Accession Protocol. Moreover, according to the Accession Protocol, the administrative law would be improved to such an extent that judicial review of administrative acts and judicial independence would be established in many fields.[34] Thus, law enforcement by administrations can be expected to be more formal and standardized.

5. Adapting China's Foreign Investment Regime towards WTO Compliance

Since the conclusion of the Sino-US agreement regarding China's WTO accession, China had been preparing its legislation for the accession. The NPC Standing Committee amended the WFIE Law, the CEJ Law on 31 October 2000. The NPC also revised the EJV Law on 15 March 2001. Accordingly, the State Council amended the Detailed Rules for the Implementation of the WFIE Law, and the EJV Regulations on 12 April 2001 and 22 July 2001 respectively. Apart from the comprehensive foreign investment laws and implementing rules, the State Council and relevant ministries have also promulgated various regulations or rules concerning foreign investment in sectors. For example, the Provisional Measures for Administration of Chinese-foreign Equity and Contractual Joint Venture Medical Institutions, the Provisional Measures for Examination and Approval and Administration of Foreign Investment in Rail Freight Transport Services, the Administrative Regulations on the Printing Industry, the Interim Measures for Foreign investment in Cinemas,[35] the Regulations on Foreign Investment in Telecommunications Enterprises, the Regulations on International Maritime Transportation, the Regulations on Foreign-Invested Insurance Companies, and the Regulations on Cinema were adopted, while the Regulations on Travel Agencies and the Regulations on Foreign-Invested Financial Institutions were amended,[36] to allow foreign participation in the medical care, rail freight services, printing, telecommunications services, maritime transportation, insurances and cinema industries, and more foreign participation in travel agency and financial services industries. The objective of the revisions is to pave the way for the Chinese government to create a more liberalised investment environment for FIEs in accordance with WTO principles after its entry to the world trade body. According to legal experts involved in drafting the amendments, the major task was to remove those clauses that contravene WTO rules from the original investment laws and regulations.

5.1. Admission of foreign investment

5.1.1. Industrial Policy

With respect to admission of foreign investment, an overview of the revision would show that the three amended basic laws relating to foreign investment and their implementing regulations or rules no longer have provisions concerning industrial policies, which are exclusively dealt with by the Guidelines and Catalogue.[37]

Secondly, admission of foreign investment is delinked with the hi-tech and export-oriented requirements. Article 3 (1) of the previous WFIE Law stipulated that: "Wholly foreign-invested enterprises shall be established in such a manner as to help the development of China's national economy; they shall use advanced technology and equipment or market all or most of their products outside China." It has now been amended as follows: "A wholly foreign-invested enterprise to be established in China must be conducive to the development of China's national economy, and be capable of achieving marked economic benefits. The State encourages wholly foreign-invested enterprises to adopt advanced technology and equipment, engage in the development of new products, realise the upgrading of products, and conserve energy and raw materials. The State also encourages the establishment of export-oriented wholly foreign-invested enterprises." The newly revised WFIE Rules further removed the requirement that a wholly foreign-owned enterprise must either meet advanced technology requirements or export 50 percent or more of its product output.

It is worth noting in this regard that the Chinese government has been reportedly revising the Guidelines and Catalogue to ensure compliance with the commitments China made concerning market access. Moreover, the government had seemingly loosen the strict ban on foreign investment in prohibited sectors before China entered into the WTO. Several foreign companies had been reportedly able to reach investment agreements with relevant Chinese partners before the formal WTO entry.[38]

5.1.2. Pilot projects

Basically as a gesture for the WTO accession, the Chinese government had launched several pilot projects to experiment with allowing foreign investment in previously restricted sectors like retailing, media and telecommunications services. For example, China had on several occasions allowed the entry of large international retailers into the Chinese market, such as Wal-Mart in Shenzhen, Carrefour, Metro in Shanghai; These moves are aimed at encouraging the development of large retail chain stores along the Wal-Mart model, and said to be intended as a solution to the moribund condition of many state-owned department stores. China approved the plan of Star Group, a subsidiary of the News Corp., to provide television services in Guangdong Province through an entertainment channel. It had also authorized the establishment of Shanghai Xintian Telecommunications Ltd. in Shanghai, a value-added telecommunications services joint venture involving the AT&T, Shanghai Information Investment Corporation, and Shanghai Telecom.

In addition, inspired by the WTO's national treatment principle, China has taken measures to level the playing field for domestic enterprises and FIEs with regard to enterprises income tax rates, tariff exemptions and other preferential treatment. The new move signified with the effort to unify the tax system long before the conclusion of the China-Us agreement on China's accession to the WTO. The tax reform in 1994 resulted in a unified enterprise tax rate of 33 percent for domestic enterprises and FIEs, although in SEZs[39] and other designated regions (such as the Economic and Technical Development Zones of open coastal cities and Central and Western China) foreign-invested enterprises still enjoy a preferential rate of 15 percent. The government has made clear, on numerous occasions, that such preferential tax treatment for FIEs will be finally removed.[40] Moreover, the special preferential tariff policies applied to SEZs had been eliminated. Contrary to the original provision that entitles all FIEs to duty exemption for their import of production equipment, parts and components as well as raw materials, auxiliary materials, components, parts and packaging materials imported for the production of goods for export, the Circular on the Adjustment of Tax Policies on Imported Equipment (1997) provides that since January 1998, only foreign-invested projects listed in the "encouraged" or "restricted category (II)" of the Catalogue may enjoy such import duty exemption. In the meantime, domestic-invested projects, which meet the requirements of the Catalogue of Major Industries, Products and Technologies Encouraged for Development in China are also entitled to the same import duty exemption.[41]

However, in an apparent effort to encourage foreign investment to boost the development of the poverty-stricken Central and Western China, this new policy will not be applied to the targeted regions for development. For example, the State Council decided on 8 December 1999 that for the three years after existing preferential tax policies end, enterprise income tax be levied at a rate of 15 percent for FIEs under the "encouraged category" that are established in central and western regions. Also, the General Administration of Customs issued a Circular Concerning Policies for Collection of Import Duties and Tax Relevant to Further Encouraging Foreign Investment, which announces exemptions from duty and VAT for equipment imports by FIEs for purposes of technological transformation, and exemptions for equipment imports by FIEs in central and western China.

It is noted that with respect to examination and approval procedures, which is an issue that the WTO has not yet touched upon, China had, prior to the conclusion of the China-US agreement, made efforts to simplify such procedures. An example is that local governments have been authorized to approve foreign investment projects that fall within the encouraged category in the Catalogue and whose approval previously belonged to the MOFTEC.[42]

5.2. Liberalization of operational environment

With respect to liberalization of operational environment, China's entry into the WTO has spelled some changes for investment vehicles. For example, China's foreign investment regime was designed primarily to address the needs of companies that get a one-time capital injection from investors or companies that have significant land and facility-based assets or companies that are generally financed by their own cash flow. It failed to meet the needs of FIEs that are preparing for public offerings, and to accommodate the structure and financing needs of high-tech startups, which have few assets, little revenue, and a limited cash flow except for the invested funds. In view of this, the Provisional Regulations on the Establishment of Foreign-invested Venture Capital Enterprises[43] provide that eligible foreign investors will be allowed to establish "foreign-invested *venture capital* enterprises alone, or "Chinese-foreign contractual venture capital enterprises" with Chinese partners. However, more vehicles need to be introduced to facilitate the operation of foreign investment as well as keep in line with China's commitments in this regard.[44]

In respect of discriminatory treatment in the operation of foreign investment, the newly revised laws and regulations or rules have relieved FIEs of the export obligation, local content requirements and forex balance requirements. In the revised EJV Law, WFIE Law, EJV Regulations and the WFIE Rules, the previous provision that joint ventures must give priority to making purchases in China has been removed. The forex balancing requirement and the export/domestic sales ratio requirement have been removed in the revised EJV Law, CJV Law, WFIE Law, EJV Regulations and the WFIE Rules.[45] For example, the original Article 9 (2) of the EJV Law, which provides "[i]n its purchase of required raw and semi-processed materials, fuels, auxiliary equipment etc, an equity joint venture shall give first priority to Chinese sources, but may also acquire them directly from the international markets with its own forex funds," has been revised to read: "[w]hen purchasing raw materials, fuels and other such requirements within the permitted scope of its operation, a joint venture may purchase the goods in China, and may also buy them on the international markets." Similar amendments have also been made to Article 15 of the WFIE Law.

So have been the provisions regarding forex balance and export requirement. For example, in the revised WFIE Rules, the previous Section 2 of Article 3, which stated that the "annual output value of export products accounts for more than 50% of the annual output value of all products, thereby realising the balance between revenues and expenditures in forex or with a surplus," has been deleted.[46] In respect to export requirement, references to export/domestic sales ratio contained in, for example, Articles 10 and 15 of the original WFIE Rules, namely "the proportion of the sales of products between the domestic market and the foreign market" and "the sales proportion between China's market and foreign markets," have been deleted. In addition, Article 45 has been revised from "In case that a wholly foreign-invested enterprise sells its products on the Chinese market, it shall conduct its sales in accordance with the approved sales proportion" to "Wholly foreign-invested enterprises are allowed to sell their products in the domestic market. Wholly foreign-invested enterprises are encouraged by the State to export their products." Section 2 of Article 46 has been amended to read: "Wholly foreign-invested enterprises may sell their own products in China or they may appoint other business organisations to sell their products." In the old version, there was no mention that wholly foreign-invested enterprises may sell their own products in the domestic market. It only stated that a wholly foreign-invested enterprise may appoint a Chinese foreign trade company to sell its products on a commission basis.

In addition, the government is making other efforts to further liberalize the operational environment. With regard to enlarging the business scope of investment companies established by foreign enterprises, for example, the Chinese government is considering granting export rights to such companies which source domestic raw materials for export. Meanwhile, encouragement will be given to enterprises engaged in R&D, and approval will be granted to investment companies to market domestically-produced goods directly.

Finally, the noteworthy improvement in transparency, such as designating official gazettes or magazine and websites to publish laws, regulations and measures, in law enforcement, as exemplified by the efforts of unified application of laws and the orientation of the judiciary and administrative officials for the WTO obligation, have the effect of facilitating foreign investment and demonstrate how China has adapted itself towards WTO compliance.

Notes

1. For an analysis of the role of foreign investment in economic development in China, see, for instance, Chen Man, An Analysis of the Effects of Introducing Foreign Direct Investment in China (in Chinese), *Strategy and Management* (*zhanlue yu guanli*), Vol. 46/3, 2001, pp.93-103.

2. See, for instance, Qingjiang Kong, Foreign Direct Investment Regime in China, 4 *Heidelberg Journal of International Law* (1997) 57, pp. 869-897.

3. There are signs, however, that the rapidly increasing foreign investment inflows of recent years are not stable. The total value of actual foreign investment inflow dropped continuously in two consecutive years of 1999 and 2000. The Asian financial crisis was partly responsible for the slowdown, as investment from other Asian countries and overseas Chinese had fallen. Chinese government officials acknowledged in late 1999 that the strict regulation of foreign business activities, particularly in the service sector, had contributed to sliding foreign investment volumes.

4. *People's Daily*, 16 January 2002.

5. For a study of the relationship between transnational trade and investment, see WTO Secretariat, Trade and Foreign Direct Investment, Press Release 57, 9 October 1996.

6. Provisions on investment protection usually refer to those provisions concerning expropriation and exchange control.

7. For a detailed discussion about the features of bilateral investment treaties, see Rudolf Dolzer and Margrete Stevens, *Bilateral Investment Treaties*, The Hague: M. Nijhoff Publishers, 1995.

8. According to a WTO Secretary study, the Agreement on Subsidies and Countervailing Measures and the plurilateral Agreement on Government Procurement also contain investment provisions. For an elaboration of the relations between the two agreements and investment rules, see WTO Secretariat, Trade and Foreign Direct Investment, Press Release 57, 9 October 1996.

9. For an elaboration of these fundamental WTO principles, see WTO Secretariat, Trading into the Future: The Introduction to the WTO, available at <http://www.wto.org/english/thewto_e/whatis_e/tif_e/fact2_e.htm>.

10. At the NPC session held in early 2000, some experts proposed that the three basic laws relating to foreign investment—the Wholly Foreign-invested Enterprise Law, the EJV Law, and Chinese-foreign Contractual Joint Venture Law—be combined into one, namely the Foreign-Invested Enterprise Law.

Officials from the Department of Treaty and Law of MOFTEC also pointed out that in many countries the utilisation of foreign investment is governed by a single law. In China, the above mentioned three laws were formulated in the early days of opening-up and reform when the country was at its infancy stage of attracting foreign investment. As time passes, China would certainly move in the direction of formulating a single Foreign-Invested Enterprise Law. But the timing was not considered ripe yet and it might take a considerable period of time before a unified piece of legislation would be introduced.

11. They are the EJV Law (1979, 1990, 2001), the Chinese-foreign Contractual Joint Venture Law (1988, 2000) and the Wholly Foreign-invested Enterprise Law (1986, 2000).

12. E.g., the EJV Regulations, the Detailed Rules for the Implementations of Wholly Foreign-invested Enterprise Law

13. E.g., the Detailed Rules for the Implementation of Chinese-foreign Contractual Joint Venture Law (MOFTEC), Provisional Regulations on Foreign Investment Guidelines (State Plan Commission).

14. E.g., Shanghai Municipal Regulations on Examination and Approval of Foreign Investment Enterprises (Shanghai Municipal People's Congress), Procedures for Establishment of Representative Offices by Foreign Enterprises in Shanghai (Shanghai People's Government).

15. China had up to 30 April 2001 concluded 97 bilateral investment treaties with countries, among which 78 had entered into force.

16. Article 5, the EJV Law.

17. See, respectively, Article 3; Article 4 and Article 5 of the Regulations for the Implementation of the EJV Law.

18. The NPC Standing Committee promulgated the Wholly Foreign-invested Enterprise Law on 12 April 1986. This Law, for the first time, provides that China restrict and prohibit foreign investment into certain sectors (Article 3). The WFIE Rules, specify, in its Articles 4 and 5, the sectors where foreign investment are prohibited or restricted.

19. See, respectively, Article 4 of the Implementing Regulations for the EJV Law, Article 3 of the Wholly Foreign-invested Enterprise Law; and Article 3 of the WFIE Rules.

20. The Catalogue was amended in 1997 and went into effect on 1 January 1998

21. China restricts investment in a wide range of the service sector, including distribution, construction, tourism and travel, shipping, advertising, legal services, and others.

22. For instance, foreign law firms can provide legal services only in the form of representative offices in Beijing, Shanghai, Guangzhou, Shenzhen, Haikou, Dalian, Qingdao, Ningbo, Yantai, Tianjin, Suzhou, Xiamen, Zhuhai, Hanghou, Fuzhou, Wuhan, Chengdu, Shenyang and Kunming only.

23. Theoretically, granting FIEs preferential treatment is also related to the operational environment of FIEs. For convenience, this subject-matter is discussed in the context of admission only.

24. While, for instance, the state-owned enterprises were taxed at a 55 percent income tax rate, the Income Tax Law of Foreign-invested Enterprises and Foreign Enterprises provides an income tax rate of 33 percent. It should be noted, however, that since 1994 the enterprise income tax rate has been levelled to a uniform 33 percent.

25. Provisional Rules on the Reduction and Exemption of Enterprise Income Tax and Consolidated Business Tax in Special Economic Zones and the Fourteen Coastal Cities, State Council, 1984. For instance, the income tax for FIEs in SEZs can be collected at a rate reduced by half (i.e. 15 percent).

26. Article 2, Decision of the NPC Standing Committee Regarding the Application of Provisional Regulations on Such Taxes as Value-added Tax, Consumption and Business Tax to Foreign-invested Enterprises and Foreign Enterprises, 29 December 1993. It should be pointed out that this preferential treatment was effective, upon approval by the government authorities, only for five years.

27. Article 13, Provisions on the Encouragement of Foreign Investment, the State Council, 11 October 1986.

28. Article 4, Provisions on the Encouragement of Foreign Investment, the State Council, 11 October 1986.

29. Article 5 of the Rules for Labour Management in Foreign-invested Enterprises (State Council, 11 August 1994)

30. The requirements are, for instance, that parent companies must have assets in excess of US$ 4000 million, have already invested US$10 million in China; will inject another US$30 million to set up the holding company; and have three or more project approvals pending.

31. In order to encourage foreign direct investment, China had granted national treatment to FIEs in forex regulation. Accordingly, FIEs were allowed to open and hold forex settlement accounts to retain receipts under current accounts, up to a maximum amount stipulated by State Administration of Forex. Receipts in excess of the maximum amount were required to be sold to designated forex banks. No restrictions were maintained on the payment and transfer of current transactions by FIEs, and FIEs could purchase forex from designated forex banks or debit their forex accounts for any payment under current transactions, upon the presentation of valid documents to the designated forex banks or SAFE for the bona fide test. FIEs could also open forex accounts to hold foreign-invested capital, and they could sell from these accounts upon the approval of SAFE. FIEs could also borrow forex directly from domestic

and overseas banks, but were required to register with SAFE later, and obtain approval by SAFE for debt repayment and services. FIEs could make payments from their forex accounts or in forex purchased from designated forex banks after liquidation, upon approval by SAFE according to law.

32. The following illustrates, for instance, China's commitments relating to the market access in some key services sectors. In respect of finance and insurance, China committed itself to full market access in five years for foreign banks. In two years foreign banks will be allowed to conduct local currency business with non Chinese-individuals. Foreign banks will enjoy national treatment, without being subjected to geographical and customer restriction after five years. From a purely legal point of view, foreign banks will be able to do whatever a Chinese bank can do in the same circumstance. With regard to value-added telecommunications services, foreign service suppliers were, upon accession, permitted to establish joint venture value-added telecommunication enterprises, without quantitative restrictions, and provide services in the cities of Shanghai, Guangzhou and Beijing. Foreign investment in joint venture shall be no more than 30 per cent. Within one year after China's accession, the areas will be expanded to include Chengdu, Chongqing, Dalian, Fuzhou, Hangzhou, Nanjing, Ningbo, Qingdao, Shenyang, Shenzhen, Xiamen, Xi'an, Taiyuan and Wuhan and foreign investment shall be no more than 49 per cent. Within two years after China's accession, there will be no geographic restriction and foreign investment shall be no more than 50 per cent. As for paging telecommunication services, foreign service suppliers will be permitted to establish joint venture enterprises, without quantitative restrictions, and provide services in and between the cities of Shanghai, Guangzhou and Beijing. Foreign investment in joint venture shall be no more than 30 per cent. Within one year after China's accession, the areas will be expanded to include services in and between Chengdu, Chongqing, Dalian, Fuzhou, Hangzhou, Nanjing, Ningbo, Qingdao, Shenyang, Shenzhen, Xiamen, Xi'an, Taiyuan and Wuhan and foreign investment shall be no more than 49 per cent. Within two years after China's accession, there will be no geographic restriction and foreign investment shall be no more than 50 per cent.

With respect to retailing services (excluding tobacco), upon accession, Zhengzhou and Wuhan will be immediately open to joint venture retailing enterprises. Within two years after China's accession to the WTO, foreign majority control will be permitted in joint venture retailing enterprises and all provincial capitals, Chongqing and Ningbo will be open to joint venture retailing enterprises.

Foreign service suppliers will be permitted to engage in the retailing of all products within one year after accession, with the exception of the retailing of books, newspapers and magazines, the retailing of pharmaceutical products, pesticides, mulching films and processed oil within three years after accession and retailing of chemical fertilizers within five years after accession

33. Article 5 of the TRIMS Agreement allows transitional arrangements to eliminate all trade-related investment measures: a two-year transitional period for developed country Members, five-year period for developing country Members and seven-year period for least developed country Members.

34. China promised that it would revise its relevant laws and regulations so that its relevant domestic laws and regulations would be consistent with the requirements of the WTO Agreement and the Accession Protocol on procedures for judicial review of administrative actions, and ensure that the tribunals responsible for such reviews would be impartial and independent of the agency entrusted with administrative enforcement, and would not have any substantial interest in the outcome of the matter.

35. The four pieces of regulations entered into force on 1 July 2000, 29 August 2000, 2 August 2001 and 25 October 2001 respectively.

36. On 5 December 2001, the State Council amended the Regulations on Travel Agencies and adopted the Regulations on Foreign Investment in Telecommunications Enterprises, the Regulations on International Maritime Transportation, and the Regulations on Foreign-Invested Insurance Companies. The former three took effective on 1 January 2002 and the fourth on 1 February 2002. The Regulations on Cinema were adopted and the Regulations on Foreign-invested Financial Institutions amended on 12 December 2001 and entered into force on 1 February 2002.

37. For instance, Articles 4 and 5 of the original Detailed Rules for the Implementation of the Wholly Foreign-invested Enterprise Law, which stipulated that wholly foreign-invested enterprises were either prohibited or restricted from the services trades such as internal commerce, foreign trade, post and telecommunications, real estate, communications and transportation, have been revised and combined into one article. The new article now reads: "Wholly foreign-invested enterprises should refer to the directions of the State for foreign investment and the Catalogue for the Guidance of Foreign Investment Industries for lists of prohibited or restricted industries."

38. For instance, Pearson Corporation, a British media giant, had reportedly reached a joint venture agreement with CTV Media, a subsidiary of China's only national television operator CCTV, and another company (Cyber Solution). The joint venture was to be set up to provide multimedia and educational programmes to Chinese cable TV subscribers. The shares for the venturers are respectively 40, 50 and 10 percent for Pearson, CTV Media and Cyber Solution. See a Xinhua New Agency report, 21 November 2001.

39. However, China indicated that there was no plan to establish any new SEZs, and thus ruled out the possibility of further expanding the differential tax treatment in association with SEZs.

40. A sign is that the newly revised investment laws and their implementing regulations or rules no longer deal with any matter related to tax reduction and exemption. For example, the revised WFIE Rules merely provides "[t]he following goods and materials imported by a wholly foreign-invested enterprise shall be entitled to tax reduction and exemption in accordance with Chinese taxation laws," thus leaving tax reduction and exemption exclusively subject to taxation laws.

41. The Catalogue of Major Industries, Products and Technologies Encouraged for Development in China was approved by the State Council on 29 December 1997.

42. See, the MOFTEC, Circular on Certain Questions concerning the Approval by Local Governments of Foreign-invested Projects That Fall within the Encouraged Category (promulgated, 15 October 1999).

43. The Provisional Regulations were promulgated by the MOFTEC, the Ministry of Science and Technology and the State Administration of Industry and Commerce and entered into force on 1 September 2001.

44. China has committed itself, in the Accession Protocol, to allowing franchising rights within three years of WTO accession and allowing foreign companies to set up branches in China. But, in the absence of a national franchising regulation and measures on branches, it may currently be difficult for foreign companies to capitalize on these new options.

45. In addition, the amendments to the EJV Regulations also address reduction of registered capital, royalties for technology transfers, supply and distribution channels, pricing, forex accounts, changes in the capital contribution rules, the joint venture's term of operation, statistical reporting and the use of RMB for accounting reports. Similarly, the new WFIE Rules have revoked such provisions as: Article 43 which provided that production and operation plans shall be submitted to the competent department; Sections 2 and 3 of Article 48 which dealt with the practice of price reporting to administrative authorities; and Article 56 which governed forex balance. All these changes signify a greater degree of autonomy for FIEs in China with respect to the operational environment.

46. Moreover, the Chinese government has further liberalized other aspect of forex control on FIEs. For example, forex transactions of FIEs in bank accounts opened in different localities have been institutionalized. FIEs with accounts in different localities will be allowed to make forex transactions among these accounts. New regulations governing forex transactions in bonded areas are reportedly also being prepared.

8

Chinese Law and Practice On Government Procurement In the Context Of WTO Accession[*]

1. Introduction

The term "government procurement" refers to purchases and consumption of goods, services and works by governments. It is a market mechanism that enables governments to maximize the use of scarce public funds. In China, both levels of governments—local and central—and related organs are significant purchasers of goods and services. For example, the goods, services and works purchased by the central government alone account for some 10 percent of the country's gross domestic product (GDP).[1] Given the large amount of funds involved and to ensure best value for money, an open, non-discriminatory and equitable procurement regime has to be instituted.[2] Such a system can also help prevent corruption.

Public procurement had existed in China well before any modern, nationwide procurement regulations were put in place. In recent years, the government has made steady effort to promote government procurement. At full-blown, the size of the procurement market, taken as a percentage of the country's gargantuan GDP,[3] can be mind-boggling.[4] While this will in turn present huge opportunities for both domestic and international trade, more interestingly, the rampant corruption inherent in the current system of government purchase will be correspondingly lessened.

* This chapter is based on an article, first published in the *Public Procurement Law Review*, 2002 (4).

Despite the growing importance of government procurement, very little has been written about the conduct of procurement activities carried out by the government. With China close to entering the WTO, it has become almost an imperative to gauge the compatibility of both the present and the evolving Chinese procurement regime with the WTO Agreement on Government Procurement (AGP). This chapter hopes to contribute to the literature in this regard.

2. A Historical Review of Government Procurement in China

Government procurement is not new to China. Early in the West Han Dynasty (circa 206 BC to 25 AD), the Han Imperial Court used "regulated purchase" (*jun shu*) to regulate commodity flow and market price.[5] In Republican China before 1949, government procurement, though different from its modern version, was already very common.[6]

In the PRC (1 October 1949-present), government procurement has its ups and downs. Basically, it can be divided into five stages. The first stage occurred when the CPC came to power. Under the influence of Marxist-Leninism, the Chinese government established a Soviet-model command economy. Then, government agencies at various levels procured goods and services from the dwindling marketplace.

The second stage started in 1956 after the Chinese government had completed the "socialist transformation of capitalist economy." At that time, nearly the entire economy was controlled by the government. The result was an economy bereaved of government procurement.

The third stage took place after the introduction of market-oriented reform in 1979. In the following years up till mid 1990s, the absolute dominance of the public sector gave way to a mixed sector where public and private enterprises co-existed; even state-owned enterprises carved out their own turf and became more independent off one another. Goods and services that government agencies needed had to be sourced from the market. Government procurement, in the broad sense, soon re-emerged. At this stage procurement was largely based on contractual negotiation by the end-users within the government structure. While this is convenient for the government agency concerned, it had very little in common with modern competitive biddings practiced in the West.

The mid-1990s saw the Chinese government importing modern Western government procurement techniques into the country. Local governments took the lead in this regard and modeled their procurement after western-style practices. Shanghai was first to experiment with the new techniques. In 1995, the Shanghai Municipal People's Government adopted, among others, the World Bank Guidelines for Procurement under IBRD (International Bank for Reconstruction and Development) Loans and IDA (International Development Association) Credits for government procurement in purchasing equipment with special government budget. This marked the fourth stage of government procurement.

Following the Shanghai practice, more and more provinces, autonomous regions and cities specifically designated in the state plan (*jihua danlie shi* or sub-provincial level cities) joined in the fray. Prior to 1999, modern methods of government procurement were exclusively carried out only at local levels. Government departments at the central level only joined in in 1999.[7] It is to be noted that before the promulgation of the Provisional Rules by the Ministry of Finance (hereinafter the MOF Provisional Rules) in 1999, and in the absence of clearly defined government procurement regulations, government agencies in many localities procured using commercial principles.

The experiments by local governments bore fruit. According to a study by the Ministry of Finance of the procurement experiments in 1998 and 1999, the average saving rate resulting from employing modern government procurement techniques was 13 percent.[8] In 2000, RMB 32.8 billion *yuan* worth of goods, services and works were procured through open bidding,[9] resulting in savings of some RMB 3.28 billion *yuan*.

The overall nationwide pattern of government procurement involves mainly goods or engineering works for office use. Experiments were first carried out in the purchase of vehicles and office equipment. Gradually, this was expanded to include engineering works, conference services, insurance for government-related activities, and installation of governmental management information system (MIS).[10] In 2000, procurement of goods, services and works accounted for 67 percent, 23 percent, and 10 percent, respectively, of all government procurements. Most purchases involved vehicles, computers and photocopiers.[11]

3. Towards a Legal Framework of Government Procurement

3.1. Emergence of a legal framework for government procurement

Following the experiments of government procurement in various localities, efforts to regulate government procurement also got underway. In 1998, the Shenzhen Special Economic Zone (SEZ) adopted the Shenzhen SEZ Regulations on Government Procurement—the first local regulations on government procurement in the country. Though 30 regions (including ten provinces, municipalities and autonomous regions) have now adopted local regulations on government procurement,[12] it is not difficult to observe that these regulations and rules have been hastily adopted in the process of experimentation. And due to inexperience, these regulations and rules lack depth and consistency, whereby procurement practices vary from locality to locality.

With government procurement expanding to central departments and institutions, regularizing and regulating the procurement activities soon became an urgent task for the central authority. In May 1999, the Administration of Office Matters of the State Council (*guowuyuan jiguanshiwu guanliju*) issued the Opinions Concerning Carrying Out Government Procurement by All Institutions of the State Council, which required institutions directly under the State Council to carry out government procurement on an experimental basis.[13] More significant was the 17 April 1999 MOF Provisional Rules promulgated by the Ministry of Finance. The promulgation of the MOF Provisional Rules signified the Chinese government's move to standardize and unify the practice of government procurement.

It is also noteworthy that the NPC has also incorporated the task of enacting a Government Procurement Law (GPL) into the Priority Items of the Legislation Plan of the 9th NPC Standing Committee. Accordingly, the Finance and Economic Committee of the NPC set up a Leadership Team for Drafting the Government Procurement Law and the first draft came out in late 2000.[14] It is expected that a law based on this draft will be passed in March 2002.

The current resurgence and regularization of government procurement in China can be seen as a response to the market economy. In the past, under a command economy, government procurement was unnecessary since public needs could be met through the command center. Later, with market-oriented reform and subsequent institutional change in the financial and taxation system, government procurement re-emerged.[15] The regularization and introduction of judicial review in the government procurement regime are in large part also the result of deepening nationwide reform as China braces up to join the WTO.

3.2. A further assessment of the legal framework for government procurement

For the purpose of implementing the MOF Provisional Rules after their promulgation, the Ministry of Finance adopted the following rules:

- Interim Measures on Bidding of Government Procurement,
- Interim Measures on the Supervision of Contracts for Government Procurement,
- Measures Governing Information Bulletin,
- Catalogue of Articles of Government Procurement,
- Interim Measures on the Operation of Government Procurement, and
- Interim Measures on Direct Disbursement of Fiscal Funds for Government Procurement.

These provisions, together with the MOF Provisional Rules, have served as the basic rules applicable to government procurement in China. It should be pointed out that all the provisions are derived from the Budget Law,[16] which provides the statutory framework for the control and management of public finances in China.

While the MOF Provisional Rules and other related rules ride on the Chinese legal structure to govern government procurement nationwide,[17] they are applicable only in localities that had helped in their formulation.[18] In other words, there exists a two-tier framework—national and local—for government procurement. Thus for government procurement by a locality, the MOF Provisional Rules and local regulations or rules shall apply complementarily. The problem arises when there is a conflict between the MOF Provisional Rules and local regulations. In such a case, even if local regulations by the province-level people's congresses are at variance with the MOF Provisional Rules—which are considered administrative rules spelt out by ministries—this does not necessarily render the local regulations or rules null and void.[19] What is problematic is that such a disparity opens the door for manipulation by local government departments and procuring entities, thus undermining the consistency of the regulations, hampering transparency and lowering the predictability level for suppliers of goods, services and works.

Another shortcoming in this regulatory framework of procurement is the lack of a national law or administrative regulations, whether introduced by the NPC, its Standing Committee or the State Council, which no local regulations or rules can contravene.[20] Yet another weakness is that existing regulations and rules are fragmented. National and local regulations and rules for government procurement co-exist with a mixed bag of rules governing general and specific applications for procurement by central departments and institutions. For example, apart from the MOF Provisional Rules and related rules, the Implementing Provisions of the Rules on Government Procurement by Central Level Institutions specifically governs government procurement at the central level. In addition, there are quite a few ministerial administrative rules in this regard,[21] which, as administrative rules, are only binding in their respective departments and industries. In the hierarchy of law in China, the legal force of these regulations and rules is inferior to the laws and administrative regulations.

4. A Comparison of the WTO AGP and the Government Procurement Regime Under the Current Legal Framework

4.1. The WTO Agreement on Government Procurement

In the Tokyo Round, the GATT—the predecessor of the WTO—formulated the Agreement on Government Procurement for open bidding in government procurement. This agreement was signed by all the GATT contracting parties and came into effect on 1 January 1981. The Uruguay Round broadened and improved the Agreement to include the idea of mutual reciprocity as well as to expand the size of the global arena open to foreign competition. Whereas the previous accord set forth rules for open and transparent bidding with regard to the purchase of goods by central governments, the Agreement expands the areas to services and construction work and covers procuring entities at sub-central government levels as well as certain public and regulated private companies. As a result, a new Agreement on Government Procurement (AGP) came into being in 1994.

China has not become a member of the AGP. Nevertheless, this does not prevent China from making reference to the AGP in preparing its GPL before its entry. A senior Chinese finance official has stated that government procurement is to be based on current national conditions, and any regime for such a purpose must conform to international law and commensurate with market economy and public finance framework.[22] If the statement reflects the official standing on procurement, the AGP is likely to play an important role in shaping the Chinese system for government procurement.

The following compares the Chinese regime of government procurement as spelt out in the MOF Provisional Rules and their derivative rules based on the AGP.

4.2. Definition of government procurement

The AGP does not provide a clear-cut definition for government procurement. As the WTO rules were framed largely by the West, particularly the United States, there is a need to look into the West's notion of government procurement. A prevailing understanding of government procurement is "purchases of goods or services undertaken by governments for their own consumption." Such a conception implicitly correlates government procurement to "public funds."

In the Chinese context, public funds have far more sources than in the West. Except for budgetary allocations, public funds can be extra-budget revenues (*yusan wai shouru*)[23] or funds owned or collected by government agencies (*ziyou zijin* and *zichou zijin*).[24] Subjecting these funds, which are currently at the disposal of the respective government agencies, to government procurement requirements would inevitably meet with opposition. In view of this, the MOF Provisional Rules and various local regulations and rules confine "government procurement" to purchases using funds from the state budget and extra-budget sources (*yusan wai zijin*) from both national and local levels.

The issue of defining government procurement is closely related to the question: Who will be required to make use of "government procurement" to purchase goods and services? The AGP provides that entities at all levels of government, including those at sub-central levels and enterprises owned or influenced by government, are required to procure in accordance with the AGP provisions.[25] Here "enterprises owned or influenced by government" refer to SOEs or those enterprises that the State controls through stakes; enterprises which are run on a commercial basis are excluded.[26]

4.3. Administrative and operational structure of government procurement

Under the AGP, national legislation can decide on whether to have a unified authority or decentralized administrative structure for government procurement. Most Western countries have a separate authority, while in China a conventional regime on government procurement has yet to be established. Before the promulgation of the MOF Provisional Rules, government procurement activities had been conducted in a decentralized manner, where the end-users had the prerogative and discretion to determine their own suppliers and forms of procurement. The central government only exercised a certain degree of control.[27]

With the promulgation of the MOF Provisional Rules, a *de facto* multi-tier administrative structure for procurement has been instituted. Government procurement is then based on the principle of "gradated administration" (*fenji guanli yuanze*). The MOF Provisional Rules require the Ministry of Finance to be responsible for the administration of procurement activities nationwide.[28] The administration of procurement of the localities is left to the discretion of governments at the provincial level in question (Article 7 of the MOF Provisional Rules). Some provincial or sub-provincial governments in turn provide, in their respective local regulations or rules, for the finance departments at or above the county or city-district level to be responsible for administration of government procurement in the localities concerned.[29] In other localities, a specially established body uniformly controls government procurement activities. In Shanghai, for example, the Shanghai Municipal Government Procurement Committee is the "leadership organ" for government procurement. It has the power to "enact procurement policies, examine and approve the procurement catalogue and coordinate the administration works of government procurement."[30] Nevertheless, the diversity in such an administrative structure for government procurement has resulted in a high level of irregularity in many localities. Many government procurement authorities are just branches or sections of finance departments.[31] Their independence is therefore questionable.

At the operational level, government procurement may take the following organizational forms: concentrated procurement (*jizhong caigou*) and decentralized procurement (*fensan caigou*).[32] The concentrated form is employed where the goods, services or works are purchased in bulk for consumption by end-users within a government department or those of related departments. The decentralized form is employed when the items to be purchased are for the use of a limited number of end-users, normally within a government department. Centralization of procurement is greater at the local than the central level; the central departments or institutions tend to conduct procurement on an individual basis.

4.4. Goods, services and works subject to procurement requirements

The AGP leaves the question of the scope of goods, services and works subject to procurement requirement to national legislation. Under the current legal framework of government procurement, there is a Catalogue of Articles of Government Procurement. However, the Catalogue is not a comprehensive list of goods, services and works that are subject to procurement, but serves more for classification and statistical purposes.[33] Ultimately the administrative authority of government procurement or the relevant procuring institution has to decide what to procure. As such, goods, services or works subject directly to government procurement requirements are quite limited.

As to the threshold value of goods, services and works subject to procurement, the MOF Provisional Rules does not provide such a threshold although such a provision listing the thresholds for the items and their different entries is provided for as an Appendix in the AGP. The lack of a threshold does not necessarily mean that all the goods, services and works that are needed are to be procured. Again, the discretion of the administrative authorities or procuring institutions is sought and they are free to decide on the scope and value of goods, services and works to be procured. However, some local regulations or rules on government procurement, e.g. the Shenzhen SEZ Regulations on Government Procurement, do set a threshold.

There are of course exemptions from the scope of procurement laid out by the government. The MOF Provisional Rules adopts the "national security" and the "emergency needs" exceptions. Worth noting is that the MOF Provisional Rules authorize the Ministry of Finance and governments at provincial level to exempt certain goods, services and works from the scope of procurement from time to time.[34]

4.5. Procedures of government procurement

The procedures for government procurement are more or less copies of the prevalent models and procedures for government procurement, such as those embodied in the UNCITRAL (United Nations Commission for International Trade Law) Model Law on Procurement. Under the Chinese legal framework, the procedures for government procurement include:

- open tendering,
- invitation for submission of tender,
- competitive negotiation,
- price inquiry, and
- purchase from designated source.[35]

The first three above are the most common means of government procurement and are equivalent to the open tendering, selective tendering and limited tendering procedures encompassed in the AGP. The last two are unique, and much discretion is left to the government departments or entities.

As far as tendering procedures are concerned, the Provisional Rules on Administration of Bidding in Government Procurement specifically sets forth the procedures in detail:

- Preparation of specification;
- Preparation of tender documents;
- Advertisement;
- Closing and opening of tenders;
- Evaluation of tenders;
- Selection of successful tenderer.

However, there is a difference between national rules and local regulations relating to government procurement. For instance, different localities have different designated publications for advertising procurement opportunities. Nevertheless, implementing the procedural provisions may prove a problem in certain cases.

First, procedures are not always strictly followed. Second, government procurements often meet with opposition. Traditionally, many officials and their government agency used their own discretion in all purchasing decisions. To require them to strictly follow procedures hence becomes something abnormal and they resist. Often, tactics used include circumventing procurement procedures like splitting contracts to fall below the threshold value, abusing technical specifications, giving short deadlines for submission of tenders, not publicizing invitations for tender, and using limited tendering. It is not rare to see local government procurements being open only to local suppliers,[36] and inconsistent screening of prospective suppliers and supervision of existing ones. Some government agencies engaging in procurement show their preference for non-public tendering (e.g. direct contractual negotiation), bearing little regard to proper tendering procedures.[37] It has been reported that some officials have even manipulated the tendering procedures in order to reap their own benefits.

4.6. Transparency

According to the AGP, making information readily available is key to a transparent regime for government procurement. That, in the first instance, means ensuring that information on procurement rules, practices and opportunities is made widely available in an easily usable form to all interested parties (particularly potential suppliers), as well as ensuring the right of access to that information.[38] To date China has no centralized system for the collection and dissemination of information on government procurement opportunities. Usually the information and invitation for tenders are directly distributed to major potential suppliers both within and outside China. Furthermore, the lack of an exhaustive database of suppliers, brands and specifications of products adds to the problem. However, the government, aware of the problem, has begun to employ modern technology to serve that purpose. The launch of the Ministry of Finance Government Procurement Website (http://www.ccgp.gov.cn) is an example.

The publication of information pertaining to the general environment for public procurement to take place and in which interested parties are expected to operate is an essential component of transparency.[39] As part of its attempt to join the WTO, the Chinese government has improved considerably its transparency with the publication of information on legislation and procedures. Nevertheless, its efforts have been undermined by the extensive discretion exercised by administrative authorities and procuring institutions (e.g. scope of procurement) in the purchase decision.

Under the AGP, transparency in government procurement also means laws and regulations being applied in a non-discriminatory basis.[40] Open bidding in which there is no limit to the number of potential bidders is the most transparent method, whereas selective and limited procedures are only justifiable when it would not be feasible or efficient to consider and evaluate a large number of potential bids. However, the preference for selective or limited bids by procuring institutions cast a shadow on the transparency of the regime.

4.7. *Ex post* supervision

For a fair, open and impartial procurement regime, public accountability is absolutely essential. Public accountability and good policy can be encouraged and nurtured by *ex post* supervision of the government procurement regime. The AGP is silent on this point, thus leaving this supervisory task to the discretion of national legislators. In the Chinese context, *ex post* supervision of government procurement is crucial to the establishment and particularly the operation of a fair procurement regime. In fact, regular checks to monitor government expenditure appear to be more effective than the annual nominal examination of government expenditure by the People's Congresses.[41]

The MOF Provisional Rules has a chapter on the supervision of government procurement. Of note here is the supervision by the public (*shehui*) in addition to supervision by auditing and supervising departments (Article 42 of the MOF Provisional Rules).[42]

4.8. Challenge and review mechanism

An effective challenge and review mechanism is another essential element of fair, open and equitable procurement procedures; the availability of such a channel for review of complaints is another element that adds to transparency of the regime. Due process requires designating a body to review suppliers' complaints about procurement processes that cannot be resolved through direct consultation with the procuring institution. The AGP requires the parties to provide for a court or an impartial and independent review body with no interest in the outcome of the procurement to hear any challenges [Article XX (6) of the AGP]. The AGP also requires that parties must provide for rapid interim measures to correct breaches of the Agreement [Article XX (7) (c) of the AGP].

The existing regulations do not pay adequate attention to the review mechanism or at least fail to provide working procedures for dispute settlement. Traditionally, according a purchase contract to a private party is entirely the prerogative and discretion of the mandarin. No one could challenge his authority. Apparently, such a mentality still persists, since many officials still believe that whom a purchase contract is awarded is a matter for the government agency and not the business of a third party. They do not understand it is their obligation to procure the needed goods, services or works through open and fair procedures and that failure to do so may result in their decision being challenged by a third party. To them, government procurement is a means of saving money; and having a lawsuit filed against them is the last thing they want. This is why some local regulations and rules confer no right to aggrieved suppliers of judicial review.[43]

The MOF Provisional Rules incorporates a provision enabling aggrieved parties in government procurement to file a complaint with the finance department (Article 41 of the MOF Provisional Rules) and a provision for administrative and judicial review (Article 48 of the MOF Provisional Rules). It should be pointed out that the provision in the MOF Provisional Rules merely states that the aggrieved party may resort to an administrative review or bring the dispute to court, leaving many areas unsaid; for example, it even fails to specify which authority the aggrieved supplier should appeal to.[44]

4.9. Treatment of foreign suppliers

In contrast to the wide experiments of domestic government procurement, government procurement involving foreign suppliers has been rather restrictive. So far, such procurement is preconditioned on the purchase being under foreign development loans[45] or given prior governmental approval (Article 6 of the MOF Provisional Rules). Usually, approval would not be granted unless the domestic goods or services procured are unable to meet the needs of the end-users. The Interim Provisions on the Operation of Government Procurement even sets strict requirements.[46] In short, when no conceivably comparable goods, service or works could be procured from domestic suppliers, the procurement involving imports of foreign goods, services or works can then be applied.[47] In order for foreign suppliers to access a particular procurement bid, they have to obtain special approval from the Ministry of Finance or the people's governments at the provincial level; alternatively, they can participate if they have access right as spelt out in international conventions, treaties or agreements to which China is a party (Article 18 of the MOF Provisional Rules).

5. Prospect of the future regime for government procurement in China

While the AGP is a useful point of reference to the evolving regime for government procurement in China,[48] the shape of the regime to come appears to have features quite distinctive from the AGP, as can be seen from the first draft of the GPL, which was released, as scheduled, before the end of 2000. The following is an elaboration of the prospect of government procurement in China.

5.1. Definition of government procurement

The current legal framework fails to deal with three problems. One is whether the social organizations (*shehui tuanti*), political parties[49] and public institutions (*shiye danwei*) should be subject to government procurement. There are a great many social organizations and political parties at different levels. Since, like government agencies, they live primarily on budgetary appropriation and extra-budget revenues, the prevailing viewpoint is that they should procure goods, services and works according to procurement rules. Public institutions that used to enjoy·similar financial status as government agencies have been undergoing reform aimed at transforming them into enterprises. In this connection, those that have been transformed successfully into enterprises will be treated as SOEs and the rest that are still subject to budgetary administration should be treated as "governments" for the purpose of government procurement legislation.

Another problem relates to SOEs. Because of the dominance of SOEs and state-controlled enterprises in the national economy, the difficulty lies in incorporating all the enterprises owned or influenced by the government and making them subject to government procurement regulations. The draft GPL suggests that SOEs, regulated monopolies and state-controlled enterprises do not need to procure in accordance with the future GPL.[50] The draft also suggests the future GPL will follow the MOF Provisional Rules and exempt entities with extra-establishment revenues from being governed by the GPL. However, such an exemption would not be feasible if the future GPL does not distinguish government procurement activities from those which are allowed and which come under administrative power.[51]

5.2. Administrative and operational structure

China is a unitary state, which ought to facilitate the setting up of a unified central authority for government procurement. However, due to the long-standing principle of gradated administration, it will be difficult to alter the administrative structure of government procurement under the MOF Provisional Rules. Of concern is the effect of the current reform to downsize the government. In view of this, it may be difficult to set up a separate and independent authority to deal with complaints.[52]

5.3. Enforcement of procedures

Law enforcement is always a problem in China. It is expected that covered entities will attempt to avoid government procurement obligations. Therefore, the weight of the future regime for government procurement would not be in full play if the follow-up supervision in the revised GPL is not strengthened.

5.4. Challenge and review mechanism

In order to establish a formal judicial review system to smooth the operation of the regime for procurement, the future GPL would need to clarify, for example, which authority is to stand in the administrative or judicial review proceedings as respondent or defendant. In this regard, the difficulty lies in attempting to institute an interim remedy, which involves having to alter the Administrative Procedural Law (APL). Any attempt to introduce such an interim remedy into the APL and the Administrative Review Law would amount to substantially changing the APL that is an integral part of China's basic legal system. Therefore, it may be more appropriate to insert a special provision in the GPL rather than trying to alter the basic administrative legal system.

5.5. Treatment of foreign suppliers

For China, "mutual benefit" is a guiding principle in its economic dealings with other states. Reciprocity is often a precondition for China to grant favorable treatment to foreign states or foreign nationals. China needs to evaluate the accessibility of Chinese goods and services to foreign procurement markets before considering its readiness to open its own procurement market to foreign traders, or to do so in the future. Ascribing to the AGP means Chinese suppliers would be able to gain access to the foreign procurement market. At the same time, the AGP requires its parties to accord national treatment to suppliers from other parties. Therefore, when China will accord national treatment to foreign suppliers primarily relies on when China will join the AGP.

The AGP is a plurilateral agreement within the WTO framework; that means, after joining the WTO, China is bound by the AGP only when it decides to join this Agreement as well.[53] The question "Will China join the AGP?" thus arises.

In the face of trade liberalization worldwide, and in order to enhance the credibility of its own trade liberalization program, China needs to seriously consider joining the AGP. As a matter of fact, China has already promised to open its procurement market to suppliers of member economies of APEC (Asia-Pacific Economic Co-operation) no later than 2020.[54] China became an observer to the AGP upon accession to the WTO. Moreover, in the process of negotiation for its WTO accession, it promised to initiate negotiations for membership in the GPA as soon as possible within two years of accession.[55] Therefore, it might consider liberalizing the market earlier.

In contrast with the slow pace of trade liberalization in the area of government procurement itself,[56] China's commitments are quite positive.

6. Concluding Remarks

The introduction of modern government procurement concepts indicates the Chinese government's effort to respond to the need for open, fair, equitable and efficient management of public expenditure. Admittedly, the existing Chinese practice of government procurement leaves much to be desired, particularly seen in the light of the AGP. Mostly the problems are structural, tied stubbornly to the Chinese political and legal systems. Fortunately, as the Chinese saying goes, once the tiger is released, it is no longer controllable. So far, progress made in promoting government procurement in the context of budgetary control calls for institutionalization *per se* of the procurement regime. As has been pointed out, the Chinese government had "fully realized the disadvantages of irregular government procurement practices and was taking an active attitude towards establishing an open, transparent and competition-friendly government procurement system."[57] With this, a new regime for government procurement that subscribes to international best practices and reinforces the principle of good governance is set to emerge in China, although one has to wait and see whether it will be workable from the operational point of view.

Notes

1. The figure is often higher if procurement of local governments and other entities is taken into account. See Bernard M. Hoekman, "Introduction and Overview," in Hoekman and Mavroidis (ed.), *Law and Policy in Public Purchasing*, Ann Arbor: The University of Michigan Press, 1997, p.1.
2. In the words of Professor Sue Arrowsmith, there are four basic principles for a government procurement regime: competition, openness, commercial criteria and transparency. See Sue Arrowsmith, "National and International Perspectives on the Regulation of Public Procurement: Harmony or Conflict?," in Arrowsmith (ed.), *Public Procurement: Global Revolution*, The Hague: Kluwer Law International, 1998, pp.15-20.
3. China's GDP in 1999 was RMB 8.2 trillion *yuan* (approximately US$1 trillion). See *China Statistical Yearbook (2000)*, Beijing: China Statistics Press, 2000, pp. 22-23.

4. Currently, the volume of government purchase is about RMB 2 billion *yuan* each day. With further promotion of government procurement, the benefits would be substantial.

5. Huan Kuan (1st Century). B.C.), *Yan Tie Lun* (Discourses on salt and iron), Edition Wang Liqi. 1992.

6. Quoted from Wang Quanxing, et al, "Zhengfu caigou zhidu yanjiu" (A Study of Government Procurement System) in Qi Duojun, *Jingjifa luncong* (Serial Theses of Economic Law 2000), Beijing: China Fangzheng Publishing House, p.72.

7. On 26 January 1999, the central authority declared that it would procure 57 computers and 17 computer auxiliary equipment through open bidding. See, "Zhengfu caigou cong zheli kaishi" (Government Procurement Starts From Here), *Jingji ribao* (Economic Daily), 27 January 1999, p.1.

8. Figure revealed in a speech by Zhang Tong, Deputy Director-General of the Department of Treasury, Ministry of Finance, at a symposium on government procurement on 17 October 2000 in Beijing. The speech is available at http://www.ccgp.gov.cn (last visited on 30 May 2001).

9. See the Department of Treasury, Ministry of Finance, *Qingkuang fanying* (Reflection of the State of Affairs), vol. 3, 2001 (3 April 2001).

10. See Wang Quanxing, *et al*, p. 73.

11. See the Department of Treasury, Ministry of Finance, *Qingkuang fanying* (Reflection of the State of Affairs), vol. 3, 2001 (3 April 2001).

12. See http://www.chinalawinfo.com (last visited on 30 May 2001).

13. Given the government structure, the Administration of Office Matters is a logistic organ serving the State Council; its Opinions are treated as internal circulars and strictly not binding to other ministries and departments.

14. See "Zhengfu caigou huhuan lifa" (Government Procurement Calls For Legislation), *Zhongguo caijing bao* (China Finance and Economic News), 10 January 2001.

15. Actually, the Shanghai experiment of government procurement in 1995 was a result of the completion of taxation reform in 1994, under which localities may retain the residue revenues after submitting its due to the central authority. See Wang Quanxing, *et al*, p.72.

16. Article 1 of the MOF Provisional Rules specifies that these rules were made "in accordance with the Budget law and other relevant laws and administrative regulations."

17. Administrative rules by ministries are only binding in their respective province of jurisdiction. So long as government procurements concern public expenditure that falls within the province of the Ministry of Finance, the MOF Provisional Rules and related rules apply (e.g. see Article 2 of the MOF Provisional Rules).

18. In the Chinese context, only the laws by the NPC or its Standing Committee and the administrative regulations by the State Council are applied and implemented nationwide. The regulations by ministries under the State Council are applicable within the work limit of the ministries concerned.

19. While the Constitution does not specify what the legal effect would be if local regulations by the people's congresses contravene ministerial administrative rules, the Legislation Law authorizes the State Council to decide which shall prevail under such circumstance [Article 86 (2)]. However, local rules by local governments and local people's congresses below the provincial level must not contravene administrative rules set by the ministries.

20. In China, all laws, regulations and rules are fixed in a hierarchy: Apart from the Constitution, the basic laws passed by the NPC are at the top of the hierarchy. Next are the laws by the NPC Standing Committee, followed by the "administrative regulations" by the State Council. Next are local regulations by the people's congresses of the provinces and the administrative rules by various ministries. Local rules by local people's congresses and people's governments are next. The hierarchy means a subordinate normative rule is null and void if it contravenes a higher one.

21. Ironically, due to the administrative structure, the MOF Provisional Rules authorizes financial departments at provincial level to adopt rules for the implementation of the Provisional Rules. Even the Implementing Provisions of the Rules on Government Procurement by Central Level Institutions that govern procurement at the central level requires that "each department enact detailed implementing measures [for the Implementing Provisions]." See, respectively, Article 55 of the MOF Provisional Rules and Article 35 of the Implementing Provisions of the Rules on Government Procurement by Central Level Institutions.

22. See Mr. Zhang Tong's speech; note 9.

23. Funds of financial nature are those which combine budget allocation and extra-budget revenues.

24. With the gradual expansion of government structure, these extra-establishment revenues (e.g. fees collected by government agency) were legalized to meet the surging administrative expenditures, resulting in many government agencies having accumulated wealth that is at their disposal. For a review of the Chinese fiscal system, see Lin Shuanglin, "Too Many Fees And Too Many Charges: China Streamlines Its Fiscal System," *EAI Background Brief No. 66*, East Asian Institute, National University of Singapore, 28 July 2000.

25. As far as a signatory party is concerned, the AGP applies only to those entities listed in schedules (Annexes) of this party. Article IX (6)(b) of the AGP explicitly calls for periodic negotiation to expand the entity coverage.

26. Article XVII of the General Agreement on Tariff and Trade provides that disciplines on "state trading enterprises" required to run on commercial considerations do not "apply to imports of products for immediate or ultimate consumption in governmental use."

27. According to valid internal provisions concerning financial management, government agencies at various levels can decide on their own as to the sources of goods for procurement purposes. But, public construction projects exceeding RMB 50 million *yuan* or foreign enterprises or joint ventures exceeding US$30 million must first get approval from the central government.

28. The Implementing Provisions of the Rules on Government Procurement by Central Level Institutions further confuses the situation for it provides that government procurement by central institutions be fixed in a two-tier structure: (1) the financial department and (2) the departments in charge (*zhuguan bumen*). The financial department is the functional department (*zhineng bumen*) of government procurement, while the departments in charge are the departments responsible for the administration of the end-users.

29. For example, Article 5 of the Provisional Rules on Government Procurement of Anhui Province provides that the "[f]inancial departments of the people's governments at or above the county level are the departments in charge for government procurement." Article 5 of the Shenzhen SEZ Regulations on Government Procurement has a similar provision.

30. Article 4 of the Shanghai Municipal Administrative Rules on Government Procurement.

31. See, for instance, Yang Juan, et al, *Zhengfu caigou: jigou shezhi ying guifan* (Government procurement: establishment of institutions should be regularized), available at http://www.ccgp.gov.cn (last visited on 30 May 2001).

32. See Article 10 of the Provisional Rules on Government Procurement. As if to confuse the situation further, the Implementing Provisions of the Rules on Government Procurement by Central Level Institutions further provides for three organizational types of procurement at the central level: (1) combined and concentrated procurement (*lianhe jizhong caigou*), (2) uniform procurement within departments (*bumen tongyi caigou*) and (3) decentralized procurement by institutions (*danwei fensan caigou*).

33. See Cai Ku (Department of Treasury, Ministry of Finance) Ordnance (2000), No.20: Circular on the Issuance of the Catalogue of Articles of Government Procurement.

34. Article 4 of the MOF Provisional Rules. This provision also excludes purchases made by Chinese missions in foreign states from the scope of procurement.

35. Article 22 of the MOF Provisional Rules.

36. Mr. Lou Jiwei, Vice-Minister of Finance, in an interview, admitted the phenomenon. See Mu Chenzhou, "Lou Jiwei on Government Procurement," *China Economic News*, Vol. XXII. 28 May 2001, p.13.

37. A typical example is Daosi Environment Protection Science (HK) Co. vs. the People's Government of Nanshan District and the Bureau of Finance. The Shenzhen SEZ Regulations on Government Procurement requires government procurement of goods, services or works worth more than RMB 100,000 *yuan* to be open to competitive bid. However, the People's Government of Nanshan District, Shenzhen City directly negotiated with the local-based Shenzhen Power Company on the construction work of the Garbage Incineration Power Plant worth hundreds of millions of *yuan*. For a report of the case, see *Zhongguo jingying bao* (China Management News), 28 February 2001.

38. Article XVII of the AGP.

39. See, for instance, Articles XIX(1), XX(3) of the AGP.

40. See, for instance, Articles III, VII(1) of the AGP.

41. According to the Constitution and the Budget Law, the People's Governments (i.e. the State Council and People's Governments at different levels) and the People's Congresses at corresponding levels both play major roles in developing the budgets at their corresponding levels. The law requires the People's Government to submit to the People's Congresses at the corresponding level its proposed budget for the next fiscal year and empowers the People's Congresses at the corresponding level to examine and approve the plan.

42. Article 8 of the Shenzhen SEZ Regulations on Government Procurement provides, more assertively, that "[g]overnment procurement shall be put under the supervision of the public. Any organization and individual has the right to inform against offending in government procurement. The people's governments of the city or district shall accord rewards to those with meritorious deeds."

43. For example, none of the regulations or rules of Guangdong, Anhui and Shenzhen contain a provision concerning complaints and their resolution. The Shanghai Municipal Administrative Rules on Government Procurement, to some extent, establishes the mechanism of administrative review by enabling suppliers to lodge a complaint to the leadership body of government procurement (Article 27). The provision, however, fails to institute a mechanism for judicial review. Moreover, even in terms of administrative review, it does not provide the procedures for lodging complaints, such as the conditions, time limitation, the manner in which to review complaints, the legal force of review.

44. In Daosi Environment Protection Science (HK) Co. vs. the People's Government of Nanshan District and the Bureau of Finance, the court ruled that the

defendants, as named by the plaintiff, should be replaced by a government agency that under the defendants' directive acted to conclude the contract with the designated Power Company.

45. As a matter of fact, since it received development loan from the Overseas Economic Cooperation Fund of Japan in 1979 and the World Bank in 1981, China has followed the loan requirements to carry out standard bidding in the procurement of goods, works or consulting services concerned. The Chinese government even adopted the Provisional Rules for Administration of Procurement under the World Bank Loans to regulate relevant procurement activities.

46. Article 31 of the Interim Provisions on the Operation of Government Procurement provides "[w]here the procuring institution needs to procure foreign products, authentication must be held by competent professional administrative departments or by an expert group consisting of professionals to certify that the foreign products concerned fail to meet the needs of the procuring institution; where an open domestic bid indicates that buying foreign products is the only choice, approval from the financial department at the same level is needed so that an open bid is conducted for foreign suppliers."

47. For example, it is common to see government procurement being applied to the imports of technologically advanced medical instrument and equipment. The military has even gone so far as to apply uniformly the practice of bidding for importing medical equipment since January 1999. See *Changjiang ribao* (Yangtze Daily), 29 January 1999, p. 5.

48. In the process of negotiation on China's accession, some members of the Working Party stated that China should, upon accession, become an observer to the AGP, and should initiate negotiations for membership in the Agreement by tabling an Appendix 1 offer within two years of accession. The representative of China responded that China would become an observer to the GPA upon accession to the WTO Agreement and initiate negotiations for membership in the AGP by tabling an Appendix 1 offer as soon as possible.

49. Social organizations are, for example, the Trade Union, the Women's Federation, the Communist Youth League, etc. Political parties include the CPC and eight "democratic parties" under the leadership of the CPC.

50. Mr. Ju Jiaren, Office Manager of the NPC Committee of Finance and Economy and Team Leader of the Leadership Team for Drafting the Law on Government Procurement, has suggested so in an interview with the reporter of *China Finance and Economic News*. See Government Procurement Calls For Legislation (in Chinese), *China Finance and Economic News*, 6 January 2001.

51. In Daosi Environmrnt Protection Science (HK) Co. vs. the People's Government of Nanshan District and the Bureau of Finance, the defendants pleaded that the plaintiff was not in a position to challenge their conduct of nominat-

ing a supplier without following the tendering procedure, because their decision to let the Power Company invest and run the Garbage Incineration Power Plant was a result of their exercising the power of macro-management and did not belong to government procurement. Actually, the defendants were taking advantage of, among other things, the lack of a clear definition of government procurement in the Shenzhen SEZ Regulations on Government Procurement.

52. Mr. Ju Jiaren has suggested in an interview that the Leadership Team for Drafting the Law on Government Procurement would not encourage the establishment of separate authorities at different levels for government procurement. See note 50.

53. It differs from a multilateral agreement that the WTO administers in that no WTO Member State stays out of a multilateral agreement, while a WTO Member State may choose to join a plurilateral agreement. The AGP entered into force on 1 January 1996. It has 12 members. Canada; the European Community and its 15 member States; Hong Kong, China; Israel; Japan; Korea; Liechtenstein; the Kingdom of the Netherlands with respect to Aruba; Norway; Singapore; Switzerland; and the United States.

54. See *Zhongguo caijin bao* (China Finance and Economic News), 5 February 2001, p. 1.

55. See Report of the Working Party on the Accession of China, VII. 4.

56. In fact, when the WTO was established, of the 12 parties of the GATT AGP, only 10 signed the AGP. Korea, which was not a party to the GATT Agreement, signed the AGP though it postponed the application of this new Agreement to 1 January 1997. Moreover, up to now, there are only 12 parties to the AGP. Even among the 12 parties, regulated sectors like telecommunications, transportation, water and energy have yet to be opened up. Trade liberalization in the field of government procurement still has a long way to go.

57. See Speech on the APEC Government Procurement Workshop by Mr. Long Yongtu, Vice Minister of Foreign Trade and Economic Co-operation, given in Kunming, China (14 to 18 July 1999).

9

China's Online Copyright Protection On the Eve Of WTO Accession[*]

The introduction and widespread use of the Internet in China is inevitably expanding the domain of traditional copyrights. However, the evolution of the copyright regime shall serve digital technology by prolonging the reach of Internet users. Therefore, a new approach has to be taken in the effort to adapt the current copyright regime to the digital environment. The WTO accession provides an opportunity to do so, and the WTO's TRIPS Agreement and the WIPO Copyright Treaty (WCT) provide references.

This effort, moreover, should seek to maintain a balance between the rights of the owners of copyrighted products on the one hand and those of the digital service providers and users on the other.

1. Copyright Law in the Digital Context

1.1. What challenge does the digital technology pose to copyright laws?

Since the invention of the art of printing, technology has been constantly

---

* This chapter is based on an article, "Old Bottle for New Wine: PRC Copyright Legislation in the Digital Context," first published in the *Issues & Studies*, 36, no. 5 (September/October 2000), and is reproduced by permission of its publisher.

affecting copyright law by bringing forth the need for adjusting the interests of different parties concerned. Just as Paul Geller pointed out that "all the copyright issues that have been explored to date should be re-examined in the Internet context," China has been host to vivid examples of interaction between digital technology and the copyright regime over the past years.[1] As a country anxious to embrace the digital era (a period which is characterized by the proliferation of computer technology in general and the Internet in particular), China cannot escape the challenge that digital technology poses to its copyright regime.

Many valuable studies have shed light on the multitude of new copyright issues to be dealt with in the digital environment.[2] Chinese lawyers, including this author, argue that the following are among the most critical issues that digital technology poses to the copyright regime from the practical point of view.[3] The first type of questions is directly brought about by digital technology. Note that the Internet enables copies of a work to be distributed to the public by transmission (*chuanbo*), which gives rise to questions of whether such transmissions fall within the exclusive distribution right (*zhuanshu faxing quan*) of the copyright owner, and whether transmission of a work into the country where the copyright is affirmed infringes upon the copyright owner's exclusive importation rights. Secondly, given that the transmission of copyrighted work is rampant on the Internet, a further question arises: How to define the liabilities of the ISPs? The third type of questions is related to the consumers of the digital data on the Internet as downloading becomes commonplace: Whether loading a protected work into a computer's random access memory is an actionable reproduction. In order to properly deal with these three interrelated issues, a fourth question regarding the principle underlining the copyright law in the digital environment has to be addressed.

Bearing the above in mind, this chapter will explore some of the fundamental questions that are addressed by the recent Chinese efforts toward the new amendment to the 1990 Copyright Law as well as some of the issues that are at the centre of the accompanying academic debate over the copyright legislation activity in the digital context.

1.2. New dimensions for "copying" in the digital context

Deliberate copying of copyrighted works is subject to applicable copyright law. Fair is to argue that the center of a copyright regime is its provisions on "copying" and "reproduction." In the light of the history of copyright law, the technology of copying is among the most important factors that affect the copyright law. Each technological innovation of copying pawns change in copyright law. For example, the emergence of the copying technology of video, which greatly reduced the cost of copying, caused heated debate over the copyright law.

Digital technology that makes copying practically penniless is a new example.[4] Before the advent of digital technology, the term "copying" (fuzhi) in copyright laws was understood as reproducing and fixing the copyrighted works onto a new, tangible medium such as paper, tape, or video tape.[5] With the wide application of the computer and Internet technologies, the term "copying" has become complicated and requires clarification.

To simplify the situation, digital "copying" will be examined from three distinct contexts: (1) the inputting of copyrighted products into the computer ("digitalization"); (2) placement of the digitalized information onto the Internet server (or in other words the "transmission" of the information over the Internet); and (3) viewing, listening, and downloading (hereinafter referred to as "downloading").

In respect to digitalization, all information is dynamic and moves within the theoretically uniform system of the Internet in the form of electronic impulse. Some electronic information is intended to land onto the physical facility of the computer network; however, no user is in a position to identify the real physical existence of the information that is available to any authorized user. As to whether digitalization amounts to an actionable reproduction of that work, Chinese lawyers are divided.

Professor Zheng Chengsi, a renowned Chinese IPRs lawyer, held that any new manner of reproducing an existing work that resulted from technological development was reproduction.[6] He was in fact in favor of the approach of treating digitalisation as a part of "reproduction" or "copying" (*fuzhi*). Others saw digitalization as a new act that is parallel to "copying."[7]

This author, however, argued that there should be a distinguishing between situations where a work is read into a computer's random access memory[8] and where a work is placed into a computer's memory. From a technical perspective, the act of reading a work into a computer's random access memory is too transitory to be treated as a tangible medium.[9] From the legal perspective, linking "transitory copying" in the technical sense and "reproduction" in the legal sense contravenes the "fixation requirement" required by the prevailing copyright regimes around the world. These regimes demand that a work be "fixed in any tangible medium of expression" in order to be copyrighted.[10]

Theoretically, random access memory has nothing to do with "tangible medium of expression," and hence the digitalized work which exists transitorily in the random access memory is not entitled to copyright protection. In addition, the work is transitorily read into the memory of a user's computer often merely as a result of the random functioning of a technical program; the situation is thus not "copying" because the action is not intentional on the part of the user. "Transitory copying" in the form of reading a work into a computer's random access memory results from, in most cases, activities concerning the user's private study, research, or self-entertainment, and hence falls within the scope of "fair use."[11] Moreover, even if "transitory copying" were treated as "reproduction," detecting when the work is reproduced in this manner would be practically impossible.

In practice, the U.S. Copyright Act is a valuable reference in this regard. The Act allows up to three copies of a work (including digital ones) to be made instead of one for preservation or replacement purposes.[12] From the present author's perspective, all these justify disconnecting "transitory copying" in the technical sense and "reproduction" in the legal sense.

As for viewing, listening, and downloading, the first two require transitory copying while downloading is basically a process of storage,[13] although all the acts involve making a "copy" of what has been stored in the computer system. As explained above, it is also controversial to hold that "downloading" fulfils the requirements of being "fixed" and "tangible."

1.3. International background for copyright legislation in the digital context

In the international regime for protection of copyright in the digital environment, there exist conspicuously two treaties: the WCT and the TRIPS Agreement.[14] The two agreements are mutually complementary: the WCT contains online rights and provides high standards with regard to substantive rights, whereas the TRIPS Agreement focuses more on enforcement. Although the TRIPS Agreement does not specifically apply to the digital context, the TRIPS provisions concerning enforcement are generally considered to be compatible with the digital environment. For example, the underlying principles of national treatment and MFN treatment, embodied in the TRIPS Agreement, lend themselves directly to the digital environment, and have already clarified and facilitated a supportive legal framework for the rapid increase in the use of digital technology. Equally, the well-established principle under the TRIPS Agreement that there should be limited exceptions to IPRs to promote such objectives as research and education apply to the digital environment, giving public policymakers an important new tool in promoting social and economic development. Furthermore, the WTO has engendered a digital agenda in the Working Programme on Electronic Commerce.[15]

As a WTO Member, China has to be bound by the TRIPS Agreement. In fact, in the effort to join the WTO, China agreed to implement the TRIPS Agreement immediately upon its accession to the WTO.[16] Given the perceived difference between the Copyright Law and the TRIPS Agreement, to align with the TRIPS Agreement became China's first and foremost obligation. As aforesaid, the TRIPS lays down specific obligation for WTO Members concerning IPRs enforcement,[17] and thus provides a benchmark for new Chinese copyright legislation.

As a member of the WIPO, China participated in the formulation of the two regulations on copyright protection under the Internet environment, that is, WCT and the WIPO Performances and Phonograms Treaty (WPPT). The WCT establishes the exclusive right of the copyright owner to digitalize and transmit his works,[18] and therefore provides a model for China to follow in copyright legislation in the digital environment. Although China has not promised to accede to the two treaties, lawmakers reportedly consulted the relevant articles in them when reviewing the amendment draft of the Copyright Law.

2. Towards Copyright Legislation for the Digital Context

As part of the effort to establish an IPRs regime, the 15th Session of the Standing Committee of the 7th National People's Congress promulgated the Copyright Law on 7 September 1990, when the notion of copyright was new to most Chinese. Naturally, the drafters of the Copyright Law could not formulate the law in such a way that the law would be able to cope with all the future challenges. As a matter of fact, immediately after the promulgation of the Copyright Law, a piece of administrative regulations, i.e. the Implementing Regulations on the Copyright Law and the Regulations on Computer Software Protection, had to be adopted in order to deal with new problems that the Copyright law could not or perceivably could not handle.[19]

Faced with an exponential increase in the number of Internet users, those concerned with the development of copyright law clearly see how the Chinese copyright regime experienced the most fundamental shift of context in the history of copyright law. The radical rise of Internet-related disputes heightened the urgency for a digital-friendly copyright regime. According to one survey, there were more than twenty online copyright-related disputes in Beijing alone that were brought to the local courts in 1999, including the high-profile case of *Wang Meng et al. v. the Shiji Hulian Communications Technology Corporation*.[20] Traditional copyright owners, such as writers, were reluctant to see their works reproduced and distributed over the Internet without their knowledge and without the due payment of royalties; however, these owners and their lawyers found difficulty in convincing the judges that copying in the digital context constitutes copyright infringement.

In this context, revising the 1990 Copyright Law became an inevitable task. However, because the issue of copyright law's protection of information in electronic form was new to the Chinese copyright regime, how to amend the 1990 Copyright Law had been a heatedly debated topic among Chinese copyright legislators, administrators, and lawyers. In December 1998, the State Council submitted to the Standing Committee of the 9th National People's Congress a draft amendment to the Copyright Law. Although, the draft amendment had been discussed nationwide for a long time, it still gave rise to debate, especially among national and local legislators, copyright administrators, and lawyers. In view of the complexity of the amendment and due to the involvement of numerous interest groups,[21] the State Council withdrew the daft amendment in June 1999 for further studies. After China successfully concluded bilateral agreements with the United States and with the European Union respectively in November 1999 and in May 2000, China started re-drafting the amendment to the 1990 Copyright Law to ensure full compliance with its commitments regarding copyright protection.[22] In October 2000, the State Council again submitted a new draft amendment to the NPC Standing Committee.

In the meantime, in order to meet the urgent needs for handling online copyright-related disputes, the Supreme People's Court promulgated the Judicial Interpretations on Certain Questions Concerning Applicable Law for Computer Network-related Disputes on 20 December 2000. The judicial interpretations were binding on courts at different levels handling on-line copyright disputes. However, given that copyright protection primarily rests on the administrative agencies, the role of these judicial interpretations is as limited as the scope of application of the judicial interpretation. Nevertheless, while they could serve as helpful reference of copyright legislation in the digital context, revising the copyright regime in a wholesale manner remained the imperative solution. After three rounds of debating and reviewing, the 24th Session of the Standing Committee of the 9th National People's Congress finally passed the amendment to the Copyright Law on 27 October 2001.

3. Old Bottle for New Wine: Adapt the 1990 Copyright Law to the Digital Context

3.1. "Right of online transmission": "right of reproduction" or "right of transmission"?

In theory, "right of reproduction" (*fuzhi quan*) and "right of transmission" (*chuanbo quan*)[23] are two of the three terms central to any copyright regime.[24] The right of reproduction serves to ensure copyright owners' control of protected works while the right of transmission centers around the author's right to control the process of disseminating his works, for example, through performance or broadcasting. In a broader sense, the right of reproduction embodies the right of transmission.[25] This is reflected in certain copyright legislation, in which the right of reproduction is established in such a manner that some of the items of the right of reproduction and those of the right of transmission overlap.

Article 10 (5) of the Chinese Copyright Law of 1990 was such an example. This article provides that the economic aspect of copyrights shall include "the right of exploitation and the right to remuneration, that is, the right of exploiting one's work by: reproduction; live performance; broadcasting; exhibition; distribution; making cinematographic, television, or video production; adaptation; translation; annotation; compilation; and the right of authorizing others to exploit one's work by the above-mentioned means and of receiving remuneration therefore." The provision was supplemented by Article 52 of the Copyright Law,[26] which defines "reproduction" as "the act of producing one or more copies of a work by printing, photocopying, copying, lithographing, making a sound or video recording, duplicating a photographic work, or by other means."[27] The reference "by other means" (*deng fangshi*) seemed to imply the term "reproduction," could be legally interpreted so as to include some of the items of the transmission right, allowing slightly different explanations to cover the transmission of copyrighted works in the traditional context, and therefore, secures to the copyright owner control over virtually any reproduction.[28]

Nevertheless, the 1990 Copyright Law did not specifically establish the right of transmission. Then, would the 1990 Copyright Law be flexible enough to be applied in the digital context? Put in another way, would it be possible to define "reproduction" to include any appearance (regardless how fleeting) of a protected work in any computer as well as any transfer of that work to, from, or through any other computer, thereby enhancing the exclusive rights in the copyright bundle so far as to give the copyright owner the exclusive right to control transmission of any work in digitalized form?

One perception was that the consequence of failure in providing for the right of transmission might be dire in the digital context. For example, e-mails, letters from newsgroups, software, photographs, music, motion pictures on FTP sites, and web pages on the World Wide Web are made available to users by transmission over the Internet. In the eyes of those who viewed the provisions concerning reproduction completely differently, the mere fact that Article 10 (5) of the 1990 Copyright Law and Article 5 (1) of the Regulations for the Implementation failed to encompass any transmission right of the copyright owner in the digital context was already a target for attack and provided grounds for change.[29] For them, the reference to "producing one or more copies of a work" in the provisions is unsatisfactory since it fails to take into consideration the distinction of online transmission. Again, the inclusion of "or by other means" in Article 5 (1) of the Regulations for the Implementation is too vaguely worded to be properly and uniformly applied to similar cases. Nevertheless, given that there are insufficient qualified professionals in the Chinese copyright administration department (and in the judiciary in particular), the defect is probably a fatal one for the purpose of prohibiting copyright infringement and protecting copyrighted products in the digital environment. Moreover, the distinction between online and traditional transmission[30] makes it difficult for the right of reproduction embodied in the Copyright Law to cover the transmission merely by way of expansive interpretation of such methods as broadcasting.

3.2. New approaches to "fair use"?

Each copyright regime establishes a limitation to the right of reproduction, usually described as "fair use." The intention of the "fair use" doctrine allows different explanations.[31] Non-commercial copying or transmission is often presumed to be a due limitation on the right of the copyright owner to reproduce his copyrighted works. The Chinese Copyright Law in 1990 was no exception.[32]

Attention should be paid to the provision of Article 22 (6) of the 1990 Copyright Law,[33] which is probably the most controversial among the provisions therein. This article allows for the reproduction of copyrighted products for "teaching or scientific purposes," thus triggering a debate between those who argue against copying for decent reasons and those who favour the legality of such copying.

Copyright owners would obviously prefer laws that maximize their own control over the works they produce. Indeed, the enhancement of the copyright owner's rights is without question in the public interest, since without strong copyright protection, there would be no information infrastructure. If authors and publishers cannot reliably control their works, they will decline to make them available at all. These individuals would clearly oppose the application of the "purpose" standard—which already exists in the printing context—to the digital environment.

However, the model is too simplistic. First, some argue that the new approach must deal with liabilities from a different perspective. Copyright owners whose works are downloaded onto the Internet can expect to reap much more than in the previous printing context,[34] especially given that the ISP must invest heavily to maintain the online service. Therefore, the rights of the copyright owners over their works transmitted online should be restricted. Second, history has demonstrated that many industries have prospered when sheltered from exceptions to copyright.[35]

Expansive exploitation of reproduction rights of copyright owners may inhibit the infant Chinese information industry. If the right of reproduction in the current copyright regime is expansively interpreted, those seeking to create a multimedia website would have to secure the following authorizations: the right to digitalize the copyrighted works, the right to place the digitalized works on the Internet server, the right to revise the works, the right to transmit the digitalized information, as well as related rights such as the rights relating to the production and video recordings and the right to authorize the online service users to view, listen to, and download the information. A typical example is a computer game software manufacturer that had to spend ten months negotiating copyright-related issues with five hundred copyright owners.[36]

Third, an appropriate copyright regime must assure the availability of the next generation of consumer electronics and computer products. Any copyright legislation in the digital environment shall provide a mechanism to assure the continued vitality of the "fair use" privilege enjoyed by teachers, students, library patrons, and all other information users. In other words, an individual user's ordinary reading, viewing, or listening to an authorized copy of a work does not infringe upon the copyright owner's rights.

Then, a question arises: would the "fair use" doctrine apply to non-commercial online transmission? However, there has been a prevailing viewpoint among Chinese copyright lawyers that commercial transmission shall be distinguished from the non-commercial. The reason for separating these two types does not seem to be rooted in the idea that the infant Internet service industry as a whole needs room for development, but rather lies more in the moral justification that public goods may be enhanced by favouring non-commercial transmission vis-à-vis commercial transmission.

Having dealt with the needs of the online service industry and its users, we can turn to the potential liabilities of ISPs and online service users. Chinese copyright lawyers generally agree that the liabilities of the ISPs and users are basically within the purview of the doctrine of liability of civil law. However, from the present author's point of view, traditional civil law might be inadequate to fully address the issue of the ISPs' liabilities.

Since online service users are often unidentifiable and an ISP and its users often interact,[37] the ISP often finds difficulty in binding the users, let alone screening and pre-excluding the contents that infringe upon the copyright of a third party. In this context, it would be unfair to the ISP and detrimental to the development of the Internet service industry to impose liabilities on the ISP based on the normal doctrine of liability for negligence.

In view of the needs resulting from the further development of the online service industry, desirable might therefore be to introduce an additional approach to dealing with the new issue.[38]

Therefore, a well-settled copyright regime as a whole should have carefully balanced the goals of strong protection and incentives for innovation on the one hand, and the goals of interoperability, fair competition, and open systems on the other. In this regard, one must be mindful of the indisputable fact that copyrights are limited monopolies created by copyright laws which undergo an unending evolutionary process of interpretation, application, and revision and that improper interpretation, application, and revision of the copyright laws could stifle competition and thereby harm consumer welfare. Important is to maintain the correct balance between protection and competition.

3.3. Overview of some proposed options for revisions to the 1990 Copyright Law

Prior to the new revision to the 1990 Copyright Law, there were various opinions concerning how to amend the copyright regime. Most agreed that there was no need for new copyright legislation in China; the existing rules only needed alteration. However, legislators and administrators were divided as to how to adapt the Chinese copyright regime to the digital environment. The following are the major opinions in this regard and the author's comments thereupon:

One possibility was to introduce a new type of right for copyright owners: the right to communicate to the public—a term used in the WCT. For the proponents, this option would allow copyright legislation to follow "world trends." China has missed every opportunity at the turns of formulation of new IPRs legislation. Given the current knowledge economy, China cannot afford to miss out on the new opportunity to participate in the formulation of a new wave of copyright rules.[39] Obviously, proponents would like to see copyright legislation develop at the same pace throughout the world and they agree that the WIPO Copyright Treaty has provided a model to follow.

A second option was to streamline the types of rights of reproduction. The 1990 Copyright Law saw reproduction as being separate from broadcasting and distribution.[40] In the digital context, distinguishing one from another becomes increasingly difficult. Therefore, it is no longer appropriate to distinguish between them. A possible approach was to substitute the differentiated types of copyright with the "right to reproduce and use" (*zaixian bing shiyong quan*).[41]

Another option was to disconnect reproduction from the form of the medium through which the copied work exists.

A fourth option was to introduce and perfect the rules of tort in the Chinese Copyright Law in 1990. The purpose is to protect copyrighted works by providing that the act of "communicating a copyrighted product of others without the permission of the copyright owner constitutes infringement."[42] Apparently the proponents of this option sought to prevent people from transmitting products copyrighted by others over the Internet. In contrast with the "right to communicate to the public," the protection that this option would afford is weaker, since the tort law does not guarantee the right of the copyright owner to communicate his copyrighted product.

Another option was to weave a net for the protection of copyrights in the digital context. For the proponents, protection of copyrighted products through copyright law is not sufficient in the digital environment; contractual protection and protection through technical means are also necessary.[43] Note that some even proposed to provide a new type of right to the copyright owner: the right to technical protection.[44] This approach would be consistent with the provisions of the WIPO Copyright Treaty.[45]

In early 2000, this author suggested that the 1990 Copyright Law need to be amended in the following respects[46]:

- The term "digitalization" should be incorporated into Article 52 of the Copyright Law in order to supplement the interpretation of "reproduction."

- The "right of transmission" should be added to the copyright bundle embodied in Article 10 of the current Copyright Law; i.e. the right of transmission or communication to the public, either by wire or wireless means, including "the making available to the public of works in a way that the members of the public may access the work from a place and at a time individually chosen by them."[47]

- In order to facilitate using works in a manner that conforms to copyright protection, advisable is to expand the scope of compulsory license embodied in Article 22 of the Copyright Law by way of collective administration of copyrights. The competent agency for collective administration of copyrights[48] should be authorized by the amendment to license the online use of the copyrighted works on behalf of the copyright owners.

• The amendment should introduce special provisions to deal with the liabilities of ISPs, a move which would supplement the relevant provisions of the General Principles of Civil Law.

• Provisions concerning "fair use" (such as for "teaching or scientific purposes") should be suitably maintained in the process of amending the current Copyright Law.[49]

Moreover, the legislation technique needed to be improved. The state of today's major copyright laws regarding reproduction rights was less than clear. First, the distribution right should be amended to reflect the idea that transmissions of copies of a work to the public fall within the exclusive distribution right of the copyright owner. Second, an amendment is required to clearly state that the transmission of a particular work infringes upon the copyright owner's exclusive importation rights. Third, the "first sale" doctrine should be repealed insofar as it might apply to transmissions. Finally, the recommended amendments should leave room for forestalling the emergence of other perceived threats to copyright owners' rights.

4. An Evaluation of the New Copyright Regime from the Digital Perspective

According to Shen Rengan, the Director-General of the State Administration of Copyright,[50] the aims of amending the Copyright Law were stated, among others,[51] as follows:

• To narrow or even eliminate the gap between the current copyright regime and international copyright treaties;

• To provide effective protection to the copyright owners while promoting the use of databanks, multimedia, and the Internet.

In retrospect, the new revision to the 1990 Copyright Law was obviously based on this perception of adapting the 1990 Chinese copyright regime to the digital environment. Article 10 (12) of the amended Copyright Law clearly created the new copyright notion: right of online information transmission (*xinxi wangluo chuanboquan*). With the advent of the notion, clearly established is a system for protection of online copyright. However, it should be pointed out first that the new revision to the 1990 Copyright Law does not lay down a complete set of rules for the protection of copyright in the digital context. Instead, the lawmakers leave this task of formulating these specific rules to the State Council.[52]

A close look at the newly-revised Copyright Law will reveal the following similarities to the TRIPS Agreement and the WCT: Firstly, a new, broadbased technology-neutral right of communication to the public, which applies to works made available on the Internet and other online services, as well as works transmitted to the public.

Secondly, the new revision strengthened the copyright enforcement mechanism, by making available detailed procedures and remedies. Although these procedures were not specifically directed at digital copying, they should be useful in enhancing copyright enforcement in the digital context.[53]

Thirdly, the new copyright regime, for the first time in the history of copyright legislation, provides for two new enforcement measures authorizing criminal sanctions and civil remedies against the use of, devices for the circumvention of technological protection measures, and the intentional removal or tampering with electronic rights management information,[54] thus making copyright protection available to the on-line technically protective measures for copyrighted information

Unfortunately, because the new revision was not intended to create a comprehensive copyright regime in the digital environment, many important issues relating to the digital context have not been addressed. For example, limitation and clarification of liability of a carrier and ISP for copyright infringements done by third parties using the facilities of the carrier or ISP were not addressed. Also noteworthy is that, while containing various provisions on "fair use," the new copyright regime fails to specify whether the "fair use" doctrine apply to the non-commercial online transmission, for example, it does not indicate whether access for libraries and educational institutions to copyright material in electronic form, including material available online, is reasonable. Needless to say, the Chinese copyright regime would have been improved if it had addressed these issues, for example, by introducing a statutory license scheme for the retransmission of free-to-air broadcasts.

5. Concluding Remarks

The ease of digital copying is likely to pose a profound challenge to a copyright regime. This challenge calls for the regulation of copying in the digital context. Fortunately, Chinese copyright legislators, administrators, and lawyers concerned with the development of the copyright regime indisputably agree that in this fast-changing digital era, copyright law should keep pace with technology. The WTO accession provides such an opportunity to do so, and the WTO's TRIPS Agreement and the WIPO's WCT provide references.

In this context, the 1990 Chinese Copyright Law has been revised to cover digital copying, with digital copying being identified as online information transmission. The reproduction right, as referred to in the traditional environment, is redefined as the "right of information online transmission," thus giving copyright owners some form of exclusive reproduction rights.

The revision is a modest one aimed at a well-balanced copyright regime rather than allowing a power grab by copyright owners. Such new efforts should repair the unintended damage that the passage of time and the growth of technology have had on the 1990 Copyright Law. As far as protecting copyrights in the digital environment is concerned, the old bottle—the Chinese copyright regime that had been amended for WTO compliance—is to hold new wine.

Notes

1. Paul E. Geller, "Conflicts of Law in Cyberspace," *Law and Arts Journal* (Columbia University), Summer 1996, quoted in Zheng Chengsi, *On Intellectual Property Rights* (in Chinese), Beijing: Law Press, 1998, p. 451.

2. Pamela Samuelson and Robert J. Glushko have insightfully pointed out that there are a series of six tools that operate on digital information that "seem likely to change significantly the contours of intellectual property law, especially copyright." These are: (1) copying; (2) transmission; (3) processing and manipulation; (4) obsolete media categories; (5) reliance on technology to see and use digital works; and (6) searching and linking capabilities. See Pamela Samuelson and Robert J. Glushko, Electronic Communications and Legal Change: Intellectual Property Rights for Digital Library and Hypertext Publishing Systems, *Harvard Journal of Law and Technology* 6 (1993): pp. 237-240.

3. For the general Chinese perspective on copyrights in the digital environment, see Li Dongtao, The Revolution of Technology vs. the Revolution of Law: Some Questions concerning the Internet (in Chinese), available at <http://www.peopledaily.com.cn/GB/channel7/35/20000704>.

4. Copying is an ongoing, necessary, and inevitable component of using electronic information. As M. Ethan Katsh observed, "Saving a file, for example, involves making a copy of what is in memory. Using a file or loading it into memory involves making a copy of what has been stored on disk. Communicating electronically involves sending a copy and not the original." See M. Ethan Katsh, *Law in a Digital World* (New York: Oxford University Press, 1995), p. 216.

5. For example, the US Copyright Act defines copying as "fix(ing) in any tangible medium of expression, now known or later developed, from which they [original works of authorship] can be perceived, reproduced, or otherwise communicated either directly or with the aid of a machine or device." See U.S. Copyright Act 1976, Section 102 (a). Worth noting is that the United States has since enacted numerous acts including the Digital Millennium Copyright Act (DMCA) 1998. All the subsequent acts constitute amendments to the Copyright Act 1976. DMCA is basically designed to implement the WIPO Copyright Treaty but also contains additional provisions addressing related matters. For the source of the Copyright Act 1976 and the subsequent amendments, look up Title 17 of the United States Code, available at <http://groton.k12.ct.us/mts/pt2a.htm3>.

6. See Zheng Chengsi, *Intellectual Property Law* (in Chinese), Beijing: Law Press, 1997, p. 401.

7. Xue Hong, Liability for Copyright Infringement on the Internet (in Chinese), *Electronic Intellectual Property*, no. 10 (1998). See the website of the online magazine at <http://www.computerworld.com.cn/magazine/eip/>.

8. "Random access memory" (RAM) represents that part of a computer's memory in which data and computer programs can be recorded temporarily. When a computer is turned off, the information stored in RAM is lost.

9. In ProCD, Inc. v. Zeidenberg, the Seventh Circuit District Court of the United States held that the defendant Zeidenberg did not violate the plaintiff's copyright by downloading the data from CD-ROM discs, of which the plaintiff ProCD, Inc. is the copyright owner, onto the random access memory of defendant's computer. For a description and analysis of the case, see C. Benjamin Salango, "Copyright Infringement in Cyberspace: Untangling the Web with Existing Law," available at <http://www.wvjolt.wvu.edu/wvjolt/current/issue1/articles/salang/salango.html>. Interesting in this regard is the drafting process of the WIPO Copyright Treaty. An earlier draft of the Treaty originally laid down a provision on "the scope of reproduction," which defined "reproduction" as including "transitory copying." The provision caused heated debate among the delegates to the Diplomatic Conference of WIPO members.

   As a result, the original provision with the controversial reference to "transitory copying" does not appear in the Agreed Statement concerning the WIPO Copyright Treaty. Therefore, the negotiators likely intended to leave to the individual member states of the WIPO the power to decide whether a transitory storage of a protected work in digital form in an electronic medium constitutes a reproduction within the meaning of Article 9 of the Berne Convention. Also see Zheng, *On Intellectual Property Rights*, pp. 562-563.

10. "Fixation requirement" is related to the notion of copyrightability of works. The US Copyright Act is an example. See U.S. Copyright Act, Section 102 (a).

11. Professor Zheng Chengsi made a similar observation. See Zheng, *Intellectual Property Law*, p. 563.

12. See U.S. Copyright Act, Section 108.

13. In practice, many ISPs allow free reading but disallow further downloading through orchestrated technical measures.

14. To facilitate the implementation of the TRIPS Agreement, the WTO concluded with WIPO an agreement on cooperation between the two organizations, which came into force on 1 January 1996. As explicitly set out in the Preamble to the TRIPS Agreement, the WTO aims to establish a mutually supportive relationship with WIPO. The Agreement provides for cooperation in three main areas, namely notification of, access to and translation of national laws and regulations; implementation of procedures for the protection of national

emblems; and technical cooperation. Article 9.1 of the Agreement requires Members to comply with Articles 1 through 21 of the Berne Convention (1971) and the Appendix thereto (the Paris Act of 24 July 1971 of the Berne Convention for the Protection of Literary and Artistic Works), both of which are administered by the WIPO.

15. The Work Programme on Electronic Commerce was adopted by the General Council on 25 September 1998. Available at <http://www.wto.org/english/ tratop_e/ecom_e/wkprog_e.htm>.

16. Under the TRIPS Agreement, all WTO Members are given some extra time, beyond the date of entry into force of the WTO itself, to adapt to the provisions of the TRIPS Agreement. While the developed countries were given one-year grace period, the developing countries and countries in transition from a centrally-planned economy to a market economy were given a further four years and the least developed countries were otherwise given eleven years in all.

17. Part III of the TRIPS Agreement spells out in detail the legal procedures and remedies that each WTO Member should make available to holders of IPRs so that they can enforce these rights effectively. The obligations in this regard include general obligations that all enforcement procedures must meet and civil and administrative procedures and remedies. According to the first section of Part III, the general procedures must meet the basic requirements of due process, such as being fair and equitable, not unduly complicated or costly, operating without unreasonable time-limits or delays, and offering the possibility of judicial review (Article 41). The second section of Part III, on civil and administrative procedures and remedies, provides for the possibility, under certain conditions, of ordering the opposing party to produce relevant evidence, and requires WTO Members to make available remedies, including injunctions to prevent infringement of rights. For instance, there must be an authority to order infringers to pay damages adequate to compensate for the injury caused by the infringement of rights, as well as legal costs. In appropriate circumstances, the remedies available through the judicial authorities should extend to the forfeiture of the infringing goods, and of materials and instruments used to produce them, and to the disposal or destruction. (Articles 42-46)

18. Article 8 of the WIPO Copyright Treaty provides: "...authors of literary and artistic works shall enjoy the exclusive right of authorizing any communication to the public of their works, by wire or wireless means, including the making available to the public of their works in such a way that members of the public may access these works from a place and at a time individually chosen by them." The Agreed Statement concerning Article 8 further explains

"[i]t is understood that the mere provision of physical facilities for enabling or making a communication does not in itself amount to communication within the meaning of this Treaty or the Berne Convention."

19. The Copyright Law came into effect on 1 June 1991. The State Council adopted the Implementing Regulations on the Copyright Law and the Regulations on Computer Software Protection respectively on 30 May and 4 June 1991. It is noteworthy that the Copyright and the Regulations on the Protection of Computer Software were amended before China's accession to the WTO.

20. The plaintiff—Wang Meng, Zhang Kangkang, and four other writers—found that their novels and poems had been put on the Internet without their knowledge by the defendant, Shiji Hulian Communications Technology Corporation. Internet surfers could, through the website of the defendant, read and download the works.
The plaintiff sued the defendant at the Haidian District People's Court for infringing upon their copyrights. The defendant argued that, first, no provision in the current Chinese Copyright Law prohibits putting the works of others on the Internet; second, the company did not profit from the services because they were provided to visitors of its website at no charge. The Haidian Court, however, ruled that the defendant had infringed upon the copyrights of the plaintiff, going against "the spirit" of the Copyright Law. For the details of the case, see <http://dailynews.sina.com.cn/ china/writers/index.shtml>.

21. In relation to copyright protection, there are various interest groups in China, such as copyright holders, copyright law experts, IT industry and "innocent" users of pirated products or services, etc.

22. In the process of negotiation for the Accession Protocol, China admitted that there were some existing differences between China's copyright laws and the TRIPS Agreement, the amendment to the Copyright Law had been accelerated. The proposed amendments would clarify the payment system by broadcasting organizations which use the recording products and also include the following provisions: rental rights in respect of computer programs and movies, mechanical performance rights, rights of communication to the public and related protection measures, protection of database compilations, provisional measures, increasing the legitimate compensation amount and strengthening the measures against infringing activities. China's copyright regime including Regulations for the Implementation of the Copyright Law and the Provisions on the Implementation of the International Copyright Treaty would be amended so as to ensure full consistency with China's obligations under the TRIPS Agreement.

23. In the legal documents, the two terms "transmission" and "communication" (*chuanshu*) are used interchangeably.

24. The third is the "right of derivation" (*yanyi quan*). See Zheng Chengsi, *Copyright Law* (in Chinese), revised edition, Beijing: China People's University Press, 1997, p. 151.

25. For an analysis of the relationship between the right of reproduction and the other two key rights, see ibid., pp. 151-206.

26. Article 5 (1) of the Regulations for the Implementation repeats the definition of "reproduction" given by the Copyright Law.

27. "By other means" is in fact a translation of "deng fangshi" in the official Chinese version of Article 52 of the Copyright Law. In the Chinese language, "deng" can be either an exhaustive or non-exhaustive expression. Therefore, the word "deng" needs to be interpreted according to context. In fact, the cited translation of "deng fangshi" as "by other means" shows the preference for expansive interpretation of the phrase. The judgment of the case of Wang Meng et al. v. the Shiji Hulian Communications Technology Corporation favoured such interpretation. See Cui Li, "Six Writers Finally Defeat the Shiji Hulian Communications Technology Corporation; Delegates of the People's Congress Invited for Appearance at the Court," (in Chinese), *China Youth News*, 15 December 1999, available at <dailynews.sina.com.cn/china/1999-12-15/42049.html>. Note that the author cites the reference "by other means" merely to comply with the well-established translation.

28. For example, in a tele-conference of the chief justices of the provincial-level supreme people's courts, the chief justice of China's Supreme People's Court instructed his subordinates to that effect. Quoted in Aster Shang *et al.*, "A Discussion about the Questions of Online Copyright" (in Chinese), available at <http://www8.bcity.com/changshi/>.

29. Xu Chao, "Some Considerations concerning the Revisions of the Copyright Law," (in Chinese), Copyright, 1999, no. 1: pp. 23- 27.

30. Online transmission is different from broadcasting in that the former is basically on-demand transmission and proceeds in accordance with the chosen time and place of the service users; the latter proceeds according to the time and place predetermined by the service providers.

31. See Zheng Chengsi, *Copyright Treaties, Copyright Protection and Copyright Trade*, Beijing: China People's University Press, 1992, pp. 118-21.

32. See Qingjiang Kong, Protection of Intellectual Property Rights in China: The Perspective of a Chinese Lawyer, 58 *Heidelberg Journal of International Law* 1 (1998), p. 197.

33. Article 22 (6) provides: "Under the following circumstances, a work may be exploited without permission from, and without payment of remuneration to, the copyright owner, provided that the name of the author and the title of the work shall be mentioned and the other rights enjoyed by the copyright owner

by virtue of this Law shall not be prejudiced: translation, or reproduction in a small quantity of copies, of a published work for use by teachers or scientific researchers, in classroom teaching or scientific research, provided that the translation or reproduction shall not be published or distributed."

34. Estimates hold that the online transmission of a work brings, for its author, economic returns several or even tens of times greater than when the work is merely placed into the market in print form. See Tao Xinliang, "A Consideration of Interest-Balancing concerning Protection of Intellectual Property Rights in the Internet Era" (in Chinese), quoted in Aster Shang, "A Theoretic Study and Case Briefing of Online Copyright Protection" (in Chinese), available at <http://www8.bcity.com/changshi>.

35. Player piano rolls became ubiquitous after courts ruled that they did not infringe upon the copyright of the underlying musical composition; phonograph records superseded both piano rolls and sheet music with the aid of the compulsory license for mechanical reproductions. The videotape rental business swept through almost every country shielded from copyright liability by the "first sale" doctrine. Even an erroneous assumption of copyright immunity can stimulate a nascent industry. The commercial photocopy shop prospered in part because of the university course pack business made possible by a supposed "fair use" privilege.

36. Quoted in Sun Tiecheng, *Computer and Law* (in Chinese), Beijing: Law Press, 1998, p. 225.

37. The user can at any time input any contents into the existing data that the ISP has provided, but the ISP can also delete the unsolicited addition. Some lawyers described the unique phenomenon of the online service with the newly-coined terms such as "uncertainty" and "instantability."

38. As a matter of fact, even the Digital Millennium Copyright Act of the United States, which is regarded as copyright owner-friendly, limits, in a general manner, copyright infringement liability of ISPs simply to transmitting information over the Internet.

39. Jiang Zhipei, deputy director of the Tribunal for Intellectual Property Cases of the Supreme People's Court, also holds this viewpoint. See Liu Haifen, "The Internet Era: Judicial Protection Meets Challenge," 105 *Chinese Lawyers* (in Chinese) 7 (1999), p. 62.

40. Article 5 of the Regulations for the Implementation defines "broadcasting," "distribution," and "reproduction." In contrast to "reproduction," "broadcasting" means "the communication of works through wireless radio waves or cable television system" and "distribution" is defined as "the provision of a certain number of copies of a work to the public through selling, renting, or other means, insofar as the said number of copies satisfy the reasonable needs of the public."

41. See Liu, "The Internet Era," p. 63.
42. Xue Hong revealed that the drafters of a previous version of the amendment to the current Copyright Law held this viewpoint. However, the approach was discarded later. See ibid.
43. Zheng Chengsi is a proponent of this approach. See ibid.
44. Shou Bu and Xue Hong share the viewpoint. See ibid.
45. Article 11 of the WIPO Copyright Law provides: "Contracting Parties shall provide adequate legal protection and effective legal remedies against the circumvention of effective technological measures that are used by authors in connection with the exercise of their rights under this Treaty or the Berne Convention and that restrict acts, in respect of their works, which are not authorized by the authors concerned or permitted by law."
46. See Qingjiang Kong, 5 *Issues & Studies* (36) 2000, p. 174.
47. Here the author quotes the reference used by the WIPO Copyright Treaty. See Article 8 of the WIPO Copyright Treaty.
48. The China Center for Copyright Protection is currently a nongovernmental organization of this kind.
49. In this respect, some scholars (Xue Hong, for example) favour this approach. See Liu, "The Internet Era," p. 63.
50. Shen Rengan, "Considerations concerning the Revisions of the Current Copyright Law," *Copyright* (in Chinese), 1999, no. 2: pp. 19-26.
51. The other stated aims were to prepare for the establishment of collective administrative agencies for copyright protection, and to make available to copyright administrations appropriate mechanisms for the enforcement of copyrights. Here, collective administration for copyright protection is regarded as being beneficial to copyright owners and users of copyrighted works. With respect to online copyrighted works, collective administration would, *inter alia*, provide an organized force for copyright protection; for the ISPs, collective administration would simplify the procedures for licensing of the copyrighted works.
52. Article 58 of the revised Copyright Law.
53. Articles 47, 48, 49, 50 and 51 of the revised Copyright Law.
54. Article 47 (6), (7) of the revised Copyright Law.

10

China's Telecom Regulatory Regime On the Eve Of WTO Accession*

1. Introduction

China is the world's fastest growing[1] and most promising telecommunications market.[2] Recent years have witnessed market-oriented reforms and new operational rules being prepared in China's telecommunications sector. Many believe that with the deepening of the market-oriented reforms and the WTO entry, this traditional monopoly sector will eventually be opened to domestic and foreign investors. As a matter of fact, many foreign companies have already begun to explore strategies for tapping the market.[3] There will certainly be an influx of capital as soon as direct foreign investment—in whatever form—becomes possible in this sector. This may account for why the newly launched telecommunications regulations have received a cautious welcome from foreign as well as domestic telecommunications operators.[4]

This chapter examines the existing telecommunications regime based on the "Regulations on Telecommunications." The analysis assesses the regime against the backdrop of China's commitments relating to WTO accession.

* This chapter is based on an article. "China's Telecom Regulatory Regime on the Eve of WTO Accession." first published in the *Issues & Studies*, 37, no. 4 (July/August 2001). and is reproduced by permission of its publisher.

2. Market-Oriented Reforms

China's telecommunications sector used to be dominated by a traditional PTT (post, telephone, and telegraph) monopoly and insulated from industrial competition in both services and operation. Prior to 1998, the Ministry of Post and Telecommunications was not only China's principal telecommunications regulator, but—through its commercial arm, China Telecom—was also the dominant operator of telecommunications business in the country. Primarily arising due to security concerns,[5] the monopoly was also a natural selection from a technological point of view.[6] With the realization of the role of the telecommunications sector in national economic[7] and technological development,[8] corporatizing the telecommunications monopoly and gradually introducing market forces into a variety of telecommunication markets became an important task for the Chinese government.

The market-oriented reforms in the telecommunications sector began with the establishment of China United Telecommunications Corporation (China Unicom and China Jitong Telecommunications Corporation (China Jitong) in December 1993 and January 1994, respectively. China Unicom and China Jitong were previously under the primary supervision of the Ministry of Electronic Industry (MEI).[9] While China Jitong focused on Internet postal services, China Unicom was designed to copy the business model of the existing China Telecom—i.e., being a full-range telecommunications service operator by providing such services as fixed line, paging, GSM[10] and CDMA[11] mobile phone communications, and Internet access service. The establishment of China Unicom and China Jitong signified the introduction of competition in the telecommunications sector, even though neither company was in a position to pose any serious competitive pressure on China Telecom. More importantly, the existence of a weak China Unicom and China Jitong made more prominent the dominant market position of China Telecom; this provided impetus for the restructuring of the telecommunications regulator and, subsequently, of China Telecom.

Accordingly, in March 1998 a new ministry—the Ministry of Information Industry (MII)—was established, replacing the MPT and the MEI, which was responsible for, among others, the computer industry. Most matters concerning information development (except for radio and television broadcasting) fall within the MII's competence,[12] reflecting the fact of digital technological convergence.

In February 1999, the old China Telecom was divided into three independent telecommunications companies—a new China Telecommunications Group (China Telecom Group) in the fixed-line business, China Mobile Communications Group, and China Satellite Communications Group (China Satcom). The paging business of China Telecom has been transferred to China Unicom. Parallel to this restructuring, the government granted preferential policies in order to cultivate fledgling players.[13] With the full support of the government, China Unicom was incorporated as the country's second largest mobile communications operator to compete with newly established China Mobile. Similarly, China Netcom Corporation Ltd. (China Netcom) was designed as a competitor of the new China Telecom Group in the field of Internet service. China Railway Telecommunications and Information Corporation (China Railcom) is now a competitor of China Telecom Group in the field of fixed-line telephony service. All these changes are part of the effort to create a competitive domestic market.

On 11 December 2001, China Telecom Group was further divided into two parts: its assets and operations in ten northern provinces would be integrated into the China Netcom; those in thirty southern provinces would be reorganized in a new China Telecom Group. China Jitong would also be merged into the China Netcom.[14] Therefore, for the first time in the history of China's telecommunications industry, there would be two parallel operators in the field of fix-lined operations.

In this regard, the change in the role of MII's predecessor and MII is noteworthy. In contrast with that of the MPT prior to 1998, the role of the MII—pursuant to the central government restructuring plan—was that of a telecommunications regulator overseeing areas relating to telecommunications, multi-media, broadcasting, satellite, and the Internet, without any mandate for directly engaging in telecommunications business.[15] The new regulator of the telecommunications sector is no longer supposed to play the role of telecommunications operator.

3. Telecommunications Regulations

Given the importance of telecommunications, a Telecommunications Law by the NPC or its Standing Committee is more suitable for governing this sector. According to the hierarchy of laws and administrative regulations, laws by the NPC or its Standing Committee are more authoritative than and superior to the administrative regulations by the State Council in terms of legal force. In fact, empirical evidence shows that important laws somewhat consistently regulate industries such as railway and electricity. However, mindful of the urgent need to establish a national regulatory framework in anticipation of China's impending entry into the WTO, a set of administrative regulations by the State Council, rather than a law by the NPC or its Standing Committee, were first promulgated to regulate the telecommunications sector. On September 20, 2000, the State Council issued the "Regulations on Telecommunications" (hereinafter referred to as *Telecom Regulations*).[16]

Nevertheless, the *Telecom Regulations* legalized the completed or ongoing reforms and more importantly revealed new reforms to be instituted in this sector. The general principles of the *Telecom Regulations* are "to regulate the telecommunications market, safeguard the legitimate rights and interests of users of telecommunications and proprietors of telecommunications business, ensure the safety of telecommunications network and information, and promote healthy development of the telecommunications industry" (Art. 1).

The *Telecom Regulations* consolidated the reform efforts in order to separate the government from business in the telecommunications sector. The *Telecom Regulations* make the department in charge of information technology under the State Council, the MII, responsible only for regulating rather than operating the national telecommunications sector. In addition, breaking monopolies, encouraging competition, and facilitating development, openness, fairness, and justice are also now the functions of the MII (Art. 4).

According to the *Telecom Regulations*, China will implement a licensing system in the telecommunications sector in line with different categories of business. All operators must apply to the central or provincial information industry administration for the license before starting up their businesses (Art. 7). The *Telecom Regulations* divide the telecommunications sector into basic telecommunications services (BTS) and value-added telecommunications services (VATS) (Art. 8). Operators of BTS must apply to the State Council's information industry administrative department for business permits.

In order to qualify for a license to operate a BTS business, at least 51 percent of the total equity of an applicant must be state-owned (Art. 10.1). Also the State Council will be the sole authority to examine and approve BTS license applications, whereas applicants for VATS license may either submit their applications to the telecommunications administrative authorities of the State Council or those of the relevant provinces or municipalities, and both authorities shall have equal power in examining and granting the license (Art. 9).

The kinds of VATS are defined in the annex to the *Telecom Regulations*, though the regulations expressly provide that the State Council may make adjustment to such definition anytime "depending on the actual situation." Pursuant to the annex, VATS include e-mail, databases, and the reselling of telecommunications services—such as Internet connection services, online data processing, and transaction processing services—to third parties. For VATS, the operators must apply to the State Council's information industry administrative department for permits if their business covers two or more provincial areas, autonomous regions, or municipalities under direct administration of the central government. Such operators can apply to the provincial information industry administration for permits if their business covers only one provincial area. For the first time, moreover, domestic private investors in China are expressly allowed to participate in the telecommunications sector through the operation of VATS.

The *Telecom Regulations* also contain pro-competitive provisions. In this regard, most noteworthy is the treatment of the relationships among the country's communications service providers, which has been a big headache for the MII because disputes between them are increasing nationwide. The *Telecom Regulations* incorporate an applicable procedure to deal with these problems, *inter alia*, by setting forth an obligation to interconnect for the "dominant telecommunications operator" (Art. 17). In addition, the

Telecom Regulations specifically prohibit actions that attempt to limit subscribers to use services of other operators, unreasonable cross-subsidization of other business, and provision of below-cost services (Art. 42).

4. WTO Disciplines on Telecommunications Services

Within the WTO framework, there are two agreements relating to the telecommunications sector. One is the General Agreement on Trade in Services (GATS) that took effect on January 1, 1995. The other agreement—the Agreement on Basic Telecommunications Services (ABTS), which was reached on 15 February 1997 and took effect on 5 February 1998—is an annex to the Fourth Protocol of the GATS.[17] The GATS, which covers trade in services, is binding on all WTO members as a multilateral agreement. As to the ABTS and its accompanying Reference Paper, participation by WTO members is voluntary, although in 1996 the forty-eight members that had then acceded to the ABTS accounted for 90 percent of the world's telecommunications revenue.[18]

A close examination of the ABTS Reference Paper reveals the following underlining disciplines:

Competition safeguards: The disciplines call for "appropriate measures" to be maintained to prevent anti-competitive practices by a dominant supplier. Anti-competitive practices include cross-subsidization, exploiting information obtained from competitors, and not making available to competing suppliers on a timely basis technical information about essential facilities and other commercial information required to provide services.

Interconnection: Because of the network externality, competing telecommunications networks often need access to existing networks to exchange traffic and allow intercommunications among users of the different systems. The WTO regulatory principles call for ensuring interconnection with a major supplier "at any technically feasible point in the network." Interconnection must be provided on nondiscriminatory terms, in a timely fashion, at cost-oriented rates, and with sufficient unbundling so that competitors need not pay for network components or facilities they do not require. Moreover, the procedures for interconnection must be publicly available and transparent. Moreover, in order to settle disputes about interconnection there must be recourse to an independent regulator with the power to resolve disputes in a reasonable period of time.

Universal service[19]: Members of the agreement have the right to establish universal service obligations, but these obligations must be administered in a transparent, nondiscriminatory, and competitively neutral manner, and not be so burdensome as to constitute a barrier to competition.

Licensing criteria: Where licenses to operate a service are required, the country must make publicly available all licensing criteria and the time period required to reach a decision about an application for a license. Signatories are also committed to make the terms and conditions of individual licenses publicly available.

Independent regulators: Regulatory bodies should be "separate from, and not accountable to" any supplier of services. Decisions and procedures of the regulator should be impartial.

Resource allocation: Procedures for the allocation of resources such as telephone numbers and radio frequencies should be "carried out in an objective, timely, transparent, and nondiscriminatory manner."

5. WTO Accession-Related Commitments by China

Having become a WTO member, China is now bound by the GATS. Under the GATS, China is required to progressively eliminate the measures restricting foreign participation.[20] Moreover, in the Sino-US agreement on China's WTO accession reached in November 1999,[21] China agreed to abide by the ABTS. China further committed to implement the pro-competitive regulatory principles embodied in the accompanying Reference Paper and Chairman Notes after the country's entry into the WTO. These principles include providing access to the public telecommunications networks of incumbent suppliers (i.e., interconnection rights) under nondiscriminatory terms and at cost-oriented rates, as well as an independent regulatory authority. China has also committed to technology-neutral scheduling, which means that any basic service may be provided through any means of technology (e.g., cable, wireless, and satellites).

Contrary to its prohibitive practice regarding foreign investment in the telecommunications sector, under this U.S.-China agreement China has for the first time agreed to allow 49 percent foreign investment in all services; 50 percent foreign equity share participation in VATS (including, for example, electronic mail, voice mail, Internet, on-line information and data base retrieval, and enhanced value/added facsimile services) and paging services two years after accession; 49 percent foreign equity share in mobile voice and data services (including all analogue/digital cellular and personal communications services) five years after accession; and for domestic and international services (including, for example, voice, facsimile, intra-company e-mail, voice and data services) six years after accession. No geographic restrictions will be imposed for paging and value-added services two years after accession, for mobile voice and data services in five years, and for domestic and international services in six years.[22]

According to the agreement reached between the EU and China in May 2000,[23] China further agreed to speed up the market access timetable. Specifically, the timetable for market opening in mobile telephone has been accelerated by two years. Foreign investment will be allowed at 25 percent on accession, 35 percent after one year, and 49 percent after three years. China will open its leasing market in three years, allowing foreign companies to rent capacity from Chinese operators and resell it for both domestic and international traffic. The liberalization of domestic leased circuit services would allow joint venture foreign telecommunications operators to create their own networks, independent of the existing ones, and to sell their capacity to clients in China. In Internet and other value-added services (including paging), foreign companies would immediately be allowed 30 percent stakes in Chinese companies in Beijing, Shanghai, and Guangzhou. Foreign ownership would be increased to 50 percent in two years when all geographic restrictions disappear.

True, neither the Sino-US agreement nor the Sino-EU agreement is worry-free. However, it is worth bearing in mind that in general the results of the two agreements are to be extended to all WTO members on a non-discriminatory basis through the MFN principle.[24] Although the agreements allow particular measures inconsistent with the MFN obligation to be maintained, "provided that such a measure is listed in, and meets the conditions of, the Annex on Article II Exemptions,"[25] China has not yet actually done so. As a result, any investor from any WTO member state will be entitled to hold China to all commitments Beijing has made in any bilateral agreement on WTO accession with any WTO member state.

6. Compatibility of the *Telecom Regulations* with the WTO

The *Telecom Regulations* and the relevant practice are to be assessed in comparison with the disciplines or principles embodied in the ABTS or the GATS, and with China's commitments concerning foreign participation in telecommunications services.

6.1. A comparison between the Telecom Regulations and WTO disciplines

With regard to competitive safeguards, the *Telecom Regulations* commendably recognize pro-competitive principles. Although China so far has no antimonopoly law,[26] the *Telecom Regulations* do establish the same competitive principles as those in the ABTS (Arts. 41 and 42). A noteworthy example is that the issuance of BTS licenses is subject to a competitive tendering process in accordance with the relevant provisions of the state.

The provisions in the *Telecom Regulations* that leave room for private initiative in the telecommunications sector[27] have also the effect of enhancing competition. While BTS is required to be at least 51 percent owned by a state-owned entity, VATS is thrown completely open to Chinese private firms.[28] Since China agreed to progressively open its telecommunications market to foreign participation, a foreign private investor should therefore be able to establish a Chinese-foreign VATS joint venture with a private domestic entity.[29]

In addition, the *Telecom Regulations* stipulates that the charges and standards of telecommunications services be set,[30] and these specific standards are designed to help hamper the telecommunications operators from using their dominant positions in dealing with services users.

However, the *Telecom Regulations* are not enough to further enhance competition in the telecommunications sector. For example, the *Telecom Regulations* fail to give details on the licensing procedures. This explains why the MII adopted the Administrative Measures for Telecommunications Services Licenses.[31] In contrast with the existing protectionist approach toward the licensing process for the BTS,[32] the new move is a positive step towards a fairer and more transparent procedures for telecommunications service licensing.

In respect to interconnection, China Telecom has not yet performed satisfactorily.[33] However, the *Telecom Regulations* provide for the interconnecting rights of telecommunications operators.[34] The "Measures for Interconnection Between Public Networks," promulgated in May 2001 by the MII, further clarified the procedures for interconnection. These provisions are obviously in line with the WTO discipline.

Regarding universal service, in telecommunications as in other sectors, China's government is concerned about geographic disparities and thus attaches importance to the concept of "universal service." Designating universal service providers is within the competence of the ABTS members. While imposing the obligation, the *Telecom Regulations* (Art. 44) failed to provide for the details.[35] Moreover, the statutory provision might prove to be a problem for foreign investors given that they are still geographically restricted in the transitional period. However, since the *Telecom Regulations* contain no provision in this regard, evaluating the compatibility between the *Telecom Regulations* and the WTO disciplines is pointless.

As for licensing criteria, the *Telecom Regulations* set out in clear terms the framework for operational licensing conforming to this WTO discipline.[36] The licensing framework contains explicit criteria to be used, and the criteria are publicly available. However, as indicated before, the licensing practice needs to be further clarified concerning the time and detailed procedures for implementation of these criteria.

In regard to regulatory independence, the *Telecom Regulations* clearly separate the regulator from the operator. However, due to the legacy of the past, the practice leaves much to be desired. First is regulatory independence of the Chinese telecommunications regulator. The MII is perceivably continuing to protect, and to exercise influence over, the major telecommunications operators,[37] as the MII is responsible for operational licensing, interconnection, the setting of telecommunications services' rates and standards, the allocation of telecommunications resources, and the selection of universal service providers. Given the close relationship between the MII and China Telecom in the past, and the perceived continuing association between the MII and the new China Telecom Group, it remains to be seen whether the MII will in practice be impartial with respect to all telecommunications operators (including new entrants) in exercising its regulatory powers under the *Telecom Regulations*. The official stance is that the current level of interference is meant only to achieve full competition, which will in turn obviate the need for the involvement of government bodies. Once this is achieved, the industry should fully realize the power of market mechanisms. More worrisome is that monopoly will not be easily broken and deregulation will be limited.[38] In reality, even after China's WTO accession, a considerable period of time may be necessary before the MII ceases exercising such biased interference and then becomes a truly independent telecommunications regulator. That the State Leading Group on Informatization (SLGI) was set up is a blessing.[39] Given that this group is in practice the policymaker of the information work and is above the somewhat interested MII, the SLGI can be expected to intervene when the MII fails to act as an independent regulator.

Resource allocation in China is governed by the "Regulations on Radio Administration."[40] These regulations put the job of spectrum allocation in the hands of a State Radio Regulatory Committee, which was made part of MII in 1998. This made the procedures for obtaining spectrum more orderly and explicit.

6.2. A comparison between the Foreign Investment Telecom Regulations and China's commitments

According to the Interim Measures on Approving Operations of Open Telecommunications Services in 1993, the so-called "open telecommunications services" that non-telecommunications domestic state-owned enterprises had been allowed to participate in, were still not open to foreign companies and foreign-invested enterprises in China.[41] Also, under the "Provisional Regulations on Foreign Investment Guidelines" and the "Catalogue of Industries for Guiding Foreign Investment,"[42] the telecommunications industry belongs to the "category of prohibitive industries," i.e., industries where foreign investment is barred. From a legal perspective, foreign participation in the telecommunications sector was still prohibited until China formally joined the WTO.[43] Note that in both the Sino-US and Sino-EU agreements, as well as other bilateral agreements on China's WTO accession, China has agreed to progressively open its telecommunications industry to foreign companies in three phases, which vary in timing over three different categories of services: VAS, paging mobiles voice and data services, and basic fixed-line services.[44] In order to align with the commitments, the *Telecom Regulations* state that foreign organizations or individuals[45] will be allowed to invest in and operate telecommunications businesses in accordance with a separate set of rules to be formulated by the State Council (Art. 80). Fortunately, the MII pronounced the repealing of the Interim Measures on Approving Operations of Open Telecommunications Services, effective on 11 December 2001. More importantly, in a subsequent effort, on 20 December 2001 the State Council promulgated the Regulations on Foreign Investment in Telecommunications Enterprises (hereinafter referred to as "*Foreign Investment Telecom Regulations*").[46] Clear is that while foreign telecommunications operators are eagerly looking forward to the upcoming regulations, the Chinese authorities obviously will not open telecommunications services to foreign investment until the last minute. Nevertheless, this was the crucial step towards honoring its commitments. The following is an evaluation of the compatibility between the *Foreign Investment Telecom Regulations* and China's commitments.

While authorizing a Chinese and a foreign party to incorporate a Chinese-foreign equity joint venture for the provision of telecommunications services, the *Foreign Investment Telecom Regulations*, as the title suggest do not contemplate the possibility of a wholly foreign-owned enterprise participating in the telecommunications industry. Contractual joint venture was also not discussed in the *Foreign Investment Telecom Regulations*.

Concerns are that notwithstanding the promise of increased access after WTO accession, the *Foreign Investment Telecom Regulations* set qualifications requirements for a telecommunications joint venture that act as a restriction in many of the potential entrants. For instance, one of the qualifying requirements for a telecommunications joint venture intending to provide national or cross-provincial BTS is to have a minimum registered capital of 2 billion RMB, a threshold which would eliminate many companies from participation in the Chinese market.[47] More noteworthy is that among the requirements for a foreign company to qualify to be the "principal foreign investor" in a telecommunications joint venture are to be licensed telecommunications operator in its own country and to have "good performance and operational experience." The criteria would not only rule out the possibility for non-telecommunications-operator foreign companies to participate in China's telecommunications services, but also subject prospective foreign investors to the discretion of the examination and approval authorities.

Nevertheless, Minister of Information Industry Wu Jichuan was reported to have assured investors that the regulations for foreign investors will provide a level playing field and China would abide by its international commitments in order to accelerate China's accession to the WTO.[48] The approval of a pilot VATS joint venture in advance of the draft regulations or the WTO accession has sent encouraging signals.[49]

In this context, clear is that, the *Telecom Regulations* and the derivative *Foreign Investment Telecom Regulations* are basically conforming to the WTO, although they reflect some vestiges of the centrally-planned economy.[50]

7. Concluding Remarks

China wants to embrace the economic development potential of information technology and the global trading system. While also wanting to retain the traditional levers of control over national industrial policy and political and social communication associated with the monopoly structure of the past, the Chinese government knows it has to respond to new necessities stemming from the development and commercialization of new telecommunications technologies. China has been restructuring the telecommunications sector, including making preparations for a new regulatory regime. As a result, the telecommunications sector is undergoing unprecedented change, with a competitive environment likely to emerge.[51] Also, in a bid to join the WTO, China has been deliberately adjusting its current industrial policies in order to make them suitable to international practice as exemplified by the WTO agreements. By setting out and implementing nationwide supervisory mechanisms for the users, operators, and regulatory organs of the industry, the *Telecom Regulations* constitute a basically WTO-compatible regime for telecommunications. Foreign enterprises will hence have the opportunity to invest in and operate local area networks with no obvious obstacles in terms of capital, technology, allocations, or service systems. Although the regulations for foreign investment in telecommunications services have not been passed, foreign private companies will have bright prospects. One example is the ability to operate local area networks for realty districts and enterprise groups, provided that the regulators are willing to distance themselves from dominant telecommunication operators.

Notes

1. According to Zhou Deqiang , president of the China Telecom Group, China now ranks second in the world in the number of fixed-line users and second in the size of its telephone network, up from 17th in the 1980s. See *China News Service*, 17 July 2000.
2. By August 2001, China boasted approximately 160 million fixed-line and 126 million cellular subscribers. China had become the biggest mobile telecommunications market in the world. Moreover, the number of Chinese Internet users was over 20 million by the end of 2000. Despite these attractive figures, only 5 percent of this market has been tapped.
3. On 13 June 2000, Vodafone and China Unicom signed an agreement on cooperating in roaming services. For details, see <http://www.vodafone.com/media/press_release/9222.htm>. Lucent Technologies has secured a CDMA project with China Unicom to provide mobile telecommunications service. See <http://www.lucent.com.cn>. Singapore Telecom is reported to have obtained permission to participate in the Internet services with the establishment of its alliance with the China Netcom.
4. For instance, Jamie P. Horsley, an attorney who lived and worked in China for thirteen years as a lawyer, diplomat, and corporate executive, hailed the "Regu-

lations on Telecommunications" as "paving the way for a WTO-compatible national law." See *The China Business Review*, July-August 2001, p. 34.
5. The openness of networks is the inherent weakness that leaves the system vulnerable to attack.
6. "Three networks" (telecommunications network, radio and television network, and computer network) used to be independent. With the development of computer technology, the demarcation between the three has become blurred.
7. Early in December 1978, Deng Xiaoping vowed to develop the telecommunications infrastructure which he saw at the time as one of the chief bottlenecks hindering economic growth. See MII, Chronicles of the Reform and Opening-Up of the Country's Telecommunications Area (in Chinese, 20 January 2001), available at <http://www.mii.gov.cn>.
8. Digital technology, a common technical platform of the "three networks," has allowed convergence of voice, data, text, image, and all other transfer services. This naturally results in pressure for cross-competition in various types of services by the three networks.
9. The founding of China Unicom was co-sponsored by the ministries of Electronic Industry, Power Industry, and Railways. The company also received capital input from such enterprises as China International Trust and Investment Corporation, China Everbright International Trust and Investment Corporation, China Resources Group, China Huaneng Group, China Merchants Holdings Company Ltd., China National Chemicals Import and Export Corporation, China Trust and Investment Corporation for Foreign Economic and Trade Relations, China National Technology Import and Export Corporation, Beijing CATCH Communications Group Co. (on behalf of the Beijing Municipal Government), Shanghai Science and Technology Investment Corporation, Guangzhou South-China Trade Center Group, and Dalian Vastone Enterprise Development Company Ltd.
10. GSM (Global System for Mobile Communications) refers to an open, nonproprietary system that is constantly evolving. One of its great strengths is international roaming capability. This gives consumers seamless and standardized same number contactability in more than 170 countries. GSM satellite roaming has extended service access to areas where terrestrial coverage is not available. See <http://www.gsmworld.com/technology/faq.html>.
11. CDMA (Code Division Multiple Access) is a "spread spectrum" technology, which means that it spreads the information contained in a particular signal of interest over a much greater bandwidth than the original signal. See the website of CDMA Technology, <http://www.cdg/tech/tech.asp>.
12. Interesting is to note that the MII had been reportedly considering merging the MII and the State Administration of Radio, Film, and Television (SARFT),

which the SAREF was disinterested in. See Hou Mingjuan, "Cable Authorities Decline Telecoms Sector's Plan to Converge Markets," *China Daily*, 23 July 2001. According to market research report by Global Information, Inc., the State Council, which has always banned the SARFT from engaging in telecommunications operations and the MII from engaging in radio and TV operations, has granted the MII regulatory authority over commercial TV broadcasting companies. See Global Information, Inc., China Telecom 2000: China's New Telecom Policy and Structure after Reorganization, available at <http://www.gii.co.jp/english/gi3557 mn_china telecom.html>.

13. While China Unicom's mobile subscriber use base (GSM) is similar to China Mobile's, China Unicom has only 5.23 million mobile phone users, compared with 40 million at China Mobile. In order to compete with China Mobile in the area of mobile communications, China Unicom decided to set up a nationwide CDMA network. The authorization for China Unicom to construct and operate a CDMA network is therefore the biggest form of governmental support.

14. Xinhua News Agency, 11 December 2001.

15. For a detailed description of the role of the MII, see <http://www.mii.gov.cn>.

16. For the text of the *Telecom Regulations*, see Gazette of the State Council 33 (2000): pp. 11-21.

17. For an elaboration of the ABTS, see, for instance, Philip L. Spector, The World Trade Organization Agreement on Telecommunications, 32 *The International Lawyer* 2 (1998): pp. 217-30.

18. See WTO Press Release, Background Note on the WTO Negotiations on Basic Telecommunications, 22 February 1996.

19. "Universal service" means the telecommunications operators must cover remote areas where communications services are needed.

20. The GATS requires progressive elimination of such measures as limitations on numbers of service providers, on the total value of service transactions, or on the total number of service operations or people employed, as well as restrictions on the kind of legal entity or joint venture through which a service is provided or any foreign capital limitations relating to maximum levels of foreign participation. See GATS, Article XVI (2). China, however, has so far prohibited foreign investment in the telecommunications sector.

21. The text of the Sino-US WTO market access agreement is available at the website of the U.S.-China Business Council, <http://www.uschina.org>.

22. China's key telecommunications services corridor in Beijing, Shanghai, and Guangzhou, which represents approximately 75 percent of all domestic traffic, will open to all telecommunications services immediately upon WTO accession.

23. For the highlights of theSinoa-EU WTO market access agreement, see the EU website at <http://europa.eu.int/comm/trade/bilateral/china/high.htm>.

24. See Article II (1) of the GATS. Also, the fourth Annex to the GATS (Annex on Telecommunications) requires WTO member states to ensure that all service suppliers seeking to take advantage of scheduled commitments have reasonable and nondiscriminatory access to and the use of public basic telecommunications networks and services.

25. See Article II (2) of the GATS.

26. In September 1993, China passed an "Anti-Unfair Competition Law" which prohibits price-fixing and prevents predatory pricing. In addition, the Price Law, the Law on Tendering and Bidding, the Criminal Law and other relevant laws also contained provisions on anti-monopoly and unfair competition. However, these laws do not intend to establish a comprehensive anti-monopoly mechanism. They are often so vague as to make enforcement difficult. For example, the Anti-Unfair Competition Law indeed has sought to prevent telecommunication operators from collecting telecommunications charges in excess of what stipulated, but the law does not have substantive or predictable procedures in place to prevent anti-competitive behaviour by the dominant operators (China Telecom), let alone challenge the longstanding monopoly in the telecommunications industry.

27. For instance, Article 13 of the *Telecom Regulations* provides that all eligible Chinese companies, regardless of state-owned or private enterprises, can operate VATS.

28. There is no requirement that a certain percentage of the equity or share capital of a VATS operator must be owned by the state. Therefore, possible is that 100 percent of the equity or share capital of a VATS operator may be owned by non-state-owned or private domestic entities.

29. Under the terms of the Sino-US bilateral agreement on China's accession to the WTO, foreign investment in VATS will be capped at 30 percent initially and at 50 percent within five to six years after accession. A non-state-owned or private entity can thus hold 70 percent of the equity initially (which may be reduced to 50 percent within five to six years of China's WTO accession) of any proposed Chinese-foreign VATS joint venture.

30. Chapter II of the *Telecom Regulations*, Section 3 (from Article 23 to Article 26) covers procedures for telecommunications charges. Chapter III (from Article 31 to Article 44) is designed to specify the standards for telecommunications services.

31. Adopted on 8 November 2001 and came into force on 1 January 2002.

32. The MII has made clear new services licenses would be granted to existing telecommunication operators and dismissed the possibility of licensing more telecommunications companies in the near future. Vice-Minister of Information Industry Zhang Chunjiang was reported to have said in relation to the new mobile telecommunications service licensing that "[t]he selections pro-

cess is still under discussion, but current telecommunications service operators are likely to be licensed." Reports widely rumored that both China Telecom and China Netcom will be allowed to provide mobile communications services. See *People's Daily*, 18 May 2000. Ironically, according to one MII official, the "current, ineffective level of competition in the industry" accounts for the need to apply selectively discriminatory policies to "support backbone enterprises in order to give them a stronger foothold in the international arena." Huang Chengqing, a senior official with the Telecom Administration Bureau under MII, made the remarks at the U.S.-China Telecommunications Regulatory Policy Forum & Roundtable, 24-25 October 2000.

33. China Telecom has been found, on numerous occasions, to have purposefully disconnected China Unicom from the national network it maintains. See Yu Hui, "An Ally Between Administrators and Operators in the Regulated Market: Examples of China's Telecommunications Industry (in Chinese)," in Zhang Xinzhu *et al.* (ed): *Regulation and Competition in China: Theories and Practice* (in Chinese), Beijing: Shehui kexue wenxian chubanshe, 2000, p. 31.

34. Chapter II of the *Telecom Regulations*, Section 2 (from Article 17 to Article 22) specifically deals with the obligations and procedures for interconnection.

35. It is reported that the MII is to adopt new rules in this regard, by which a "universal Service Fund" is to be set up. All telecommunications operators will be required to contribute to the Fund. The government will use the fund to subsidize or compensate any company that wants to invest in less-developed regions, but suffers a loss in doing so. *China News Service*, 23 January 2002.

36. Chapter II of the *Telecom Regulations*, Section 1 (from Article 7 to Article 16) deals in detail with the operational licensing.

37. According to a 2000 study on telecommunications competition in China, the MII "still significantly influences strategic issues such as pricing, assets, and personnel matters at both China Telecom and Unicom." See Bing Zhang and Mike W. Peng, "Telecom Competition, Post-WTO Style," *China Business Review*, May-June 2000, p. 16. For an elaboration on how the regulator might collude with operators in the telecommunications industry, see Yu, "An Ally Between Administrators and Operators," pp. 23-34.

38. First, for telecommunications security, the openness of networks is the inherent weakness that leaves the system vulnerable to attack. The MII may be unwilling to take the risk of undermining telecommunications security. Second, the regulations on the separation of government from enterprises generates a dilemma: as the government's role is separated from that of enterprise operations, the MII will have less power to directly weaken China Telecom Group's monopoly. See *Zhengquan shibao* (Securities Times), 16 July 2000.

39. The State Council set up the Leading Group of Informatization in 1996. It had the Office of the Leading Group of Informatization as its administrative body. In 1998, the Office of the Leading Group of Informatization and the former State Radio Regulatory Committee became two divisions of the newly established MII. Recently, the LGI was reorganized into a higher-ranking SLGI, with Premier Zhu Rongji as its head. See *Ming Pao* (Hong Kong), 27 September 2001.

40. The State Council and the Central Military Commission issued the "Regulations on Radio Administration" in September 1993.

41. China prohibited foreign participation in telecommunications network ownership, operations, and management. However, China Unicom, the second largest telecommunications operator, and its incorporators devised a model—the "*Zhong-Zhong-wai*" (Chinese-Chinese-foreign) mode—to circumvent this regulation. In a "*Zhong-Zhong-wai*" arrangement, a foreign investor (Foreign) forms a joint venture with Chinese partners (Chinese) which is either the incorporator of China Unicom or the companies designated by China Unicom (these Chinese partners are not in the field of telecommunications sector). The joint venture will build the network and sign revenue sharing and other network services agreements with China Unicom (Chinese). The foreign investor typically contributes the majority of the funding needed for network buildup and in return shares the revenue allocated to the joint venture from China Unicom. In this way, the foreign investor seemingly could reap "equity-like" returns without breaking Chinese rules. According to one study, during the four years from 1995 to late 1998, nearly fifty "*Zhong-Zhong-wai*" projects were established, involving US$1.4 billion of foreign investment from companies from the United States, Canada, Germany, France, Italy, Japan, South Korea, and Singapore. In September 1998, the Chinese government issued a decree calling for the ban of the "*Zhong-Zhong-wai*" investment model. The move was apparently a major setback for foreign investors who were using this model to circumvent the Chinese government ban on foreign participation in the telecommunications services industry. See He Xia, "Strategic Selections for Financing China's Telecommunications Industry," in above Zhang Xinzhu *et al.* (ed.), pp. 310-312.

42. The Guidelines and the accompanying Catalogue were promulgated in 1995, while the Catalogue was amended in 1997.

43. Investors, especially foreign venture capital suppliers, report being confused by China's current policies concerning investment involving Internet content and service providers. Although many of the country's Internet content and service companies have won capital support from foreign investors, the official stance is still one of "prohibition."

44. This is another aspect where the *Telecom Regulations* are not free from criticism in relation to the definition of BTS and VATS. The definitions of BTS and VATS are not inconsistent per se with the GATS and the Basic Telecommunications Agreement. The Services Sectoral Classification List, an informal note by the GATT on 10 July 1991, divides telecommunications services into fifteen subsectors. Although the WTO ABTS does not provide a definition of BTS, the first six subsectors of the list (voice telephone services, packet-switched data transmission, telex services, telegraph services, fax services, and private-circuit services) as well as certain mobile communications and other services are in the catchall "other" category, as BTS. However, technological development may outdate the distinction and lead to misconceptions. The definition of BTS under the "Classification Catalogue of Telecommunications Services" would appear to be broad. For example, the meaning of certain services included as part of BTS—such as network bearer services and network outsourcing services—is not immediately obvious. Network outsourcing services, paging services, and resale of BTS would appear to be value-added in nature but have been included as part of BTS and are subject to the more stringent licensing requirements under the *Telecom Regulations*. Amidst the calls for clarification, on June 11, 2001 the MII substantially revised the catalogue in a "Circular on the Adjustment of the Classification Catalogue of Telecommunications Services." According to the new catalogue, some telecommunications services that used to belong to the BTS under the original catalogue—such as network outsourcing services, paging services, and resale of BTS—are treated as reference to VATS, thus giving clear-cut definition of various telecommunications services. However, the lease or sale of products that presumably should not constitute telecommunications business is still included in the definition of BTS, and are thus subject to the licensing regime introduced by the *Telecom Regulations*.

45. For the purpose of the *Telecom Regulations*, "origin investors" include those from Hong Kong, Macau, and Taiwan.

46. The Regulations on Foreign Investment in Telecommunications Enterprises was adopted on 5 December 2001 and entered into force on 1 January 2002.

47. An unofficial draft, circulated in late 2000, created uproar by imposing restrictive conditions on foreign applicants as well as their Chinese partners. According to a Coudert Brothers report, this is a criterion which would eliminate many companies from participation in the Chinese telecommunications market. See Vivienne Bath and Cindy Chong (Coudert Brothers, Hong Kong Office), "China's New Telecommunications Regulations," *Asia Legal Briefing*, November 2000.

48. Wu made the remarks at a press conference held by the State Council Information Office on 30 September 2000.

49. In December 2000, a VATS joint venture involving the AT&T, Shanghai Information Investment Corporation, and Shanghai Telecom—Shanghai Xintian Telecommunications Ltd.—was set up and would provide broadband Internet services in Shanghai's Pudong area.

50. The *Telecom Regulations* provide for obligations in association with social control. One example is the state control provisions. True, non-state-owned or private entities are now allowed for the first time to hold up to 49 percent of the equity or share capital of a BTS operator within five to six years of China's WTO accession; the requirement that 51 percent of the equity or share capital of a BTS operator must be owned by the state reflects, however, the Chinese government's determination to retain control over the operation of BTS. Unless a potential foreign investor is willing to accept an ownership interest of less than 49 percent in any proposed Chinese-foreign BTS joint venture, the chances of the foreign investor successfully partnering with a non-state-owned or private domestic entity would therefore appear to be minimal. Another example is that, because the MII intends to exercise a certain degree of social control in association with telecommunications services, all telecommunications companies are required to provide universal service.

51. As the commercialization of third-generation telecommunications technology (3G) nears, the selection of 3G operators has been on the MII's work agenda. The ministry has set up an expert panel to research and study how to distribute China's 3G licenses. Reports held that the Chinese government would announce the final 3G operators during the second half of 2001 and the first half of 2002. Recently, wireless application protocol (WAP) technology has received enormous publicity, while private Internet companies can use their existing networks to participate in WAP operations as their first step in edging into the telecommunications sector.

11

Where Will China's Internet Regulation Go After WTO Accession?

1. Introduction

With no escape from the age of information, China has chosen to embrace the Internet without a lot of fanfare.[1] As in the West, one big theme facing the government is the regulation of the Internet.[2] As a result, recent years saw the promulgation of numerous regulations on the Internet[3].

The WTO negotiations, in addition, served as a catalyst to strengthen and consolidate liberalizing forces in the economic arena. While international observers habitually notice the Chinese government has already taken measures to regulate the Internet, they fail to perceive the inter-linkage between the new rules and the bureaucratic obstacles to open market competition in the telecommunication industry. It is also easy to underestimate the inherent power of the Internet and, particularly, to ignore the ambition of the Chinese government to adapt to the technological opportunity. As the government is readily embracing information technology (IT) revolution and preparing for the WTO accession, the Internet rules would not be so restrictive as to deny free access to the Internet. It is undoubtedly meaningful to have an overview of the Chinese approach to the regulation of the Internet at the turn of WTO accession.

2. An Overview of the Internet Rules

It is not difficult to find that the rules regulating the Internet come from two sources: specific rules for the Internet regulation and general rules for telecommunications regulation.

Among the specific regulatory rules, the Interim Provisions on the Administration of International Wiring of Computer Information Networks (*jisuanji xinxi wangluo guoji lianwang guanli zhanxing guiding*), which the State Council promulgated on 1 February 1996, are the principal rules from which the rest derive. As the term "administration" or "*guanli*" indicates, the purpose of the regulations is to strengthen the administration of international wiring of computer information networks.

The Regulations on Telecommunications, which the State Council promulgated on 20 September 2000, have been the only comprehensive governing rules in the field of telecommunications regulation. The Regulations on Telecommunications basically focus on the operation of telecommunications services, and the operation of Internet services naturally falls within the Regulations' scope of application.

In general, rules regulating the Internet can largely be divided into three inter-related categories: rules governing Internet content censorship, those governing operations of Internet service and those governing users of Internet services.

2.1. Rules for Internet content censorship

Of the three categories of Internet rules, the most controversial is the rules for Internet content censorship. In this regard, particular attention should be paid to the Administrative Provisions on Secrecy of Computer Information Systems (*jisuanji xinxi xitong baomi guanli guiding*), which deal with state secrets on the Internet.

The Administrative Provisions, which some international observers see as "a disaster for the Chinese Internet revolution,"[4] ban individuals and institutions from discussing or disseminating any information that is considered "state secrets."[5] As to what "state secrets" mean, the Administrative Provisions, however, fail to provide any definition. Presumably, the State

Secrecy Law should be referred to in this regard, which provides that "state secrets are matters relating to the national security and benefits whose access is, in accordance with the legal procedures, limited to persons of a certain scope in a certain period."[6]

It is intriguing that the Administrative Provisions on Secrecy of Computer Information Systems provide that state approval should be obtained from relevant authorities for the distribution of information on the Internet.[7] This requirement probably is most likely to give rise to criticism in the Administrative Provisions on Secrecy of Computer Information Systems in that, among other things, it fails to notice the difference between information flow over the Internet and information transmission over the traditional media such as newspapers and television. It dictates as tight a censorship on the Internet contents as on the traditional media materials.[8] It in letter is so prohibitive to the ISPs that the implementation of this requirement to the letter would mean not only devastating China's emerging Internet industry but a giant backlash.[9] However, as observed by numerous Internet analysts, it would be too costly and impractical to do that.[10] Nevertheless, the self-censorship among the ISP can also be an expected result of the strict implementation of the requirement.[11]

In addition to state secrets, pornographic information is also on the list of Internet content censorship.[12] However, while dictating rigid censorship, the Internet rules are far from complete. A clear indication is that they fail to address the issue of privacy protection, which in western democracies is viewed as crucial to human rights of individuals. Apparently, the drafters of the Internet rules realized that transmission of both state secrets and pornographic information is harmful to the state interests or public goods but overlooked privacy protection. The adoption of censoring state secrets and pornographic information by the Internet rules and its failure to incorporate rules for protection of privacy in a similar way clearly reflect the values of the typical oriental rule makers.[13]

2.2. Rules governing operations of the Internet service

Rules governing the operation of the Internet services are divided into two categories: rules governing licensing or registration and rules governing wiring. As pointed out before, the Regulations on Telecommunications regulate the operation of telecommunications services. Pursuant to the Regulations on Telecommunications, the State Council) adopted the Administrative Measures for the Internet Information Services (*hulianwang xinxi fuwu guanli banfa*) on 20 September 2000 to further specify the conditions for the licensing and registration of the Internet services.

According to the Administrative Measures for the Internet Information Services, Internet services are divided into two categories: profit-making services and non-profit-making services. While non-profit-making services providers need to file registrations with the competent authorities before operating, profit-making services providers must obtain licenses from the authorities.[14] For the profit-making Internet services, the Administrative Measures set forth stiff licensing requirements in addition to those stipulated in the Regulations on Telecommunications.[15] These additional requirements include: business development blueprint and corresponding technical support plan, "healthy and complete" network security safeguard measures. The vague licensing requirements seemingly leave much room for the authorities, thus creating difficulty for the starters.

The Interim Provisions on the Administration of International Wiring of Computer Information Networks establish a complex four-tier system for international wiring. The first is the gateway for International wiring. The Interim Provisions require that all traffic to the computer networks outside China be effectuated through the gateway maintained by public telecommunication networks, that is, the networks maintained by the China Telecom and other approved public networks.[16] The Rules for the Administration of International Wiring Gateway for Inbound and Outbound Computer Information (*jisuanji xinxi wangluo guoji lianwang churukou xindao guanli banfa*), adopted by the former MPT, reaffirms the privileged role of the China Telecom network as the gateway.[17] No persons or units may establish or use other gateways for Internet traffic without prior approval from the government.[18] In addition to ChinaNet of China Telecom, the approved networks include CERNET of Ministry of Education, CSTNET of Chinese Academy of Sciences, GBNet of China Jitong, UNINET of China Unicom, CNCNET of China Netcom, CIET of the Ministry of Foreign Trade and

Economic Cooperation, CMNET of China Mobile, CGWNET of the People's Liberation Army and CSNET of China Satcom.[19] Nevertheless, this international gateway requirement facilitates the filtering of the information offensive to the regime. The second is those computer information networks directly wired with the gateway. It is required that only those approved "inter-wired networks" can carry out international wiring directly through the gateway. The third is "wired networks" that are defined as computer information networks that carry out international wiring through the "inter-wired networks."[20] In practice, most maintainers of inter-wired networks also act as those that maintain wired networks. They both constitute the ISPs.[21] The Interim Provisions require that any entity intending to be connected with the Internet has to file an application with the relevant government agencies for Internet wiring; an entity intending to operate business on the Internet has to procure a license.[22] Individuals are excluded from the scope of ISP. The last tier consists of the Internet users that are individuals or entities.

According to the Interim Provisions, individuals and entities engaging international wiring, shall, in compliance with the relevant state laws and administrative regulations, not commit violations or crimes concerning endangering national security, disclosing state secrets, and refrain from making, checking, copying and transmitting pornographic information.[23] Also, according to the Regulations on the Safeguard of Computer Information System, endangering the security of computer networks, is also punishable.[24]

It is worth noticing that the Interim Provisions here suggest that the other laws of China, the Criminal Law in particular, also apply to the ISPs. Moreover, the vaguely worded provision may even leave room for the government to deal with cases that otherwise may be dealt with on other grounds, e.g. tort. Moreover, the NPC Standing Committee adopted the Decision on Safeguarding the Internet (*weihu hulianwang anquan de jueding*) on 28 December 2000. The Decision provides in detail that 15 online acts are criminal offences, and thus has remedied the defect in this regard. However, it is worthy noting that the Decision on Safeguarding the Internet goes so far as to provide that a website keeper who links to pornographic information websites is criminally chargeable.[25]

Nevertheless, there is a risk for the police, i.e. the Ministry of Public Security (MSB) and its local branches—Public Security Bureaus (PSBs), to tend to charge the violating business on the intimidating ground of endangering national security.[26] An example is that a private Internet service provider was prosecuted for the alleged endangering national security by disclosing the e-mail addresses of his clients to an overseas institution identified as an anti-government organization.[27]

Fortunately, there are signs that the Chinese courts are not always willing to support the accusations of the ISPs based on the "endangering national security" provisions. It is interesting to note a high-profile case in Fujian Province. The Chen brothers who are Internet users of China Telecom set up a phone service via the Internet, selling calls to the United States at a fraction of the state monopoly's price.[28] Acting on requests from China Telecom, the local police arrested the brothers, seized their property including their computer and accused them of "endangering national security" and committing "a new type of crime." The brothers responded by suing the police, arguing that their actions were not criminal because there was no law banning Internet phone service.[29] The brothers won the case.[30]

In this regard, it should be pointed out that the Regulations on the Administration of Commercial Encryption, which govern the development, production, sale and use of commercial encryption has also an adverse, indirect impact on the operation of the online services. On 7 October 1999, the State Council adopted Administration of Commercial Encryption Regulations governing the sale, distribution, use and production of commercial encryption products in China, including a ban on the sale of all foreign products.[31] On 31 January 2000, the Chinese government began to implement the Encryption Administration. As originally proposed, the rules were viewed to have a stifling effect on the development on the Internet and e-commerce in China and foreign companies seeking market access. The Chinese government, realizing the practical and commercial implications of implementing such a broad regulatory regime, recently issued a statement clarifying its commercial encryption policy. According to the March 2000 statement by the National Commission on Encryption Code Regulations (NCECR), the Encryption Administration would be limited to "specialized hardware and software products for which encryption and decoding operations are its core functions." Wireless phones, Windows software, and browser software are not covered. Registration requirements are also relaxed. In addition, the regulations are being researched and will be revised "in accordance with WTO regulations and promises to foreign governments."

2.3. Rules for users of Internet services

In relation to users of Internet service, individuals and entities, intending to plug on to the Internet is required to register with the police. Failure to register may result in forced de-wiring by PSBs.[32]

Internet users are also not allowed to publish, discuss and spread any "state secrets" through the e-mail systems, chat rooms or electronic bulletin boards.[33] The MII even adopted the Administrative Measures for Services on Electronic Bulletin Boards (*hulianwang dianzi gonggao fuwu guanli guiding*) to specify the conditions for the provision and use of services through electronic bulletin boards. For example, operations of services through electronic bulletin boards must be approved or registered,[34] the operators must keep the service records for 60 days for official inspection.[35]

3. Departments in Charge of the Administration of the Internet

In this regard, it should be borne in mind that in practice the unstreamlined Chinese bureaucratic structures make the regulation of the Internet in China a more complicated picture.

According to the Interim Provisions on the Administration of International Wiring of Computer Information Networks, an agency, i.e. the Leading Group of Informatization (LGI) under the auspice of the State Council, was established. The LGI is entrusted with wide range of powers, including making detailed rules for the implementation of the regulations, regulating the rights and duties of channel providers, ISPs and users, and supervising and inspecting the international wiring of networks.[36] It had the Office of the Leading Group of Informatization as its administrative body. In 1998, the Office of the Leading Group of Informatization and the former State Radio Regulatory Committee became two divisions of the newly established MII. Recently, the LGI was reorganized into a higher-ranking State Leading Group of Informatization (SLGI), with Premier Zhu Rongji as its head.[37]

However, as shown from the Internet regulations that come from various ministries, the LGI is not the sole responsible administrative authority on the Internet. Among the competent authorities, the MII, the MSB and the State Secrecy Bureau (SSB) are particularly worth mentioning. Though the regulatory power has been shifted officially from the Ministry to the IWLG in the field of Internet administration, these bodies are, to some extent, still intertwined. MII is the governing department of China Telecom and is vested with the power to regulate the telecommunication industry. It is believed that drafting the regulations to govern operations of ISPs actually rests on MII rather than IWLG, which is only in charge of writing rules for Internet content providers. As for the MSB and PSBs, which are traditionally seen as "dictatorship organs (*zhuanzheng jiguan*)," they are empowered with a wide range of administrative and quasi-judicial authorities on the Internet.[38] With the Administrative Provisions on Secrecy of Computer Information Systems, one has reason to believe that the police works in close collaboration with the SSB in patrolling the Internet. It is fair to argue in this regard that the enforcement of the Interim Provisions on the Administration of International Wiring of Computer Information Networks rests primarily on the police.

In this context, it is important to bear in mind that in China rules and their implementation often differ. For example, registration and annual renewal with the police is a prerequisite in many localities for end users to plug on to the Internet.[39] However, the personal experience of the author, an enthusiastic user of the Internet, shows the reality is not the same. The author has never renewed registration since 1997 and no de-wiring has been imposed by the local PSB. In other words, there is a possibility that, though the Internet rules feature the usual restrictive rhetoric, they might not generate unwanted fruits.

4. Hidden Agenda behind the Tight Internet Rules

Indeed, governments tend to favour regulation although others see the Internet in a different way.[40] In the West, the government has traditionally had an interest and is allowed to regulate access to such issues as indecency in the following way: it can block out minors as long as it keeps access open for adults.[41] The ground behind is that the government may serve the good of the society as a whole. However, anti-government and political content has been limited or outlawed mainly in nations that traditionally have either not recognized, or given little protection to, freedom of speech.[42] From these governments' perspective, controls are needed to reduce to a minimum the adverse effect of the Internet to the society as a whole.

In China, the government regulation of the Internet is taken for granted. The justification should be traced back to the unique and delicate Chinese culture. In China, the advent of new forms of technology is always a cause for public anxiety and unease. The age-old mantra was *zhongxue weiti, xixue weiyong*, or, Chinese thinking for our essence, western learning for application, is evidence. Historically, the government never hesitated to block access of its people to information it deems politically or culturally suspect. For the Chinese government that deems maintaining stability as its paramount challenge, it is understandable that it attaches ever greater importance to what it calls security of information inflow. A tight censorship has long been established to control the traditional media. The Internet, with its staggering ability to disseminate information quickly and to give an amplified voice to minority views, would pose a fundamental challenge to China's tightly run society. In this connection, it is the natural reaction of the government to design to address politically sensitive issues and combat "spiritual pollution."[43]

However, the Internet rules are also a result of pressure from the monopoly in the telecommunication industry. China Telecom, which used to be the commercial arm of the MPT, has long enjoyed monopoly. Facing the enormous potential that the Internet will bring forth, they are naturally reluctant to lose their monopoly. Their ambitions are reflected in the new regulations,[44] both because of the influence of the monopolies and their allies in the administration and because of the vesting of the regulatory power in the industry.

5. External Pressure for Liberalizing the Internet Regulation: Implications of China's WTO Accession

According to the Provisional Regulations for Guiding the Direction of Foreign Investment and its companion Catalogue for Guiding Foreign Investment in Industry, the telecommunications industry is one of those where foreign investment is prohibited. Although both the Regulations on Telecommunications and the Administrative Measures for the Internet Information Services have been promulgated, neither of them has answered the crucial question of how China should open the telecommunications and Internet sectors to foreign investment. In principle, therefore, there has been almost no direct role for foreign companies in Internet service provision, although foreign portfolio investments have been active in the state-controlled Internet service companies.[45]

In the effort to join the WTO, China has made substantial commitments regarding opening, *inter alia*, the Internet services to foreign participation. The main accession terms relevant for the Internet services sectors, as initially negotiated in the bilateral agreements with the United States and the EU and later incorporated in the Accession Protocol, are:

1. Permit up to 50 percent foreign ownership in value-added and paging services (including Internet, e-mail, voice mail, online information, data retrieval, and enhanced fax) four years after accession (30 percent upon accession) and remove all geographic restrictions on the participation by foreign companies in such services two years after accession.

2. Adhere to the pro-competition and level playing field regulatory principles embodied in the Agreement on Basic Telecommunications Services (ABTS) concerning pricing, interconnection rights, technology-neutral scheduling, domestic leased-circuit services, and independent status of the regulatory authority.

In addition, China agreed to eliminate all current restrictions on domestic distribution and trade, as well as import and export quotas applicable to foreign companies operating in China, by 2003, remove all export requirements, as well as local content restrictions on foreign-invested companies upon accession, and apply all taxes and tariffs uniformly to companies regardless of ownership upon accession.

The long-term social, political, financial, and economic consequences of full implementation of China's commitments are likely to be great. China's pending WTO accession will fundamentally change the landscape of Internet services, and the Chinese market for Internet services will be one of the most open in developing countries.

If fully implemented, China's commitments will also enhance competition. Currently, state-owned telecommunications companies, which are regulated and controlled by the MII, dominate the market for ISPs. The dominant ISP is ChinaNet of China Telecom, which controls 83 percent of all current Internet connections. Many small, local Internet companies exist, but most are struggling financially, in part because of the high rates charged by China Telecom. In the post-WTO era, with foreign participation, the monopoly on the Internet service will unlikely be maintained in the long run. In fact, in order to gain a strategic foothold, many major multinational telecommunications and Internet companies in the world have already begun making investment in China's Internet services sector.[46]

6. Unsettled Issues

Given the restrictive feature of the Internet regulations, a question normally arises whether there are any risks that China will build the electric equivalent of the Great Wall or that the Chinese government will facilitate all sorts of filtering of all sorts of content, at any level on the distributional chain, turning the Internet from this great space of freedom and openness into a space of maximum regulability.

The question has to be explored in the contexts of market-oriented reform and technological aspect of the Internet. It is fair to assert that the Chinese government envisions its relationship with the Internet as one entirely geared towards business, where it serves as a tool to spur China's economic development. In the tech-minded leadership, the Internet is considered a technological area *vis-à-vis* the traditional media that is more restricted. Early in the 1990's the Chinese government began introducing and promoting the application of the Internet, seeing it as strategic in restructuring the economy towards gaining competitive edge. As a matter of fact, the above-mentioned ministerial level body LGI was accordingly established to ensure the widespread application as well as the regulation of the Internet. Given that technology and competitiveness are deeply linked and that the Internet can serve the purpose of making China competitive, what concerns the leadership most is how to get Chinese onto the Internet in an orderly way and how best to explore the Internet, not how to keep the Internet off altogether.

From the technological point of view, it is unlikely that China would be able to resort to the same tight censorship as it used in the traditional media to architect an Intranet whose essence is the control of access and content.

Still, another issue remains to be clarified. While China has pledged to allow 30 percent global stakes in Internet, paging and other value-added services upon accession, rising to 49 percent after one year and 50 percent after two years most Web start-ups in China have upwards of 90 percent outside capital. Will they readjust their portfolio structure in the post-WTO era? Will they survive loopholes and slack enforcement? Almost none of China's major Web sites began as Chinese firms with pre-existing revenues. It is noted that lower incomes, lack of well-established payment infrastructure and consumer reluctance to pay for content have been the main hurdles to the development of the Internet industry, and that all have depended mainly on other investment to survive.

7. Concluding Remarks

As China is readily embracing the IT revolution, it has to deal with an accompanying problem: the regulation of the Internet, which cuts to the heart of issues that are key to China's future, such as how much market competition will be allowed and whether the free flow of information, crucial for economic development, will be hindered by political concerns. China's WTO accession provides a badly needed dimension for Internet regulation. With foreign participation guaranteed by the WTO commitments, the Chinese rules on the Internet, though featuring the usual restrictive rhetoric, should not be so restrictive as to deny free access to the Internet.

In concluding, the Internet regulations in China will serve more than merely as the legal techniques of political control on the Internet in that the government perceives the Internet as a means to its economic end. However, the real challenge is for the Chinese government to balance the need to promote Internet development and its efforts to control the information flow.

It is proposed, in relation to the regulation of the Internet, that special information zones be established with open competition and uncensored Internet access, much like the special economic zones of the 1980s that allowed China to experiment with western ideas and institutions. This has to be prompted by the desire of the government to tap the benefits of the Internet and shows the most revolutionary features of China's information openness. It is also inspiring to note that the Chinese government has reportedly granted the News Corporation and AOL Time Warner, two leading media giants in the world, the concession to access the media market in Guangdong Province, which might signify a gradual relaxation of control on the Internet.[47]

Notes

1. Some small, local Internet experiments started in 1987. China's Internet was formally launched in 1991. It was initially limited to interconnections between university research laboratories, but it has since been expanded nationally. According to China Internet Network Information Centre, in 1994 the use of the Internet was only limited to a small group of computer scientists and students. By 31 December 2001 there were already 33.70 million Chinese with access to the Internet. The Internet monitoring company expects that China will become one of the leading Internet-related markets in the world in ten years.

2. For the past 25 years, the US government administered the overall activity of the Internet with the actual work parceled out to DOD contractor think tanks. During most of this period, the arrangement worked well, since the Internet was owned and operated first exclusively by DOD, then later jointly by DOD together with government science agencies. For important national security

and research reasons, network-wide policies were established, registrations accomplished, databases maintained, and public directory services made available.

3. Among them are the Regulations on the Safeguard of Computer Information System (the State Council, 18 February, 1994), the Interim Provisions on the Administration of International Wiring of Computer Information Networks (1 February 1996, revised on 20 May 1997), the Rules for the Administration of International Wiring Gateway for Inbound and Outbound Computer Information (Ministry of Post and Telecommunication, 9 April 1996), Circulars of the Ministry of Public Security on the Recording of the Internationally-wired Computer Information System (29 January 1996), the Interim Rules on the Connection between Specialized Networks and the Public Network (Ministry of Post and Telecommunication, 24 July 1996) and the Administrative Provisions on Secrecy of Computer Information Systems (State Secrecy Bureau, 1 January 2000).

4. Jasper Becker, Mainland clamps down on Net, *South China Morning Post*, Internet Edition, 27 January 2000.

5. Article 6, the Administrative Provisions on Secrecy of Computer Information Systems.

6. Article 2 of the State Secrecy Law.

7. Article 9 of the Administrative Provisions on Secrecy of Computer Information Systems.

8. It is no secret that in China not only is the traditional media used by the CPC and the government as state instruments for blatant political propaganda, but it is also put under strict monitoring. According to a study, all materials are reviewed by the CPC officials. See Suzanne Ogden, *China's Unresolved Issues* (3rd ed.), Englewood Clifts, N.J.: Prentice Hall, 1995, p. 150.

9. For instance, it may frighten off foreign investment that is badly needed to nurture the nascent Chinese Internet industry and kill hopes that China's entry into the World Trade Organization will signal a new openness to technological advance and Internet use.

10. For instance, see Carolyn Ong, *et al.*, Taming the web, *South China Morning Post*, 27 January 2000.

11. A member of the News Department of Sina.com, a leading Chinese ISP, admitted that it had to wait for an official organization to release sensitive news before it could upload the information on its website. See Mark O'Neill, Battle of new and old media, *South China Morning Post*, the Internet Edition, 19 February 2000. As a matter of fact, the self-censoring is also a natural response of the ISPs in the context that it is up to the government to determine whether or not to approve the listing of the ISPs, which are starters and badly need capital from the financial market.

One Chinese scholar even proposed that besides self-censorship the ISPs have the following obligations: 1) regular check. The ISPs shall check the on-line information released by their domestic clients to ensure that it is proper; 2) monitoring and screening .The ISPs shall monitor regularly foreign Websites or on-line information sources and screen that "politically reactionary" or pornographic or "not really useful"; 3) notification and reporting. The ISPs shall notify the relevant government authorities of any release of prohibited information and "unfit" foreign Websites the fate of which will be left at the disposal of the government; 4) cooperation. The ISPs shall cooperate with the relevant authorities in regulating the Internet and investigating on-line crimes. See Sun Tiecheng, Legal Problems of Computer Networks, in The Editing Group of Jurisprudence Frontiers (in Chinese), *Jurisprudence Frontiers*, Beijing: Law Press, 1999, pp. 99-100.

12. Article 13, the Interim Provisions on the Administration of International Wiring of Computer Information Networks.

13. It suffices to mention that same rigid censorship applies on the Internet in Singapore. See Garry Rodan, The Internet and Political Control in Singapore, *Political Science Quarterly*, 113 (1998), pp.71-76.

14. Article 4, the Administrative Measures for the Internet Information Services.

15. Article 6, the Administrative Measures for the Internet Information Services.

16. Article 6, the Interim Provisions on the Administration of International Wiring of Computer Information Networks. When the Interim Provisions on the Administration of International Wiring of Computer Information Networks were promulgated, China Telecom was a department of the MPT, which was later renamed "MII." Therefore, Article 6 referred to the "public network maintained by the MPT" as the international gateway.

17. Article 2 of the Rules for the Administration of International Wiring Gateway for Inbound and Outbound Computer Information.

18. Article 6 (2), the Interim Provisions on the Administration of International Wiring of Computer Information Networks.

19. When the Interim Provisions on the Administration of International Wiring of Computer Information Networks were promulgated, there were only four gateways, i.e. ChinaNet, CERNET, CSTNET and GBNet. Therefore, Article 7 recognized these four existing inter-wired networks.

20. Article 10, the Interim Provisions on the Administration of International Wiring of Computer Information Networks.

21. Up to the end of 1999 there were 520 ISPs in China. Reuters, 15 February 2000.

22. Article 8, the Interim Provisions on the Administration of International Wiring of Computer Information Networks.

23. Article 13, the Interim Provisions on the Administration of International Wiring of Computer Information Networks.

24. Article 7, the Regulations on the Safeguard of Computer Information System.
25. Article 3.5, Decision on Safeguarding the Internet.
26. According to the Criminal Law, a person may be sentenced to 10 years' imprisonment or even life imprisonment.
27. The facts were reported by media in China and abroad. See generally, *Lianhe Zaobao*, 6 December 1998, the Internet edition. It may be interesting to observe that it is apparently illegal even in the West for a business to disclose, without prior consent, its clients' information obtained through commercial channels. However, the difference in approach, taken by China and the West in dealing with this issue, is striking. It should be noted that the competent Chinese authority would not find itself in a position to charge the violating business—because there is no applicable rule of torts.
28. The Chen Brothers apparently violated the provision that only entities are entitled to act as the ISPs.
29. Unfortunately, such a regulation was approved, apparently only to maintain the telecommunication monopoly, in September 1998, nine months after the business of Chen brothers was shut down.
30. John Pomfret, China's Telecoms Battle, *International Herald Tribune*, 26 January 1999.
31. Article 13 of the Order provides that imported Commercial Encryption Codes (CEC) products, imported equipment containing CEC technologies and exported CEC products must be approved by the National Commission on Encryption Code Regulations (NCECR) and that no work units or individuals may sell foreign CEC products. Article 15 further provides that foreign organizations or individuals using CEC products or equipment containing CEC technologies within the borders of China are required to report these products and their use to the NCECR and obtain approval.
32. Article 20(2), the Regulations on the Safeguard of Computer Information System.
33. Article 10, the Administrative Provisions on Secrecy of Computer Information Systems; Article 2, the Decision on Safeguarding the Internet.
34. Article 5, the Administrative Measures for Services on Electronic Bulletin Boards.
35. Article 14, the Administrative Measures for Services on Electronic Bulletin Boards.
36. Article 5, the Interim Provisions on the Administration of International Wiring of Computer Information Networks.
37. See *Ming Pao News*, 27 September 2001.
38. The police is vested with the quasi-judicial power to issue warnings, order the cessation of wiring, and impose a fine of no more than RMB 15,000 *yuan*

(US$1,800) for, among other things, violations of the requirement to use the public gateway for international wiring, violations of the requirement that wired networks must carry out international wiring through an interconnected network; and violations of the requirements that Internet users must carry out international wiring through a wired network. See Article of 14, the Interim Provisions on the Administration of International Wiring of Computer Information Networks.

39. For instance, Zhejiang Province. Apparently, this local measures (*tu banfa*) regarding annual renewal are further restraints in addition to the Article 20(2), the Regulations on the Safeguard of Computer Information System.

40. For them cyberspace is itself a regulator and governmental regulation is redundant and therefore conventional politics should not apply to the Internet. Technically, if the unfettered access to the Internet is being threatened, the dream of universal access will remain only a dream. Politically, without free and unfettered access to the Internet, this exciting new medium could become little more than a souped-up television network. Internet is "the most participatory form of mass speech yet developed," and should be entitled to "the highest protection from governmental intrusion." In view of this, they firmly hold that government censorship of the Internet violates the freedom of speech.

41. Pornography is almost universally criticized. Governments of almost every nation which has access to the Internet have pronounced certain limitations on the transmission of pornographic materials over the Internet. For instance, on 8 February 1996 the US President, Bill Clinton, signed into law the Telecommunication Act of 1996, which includes the Communications Decency Act of 1996 (CDA)—an exclusively Internet-related section. The CDA declared that ISPs would be criminally liable for transmitting "indecent" material without restricting access to minors. In 1997 the Federal Republic of Germany adopted a similar law on the Internet, which authorizes the punishment of ISPs failing to comply with the "decent" rule. See U.S.C. § 223 (a)-(h); Compuserve Deutschland GmbH case, see, generally, Determann Lothar, The New German Internet Law, *Hastings International and Comparative Law Review*, Vol. 22 (1998), pp. 117-124.

42. See, for instance, Wayne Arnold, Cyberpatrols: Censoring the net isn't easy, but it can be intimidating, in *Asian Wall Street Journal*, 11 September 1996, p.1.

43. The term "spiritual pollution" normally refers to, among other things, political dissent and pornography.

44. For instance, Article 2, the Administration of International Wiring Gateway for Inbound and Outbound Computer Information.

45. For instance, all the three major Internet portals, i.e. Sina.com, Sohu.com and Netease.com, are primarily financed by foreign venture capitals and have been listed in Nasdaq over-the-counter market. The scenario is even more impressive if consideration is taken of the Hong Kong initial public offerings of China Telecom, through which the government decides to sell more of the shares it holds in this state-controlled Internet gateway and services giant.

46. On 24 September 1999, the US Internet player Yahoo! launched Yahoo!China. This enterprise is a joint venture between Beijing Founder Electronics Co., a leading Chinese computer company, and Yahoo! to provide Chinese online information and advertisement services: see Reuters 24 September 1999. On 11 June 2001, AOL Time Warner, the largest media corporation, and the Chinese computer maker Legend Holdings set up a US$200 joint venture to provide online services in China. The venture is 51 percent owned by Legend and 49 percent owned by America Online, a subsidiary of AOL Time Warner. Reportedly, the joint venture partners hope to combine AOL's marketing and technology expertise with Legend's leadership and brand recognition in the Chinese market for personal computer for consumers. However, since China has so far prohibited foreign ownership of content providers, AOL will initially have to provide technical support and consultation. See *China Daily*, 12 June 2001.

47. *The New York Times*, 5 September 2001, Internet Edition, available at http://college1.nytimes.com/guests/articles/2001/09/05/866101.xml.

12
Judicial Protection of Intellectual Property Rights in China: On the Eve of WTO Accession*

1. The Overall Situation of Intellectual Property Protection

Protection of intellectual property rights (IPRs) in China has been the subject of domestic and international attention during the past few years. On the one hand, the Chinese government recognized the importance, for its sustainable growth, of protecting IPRs and therefore has been striving to develop its IPRs law system. On the other, inadequate protection of foreign IPRs in China[1] once constituted one of the biggest obstacles to China's accession to WTO and has remained a source of external pressure. In this context, China started upgrading its IPRs laws when the bilateral IPRs agreements with the United States were concluded in 1992 and 1995.[2] On the eve of its WTO accession, the first major revision to its overall IPRs regime is coming to an end and accordingly,[3] an IPRs regime is emerging that provides a high standard for protection of IPRs comparable to that of the Agreement of Trade-Related Aspects of Intellectual Property Rights

* This article was first published in the November 2001 issue of *The Journal of World Intellectual Property* (Vol. 4, No. 6) and is reproduced by permission of its publisher.

(TRIPS). It is fair to argue that China has so far established a comprehensive and high-standard IPRs regime that is modeled on international standards. As a matter of fact, China's IPRs laws not only meet, but also, on some points, exceed the standards of the principal international treaties. In parallel with the effort to update its IPRs law, China has taken aggressive steps in recent years to improve IPRs enforcement. Amid the cry for protection of IPRs, the State Council promulgated a Decision Concerning Further Strengthening of Intellectual Property Rights Protection Work on 5 July 1994. Since then, there have been attempts by the government on capacity building for IPRs enforcement. There are signs that the Chinese government wishes to strengthen its hand administratively in the field of law enforcement. In April 1998, the Patent Administration Office was transformed into the State Intellectual Property Office, a move some observers believe is the first step towards unifying the regulators in the field of IPRs. In December 1999, the Administration of Industry and Commerce was restructured to the effect that an Administration of Industry and Commerce is directly responsible to the Administration of Industry and Commerce above, rather than to the local government. The reform strengthened the power of Administrations at higher levels, thus making it easier for local administrations to carry out the orders of the higher Administrations and to shun off local protection in regard to trademark infringement and unfair competitive acts.

In addition, enforcement of IPRs is now characterized with a combination of the launches of enforcement campaigns and regular enforcement. For instance, in 1997 and 1998 alone, China closed down at least 72 illegal makers of compact disc. In 1999, the State Administration of Industry and Commerce and its local branches dealt with 16,938 cases of counterfeiting, 1810 of which involved infringement of foreign trademarks, the total fine was RMB 106 million *yuan* and ordered compensation was RMB 5.717 million *yuan*. Twenty-one persons were subjected to criminal prosecution. In 1999, the General Administration of Customs and its local offices dealt with 178 cases of trademark infringement worth RMB 61.98 million *yuan*. In 2000, the patent administrative authorities of provinces and the main cities accepted 802 cases of patent disputes in total.

In addition, several administrative enforcement authorities join forces to act against infringement of a specific IPRs. In March 2000, for instance, the State Press and Publication Administration (SPPA), the National Copyright Administration of China (NCAC), the Ministry of Public Security (MPC), and the State Administration of Industry and Commerce (SAIC) issued an urgent joint circular to urge every provincial, regional and municipal government authority to launch a special campaign against DVD piracy in China. In the same year, the State Intellectual Property Office (SIPO), the MOFTEC, the General Customs Administration of China (GCAC), the SAIC and the State Administration Bureau of Entry-Exit jointly issued "the Notification of Carrying on the Actions of Attacking the Acts of Counterfeiting UL Mark."[4] In an effort to bring IPRs enforcement into WTO compliance, for example, China established a new National Anticounterfeiting Coordination Committee, chaired by Deputy Premier Wu Bangguo.

As a result, infringement of IPRs has been substantially reduced. The production of pirated copyrighted works, for example, has dropped dramatically since 1996.[5]

More importantly, however, China has agreed in the context of the negotiations on accession to the WTO to implement the TRIPS Agreement without recourse to any transition period. Honoring the commitment means making available enforcement measures and sanctions able to deter further infringing activity and this move is expected to strengthen the protection of IPRs.

In this context, the latest revisions of the IPRs laws, which lend support to enforcement, including specifying detailed procedures for litigation, granting more power to local officials to investigate cases of infringement, and offering more compensation for infringement, serve an encouraging example of China's determination to honor the commitment.[6]

Despite the achievements, enforcement of foreign IPRs still remains a problem. End-user piracy of business software, trademark infringement, and retail piracy and counterfeit goods remain widespread in China—although pirated products are mainly imports.[7] Moreover, obtaining administrative protection for pharmaceuticals is still a persistent problem. This is partly because of the inadequacy of deterrent sanctions, including less harsh criminal penalties, due in some part to the opaque structure of IPRs administration and enforcement in China.[8]

It is not difficult to note that enforcement of IPRs is generally shared by administrative organs and the judiciary.[9] However, due to the uniqueness of the Chinese society—dominance of the administrative authority, and the reluctance to resolve disputes through methods other than litigation, the administrative organs have so far played a much more important role than the judiciary. It is a blessing that judicial enforcement by Chinese courts, which used to be useless particularly in infringement of trademark cases, has become increasingly competent in recent years, since around the mid 1990s. Amidst the efforts of the Chinese authorities to improve the enforcement of IPRs in 1994, the Supreme People's Court (SPC) promulgated the Circular on Further Strengthening Judicial Protection of Intellectual Property, a milestone in the history of judicial enforcement of IPRs in China.

It is particularly worthwhile to mention the special role of the SPC, the highest judiciary body in China. By hearing a bunch of appeal IPRs cases, the SPC sets the example of enforcing IPRs, and the cases it adjudicates serve as references for all courts across the whole country. In addition, the SPC has made quite a few judicial interpretations on IPRs that are binding on all the courts.[10]

Table 12.1 The IPRs (Civil) Cases
Accepted by the People's Courts (1996–1999)

	Number of Civil Cases in:					
	Copyright	Technology contract	Patent	Trademark	Know-how infringement	Total
1999	750	942	1,485	460	645	4,282
1998	571	1,175	1,162	527	658	4,093
1997	411	936	1,045	338	914	3,644
1996	436	1,221	1,184	320	600	3,761

Source: Compiled by the author from *China Law Yearbook*, Law Press, Beijing, 1997, 1998, 1999 and 2000.

Judicial enforcement of IPRs is realized through case handling by the courts. Chinese courts deal with civil cases where the IPRs proprietors file suits with the court against infringers, criminal cases where prosecutors file criminal charges against suspected infringers, and administrative litigation cases where the parties who are dissatisfied with administrative acts by authorities for IPRs administration, initiate administrative litigations. A statistical analysis of the cases handled by Chinese courts in recent years shows that the total number of cases that the judiciary has accepted is steadily going up, which reflects the fact that the judicial enforcement of IPRs has gradually gained more weight.

2. Institutional Characteristics of Judicial Enforcement of Intellectual Property

Judicial enforcement of IPRs requires highly specialized and professional adjudicators. Therefore, early in 1992, the SPC designated certain Intermediate People's Courts as the first instance courts for patent disputes. These are often better staffed with more knowledgeable judges than other Intermediate People's Courts or the basic people's courts.[11] More importantly, in August 1993, the first Intellectual Property Tribunal in the Beijing Municipal Intermediate People's Court was set up in China. This triggered the trend of forming specialized IPRs tribunals within the existing court system. In October 1996, the SPC set up an IPRs division in order to improve the quality of such trials throughout China. This move has been followed by high people's courts or intermediate people's courts in more than twenty provinces and major cities that decided to set up similar tribunals. Up to August 2001, there were 50 such specialized tribunals.

Among the important courts now prepared to deal effectively with IPRs cases, are those in Beijing, Shanghai, Tianjin and in the provinces of Guandong, Fujian, Jiangsu, Hainan, Sichuan, Chongqing, Henan and Liaoning. In certain jurisdictions, specialists in IPRs law also work in the Intermediate People's Courts in the capitals of some provinces, as well as in the special economic zones of Shenzhen, Zhuhai, Shantou and Xiamen. Some basic people's courts even set up IPRs tribunals, for example, in the Haidian District of Beijing, or the Pudong and Huangpu Districts of Shanghai. Within the existing Chinese court framework, these specialist tribunals only handle IPRs cases.

In the jurisdictions where no specialized IPRs tribunals have been established, given the comparatively few cases, Intermediate People's Courts have become the first instance courts for civil IPRs cases, a symbol for higher level judiciary protection.

Generally speaking, specialized IPRs tribunals and other courts that have the power to adjudicate IPRs cases are staffed with new-generation judges who have received a better education in science, engineering and foreign languages and who are eager to deal with IPRs issues in a way that meets international standards. By trying IPRs cases through the special tribunals, a degree of consistency in law enforcement is assured. As a result of experience thus accumulated, the judges are able to raise the quality and accuracy of cases involving IPRs. Many of them receive on-the-job training, and some are sent abroad for further study.[12] In all, this practice serves two functions: it creates models for legal reform throughout the larger Chinese legal system and provide a foundation for a cadre of legal experts well versed in IPRs rules and procedures.

Nevertheless, the judicial enforcement of IPRs is crippled by institutional defects. One defect is that, under the current court system, administrative and criminal cases are held before the administrative and criminal tribunals. When these types of proceedings are related to IPRs, the administrative and criminal tribunals may be unfit for adjudicating these cases due to lack of expertise.

To make it worse, the adjudication committee system further produces an obstacle.[13] Apart from the fact that judicial independence may be undermined, the adjudicating committee that often consists of non-professional ranking officials is often not in a position to handle sophisticated IPRs cases.

Another institutional failing is that the judicial review system has not been firmly established. Article 12 of the Administrative Procedural Law (APL) provides that courts shall not accept any suits against "specific administrative acts that shall, as provided by law, be finally decided by an administrative organ." This provision is clearly inconsistent with TRIPS rules allowing judicial review.[14] Indeed, the Patent Law has been amended to the effect that judicial review will be allowed regarding the decision of the patent authority on utility models and designs. However, since the APL is one of the basic laws made by the NPC, which in the hierarchy of the Chinese law system, are superior in force to the laws by NPC Standing Committee. The Patent Law, the Trademark Law and the Copyright Law being these inferior laws, it is not clear whether all the tribunals and courts will faithfully enforce the new provisions in these amended IPRs laws.

A further defect is that adjournments in the adjudicating process of utility models and designs cases often cause "delayed justice." When handling cases involving conflicting claims on the propriety of the disputed utility models and designs, Chinese courts tend to adjourn the cases until the pertinent administrative authorities have decided on the rights according to the invalidation procedure. If the IPRs conflict still remains unsolved following the relevant invalidation procedure, after three months from the date of filing a request by the party without justified reason, Chinese courts apply the principles of honesty and provide the protection to the earliest granted IPRs holder or the prior user. This practice prolongs the proceedings. Moreover, the real infringer could thereby defer the proceedings merely by making a counterclaim that the IPRs concerned was invalid.[15]

3. Procedures for Judicial Enforcement of Intellectual Property Rights

In addition to seeking administrative sanction, any person or organization whose IPRs have been infringed may sue in a Chinese court to ask for judicial protection. A court trial is a final resort and may be pursued when necessary. Judicial enforcement is afforded in three ways. One is a civil remedy, which includes an order to stop infringement, to pay damages or to issue an apology. Another is a finding of criminal responsibility. This includes a fine or a fixed term of imprisonment imposed upon the person found guilty of infringement. The third way is to initiate an administrative litigation where the IPRs holder's interest is affected by the act of an administrative authority.

In civil cases, the party whose IPRs have been infringed has several remedies open to him. For example, the IPRs holder may ask the court to render judgment to stop infringement, to award damages and/or an apology for infringement.

In view of the high professional requirement needed for IPRS cases, Chinese courts require the parties to submit supporting evidence before the opening of a hearing. The submitted evidence is exchanged among the parties. The evidence relating to facts including professional opinion has to be questioned in court in the parties' presence for it to be accepted by the court. In one case, the SPC ordered a High People's Court to form a new panel and re-try the IPRs case involving admission of evidence which had not been cross-examined in court.[16]

Chinese courts have gained increasing judicial power to act against IPRs infringement through strengthened procedures. The Civil Procedure Law (CPL) has no specific reference to "preliminary injunctions." However, when a Chinese court is determined that evidence should be preserved as a protective measure, where there is a likelihood that it may be distorted, lost or become difficult to obtain later, provision is made for preservation of evidence.[17] In these cases evidence can be confiscated, or property can be legally impounded. Moreover, the newly amended Patent Law authorizes, for the first time in the history of IPRs legislation, judicial protective measures[18] amounting to "preliminary injunction" and "provisional measures," terms used to denote that the court is acting in advance of a final judgment because of the fear that the applicant's livelihood or production operations could be harmed if the court failed to take action while the case was under consideration.[19] The SPC further specified the procedures for such provisional measures in association with patent infringement.[20] Chinese courts may take such actions at the request of any party in order to provide temporary protection, or the courts may act on their own initiative when necessary. Evidence or property protection and advance execution measures have proven rather effective in a number of cases. For example, in the case of Microsoft v. Beijing Juren Computer Company *et al.*, upon the request of the plaintiffs and on the condition that they provided valid security, the Beijing Municipal People's Intermediate Court ordered evidence and property protection measures. Seven computers and 366 floppy disks were impounded as the case proceeded to judgment.[21]

The CPL and the Criminal Procedure Law empower courts to address IPRs infringement through measures to stop the infringement, preserve property before and during litigation,[22] and to order the infringer to provide compensation to right holder for infringement. In addition, the courts also act to preserve evidence to permit effective litigation.

According to law and the judicial interpretation of the SPC, there are three methods of calculating compensation for IPRs infringement: The first one is to take the actual losses caused by infringement as the criterion for the computation of compensation. The second is to take the illegal income of the infringer as the criterion, and the third method is to take more than a fair and reasonable royalty or transfer fee for the infringed IPRs as the criterion. In addition, Chinese judges have also created and accumulated other methods of calculating compensation for these types of cases. For example, when calculating the loss for trademark infringement, the number of infringement products multiplied by the reasonable profit per brand product of the trademark owner might be taken. It is worth mentioning that the concept of "statutory damages" has also been used to decide a fixed amount of compensation when both the actual loss by the IPRs owner and the profits of the infringer are too difficult to be proved. The fixed amount of compensation ranges from RMB 5,000 *yuan* to RMB 500,000 *yuan* at the court's discretion, taking into account the type and appraised value of the infringed IPRs, the time-frame of the infringement, the damages suffered by the IPRs owner, etc. Under certain conditions, Chinese judges may also award the IPRs owner a reasonable amount for attorney's fees and the costs of stopping and eliminating the infringement. Given the discretionary power, some courts (for example in Guangdong Province) are prepared to award more compensation than others. This is a welcome sign for IPRs holders.

Criminal charges concerning IPRs are limited to infringements that endanger the social or economic order or the national interest. Criminal charges could be filed in the following cases: the counterfeiting of patents;[23] the counterfeiting of trademarks;[24] the unauthorized reproduction of another person's works, including published materials, records or video tapes; making and/or selling a work of fine art with a forged signature of another author. Equally, it is a crime to knowingly sell infringed works.[25] However, the procedures for criminal indictment are not always so clear as to follow. Fortunately, the SPC and the Supreme People's Prosecutorate have moved a step forward by issuing, in April 2001, judicial interpretation and prosecution guidelines which establish new and clearer standards for criminal liability in counterfeiting cases.[26]

4. A Selection of Cases Handled by the Judiciary

4.1. Cases of copying

One major type of infringement commonly found in China is the outright copying of other's patent, registered marks or copyright. Another often encountered type is passing-off. The following four cases illustrate.

Case 1: *Walt Disney Company v. Beijing Publishing Company*
Walt Disney v. Beijing Publishing Company[27] was a case of outright copyright piracy. In 1995, Disney charged that the Beijing Publishing Company, Beijing Children's Press and New China Bookstore had illegally reproduced and sold its Disney Virtue Story Series books, and petitioned the Beijing Municipal People's High Court to stop the infringement, make a public apology in the media and order compensation of RMB 177,000 *yuan*. The defendants argued that it had procured from Maxwell, a Hong Kong-based company, the consent for publishing the books. The court ruled that Disney enjoyed copyright to the artistic work of cartoon images in the United States and, since the coming into force of the Sino-US IPRs MOU in 1992, the copyright need to be protected in China. The infringement was, therefore, held established. According to the MOU, however, the US copyrighted products were not protected in China prior to 1992. Therefore, the compensation needed to be reduced accordingly. In the end, Beijing Publishing Company and the other defendants were ordered to stop infringement and to pay the plaintiff RMB 227,000 *yuan* as damages, and to make a public apology in newspapers and magazines.

The high-profile case set an example for judicial enforcement of foreign IPRs following the historical bilateral agreement on IPRs. However, in a similar outright infringement case, the court seemed to be influenced by domestic opinion.

Case 2: *Microsoft v. Yadu Technology Corporation*

Microsoft is the copyright owner of the computer software MS-DOS, MS-Windows 95 (Chinese edition), MS-Window 95 (English edition), etc. After an investigation (the result was notarized), more than fifty computers were found installed with pirated software at the Beijing Yadu Technology Corporation (Yadu). Microsoft, who had been grilled in the antitrust action in the United States, sued Yadu for copyright infringement at the Beijing No. 1 Intermediate People's Court in April 1999.[28] The case was seen as a landmark copyright suit in China and a test of Beijing's activism in pursuing IPRs abuses, following its bilateral agreement with the United States regarding accession to the WTO reached in November 1999. A Microsoft announcement that IPRs protection is critical to the development of knowledge economy, was therefore perceived as not only putting pressure on the Court to protect the copyright, but also interpreted as hinting at its expectation of the outcome of the suit. However, many Chinese viewed it differently, some even cried to "Strike Microsoft's Intellectual Hegemony." The dispute was heard at the Court in a mixed atmosphere. At the hearing, the plaintiff alleged that the defendant's act had reduced its own costs of operation by tens of thousands of RMB *yuan*. That is, the defendant had illegally gained extra profit of the said amount, and had directly inflicted on the plaintiff a loss of over RMB 800,000 *yuan*. The plaintiff petitioned the Court to make a judgement in its favor by ordering the defendant to stop the infringement, make a public announcement of apology, and pay it RMB 1,500,000 *yuan* in compensation as well as other reasonable litigation fees. The defendant argued that it should not be cited as the defendant and copyright infringer because it had never reproduced and used the allegedly infringed software. The defendant also argued that the notary paper, provided by the plaintiff as evidence, was illegal. After court investigation and debate, the Court sponsored a mediation between the parties concerned. The mediation could not generate an agreement of settlement, so the collegial bench announced the adjournment of the case hearing. The court announced the decision on 21 December 1999, ruling that Microsoft had not provided sufficient proof that it was suing the right company. In such a case, a plaintiff like Microsoft whose software piracy case had been surprisingly thrown out would naturally tend to suspect that the Court had acted under the domestic pressure for striking what was termed as arrogant hegemonism. Although the court was not to be faulted ruling after the hearing,[29] its sponsoring the mediation and then adjourning the announcement of the verdict might have been perceived as being prejudiced against the plaintiff.

Case 3: *Shijiazhuang Falande Development Company v. Beijing Mitian Jiaye Jimao Company*

The *Shijiazhuang Falande* case is a pass-off case. The plaintiff is the registrar of the PDA trademark, which was registered in Class 9 on March 1997. In late 1998, the plaintiff, trying to reserve the Internet domain name <pda.com.cn> discovered, for the first time, that the defendant, without its authorization, had already reserved the domain name at the China Internet Network Information Center (CNNIC) and established a Website for advertising and selling the laptop computers made by other producers; moreover, there was a "PDA" logo on the home page. The defendant's reservation of the domain name had precluded the plaintiff from reserving the same domain name which incorporated its registered trademark. After failing to get the domain name, the plaintiff brought an action against the defendant on the basis of trademark infringement and unfair competition at the Beijing Municipal No. 1 Intermediate People's Court. The defendant argued that the trademark infringement and unfair competition could not be established because "PDA" is the acronym of " personal digital assistant" (the generic name for personal lap top computers); and "PDA" was an entry in some English-Chinese dictionaries and was widely used in the industry. This meant, it has been in the public domain and therefore could not be monopolized by the plaintiff as a trademark. In the judgement, the court decided that trademark infringement and unfair competition were not established because: (a) using a registered trademark as a part of a domain name is not the trademark owner' exclusive right and it is also outside the scope of trademark infringement according to the Trademark Law; (b) "PDA" is the generic name of laptop computers and the plaintiff has not proved it is a well-known trademark and that the public has been misled because of the defendant's act."[30]

The case became well-known throughout China and caused anxieties in the trademark and Internet circles, because at that time the Trademark Law and Unfair Competition Law did not provide specific clauses concerning trademark protection on the Internet. At the same time, there are different opinions and heated debates among the experts of the trademark and Internet circles. Some trademark owners who want to use their marks as domain names will certainly have found that unrelated persons have already taken the best names. And it is also generally recognized that it is very difficult for them to find the best legal means to solve this problem at the present time. Given that the trademark "PDA" was later revoked, the impact of the judgment died out. However, one might have to ask what would happen if the trademark concerned is well secured under the Trademark Law. Fortunately, a similar case heard by the same court somewhat reduced the worries.

Case 4: *Procter & Gamble Company v. Beijing Tide Electronic Engineering Corporation*

In the *Procter & Gamble v. Beijing Tide* case,[31] the plaintiff, a consumer product company, is the registrar of the trademark "Tide" in China. When trying to register the Internet domain name <www.tide.com.cn>, the plaintiff discovered that the defendant, without its authorization, had already reserved the domain name at the CNNIC and established a Website for advertising and selling its electronic products. In the negotiation initiated by the plaintiff, the defendant agreed to "transfer the domain name" to the plaintiff for over RMB 1 million yuan. In response, the plaintiff brought an action against the defendant for infringing its well-known trademark and for unfair competition at the Beijing Municipal No. 1 People's Court. The defendant argued that accusation of trademark infringement and unfair competition were not grounded, for as the plaintiff's trademark is for washing powder and related products, its registration of the domain name for a company of electronic products did not constitute infringement of that trademark. It further added that the trademark "Tide" was not entitled to the protection accorded to well-known trademarks because the State Administration of Industry and Commerce had never publicized that it was a well-known trademark. In the judgement, the court decided that the trademark infringement and unfair competition were established because: the Paris Convention on the Protection of Industrial Property applied in this case; despite the provision concerning recognition of well-known trademarks by the State Administration of Industry and Commerce, the court itself has the power to determine whether a trademark in question is a well-known trademark; and the trademark "Tide" is a well-known trademark and entitled to special protection and in this case, the owner of the well-known trademark should be protected against unauthorized use of the trademark on the Internet, regardless of the type of product the trademark is used for.

In this case, it is particularly noticeable that the court asserted its own power, instead of general practice of letting the trademark authority determine whether a trademark is a well-known trademark and was well able to enforce the rights accorded to well-known trademarks by the Paris Convention.

4.2. New types of problems

The following two cases show how Chinese courts deal with new problems arising from enforcement of IPRs. They have demonstrated the ability to absorb the advanced legal knowledge for that purpose and the audacity to assert the due power of the court.

Case 1: *Chen Weihua v. Chengdu Computer Business Information*
The *Chen* Weihua case[32] is the first Internet-related case of copyright infringement in China. The plaintiff maintained a personal home page, "Talking about 3D," in his pen name "Wu Fang." Since January 1998, files have been uploaded onto this personal home page, mainly articles on 3D. On 10 May 1998, an article entitled "Talking about MAYA Dramatically" was uploaded onto this homepage. The author was also mentioned as "Wu Fang." A copyright statement saying "Copyright Reserved" accompanied the work

online. On 16 October 1998, the defendant published this article in its newspaper, Computer Business Information, with the author being named as "Wu Fang." The plaintiff sued the defendant for copyright infringement at the Haidian District People's Court of Beijing, asking the court to make a judgement in his favor by ordering the defendant to: apologize publicly; pay a remuneration of RMB 231 *yuan*, and pay punitive damages of RMB 50,000 *yuan*. The court held that the copyright infringement was established and the defendant was the infringer. The court made its ruling of first instance on 28 April 1999; the defendant was to: stop its infringing act; make an open apology in the Computer Business Information; and pay a compensation of RMB 924 *yuan* to the plaintiff.

The court failed to provide for compensation as requested by the copyright owner and, more importantly, it is still open to debate whether the court was correct in linking copyrightable works to being reproduced in a tangible medium.[33] However, it set an example for enforcing copyright on works on the Internet in the absence of specific regulations. Copyright is, by nature, an exclusive right that the author is entitled to for his work. The court gave an expansive interpretation of the term "works" in the Copyright Law, which means intellectual creations with originality in the literary, artistic or scientific domain in so far as they are capable of being reproduced in a tangible form. It held that an intellectual creation should be fixed in a tangible medium of expression and kept stable enough to permit it to be reproduced or contacted by the public directly or with the help of some machines. It reasoned that the work in question could be fixed in a digital style in the hard disc of the computer, uploaded onto the Internet through a <www> server and kept stable enough to be accessed and reproduced by the public via any host. Therefore, this work was deemed to be a copyrightable work. The defendant put the work in its newspaper with some advertisements-that is, without the plaintiff's permission, and for a commercial purpose-obviously violating the plaintiff's right of exploitation and the right to remuneration.

The result of this case is a clear sign that Chinese courts are prepared to ensure protection of new types of IPRs, despite the absence of relevant laws and regulations.

Case 2: *TMT Company v. Guangdong Light Industry Products Import & Export Company*

The trademarks TMT, TMC and SMT were designed and first used and registered abroad by the TMT Company, a Hong Kong-based firm. In 1979, TMT Company authorized Guangdong Light Industry Products Import & Export Company to produce articles bearing those trademarks. All these articles were exported for sale by TMT Company. In 1980, as a foreign firm, TMT Company failed to register the trademarks in China under the trademark regulations then, and authorized Guangdong Light Industry to register the trademarks with the Trademark Bureau of China in its own name. In 1997, the long-standing cooperation between the two firms broke up and TMT named another Chinese firm to replace Guangdong Light Industry. Guangdong Light Industry submitted an application to the Customs, in the name of the owner of the trademarks, for an injunction on exports bearing the trademarks and claimed royalty for use of the trademarks from TMT Company. Subsequently, TMT Company brought a suit before the High People's Court of Guangdong Province for termination of the agency between the two firms and claimed damages. The High Court rendered a judgment in favour of TMT Company. Guangdong Light Industry appealed to the SPC. It pleaded, among other things, that the High People's Court did not have jurisdiction over this case because it was about the ownership of trademarks. Regardless of the statutory provisions asserting the decisions of the Trademark Bureau of China are final concerning the proprietary of trademarks, the SPC seized the jurisdiction and pronounced a judgement by holding that disputes over propriety of trademarks belong to disputes over civil rights.[34] This case shows how the SPC took initiative in applying law by reference to the general principle of judicial review from the jurisprudence of other countries.

Case 3: *Beijing Golden Human Computer Co. Ltd. v. Huistt Science and Technology Development Centre*

In the *Huistt* case,[35] the plaintiff developed the software "*Gu Sheng*" (*God of Securities*) in 1997 and in the following years the software sold well. In 1999, it filed for software copyright registration with the NCAC. In the

the same year, it applied to the Trademark Office for registration of the trademark "*Gu Sheng*" in Class 9 of the international classification system, which stands for computer hardware. The Trademark Office later made a preliminary approval.[36] In 2000, the defendant opposed the application to the Trademark Office following gazetting of the trademark, claiming it was unjustifiable and the Trademark Office's review of the objection was pending when the dispute was referred to the Haidian People's Court in Beijing. Early April 1999, the defendant produced its software "*Gushi Jingdian*" (Classics of Securities Market). However, the software packages was labeled as "*Gu Sheng 2000*" as well as "*Gushi Jingdian Qianxi Ban*" (Classics of Securities Market, Millenium Edition). The court ruled that the plaintiff enjoyed the trademark "*Gu Sheng*" in relation to commodities in Class 9 of the international classification system unless the Trademark Office authorized the opposition by the defendant. The commodities that the defendant promoted with the mark of "*Gu Sheng*" are softwares which do not fall within Class 9, but they are closely related to computer hardwares in that both are indispensable to the running of computers. The defendant's acts amounted to "using a trademark that is identical with or similar to a registered trademark in respect of the same or similar goods without the authorization of the proprietor of the registered trademark" therefore infringing the exclusive right of the plaintiff to use the registered trademark (Article 38(1) of the Trademark Law). In the meantime, the defendant had committed an unfair competition act by using for a commodity without authorization, a unique name, package, or decoration of another's famous commodity, or using a name, package or decoration similar to that of another's famous commodity, thereby confusing the commodity with that famous commodity and leading the purchasers to mistake the former for the latter (Article 5(2) of the Unfair Competition Law). In the end, the defendant was ordered to stop infringement, and to apologize to and compensate the plaintiff.

It seems that in this case the court duly used its discretion in interpreting the Trademark Law provision concerning the scope of protection of a specific trademark.

5. Factors Hindering Judicial Enforcement of Intellectual Property

Recent Chinese court practice suggests a substantial improvement in judicial enforcement of IPRs protections.[37] This is a good sign for future judicial enforcement of IPRs. Furthermore, TRIPS Agreement prescribes minimum national standards of IPRs laws, enforcement standards, and a binding dispute settlement process. Now that China is a WTO Member, it needs to phase these provisions into judicial enforcement. However, it might be a little bit early for foreign IPRs holders to sigh with relief; there still exist factors affecting the judicial enforcement of IPRs in China, including high standard IPRs laws and operationality of the laws. The unprecedented efforts to establish the comprehensive legal framework signifies the first step towards effective protection of IPRs. Unfortunately, the operationality of IPRs laws, which is closely related to the specificity of the provisions, remains a problem. Experience with the Sino-US IPRs MOUs demonstrates that rules are enforced most satisfactorily when obligations are concrete, specific, and open to monitoring.[38] On the contrary, where lack of specific clauses in IPRs laws exists, the ambiguity of the provisions of the laws may act to hinder judicial enforcement. Take the copyright law and regulations as an example. Despite several amendments to the Copyright Law since its promulgation in 1991, there are still ambiguous provisions such as: "noncommercial objectives," "banned from publication receiving no copyright protection," or the "knowingly standard, allowing ignorance of infringement to be a defense in the Computer Software Protection Regulations." All these might as well be manipulated by infringers to prevent Chinese courts from enforcing IPRs.[39] Similarly, in the area of trade secrets-which are the new gold of the market place in the information age-there are also ambiguities as shown in the following hypothetical example: whether the customer list is included in the trade secret description poses a real hindrance as regards protection of such lists. The plaintiff is Airline A. The defendant is a former employee of the plaintiff. For three years, the defendant has been a sales representative for the plaintiff in Beijing. On 1 October 1998, the defendant left Airline A and began work as a sales representative for Airline B, a competitor of the plaintiff. The defendant concluded an agreement with Airline A when he resigned. According to the agreement, he promised to keep all trade secrets after his resignation. Shortly after he left Airline A, the defendant began contacting, on behalf of Airline B, the old customers he sold tickets to in Airline A on the same business. Because of his efforts, some of the plaintiff's customers began ordering tickets from Airline B. In January 1999, the plaintiff sued the defendant for trade secret infringement because he had abused the customer list. The defendant argued that customer list was not the plaintiff's trade secret and he was innocent. If anyone wants to apply the trade secret law to protect his customer list, he must prove it is a so-called trade secret: the existence of secrecy and competitive advantage. In modern society, it is clear that customers are extremely price-sensitive and everyone hopes to find a better deal. In this case, although the plaintiff signed an agreement on trade secret protection with the defendant, it did not prove why the customer list was its trade secret: the agreement being used as evidence is not enough.

Notes

1. For instance, the US software industry reported that up to 98 percent of the copies of US software products sold in China were unlicensed or "pirated" copies.

2. In this regard, it is not difficult to note that foreign pressure serves as a useful tool to persuade China to upgrade its intellectual property laws. The most famous example is the credible leverage of carefully targeted US Section 301 retaliation being used to reach agreement with China in February 1995 on enforcement of its intellectual property protection laws, and again in June 1996 to secure effective compliance with that agreement.

3. The Intellectual Property Working Meeting under the State Council, a coordinating body in this area that was set up in 1996, is overhauling all of China's intellectual property legislation to bring it fully in line with the TRIPS. On 25 August 2000, the 17th Session of the Standing Committee of the 9th National People's Congress (NPC) passed the amendment to the Patent Law and the amended Patent Law came into effect on 1 July 2001. Also, the 24th Session of the Standing Committee of the 9th NPC amended the Trademark Law and the Copyright Law on 27 October 2001. The new Copyright Law came into force on 27 October 2001 and the new Trademark Law on 1 December 2001. The Regulations on Computer Software is also being revised.

4. The UL marks are registered certification marks of Underwriters Laboratories Inc. They may be only used on or in connection with products certified by UL and under the terms of written agreement with UL. According to statistics, the State Administration for Entry-Exit Inspection and Quarantine supervised the destroying of counterfeit UL goods valued RMB 2 million *yuan,* imposed fines approximately RMB 800,000 *yuan,* and transferred about 10 cases to the administrative authorities for industry and commerce and public security bureaus at various levels. Each port of the customs investigated about eighty lots of exporting goods bearing the UL mark.

5. One example is that production of pirated compact discs in China has been so reduced that the United States, in April 1997, removed China from its "priority watch list" under the US Special 301 trade legislation that authorizes the United States to impose trade sanctions on countries not meeting its standards.

6. Even before China became a WTO Member, it had already put into effect the newly amended Patent Law, which was deemed consistent with the TRIPS Agreement.

7. In the past, some infringers outside the borders would conspire with infringers inside, to install underground production lines, rather than directly smuggle pirated products.

8. Special 301 on Intellectual Property Rights, Fact Sheet released by the Office of the U.S. Trade Representative 1 May 2000.

9. The State Intellectual Property Office (SIPO) was responsible for patent approval; the Trademarks Office under the State Administration for Industry and Commerce (SAIC) was responsible for trademarks registration; the Copyright Office was responsible for copyright policy making; SAIC was responsible for anti-unfair competition, including the protection of trade secrets; the State Drug Administration (SDA) was responsible for administrative protection of pharmaceuticals; the General Administration of Customs was responsible for border measures; the Ministry of Agriculture and the State Administration of Forestry were responsible for protection of plant varieties; the Ministry of Information Industry was responsible for the protection of layout designs of integrated circuits; and the State General Administration of the People's Republic of China for Quality Supervision and Inspection and Quarantine and SAIC were responsible for combating counterfeiting activities. Other agencies like the agency for press and publications, the people's courts and police were also involved in the protection of IPRs in China.

10. The SPC, for instance, promulgated the Interpretation Regarding Certain Matters of Law Application to Cases of Computer Net Copyright Disputes in December 2000. This judicial interpretation offers applicable rules for treat-

ment of issues such as the jurisdiction of the cases concerning the network copyright disputes, the digitalization of works, the description of copyrights, the cognizance of violations, the legal liability, as well as the application of the damage-compensating responsibilities, which the General Principle of Civil Law, Copyright Law, and the CPL have not covered.

11. In the Chinese court system, the Basic (ground-level) People's Court is the first instance court for civil cases. However, the Intermediate People's Court may become the first instance court for such cases as, among other things, those "determined by the SPC as coming under its jurisdiction": see, respectively, Articles 18 and 19 of the CPL.

12. So far, over three thousand specialists have benefited from such training activities.

13. There is an Adjudication Committee consisting of ranking judicial staff in each Chinese court. The Adjudication Committee analyzes and decides cases which are difficult and complex. Jiang Zhipei, Director of the Intellectual Property Tribunal (renamed the 3rd Civil Trial Tribunal) of the SPC, revealed, in his presentation at the AIPLA Annual Meeting 1999, that in relation to patent cases alone, each year one or two important cases are submitted to the Adjudication Committee of the SPC for discussion and approval.

14. Article 41 (1) of the TRIPS Agreement also sets out the obligations of Member governments to provide procedures and remedies under their domestic law to ensure that intellectual property rights can be effectively enforced, by foreign right holders as well as by their own nationals. The purpose of these provisions is, *inter alia*, to put in place proper judicial procedures, which are the basic components of any judicial system. It is true that the WTO Agreements do not require instituting such tribunals or procedures inconsistent with a constitutional structure or the nature of its legal system. However, for some Member States, the provisions regarding the judicial system set out in a surprisingly detailed way amount to an obligation to substantially revise their judicial systems, particularly their judicial review system.

15. The newly amended Patent Law has, to some extent, taken the first step towards remedying the defect, which provides that the court adjudicating the case may require the provision of a retrieval report by the intellectual property authority. For a detailed discussion of how the newly revised Patent Law would affect the infringement cases, see Li Wei, New Patent Law Will Bring Substantial Impact on the Patent Litigation (in Chinese), *China Intellectual Property*, 2000, no. 2, p. 35.

16. In the appeal copyright infringement case of *Pacific Unida Ltd. et al, v. Avon (China) Corp.*, the SPC ruled that the Guangdong High People's Court should re-form a tribunal and re-try the case on that ground. See The SPC, Min Shi

Cai Ding Shu (Civil Award), (1998), Zhi Zhong Zi No. 6. Available at http:// www.chinaiprlaw.com/wsjx/wsjx10.htm.

17. Articles 74, 92, 93 and 97 of the CPL.

18. Article 61 of the Patent Law.

19. Advance execution (*xian yu zhixing*) is provided in the CPL.

20. On 5 June 2001 the SPC promulgated the Certain Provisions on Questions of the Application of Law concerning Preliminary Injunctions in Patent Infringement Cases, which entered into effect on the same date when the Patent Law came into force, i.e. 1 July 2001.

21. See, Jiang Zhipei, Judicial Protection of Copyright and Neighboring Rights in China, available at http://www.chinaiprlaw.com/english/forum/forum1.htm.

22. In order to facilitate implement the property preservation concerning registered trademark, the SPC promulgated a judicial interpretation on 21 January 2001.

23. Article 63(1) of the Patent Law.

24. Article 40(1) of the Trademark Law.

25. Articles 1 and 2 of the Decision of the Standing Committee of the National People's Congress on Punishing Copyright Infringement Crimes.

26. The Interpretations on Certain Issues concerning the Concrete Application of Law in Handling Criminal Cases Involving the Manufacture and Sale of Fake and Substandard Commodities.

27. For the case description, see the Gazette of the Supreme People's Court, 1996, No. 4, pp. 136-140.

28. For a description of the case, see Li Dongtao, Microsoft Went to Court Again, available at http://www.cnc.ac.cn/law/dongtao_e2_991123.html.

29. According to the CPL, agreement in mediation must be reached between the two parties of their own accord, no coercion is allowed, and the contents of the agreement shall not go against the law; where mediation has failed to reach agreement or one party goes back on his word before the delivery of the bill of mediation, the people's court shall make an adjudication promptly.

30. Beijing Municipal No. 1 Intermediate People's Court, Min Shi Pan Jue Shu (Civil Judgment), Yi Zhong Zhi Chu Zi No. 48, available at http:// www.chinaiprlaw.com/wsjx/wsjxdi33.htm.

31. The Beijing Municipal No. 1 Intermediate People's Court, Min Shi Pan Jue Shu (Civil Judgment), (2000) Yi Zhong Zhi Chu Zi, No. 49, available at http:// www.chinaiprlaw.com/wsjx/wsjxdi13.htm.

32. For the case description, see the Gazette of the Supreme People's Court, No. 5, 1999, pp.173-175.

33. For a discussion about enforcement of copyright relating to the Internet, see Qingjiang Kong, Old Bottle for New Wine: Copyright Legislation in the Digital Context, 36 *Issues & Studies* 5, 2000, pp.158-175.

34. See SPC, Min Shi Pan Jue Shu (Civil Judgment), Fa Gong Bu (2000), No. 25, available at http://www.rmfyb.com.cn/.
35. For the case description, see the Gazette of the Supreme People's Court, 2000, No. 2, pp. 63-65.
36. Applications will be preliminarily approved and a preliminary approval number allocated if a mark is considered by the examiner to be registrable pursuant to the Trademark Law, and if no other conflicting applications or registrations are found.
37. Professor Zheng Chengsi, a renowned intellectual property expert, even asserts that in the field of intellectual property, the judiciary has gone further than the legislation; in the meantime, the legislation has gone further than the academic. He attributed the improvement of the Chinese judiciary to the intellectual property judges' relentless observation of the practice of foreign courts and their ambition to adopt the successful practices of the foreign courts: see Zheng Chengsi, Certain Questions on the Studies of Intellectual Property Rights in Our Country (in Chinese), available at the Website of People's Court Daily; http://www.rmfyb.com.cn.
38. See Enforcement of The U.S.-China WTO Accession Deal, The White House Press Release, 8 March 2000.
39. The "knowingly" standard in Article 32, for example, is one important ambiguity. This is not in accordance with the strict liability provisions of international standards, as any user could falsely claim that he was unaware of infringement of other copyrighted products to avoid liabilities for infringement.

Part IV

Conclusion

13

Enforcement of WTO Agreements in China: Reality or Illusion?*

1. Introduction

Enforcement of WTO Agreements[1] has engaged attention in trade and legal circles. The concluding of the comprehensive market accession agreements between China and the WTO Members heightened the issue of the prospect of enforcing WTO Agreements in China. Although any conclusive findings must await the availability of more empirical information, this article explores the theoretical aspects of WTO Agreements enforcement, examines the practice of implementing international treaties in China with a view to helping shed light on the prospect of enforcing WTO Agreements in China.

China began negotiating trade treaties with major countries when it adopted the open door policy in late 1970's. At the bilateral level, it has entered into trade agreements or other agreements on economic technical co-operation with practically every country that it maintains diplomatic relationship with.[2] China is good at bilateral trade bargaining because, as a large country, it is often able to gain what it needs. Through the most-favoured-nation provisions in the bilateral agreements, China has in fact enjoyed the

* This chapter was first published in the *Journal of World Trade*, 2001 (pp.1187-1220) and is reproduced by the permission of the publisher.

same trade treatment vis-à-vis a WTO Member as other WTO Members may gain from that WTO Member.

At the multilateral level, China has acceded to or participated in the making of numerous multilateral treaties. From 1982 on, China participated in the entire process of the Multi-Fibre Agreements, which has been replaced by the Agreement on Textiles and Clothing, within the framework of WTO. As an observer, China was also a participant of the Uruguay Round negotiation.

Despite these trade advantages China has long desired entry into the WTO, and in July 1986 officially applied to the GATT, the WTO's predecessor, to resume its status as an original contracting party. After a series of bilateral and multilateral negotiations, China's specific obligations upon entering the WTO were incorporated into an Accession Protocol and accompanying schedules, which were multilateralized (or extended to all WTO Members), upon its accession. With their breadth and scope, and a strong enforcement mechanism, the WTO Agreements are the backbone of the trade treaties that bind China.

2. WTO Agreements and Their Enforcement in International Law

2.1. The nature of legal obligations under the WTO Agreements

For fifty years, the GATT system has fostered the development of liberal multilateralism. The GATT, originally negotiated as part of the Havana Charter for the Proposed International Trade Organization, was intended to be applied provisionally between just twenty-three "original" Contracting Parties. Because of the failure of US Congress to ratify the Havana Charter, this short set of rules had governed trade ties for 47 years,[3] and finally evolved into a number of well formulated international treaties and a charter-based international organisation.

Due to its "provisional" status, the GATT showed significant ambiguities concerning the legal status of particular texts, thus affecting its function as international law. As a matter of fact, even the Tokyo Round results, usually called "side codes," which preceded the WTO Agreements on safeguard and antidumping, were optional. The legal structure of the WTO Agreements has remedied the birth defects of the GATT.[4] In contrast, the WTO is bestowed with a founding charter and clarified rules of procedure for decision-making by the Members and a genuine secretariat. All these vastly improve the system's institutional strength.

More importantly, the world's pre-eminent trade institution administers many mandatory agreements that impose binding obligations on all Members of the WTO.

Noteworthy here is that the WTO Agreements departed from the Tokyo Round approach of "pick and choose" side codes and reinforced the "single package" conception.[5] This requires all WTO Members to accept as binding international law obligations all of the WTO Agreements except the optional Pluralateral Trade Agreements. Similarly, the WTO dispute settlement procedures unified most of the multiplicity of dispute settlement procedures under the pre-1994 GATT and its many side codes, thus strengthening the binding nature of the WTO Agreements as a whole.

In addition, the decision-making rules of the WTO differentiate the WTO Agreements from the pre-1994 GATT. The latter operated on "consensus." If one Contracting Party complained that another Contracting Party's trade measures were inconsistent with the GATT obligation, and a GATT panel, after studying the matter, ruled in favour of one Contracting Party, the losing party could, by simply withholding its agreement, prevent the adverse GATT panel findings from being implemented. In the case of the WTO, under the DSU, unless there is a consensus against the establishment of a panel, the panel shall be established where a dispute is not settled through consultations (Article 6.1. of the DSU). More importantly, unless there is a consensus to reject the findings of the DSB,[6] the losing party will have to bring its practices into conformity with the WTO Panel Reports or face compensation or unilateral retaliation by the other party in the form of suspending concessions (Article 22.1.) of the DSU).

In the light of the history of the pre-1994 GATT and the WTO, it is not surprising to find that the essential characteristic of the WTO Agreements is their bindingness.

2.2. Enforcement of the WTO Agreements

From the perspective of WTO Members, enforcement of the WTO Agreements consists of two aspects: internal implementation by the Members and external overseeing by the institutional WTO.

The obligations under the WTO Agreements rely primarily on the WTO Members to be fulfilled. While WTO Members enjoy applying the domestic safeguard measures that are allowed by the WTO Agreements, they are bound to perform their obligations under the WTO Agreements by taking domestic measures. Such measures include mainly translating WTO Agreements into domestic law or regulations, amending inconsistent domestic laws, and uniformly administering trade-related measures. The Agreement Establishing the World Trade Organisation requires that "(e)ach Member shall ensure the conformity of its laws, regulations and administrative procedures with its obligations provided in the annexed Agreements."[7]

The WTO oversees the internal implementation by the Members. The overseeing mainly takes the forms of dispute settlement mechanism and policy review.[8]

The dispute settlement mechanism is the central element in providing security and predictability to the multilateral trading system.[9] It is essential to the enforcement of WTO Agreements.[10]

The WTO established a DSB charged with creating panels, adopting panel and appellate body reports, and monitoring compliance with decisions and recommendations. Only Members can initiate WTO dispute settlement against other Members. Refusal to take recommended compliance measures by a WTO Member involved in a dispute, which a WTO panel has dealt with, would lead to unilateral retaliation.

In this regard, a further question needs clarifying: Can a WTO Member make a defence for breaching the obligation of a WTO agreement by arguing that it acted in such a manner that it was following the dictates of a domestic law? The Vienna Convention on the Law of Treaties (Vienna Convention)[11] provides the answer. Article 26 of the Vienna Convention provides that in so far as treaties are concerned, a party may not invoke the provisions of its internal law as justification for its failure to carry out an international agreement.

A more complicated question is whether DSB reports can be enforced in the domestic law of the losing Member. After all, enforcing the DSB reports in the losing Member's domestic court provides another alternative to the injured Member. Since the DSU does not provide answers to this issue, arguably this is a question to be decided under the domestic law of the losing Member.[12]

It should be also pointed out that the WTO Dispute Settlement Mechanism could result in sanctions even where it is a provincial or municipal government rather than the central government that is responsible for the breach.

3. Factors Affecting China's Future Compliance with WTO Agreements

3.1. Positive factors affecting China's compliance with WTO Agreements

3.1.1. Market reform and economic liberalisation
China has been on the way to market-oriented reform for two decades.[13] The Chinese government has recognised that economic reform and market openness are cornerstones of sustainable economic growth. China realized that pro-market-reforms as suggested by the WTO are critical to China's growth. Nonetheless, these reforms have been difficult for certain constituencies, particularly in the ageing industrial sector and the heavily protected agricultural sector.

However, it is fair to argue that China's accession agreement per se is evidence of a China formally committed to further the WTO-mandated reforms. It is therefore expected, as genuine difficulties arise, that the Chinese government will rely upon WTO-consistent methods to address them. China's WTO accession will deepen and entrench market reforms—and strengthen those in China's leadership who want their country to move further and faster toward economic freedom. Failure by China to honour its commitments would erode the confidence of foreign investors who are playing an important role in China's modernization.

3.1.2. Recent Chinese practice of enforcing international treaties

Since 1979, the United States and China have reached some twenty trade agreements, ranging from civil aviation and satellite exports to agriculture and IPRs protection.[14] Among the most significant are the IPRs MOUs in 1992 and in 1995. The historical record of China's implementation of the two IPRs agreements can perhaps be used to shed light on the question whether China will comply with the WTO rules after its accession.

Vigorous enforcement of the bilateral agreements between the United States and China has resulted in significant improvements in both IPRs protection and market access. Before the IPRs agreements in 1992 and 1995, and the enforcement action in 1996, China was one of the world's largest IPRs pirates. Since then, it has improved its legal framework—and it has virtually shut down the illegal production and export of pirated music, video CDs and CD-ROMs. Enforcement of IPRs rights has become part of China's nation-wide anti-crime campaign, and the Chinese police and court system have become actively involved in combating IPRs piracy. China's efforts to honour the commitment to strengthen IPRs protection is evident in that the Patent Law, the Trademark Law the Copyright Law have been amended. The revisions were intended to bring the law into conformity with the TRIPS Agreement and other international IPRs standards covered under the WIPO treaties.

However, other issues concerning the implementation of the agreements still have to be resolved. Local and foreign IPRs owners suffer from, for example, counterfeiting of brand name products and Internet domain names. While regional co-operation on enforcement of IPRs has improved, it is still problematic. Difficulties with enforcement at the local level include local protectionism and corruption, reluctance to impose deterrent level penalties, and a low number of criminal prosecutions.

3.2. Negative factors affecting China's compliance with WTO Agreements

There are some factors that might lead to China violating WTO rules on some occasions and which therefore might lead to disputes.

3.2.1. Legal culture

Also undeniably, among the factors affecting the implementation of international treaties are the nation's fundamental attitudes towards law and its attitude towards international law. Therefore, it is necessary to probe into the unique Chinese legal culture and practice.

It is widely observed that China has no tradition of the rule of law. Rather the rulers of different time have demonstrated their preference for a rule of man (*ren zhi*). The distinguishing feature of the rule of man can be described as "law being conceived of as an instrument of the ruler."[15] This conception of rule of man fully resonated with Marxist dogma and thus was strengthened when the People's Republic of China was founded. The practice of the rule of man culminated in the Cultural Revolution.

In the wake of the chaos and accompanying poverty, people became aware of the devastating force of the rule of man and began to study the institutional shortcomings. Accordingly, *fa zhi* (legality) was proposed as a substitute for *ren zhi* (the rule of man). Since 1979 when China targeted legalism, it has made remarkable progress in the development of its legal system. China's significant and ever-growing body of legislation is clear evidence of the achievement. However, the over-arching principle is still legal instrumentalism. It is fair to argue that the feature of this legalism is the use of liberal language, rhetoric and the ritual of law to pursue distinctly illiberal political and social objectives; it is the rule through law rather than the rule of law.

Another unique legal culture is that enforcement of law, to a certain degree, relies on the *guanxi* (social connections) and *mianzi* (face).[16] *Guanxi* can either assist in enhancing law enforcement, or be used to avoid compliance of law (severe violation may be deemed as slight violations and heavy fines may be reduced to light ones).[17] Similarly, law enforcement may also be related to the psychological assessment of saving face or losing face by the persons against whom law is enforced. For example, causing loss of face can impede law enforcement.[18]

3.2.2. Political considerations

Given the prospective enormous impact of WTO Agreements, enforcing them will give rise to as much concern as joining the WTO. In the process of implementing the WTO Agreements, the Chinese government will inevitably face pressures from internal interest groups.[19] To explain in detail interest groups and their role in policy-making is beyond the scope and length of this article. As far as the same leadership that decided to join the WTO and will implement the WTO Agreements is concerned, the political pressure primarily comes from industries, local governments, prospective lay-offs, farmers as well as the conservative forces within the party. Except for deplorable lay-offs and farmers who may have to strive for a way to make the Party leadership consider their grievances, all these interest groups either are organised or have institutional channels at their disposal for their voice to be heard. They will push either for or against implementing the WTO Agreements. The government's determination to implement WTO Agreements might sway under the pressure combined with fermenting nationalism.[20]

Closer trade ties with other WTO Members after the accession of China to the WTO will create conditions for smoothing rugged political relations with its major trade partners, and the United States in particular. As a matter of fact, concluding the Sino-US Market Access Agreement seemed per se to be motivated by the Chinese expectation that trading with the United States would be free from political interference. However, the international business community is more concerned with the possibility that China's political considerations affect its trade policy towards its trade partners.

In the process of pursuing economic prosperity, China has learned that it needs to treat economic and political issues differently. The decision to join the WTO *per se* is an example. However, from time to time, Chinese practice in diplomacy as well as in domestic affairs shows China has not utterly given up its longstanding practice of "putting political concerns above all (*zhengzhi guashuai*)," particularly when it comes to the question of Taiwan. It is still seen using trade measures as a way of either punishment or reward for its trading partners. Therefore, no one can rule out the possibility that China, after joining the WTO, will relinquish that practice.[21]

To be fair, it should be pointed out that China is not the only country whose trade policy is subject to political concern. In the eye of China, the US Congress has demonstrated its inclination to politicise trade issues.[22]

The difference between the practice of China and that of some of the WTO Members is in degree. In other words, Chinese trade measures are more influenced by domestic political struggle than those of most WTO Members. Given that politicisation of trade measures might elicit reciprocal responses from its partner, the risk should not be underestimated. Among the political considerations that may affect China's implementation of WTO Agreements are domestic pressure primarily from interested industries, as well as the question of Taiwan.

With respect to the Taiwan issue, Taiwan acceded to the WTO after China's accession. The cohabitation of China and Taiwan in the same international organisation on the one hand will provide chances for both China and Taiwan to deal with each other, and on the other will host friction if either side is interested in promoting its international stance in the forum. Despite the rest of the WTO Members' attitudes towards this issue,[23] there will still be a risk that political concerns on the Chinese side will interrupt the trade body's agenda and China's enforcement of the WTO Agreements.

In respect to domestic political pressure, many state bank and factory managers, for example, fear foreign competition and the free market. Some already warn that moving too quickly will bankrupt their enterprises and abolish jobs, leading to dangerous social unrest. Beijing must heed these voices and will almost certainly apply WTO terms erratically at best bringing fresh foreign complaints about China evading its treaty obligations.

Fortunately, with the stabilisation of the reform-minded leadership, the practice of letting domestic political caprice or Party whims affect rule-based trade issues will gradually be phased out.

3.2.3. Institutional defects

Ambivalence of law, compartmentalisation of law-making and enforcement. A comprehensive legal framework, coupled with adequate prior notice of proposed changes to laws and regulations, and an opportunity to comment on those changes, greatly enhances business conditions, promotes commerce, and reduces opportunities for corruption. The WTO system assumes that a lack of transparency about rules or regulations affecting imports could have the same effect as a quantitative restriction (Article XI of GATT 1994) and thus requires Members' laws, regulations, and administrative and legislative processes be transparent (Article X of GATT 1994). This is crucial to the effectiveness of many of the WTO's main principles. For example, transparency relates to national treatment (Articles III of GATT 1994), which inherently requires that both domestic and foreign producers know the rules of the game. If the relevant rule is only known to domestic producers, foreign producers cannot have knowledge of whether or not the rule is discriminatory in its effect, and whether the rule can represent its interests or not. In addition, as will be discussed infra, any meaningful discipline on state enterprises also entails transparency.

However, statutory provisions in China[24] often leave many questions unanswered. In China, laws and regulations are promulgated by a host of different ministries and governments at provincial and local levels, as well as by the NPC, its Standing Committee and the State Council. As a result, laws and regulations are frequently at odds with each other.[25]

To make matters worse, there is a bureaucratic tendency in China that once a law is passed, the problem which the law is supposed to address is assumed to have been addressed and this bureaucracy adds to a lasting ambiguity of statutory provisions.[26]

The lack of a clear and consistent framework of laws and regulations is an effective barrier to the participation of foreign firms in the domestic market.

Reliable and impartial law enforcement may be the *sine qua non* of equitable trade relationships. However, under the Chinese legal system, the implementation of law constitutes a major problem. Law enforcement, to a large degree, depends on bureaucracy. Given the inconsistency between relevant laws and regulations derived from different departments, these statutory provisions often leave room for discretionary application[27]—either through honest misunderstanding or through selective application—or are ignored outright. Some ministries that see their interests threatened, for example, may be reluctant to enforce the laws concerned[28].

Credibility of dispute resolution mechanisms. The WTO system implicitly expects that members will have an effective and impartial judicial system, which is crucial to the effectiveness of many WTO obligations. For example, it is difficult to see how a country with a judicial system that is slow, corrupt, or not independent of domestic political influence could offer reliable and impartial enforcement of its laws. The highly personalised nature of business in China often makes arbitration or other legal remedies impractical. Even when they have strong cases, people often decide against using legal means to resolve disputes out of concern over permanently alienating critical business associates or government authorities.

Scepticism about the independence and professionalism of the Chinese judiciary[29] and the enforceability of judgements and awards remains high in the international community. This has often caused both foreign and domestic companies to avoid enforcement actions through the Chinese courts.

A weak judicial system is troubling. The fact that a WTO dispute settlement panel lacks the means and is not willing to condemn an entire legal system as ineffective or lacking impartiality adds to concerns on the credibility issue.

It might come as a relief that the Chinese government is moving to establish consistent and reliable mechanisms for dispute resolution through the adoption of improved codes of ethics for lawyers and judges and increased emphasis on the consistent and predictable application of laws.

Non-institutional central-local relationship. China is a vast, multiethnical, unitary country. In theory, all the powers of localities stem from the centre. Even in regions with ethnical minorities where a certain degree of self-government is instituted, they still cannot possess similar powers as sub-federal entities in federal nations. With the introduction and development of reform that aims at economic mobility, the localities have been given more powers and thus more resources to administer the state economy in the localities. Driven by local interests, the local leaders have gradually become less obedient to the centre. As a result, at the local level, the laws and regulations promulgated by the centre are unevenly implemented to their letters.[30] For example, governments in some localities lack the incentive to implement laws and regulations that will not bring benefits to the locality concerned[31].

The extent to which sub-central government authorities refuse to obey central government rules in China, and the apparent impotence of the central government to change that behaviour is not new to the outsiders. The relative weakness of the central government is likely to reduce the effectiveness and meaningfulness of WTO commitments.

3.2.4. Chinese attitudes towards international law

The Chinese attitude towards international law is the other facet of the coin called "rule of law." In the Mao era, China, though too weak and too self-isolated to pose any threat to the international law and order, still had fame in the eyes of some critical Western observers as an outlaw vis-à-vis international society. Thanks to the unhappy historical experience with international law, it was not difficult to find among Chinese experts on international relations an absolute negation of international law.[32] However, China's international behaviour in the post-Mao era has demonstrated the noteworthy change in its attitudes towards international law.

In general, the Chinese attitude towards international law can be fairly described in this way: while emphasising the principle of absolute sovereignty,[33] it recognises the existence of generally recognised international law and its universal applicability.[34]

In respect to treaties, the Chinese acknowledges the doctrine of *pact sunt servanda* but argues "unequal treaties"[35] are null and void. With the consecutive return of Hong Kong and Macau to Chinese sovereignty, this voice has died out. It may be interesting to note that the Chinese treats international treaties differently from customary international law.[36] Nevertheless, the recognition of a body of generally recognised international norms is a positive phenomenon. In this regard, it is particularly noteworthy that reference to international customs and practice (*guoji guanli*) can be found in some laws and regulations.[37]

Take international jurisdiction over states as an example. Before it signed the Sino-US agreement, the Chinese practice had been consistent in rejecting compulsory international jurisdiction over it. China does not belong to the category of countries, as referred to in Article 36 (2) of the Statute of the International Court of Justice (ICJ), which recognises as compulsory ipso facto and without special agreement, in relation to any other state accepting the same obligation, the jurisdiction of the Court in all legal disputes.[38] As a matter of fact, it has never subjected itself to the jurisdiction of the ICJ since it resumed the seat of China in the United Nations in 1972. It had firmly maintained that unless it granted specific consent, it would not be subjected to any jurisdiction of international tribunals.[39]

Another example is its attitude towards the role of private parties in international law and private enforcement of international treaties in particular. Chinese publicists in their writings do not recognise individual and non-governmental entities such as companies as having legal personality under international law.[40] It may be fair to argue that the prevailing scholastic opinion in this regard represents that of the Chinese government.[41] The Chinese practice, however, has shown its deviation from its long-standing negative attitudes towards foreign private enforcement. It has even acceded to or taken part in the making of many international treaties that specifically authorise foreign private enforcement against the Chinese government. The 1985 accession to the United Nations Convention on the Recognition and Enforcement of Foreign Arbitral Awards (New York Convention, 1958) signified the staring point,[42] the 1992 accession to the Convention on the Settlement of Investment Disputes between States and Nationals of Other States (ICSID Convention) left room for private enforcement,[43] while the 1999 conclusion of the Sino-US Market Access Agreement was the decisive step towards foreign private enforcement of China's commitments under an international agreement.[44]

In conclusion, the Chinese attitude towards international law and China's international behaviour will be heavily influenced by many factors in addition to generally recognised international law. Among the factors that influence China's attitude towards international law and international behaviour are China's perceived national interests and the current international situation, domestic concerns and policy and China's historical experience with international law.

By declaring that the "Open Door" policy is a cornerstone of its overall policy (*guo ce*), China has acknowledged that its interests lie in trade with the rest of the world. It also knows that expanding trade is only possible by adapting itself to, rather than by changing, the existing multilateral trading system. In the meantime, its self-identification also has an impact on its international legal behaviour. It views itself as a weak developing country vis-à-vis developed countries and a responsible and trustworthy agent of the developing countries. In view of this, China reiterates "supporting any effort to build up a fair, safe and non-discriminatory multilateral trade system,"[45] in which the special interests of the developing country should be adequately addressed and it may play the role of "one of the multi-poles." Consequently it has shown strong interest in participating in rule-making. It may be argued that China's desire to play a role in international rule-making, if properly nurtured, would be conducive to enhancing China's willingness and capability to abide by recognised rules of international law.

On the other hand, the Chinese government has gradually become convinced of the need to use at its disposal the instrument of international law to meet the numerous challenges posed by the unpredictable international environment.

3.2.5. Difficulty of economic restructuring

Moreover, daunting as these factors may sound, they represent only the "tip of the iceberg." The greatest challenge facing Chinese leaders during the implementation process will be the task of maintaining employment and family incomes at socially acceptable levels—as tens of thousands of inefficient state-owned enterprises face new pressure from foreign competition, and hundreds of millions of farmers cope with declining commodity prices due to new imports of agricultural products. If unemployment gets out-of-hand, and if a viable safety net cannot be established and maintained, then Chinese leaders may be forced to choose between domestic turmoil and deferring implementation of some of their WTO commitments.

4. Some Factors Affecting the Likelihood of WTO Dispute Settlement Proceedings Involving China

The accession of China to the WTO may increase dissatisfaction of some Members with the fact that some subject matters are not regulated by the WTO rules. The following will identify several sources that are not adequately addressed by WTO Agreements, but may prove essential to the interests of the rest of the WTO Members.

4.1. Market rule v. dominant role of state-owned enterprises

The draftsman of the GATT, who designed an article (i.e. Article XVII) to discipline activity by state enterprises, could never have anticipated that this article and the GATT as a whole would not sufficiently address problems created by the accession of a country as big as China and with such a big role for state enterprises.

Even according to the most generous estimates of the extent to which China's market has liberalized, at least thirty-five percent of Chinese gross domestic product is still produced by SOEs. Therefore, problems relating to SOEs will definitely be encountered in China. The risk is that action by SOE has the potential to undermine the fundamental rules of the GATT. For the most part, the GATT assumes that economic decision-making is made by producers and consumers based on price, but SOEs do not always make decisions based on price. It is not difficult to see SOEs that consume computer chips purchase all of their computer chips from state-owned chip manufacturers. This would not only contravene the primary requirement of Article XVII, that is, state enterprises shall make purchases or sales "solely in accordance with commercial considerations," but also effectively undermine the GATT's Article III national treatment provision. Similar arguments can be made about how SOEs may engage in behaviour that would undermine the GATT Article I commitment of MFN treatment, the Article II commitment to a schedule of concessions, and the Article XI commitment against maintaining quantitative restrictions. Given that the reason for purchases or sales by state enterprises is not transparent, none of these disciplines could be effective.

4.2. Lack in corporate disciplines v. monopoly, corruption, low environment and labour standards

China has not yet established any meaningful competition system[46] and the WTO system does not require a Member to have a competition policy. While complaints about anti-competitive activities can already be heard in China, it does not take great imagination to see that such problems could culminate in the future. Furthermore, in view of the pattern that has been followed in some other Asian countries and in Eastern Europe, the Chinese government could even decide to give a legal monopoly to certain SOEs, particularly in the early phases of privatisation. Monopoly or monopolistic behaviour that is analogue to discriminatory behaviour by SOEs can eviscerate the effectiveness and meaningfulness of basic GATT rules.

The existence of widespread corruption in China highlights the worry that it can undermine the effectiveness of the WTO Agreements. Rampant corruption practice by Chinese businesses in purchasing, investment, procurement, and regulatory administration (including customs) has been cited as an example which undermines the MFN treatment. The absence of WTO disciplines on corrupt practices, combined with restrictions on such activities by nationals of some foreign countries like the OECD Members[47] can yield a different business environment in China. That is also detrimental to the national treatment envisaged by the WTO Agreements.

The WTO lacks rules to ensure minimal standards of environmental and social regulation in Members. This raises the possibility that big differences in the stringency of regulatory regimes across WTO Members may attract investment and jobs away from countries that have relatively stringent standards towards countries, like China, that have relatively lax environmental or workers' rights standards.

4.3. Limited WTO rules on investment and China's investment screening

China has so far maintained its practice of foreign investment screening. Under this practice, any proposed foreign investment or participation project is subject to state examination and approval. The investment screening, which involves multi-level governments and multi-agencies and both procedural and substantial requirements,[48] leaves ample room for manipulation and constitutes a major barrier for foreign investment participation.

Indeed, the TRIMS Agreement sets forth disciplines on trade-related investment measure and other WTO rules disciplining non-national treatment, and the application of domestic rules on licensing and technical regulations may also help to remove hidden barriers to establishment of businesses in China. However, this Agreement, and the WTO Agreements as a whole, may not provide effective discipline on China's unexceptional case-by-case screening.

5. The Implementation of the International Law in Chinese Domestic Law

5.1. The sources of Chinese law

It is helpful to note that as various organs exercise, to some extent, the legislative power in China, "domestic law" in the Chinese context refers to numerous sources of laws, regulations and rules that are in a hierarchy.

5.1.1. Basic laws by the NPC

According to the Constitution of the People's Republic of China, the NPC is the highest authority of the State. The Constitution provides that NPC has the power to enact and amend "basic laws (*jiben fa*)." In principle, "basic laws" refer to such laws as General Principles of Civil Law (GPCL), the Civil Procedural Law (CPL), the Criminal Law, Criminal Procedural Law, Administrative Procedure Law (APL), and the Law for Self-government in the Minority Autonomous Regions, etc.

5.1.2. Laws by the NPC Standing Committee

The NPC Standing Committee is the permanent organ of the NPC. It exercises the legislative power when the NPC adjourns. The NPC Standing Committee has the power to enact and amend "laws other than basic laws," supplement and amend to some extent laws made by the NPC.

5.1.3. Administrative Regulations by the State Council

Under the Chinese Constitution, the State Council is the highest administrative organ of the State. It has the power to enact "administrative regulations (*xingzheng fagui*)" "in accordance with the Constitution and laws."[49] Like the basic laws and laws, the "administrative regulations" are binding nationwide.

It should be noted that that in China most of the normative rules take the form of administrative regulations. Given this, the role of the administrative regulations should by no means be underestimated.

5.1.4. Local regulations by Provincial People's Congresses

The people's congresses at the provincial level and their standing committees have the power to draw up "local regulations (*difangxing fagui*)," "provided that they do not contravene the Constitution, laws and administrative regulations"[50]; but the regulations are required to be reported to the NPC Standing Committee for the record. People's congresses in minority autonomous regions have the power to work out autonomous regulations and special regulations. It is noted that in 1992, 1994 and 1996, the NPC Standing Committee authorised the people's congresses and the people's governments of four Special Economic Zones (i.e. Shenzhen, Zhuhai, Shantou and Xiamen) to enact "local regulations." Local regulations are binding only in the provinces and the SEZs concerned.

5.1.5. Local rules by people's congresses at sub-provincial levels and local governments

The Constitution provides no reference to the power of local people's congresses at sub-provincial levels and local governments to enact regulative rules. The 1986 Organic Law of the Local People's Congresses and Local People's Governments, however, provides that the local people's congresses and local people's governments of cities where the provincial governments are situated and of "large-sized cities" have the power to work out local rules (*guizhang*). These local rules are binding only in the localities concerned.

5.1.6. Administrative rules passed by Ministries

The Constitution provides, subject to their respective authority, ministries and ministerial-level commissions may enact "administrative rules" (*xingzheng guizhang*) "in accordance with the laws and administrative regulations of the State Council."[51] Administrative rules are binding nationwide on the matters concerned, and may serve as reference for application when courts at different levels adjudicate relevant cases. Given the predominant role of the ministries in the economic life of China, however, the importance of the administrative rules of ministries should not be underestimated.

5.2. The hierarchy of sources of domestic law observed by courts

Courts across the country must observe basic laws, laws and administrative regulations, and those within a province or SEZ must observe local regulations. According to relevant judicial interpretations of the Supreme People's Court (SPR), courts may invoke "rules (*guizhang*) and other normative guidelines (*qita guifanxing wenjian*)"[52], which refer to administrative rules by Ministries, local people's congresses and governments of cities where provincial governments are situated, and provincial governments.

All these laws, regulations and rules are fixed in a hierarchy: Apart from the Constitution, the basic laws passed by the NPC are at the top of the hierarchy. Next are the laws by the NPC Standing Committee. Then follows "administrative regulations" by the State Council. Next are local regulations by the people's congresses of the provinces and administrative rules by Ministries. Subsequently follows local rules by local people's congresses and people's governments.

The hierarchy means, subordinate normative rule is null and void if it contravene with a higher one. For example, the local regulations by the provincial-level People's Congress are binding in the provinces concerned only if they do not contravene the laws and regulations by the NPC and the State Council.

Noteworthy here is that in the Chinese domestic legal system, the organ adopting a higher normative rule has the power to determine whether such a conflict occurs between that rule and a subordinate one and hence declare the subordinate rule null and void. In other words, the NPC has the power to modify or repeal inappropriate resolutions made by the NPC Standing Committee; the NPC standing Committee possesses the authority to annul administrative regulations by the State Council and revoke local regulations by local organs of state power; the State Council has the power to annul the rules by Ministries and local governments; etc. On the other hand, a competent court possesses no authority to mend the inconsistency between two normative rules at different levels by repealing the lower rules. Moreover, according to the Legislation Law of the People's Republic of China (2000), the court is not among the competent authorities that have the power to take the initiative to make, amend or annul a statute, and therefore is presumably not in a position to refer the statutory provision to the competent authority for amendment.

It should be borne in mind the status in Chinese law of a directive of the Supreme Peoples Court. The Constitution does not specify whether they have legal force. However, for the purpose of uniform application of laws, the NPC Standing Committee authorises the SPR to interpret laws and decrees relating to their specific application at trial.[53] Moreover, the SPR has asserted the authority to give courts at different levels directives, in the form of judicial interpretations, concerning the application of laws and regulations in relevant cases. As a matter of fact, its directives are binding on the courts across the country, thus assuming the same legal effect as laws and regulations.

5.3. Chinese law and practice on the ratification of treaties

According to the Chinese Constitution, the State Council is responsible for "conducting foreign affairs and concluding treaties (*tiaoyue*) and agreements (*xieding*) with foreign states."[54] The power to ratify and abrogate "treaties and important agreements" rests with the NPC Standing Committee.[55] According to the Law of Procedures for Concluding Treaties of the People's Republic of China (1990), "treaties and important agreements" are referred to, among other things, treaties and agreements that differ from the laws of the People's Republic of China.[56]

The constitutional provision suggests international agreements that are not "important" are not subject to approval by the NPC Standing Committee. As a matter of fact, the Law of Procedures for Concluding Treaties confirms that all the other legal instruments shall be checked and approved by the State Council.[57] Nevertheless, for the treaties and important agreements, constitutionally it appears to be a possibility that the NPC Standing Committee might refuse to ratify such a treaty referred to it for ratification.

In practice, due to the political structure and power operation, negotiating or entering into a treaty or an important agreement and then ratifying it always follows the decision made by the Chinese leadership with the Politburo at its top to accede to that treaty or important agreement. It can be normally presumed that where a treaty has been entered into in the name of the State Council, the NPC Standing Committee does not possess the real means to table an agreement referred to it for ratification. A typical example is the signing and subsequent ratifying the United Nations Covenant on Economic, Social and Cultural Rights.[58] As a matter of fact, there has been no case yet in which the NPC Standing Committee refused to ratify an international treaty submitted to it by the State Council for ratification.

5.4. The status of treaties as a source of law in Chinese domestic law

The legal status of international treaties is examined in the context of their relationship to domestic law. Essentially, this is determined by a particular domestic system's constitutional structure, unless otherwise provided in the treaties concerned.

An international treaty concluded and ratified in due course has the force of law within a Contracting State, but it does not necessarily form an integral part of the legal order of the State. In some States, treaties themselves are not part of the domestic law. They become part of domestic law only when some domestic legal instrument makes the treaty into a part of domestic law. In other countries treaties are automatically part of domestic law without any special act of domestic law. The former category of States belong to the Monist system in the theory of international law, the latter the Dualist system.

In this regard, it should be noted that even in a State that takes a Monist approach, a treaty is not necessarily directly applicable since there is a distinction between "self-executing" and "non-self-executing" treaties (in some countries, the terminology used is "directly applicable" and "non-directly applicable" treaties). According to conventional usage of the terms, a "self-executing" international treaty can be applied directly without further legislative or other measures to implement it, a non-self-executing agreement cannot be directly applied, but must be implemented by legislative or other measures.

Although one may argue that an international treaty may be directly applicable if its provisions are unconditional and sufficiently precise,[59] whether a treaty is self-executing or not is always a question of domestic law of the particular State, unless otherwise provided in the treaty. The practice of domestic law in dealing with this issue varies from nation to nation.

In the Chinese context, one has difficulty defining whether the State belongs to the Monist or Dualist system. On the one hand, there exists no statutory provisions that characterise treaties as part of the domestic legal system; on the other, from time to time, international treaties are directly applicable in practice. The Constitution remains silent as to the legal status of an international treaty in Chinese domestic law, numerous laws provide that the international agreement shall prevail in case of conflict between Chinese law and an international treaty. For example, the GPCL provide, "[i]f any international treaty concluded or acceded to by the People's Republic of China contains provisions differing from those in the civil laws of the People's Republic of China, the provisions of the international treaty shall apply, unless the provisions are ones on which the People's Republic of China has announced reservations."[60] In view of this, it can be held that in case of disagreement between an international treaty provision that allows no reservation and the relevant Chinese statutory provision, the international treaty provision shall prevail over relevant statutory provision and apply.

In the meantime, however, the provisions appear to limit the effect of international treaties in the domestic legal order. They suggest that an international treaty be applied only when the relevant law is inconsistent with the treaty. In other words, framers of these laws would be pleased to see that domestic law plays main role where the issue concerned is covered by both an international treaty and a relevant law. Therefore, inherently, there is a risk that courts do not bother seeing if the relevant law is consistent with a treaty before determining the appropriate "applicable law."

5.5. The place of treaties in the hierarchy of source of Chinese law

A question whose answer cannot be found from the above-mentioned statutory provisions regarding precedence of a treaty provision over a relevant domestic provision is: whether implementation of a higher domestic law and a fundamental domestic law in particular is a ground for ignoring its international obligations? For example, the Law for Self-government in the Minority Autonomous Regions (Law for Self-government) is a basic law in multi-ethnical China. According to the Law for Self-government, in minority autonomous regions the organs of self-government, (i.e. the local people's congresses and governments) may modify laws and administrative regulations in accordance with the local requirements. Supposing the law or regulations the local self-government region modified are those that had already been fully translated from a WTO Agreement, doesn't it mean that the international obligation under an international treaty is annulled on the grounds of the higher domestic law?

The place of an international agreement in the hierarchy of source of Chinese law depends on whether the agreement is a treaty (so is an important agreement) or a non-important international agreement. A treaty or an important international agreement does not come into effect until it is ratified by the NPC Standing Committee, while the latter comes into force when the State Council has entered into and then promulgate it. Therefore, in the hierarchy of the domestic law, a treaty or an important international agreement presumably has the same place as laws which are adopted by the NPC Standing Committee; an international agreement other than treaties and important agreements presumably is at the same place as administrative regulations by the State Council. It maybe advisable to identify the place of an international agreement in the hierarchy merely by observing whether the agreement concerned is ratified by the NPC Standing Committee or executed by the State Council.

It should be pointed out that where a law that the NPC or its Standing Committee adopted conflicts with an international agreement, whose coming into effect does not depend on the ratification of the NPC Standing Committee, the international agreement may be prejudiced in relation to application.

In this regard, it is also helpful to mention that, administrative regulations the State Council adopts for the purpose of implementing international agreements are in lower place than the laws the NPC Standing Committee adopts for the same purpose. According to the Constitution, laws are enacted by the NPC or its Standing Committee while the State Council is responsible for adopting administrative regulations. Laws shall prevail in case of conflicts between laws and administrative regulations. This leaves room, in case of conflicts between international agreements and domestic laws, that the implementing regulations of the agreements could not ensure the implementation of the agreements. For the purpose of the implementation of an international agreement to which China is a party, preferable is not to adopt implementing administrative regulations by the State Council, but the implementing law by the NPC standing Committee.[61]

6. The Enforcement of WTO Agreements in Chinese Domestic Law

6.1. How did China ratify WTO Agreements?

In the process of negotiation of the Accession Protocol, China made clear that the WTO Agreements and the Accession Protocol specifying the terms and conditions for China's accession to the WTO fall within the category of "important international agreements" subject to the ratification by the NPC Standing Committee.[62] The perceivable substantial difference between the WTO Agreements and relevant Chinese laws had led to speculation whether the NPC Standing Committee should ratify the Accession Protocol negotiated by the State Council.[63] In fact, there was even no formal debate in the NPC or its Standing Committee; the NPC Standing completed its ratification formality even before the completion of the Draft Protocol on 17 September 2001.[64]

6.2. How does China implement WTO Agreements into Chinese domestic law?

6.2.1. Theoretical approach
The Chinese Constitution and laws again remain silent on whether a treaty shall be applied directly or through domestic law. Therefore, the Chinese practice is the only source for determining their position.

Unfortunately, practice in this regard is not consistent. When China joined the international copyright conventions in accordance with its commitments under the 1992 Sino-US IPRs MOU, the State Council promulgated regulations to implement the agreement.[65] When China joined the Patent

Co-operation Treaty in 1993, it took a similar measure to implement the agreement.[66] Sometimes the NPC Standing Committee adopts a Law (statute) to implement the provisions of a treaty. The typical example is that in 1986 the NPC Standing Committee adopted a special law—Regulations on Diplomatic Privileges and Immunity- for the purpose of implementing the Vienna Convention on Diplomatic Relations.[67] It seems from the empirical evidence that the organ with legislative power prefer to implement international treaty obligations through domestic law.

In contrast, the judicial practice shows a preference for direct application of international treaties. The SPR in certain circumstances instructs the courts across the country to apply directly the provisions of international treaties. For example, on 10 April 1987, in the Notice on the Implementation of the Convention on the Recognition and Enforcement of Foreign Arbitral Awards to Which China Has Acceded, the SPR required the courts which receive an application or a request for judicial assistance to conscientiously handle the matter strictly in conformity with the provisions of the treaties which China has concluded or acceded to.[68] Even in the absence of judicial interpretations by the SPR, courts from time to time apply directly international treaties or permit direct invocation of international treaties by parties to litigations.[69] For example, two cases involving application of the Hague Rules (i.e. International Convention for the Unification of Certain Rules of Law Relating to Bills of Lading) may help understand court practice in this regard. One is *China National Supply Corp. of Xiamen Special Economic Zone of Fujian Province vs. Europe Overseas Steamship Lines NV Belgium*, the other *Japan Sea Fire Insurance Co. Ltd vs. Tianjin Branch of China General Foreign Trade Transportation Co*. In the former case, the plaintiff did not invoke the Hague Rules but the court applied them: in the latter, the plaintiff invoked the rules and the court upheld them.[70]

In this regard, it should be noted that the SPR's judicial interpretations that favour direct application of an international treaty can only play a part where the NPC Standing Committee or the State Council has not acted to enact an implementing law or regulations for the treaty.

6.2.2. Current practice

In the Accession Protocol, China made clear that it would implement the WTO Agreements "through revising its existing domestic laws and enacting new ones fully in compliance with the WTO Agreement(s)." China therefore needs to transform or translate the obligations under WTO Agreements into domestic sources of law. This involves the examination and review of all existing laws, regulations and rules. In principle, those which are found inconsistent with WTO Agreements have to be amended or repealed; where no provisions can be found corresponding to relevant WTO Agreements, new laws or regulations will be enacted pursuant to the WTO Agreements.

Amending or repealing inconsistent domestic law. Amending laws and regulations in line with WTO Agreements has been a major problem at the turn of accession to the WTO. WTO Agreements cover a great number of issues that traditionally are within the exclusive domestic administrative jurisdiction, such required amending is unprecedented in the Chinese history of legislation and administration.[71]

Here noteworthy is that the domestic sources of law that need to be amended or repealed include not only those which are directly inconsistent with WTO Agreements, but also those which require the Chinese government to act in a way that is inconsistent with WTO Agreements. The former is obvious. For example, provisions of the previous Patent Law and Trademark Law supporting final decisions by administrative organs should be repealed to keep in agreement with TRIPS rules allowing judicial review. An example of the latter is that implementation of the domestic laws on Special Economic Zones would result in conflict with the disciplines of uniform administration embodied in the Agreement Establishing the World Trade Organisation.

As a matter of fact, up to 31 December 2001, the NPC and its Standing Committee was found to have revised primarily six laws that contain provisions inconsistent with the WTO Agreements, that is, the Chinese-foreign Equity Joint Venture Law, Chinese-foreign Contractual Joint Venture Law, Wholly Foreign-invested Enterprise Law, the Patent Law, the Trademark Law and the Copyright Law. The State Council cleansed 756 pieces of administrative regulations that had been adopted before the end of 2000 and repealed 71 pieces and declared 80 pieces void in October 2001. In addition, various regulations including the Regulations on Travel Agencies and the Regulations on Foreign-invested Financial Institutions were amended. The Ministries also acted to this end. For example, the State Development Planning Commission (SDPC) had, among a total of 341 regulations and instruments released before the end of 2000, dumped 124 price regulations and will further revamp another 51 price regulations in order to fit its price laws into the framework of the WTO.

An issue directly relevant here is the appropriate authority to mend the inconsistency between Chinese law and WTO Agreements. Since legislative power is shared by numerous organs at the central and local level, it is important to identify which entity has the authority to amend or repeal WTO inconsistent provisions. Of course, with respect to the amending or repeal of laws, the NPC and its Standing Committee in particular will have to act. According to the Legislation Law, the NPC and its Standing Committee possess the exclusive legislative power regarding the State's fundamental economic system and the basic systems of finance, taxation, customs, monetary affairs and foreign trade.[72] Indeed, some relevant laws appear to require that courts in China are under an obligation to apply WTO Agreements vis-à-vis relevant domestic law. However, in accordance with the Constitution, except for the NPC Standing Committee,[73] no organ and no one can declare a law is null and void. In fact, even a court, which has identified a discrepancy between a WTO Agreement and a relevant law, is not in a position to annul the conflicting law. In case of inconsistent administrative regulations and rules, the court is not empowered to take measures to repeal the inconsistent provisions either.

Nevertheless, it would have been preferable if one authoritative organ had been solely responsible for amending or repealing inconsistent provisions in other sources of law. Unfortunately, in practice, such task has so far not been carried out in a unified manner. For example, although the State Council is in a position to mend the inconsistency between WTO Agreements and all the sources of law except the basic laws by the NPC and the laws by the NPC Standing Committee, all that it has done was to revise its own administrative regulations, leaving the rest up to their respective enactors: the ministries and local people's congress and local people's governments.[74]

It should also be pointed out that the process of identifying which law is inconsistent inevitably involves some discretion permitting a government department, agency or official to act in a way that violates the WTO Agreement. Furthermore, in view of the massive changes required [75] there still exist quite a few gaps or inconsistent laws and regulations after the accession. In this context, where new provisions have not yet been enacted, or inconsistencies not mended, Article 142 of the GPCL shall be applied to ensure the prevalence of relevant WTO Agreements over inconsistent domestic laws, regulations and rules.[76] In the Accession Protocol, China confirmed that revising be made "in a timely manner so that China's commitments would be fully implemented within the relevant time frames"; "If administrative regulations, departmental [ministerial] rules or other measures were not in place within such time frames, authorities would still honour China's obligations" under the WTO Agreements and Accession Protocol.

Translating WTO Agreements into domestic law. In the Accession Protocol, China has committed itself to opening to foreign investment various industries that had been prohibitive or restrictive to foreign participation. Since the existing laws and regulations could not provide WTO-consistent rules in this regard, the State Council adopted the Provisional Measures for Administration of Chinese-foreign Equity and Contractual Joint Venture Medical Institutions, the Provisional Measures for Examination and Approval and Administration of Foreign Investment in Rail Freight Transport Services, the Administrative Regulations on the Printing Industry, the Interim Measures for Foreign investment in Cinemas, the Regulations on Foreign Investment in Telecommunications Enterprises, the Regulations on International Maritime Transportation, the Regulations on Foreign-Invested Insurance Companies, the Regulations on Cinema, to allow foreign participation in the medical care, rail freight services, printing, telecommunications services, maritime transportation, insurances and cinema industries. It is advisable to translate WTO Agreements into domestic law and let the domestic law take the main task of transforming the international obligations under WTO Agreements into domestic sphere where the status of treaties as a source of law in Chinese legal system is not assertive. Given the extensive coverage of WTO Agreements, incorporation is no easy task.

Uniform administration. According to the GATT (1994), each WTO Member "shall take such reasonable measures as may be available to it to ensure such observance by regional and local governments and authorities within its territory."[77] The understanding on the interpretation of this provision further strengthens the requirement for uniform administration by introducing the WTO Dispute Settlement Mechanism and even sanctions where the central government of a WTO Member fails to mend a breach by a regional or local government.[78]

Although China is a unitary State, the regions are different in terms of economic prosperity, degree of openness, tradition and governance structure, etc. The law enforcement varies from region to region, not only because of differing local regulations and rules, but because of the discretionary application from region to region. This poses great difficulty for uniform implementation of WTO Agreements. For example, as a result of the implementation of the Law for Self-government in the minority autonomous region, the relevant law or regulations incorporating the obligation under a WTO Agreement will not be applied in its entirety in these regions.

Unifying laws and regulations and rules and ensuring their uniform implementation is a task facing China. Despite difficulty, the de facto supremacy of Party Central Committee and its Politburo in the power structure and the leading role of the State Council in administrative structure should facilitate uniform administration of WTO Agreements in its entire territory of China.

The promulgation of the Legislation Law in 2000 has provided a possibility for clarifying the legislative power delimit, thus contributing to the uniform application of law. The latest subsequent adoption of the Regulations on the Procedures for Enacting Administrative Regulations and the Regulations on the Procedures for Enacting Ministerial Rules On 26 November 2001, and the Regulations for Filing Regulations for Record on 21 December 2001, which became effective on 1 January 2002, will further facilitate the uniform application of law by providing the procedures for the State Council to adopt administrative regulations and for the ministries to adopt and file for record ministerial rules.

Nevertheless, more clarification is needed, for example, by way of promulgating a law amending the Law for Self-Government and regulations concerning the grant of special treatments to SEZs so that the latter do not extend to the WTO Agreements.

6.3. Outstanding problems and issues

6.3.1. Appropriate authority to mend the inconsistency
Since the real legislative power is shared by numerous organs, at the central or local level, it will be appropriate if one authoritative organ is solely responsible for amending or repealing inconsistent provisions for the purpose of keeping in line with WTO Agreements. As far as the regulations and rules are concerned, such an arrangement can become a reality in the current administrative structure. The Constitution provides that people's governments at all levels are under the leadership of the State Council, which has the power to delimit the power of the administrative organs at the central and provincial levels.[79] Hence, the State Council should be able to control the amending or repeal of the rules by Ministries and by local people's governments as well as the administrative regulations by itself. Moreover, given that the rules by the local people's congresses shall not contravene with administrative regulations, the State Council should also be able to exercise control over the amending or repeal of the rules by local people's congresses.

With respect to the amending or repeal of laws, the NPC and its Standing Committee in particular should take the charge. According to the Legislation Law, the NPC and its Standing Committee possess the exclusive legislative power regarding the State's fundamental economic system and the basic systems of finance, taxation, customs, monetary affairs and foreign trade.[80]

Indeed, some relevant laws appear to require that the courts in China are under an obligation to apply WTO Agreements vis-à-vis relevant domestic law. However, in accordance with the Constitution, except for the NPC Standing Committee,[81] no organ and no one can declare a law is null and void. In fact, even a court that, in adjudicating cases, has ascertained a discrepancy between a WTO Agreement and a relevant law, is not in a position to annul the conflicting law. In case of inconsistent administrative regulations and rules, the court is not able to take measures to repeal the inconsistent provisions either.

6.3.2. Law reform in broad terms

To some extent, WTO Agreements reflect the requirements of market economy and can function well in the prevailing legal system of the established market economies. An important aspect is that the implementation of law heavily relies on an independent, fair and effective administrative legal system and a judicial review system. In view of this, WTO Agreements set out corresponding requirements. For example, the General Agreement on Trade in Services provides that "(e)ach Member shall maintain or institute as soon as practicable judicial, arbitral or administrative tribunals or procedures which provide, at the request of an affected supplier, for the prompt review of, and where justified, appropriate remedies for, administrative decisions affecting trade in services."[82] The TRIPS also requires that Members accord to parties an opportunity for review by a judicial authority of final administrative decisions.[83] In contrast, the APL provides that no organ or no one can even challenge before the court any administrative rules, orders and acts of a binding nature.[84] Some other laws even provide that certain administrative acts shall be finally decided by relevant administrative organs. The APL further strengthens the regime by providing that courts shall not accept any suits against "specific administrative acts that shall, as provided by law, be finally decided by an administrative organ."[85] These are in conflict with the WTO Agreements.

WTO Agreements have begun to cover those matters that are traditionally within the exclusive domestic jurisdiction. From the Chinese perspective, such issues are politically sensitive since such systems might undermine the foundation of the regime based on Party and administrative control. From the perspective of the West, however, China could accommodate the demands of WTO Members only when such institutions are established in China. Therefore, China will have to face the challenge to introduce such law reform.

The objective of such law reform is to institute a uniform set of modern administrative law system. Of course, a pragmatic Chinese leadership could initiate the reform by instituting less sensitive procedures. For example, the Chinese government can introduce judicial review as required by the TRIPS through incorporating the TRIPS provisions into the intellectual property laws. This goal is easier to achieve since in China IPRs law reform aimed at rigid protection of IPRs started in early 1990's and people are used to the reform.

7. Reflections and Perspectives

7.1. Prospect of implementing WTO Agreements in China

Under international law, China will be bound by WTO Agreements and its commitments. Seen from the measures taken by the Chinese authority to revise its domestic law that conflicts with the agreements, China would not make the agreements directly applicable; instead, it would prefer incorporating its international commitments into domestic law. In this connection, for the purpose of implementing WTO Agreements, it may be desirable for China to translate the WTO Agreements and its commitments into domestic law by adopting a special law. Since the WTO Agreements require Members to take measures to ensure the implementation of the agreements,[86] that measure might be appropriate.

For the Chinese government, the translation of WTO Agreements into domestic laws and policies is the easy part, it is the non-market factors and domestic legal restraints that pose the greatest challenge to the implementation of the agreements.

In the long run, for the purpose of the implementation of China's international obligations under WTO Agreements, the traditional Chinese attitude towards international law needs to undergo a further change. It is submitted that, in order to eliminate the remaining negative effect of its attitude towards international law, China needs first to unify its practice in applying treaties by domestic judicial and administrative organs. It may even consider revising domestic statutory provisions to the effect that the legal force of international treaties and their direct application are clearly stated.

7.2. Prospect of China's behaviour relating to the Dispute Settlement Mechanism

As Professor Jackson pointed out, "[a] very important consideration affecting a nation's willingness to accept the WTO dispute procedures is that nation's view of the role that the treaty and its institutions should play in its international economic diplomacy."[87] Due to its culture, China is never shy to express its preference for amicable means of dispute settlement in diplomacy.[88] That attitude might discourage China from using, or even accepting, the adjudicating method used by WTO panels for dispute settlement, which is arguably the strength of the WTO dispute settlement mechanism.[89]

With its accession to the WTO, however, China is now bound by the WTO Agreements including the DSU. Unlike other international organs for dispute settlement, the jurisdiction of the DSB is compulsory. Whenever China's partner feels China's trade measures are violating the WTO Agreements, it can bring China to the DSB without prior procurement of China's consent. China cannot challenge the jurisdiction of the DSB that receives the application of that Member.

As a matter of fact, since the inauguration of the WTO, the DSB has been successful and efficient in settling trade disputes between Members. Needless to say, in cases where a complainant can show that China has violated WTO rules, the WTO dispute settlement system mechanism will be in a position to recommend that China change its behaviour and comply; moreover, if compliance is not forthcoming, the DSU will ensure an automatic right to retaliation by the injured WTO Member.

In this regard, it is important to remember that the WTO dispute settlement mechanism can only play a role in areas covered by WTO Agreements. As discussed above, part of the reality is that many dimensions of China's political-economic system are not accounted for by current WTO Agreements. Where such practice culminates in a dispute between a WTO Member and China, the DSB might be frustrated in dealing with it.

Nevertheless, subjecting itself to the dispute settlement mechanism— no matter how unwilling China might be—would result in a desirable side effect per se: China may develop an interest in defending its rights through a generally viable and fair quasi-judicial body.

7.3. Prospect of private enforcement of China's commitments

It should be observed that while most treaties are designed to create rights and obligations between the contracting parties, many international treaties, represented by the WTO Agreements, leave room for private parties to enforce their rights under the agreements. The TRIPS is an example. It requires Members to provide private entities with legal remedies under domestic law, thus making available enforcement to private parties. In this regard, it should be borne in mind that the private enforcement of WTO Agreements against a WTO Member is different from private participation in a WTO Member's enforcement of WTO Agreements against another Member in the context of WTO dispute settlement mechanism.[90] Moreover, private enforcement of WTO Agreements, theoretically, encompasses two situations: enforcement by a private party against its own state and enforcement by a private party against another WTO Member either in the jurisdiction of that country or in an international forum. However, the answer in both circumstances falls completely within the municipal jurisdiction of the WTO Member concerned.

As explained before, Chinese practices regarding the New York Convention, ICSID Convention and the Sino-US Market Access Agreement show changing attitudes towards recognising foreign private party's right to enforce their rights in China under international treaties.

While under the ICSID Convention, China's submitting itself to international arbitration is still conditioned on its consent where a dispute arises, it has expressly agreed, under the Sino-US Market Access Agreement, to foreign private enforcement wherever a dispute arises and the foreign private party desires to do so. Nevertheless, the provision in the Sino-US Market Access Agreement leaves room to presume that China recognises foreign private party's right to enforce WTO Agreements.

It is important to note that the Sino-US Market Access Agreement provides that a foreign "minority shareholder" shall enforce his rights in the investment "under China's laws, regulations and measures." It should also be noted that the provision of the Sino-US Market Access Agreement leaves an important question unanswered: whether the foreign private party can only enforce his right in China. Since the right of the "minority shareholder" is presumably based on China's commitments (i.e. international treaties), the "Chinese laws, regulations and measures" should not refer to the substantive Chinese rules that might contravene with its commitments, but the procedural rules,[91] which provide that aggrieved companies and individuals may resort to administrative reconsideration and/or litigations.

Here comes a question: Can a private party bring an administrative proceeding against the Chinese government for damages incurred as a result of the non-compliance of WTO Agreements by the government? The APL provides that individual, Chinese or foreign,[92] may bring administrative proceedings against the government agency hose "specific administrative act" causes damages to the individual. The same law commands courts to reject suits against administrative orders with general binding nature.[93] In this connection, private party may take administrative actions against the government for damages incurred as the non-compliance if the non-compliance constitutes a "specific administrative act"; where the Chinese government infringes the interests of private parties in implementing laws and regulations that contravene the WTO Agreements, the private parties do not have access to judicial remedy.

The Chinese procedural law rules give no reference as to whether the foreign private party can enforce his right against the Chinese government outside China. Given that the Chinese government holds that it and its property enjoy immunity in its international law practice,[94] the Chinese intention in the above-mentioned provision may be understood to exclude foreign enforcement unless international treaties, e.g. the ICSID Convention allows such enforcement.

A further question regarding private enforcement of WTO Agreements is related to the WTO dispute settlement mechanism. As explained before, WTO Panel and Appellate Body Reports are presumably binding in Chinese law. Then it follows whether a foreign private party, attempting to defend its interests vis-à-vis Chinese trade measures, which the Panel has found to be inconsistent with the WTO Agreements, can enforce the findings in a Chinese court? Given the recent judicial practice in admitting enforcement requests brought by interested individuals,[95] Chinese courts are unlikely to discourage, by merely denying the appropriateness of the foreign private party for litigation subjects, the foreign private party from doing so.

8. Concluding Remarks

There are fundamental questions about the Chinese ability to implement and enforce WTO Agreements. Internally, real tensions exist between application of laws and procedures on one hand, and constitutional and political/ideological considerations on the other.

Moreover, the huge gap between Chinese culture-legal, political and economic-and that of the West, suggests difficulties for the enforcement of WTO Agreements in China. From the perspective of major WTO Members which will inevitably pursue interests endorsed by the WTO Agreements regardless of whether this causes political tensions, however, the difference does not command that the rest of the world must accept the uniqueness of Chinese culture, but not the culture of the WTO Agreements itself. Therefore, unless China is fully prepared to accept the culture of WTO Agreements, trade disputes and political tensions will likely accompany the West's efforts to enforce WTO Agreements in China.

At the diplomatic level, it may not be wrong to frequently remind the Chinese side that WTO laws and procedures were written to be used. It is unlikely that just because one State, China or other, has different ways of approaching dispute settlement, the other states should bow to these specific needs and ignore the mechanism at their disposal, such as sanctions. On the other hand, it might be useful to remember that patience will pay off in dealing with a country like China.

Fortunately, China has no reason to disregard its commitments. The WTO succeeded the club-like atmosphere from the GATT. As a matter of fact, WTO Members are becoming ever more engaged with the detailed process of the WTO, especially its dispute settlement procedures. A pragmatic China knows that if it wants to protects its interests as a club member and play a role in the club, it will have to treat its obligations under WTO Agreements seriously and reform its domestic legal structure.

Notes

1. According to the Vienna Convention on the Law of Treaties, a "treaty" means "an international agreement concluded between States, whether embodied in a single instrument or in two or more related instruments and whatever its particular designation" (See Article 2 (1)). In the Chinese context, however, a "treaty" refers only to a legal instrument bearing the title of "*tiaoyue*" as concluded between China and other states, and "*xieding*" all the rest of the legal instruments. An empirical experience of treaty practice shows, as one Chinese scholar points out, the name of "*tiaoyue*" is used to designate the most important of international documents, regulating political, economic or other relations between contracting parties. See Wang Yaotian, International Trade Treaties and Agreements (*Guoji maoyi tiaoyue he xieding*), Beijing: Finance and Economics Publishing House (*Chaijing chubanshe*), 1958, p. 12.

   It should be made clear that international treaties and agreements are used interchangeably in this article. When it comes to multilateral trade treaties concluded under the auspices of the GATT and the WTO, this article follows the customary reference "agreements." On the other occasions, "international treaties" is used.

   WTO Agreements or WTO-administered agreements refer to those agreements that were concluded under the auspices of the Uruguay Round of the GATT and those concluded subsequently under the auspices of the WTO.

2. The most prominent bilateral trade agreements are the China-Japan trade agreement (1978), China-US trade agreement (1979) and China-EC Trade and Economic Cooperation Agreement (1985).

3. For an analysis of how the GATT was negotiated and "provisionally" applied for 47 years, see, for example, David Palmeter and Petros C. Mavroidis, *Dispute Settlement in the World Trade Organization*, The Hague, London, Boston: Kluwer Law International Law, 1999, pp. 1-7.

4. See John H. Jackson, *The World Trade Organisation: Constitution and Jurisprudence*, London: The Royal Institute of International Affairs, 1998, p.37.

5. "Single package" means that in order to become Members, the prospective WTO Members have to accede to or accept both the Agreement Establishing the World Trade Organisation and all the Multilateral Trade Agreements in the four Annexes, rather than acceding to or accepting one or more of these agreements. The conception is embodied in Article XII (1) and Article XVI (4) of the Agreement Establishing the World Trade Organisation.

6. Article 16 (4) of the DSU provides that, unless the DSB rejects the Panel Report with a consensus, the losing party shall adopt the Report.

7. Article XVI (4) of the Agreement Establishing the World Trade Organisation.

8. The Trade Policy Review Mechanism (TPRM) was confirmed as an integral part of the WTO in Annex 3 of the Agreement establishing the World Trade Organization. Its purpose is to "contribute to improved adherence by all Members to rules, disciplines and commitments made under the Multilateral Trade Agreements and, where applicable, the Plurilateral Trade Agreements, and hence to the smoother functioning of the multilateral trading system, by achieving greater transparency in, and understanding of, the trade policies and practices of Members."

9. Article 3 (2) of the DSU.

10. Confidence in the system is borne out by the number of cases brought to the WTO—167 cases by March 1999 compared to some 300 disputes dealt with during the entire life of GATT (1947–94).

11. China ratified the Vienna Convention on 3 September 1997, with, among other things, a reservation to Article 66 concerning submitting disputes to the International Court of Justice for judicial settlement and other procedures for arbitration and conciliation.

12. Professor John H. Jackson observed that failure of a WTO Member concerned to implement the DSB recommendations should be deemed as a breach of international law. See John H. Jackson, The WTO Dispute Settlement Understanding-Misunderstanding of the Nature of Legal Obligations, 91 *AJIL* 60 (1997), pp. 60-64.

13. Most commodities on the Chinese market used to be priced by the state. As a result of the price reform carried out step by step and according to plan, by July 2001 90 percent of retail, agricultural and capital goods had been priced by the market rather than the state. Only 13 products or services remain under state pricing control, compared with 141 in 1992: See Fu Jing, Prices of more goods, services liberalized, *China Daily*, 12 July 2001.

14. United States Department of Commerce, U.S. Trade Agreements with China, available at < http://199.88.185.106/China/Agreements.htm>.

15. A typical example is that in a nation-wide crime crack-down campaign of 1983, the NPC Standing Committee substantially shortened, merely by issuing a decree, the period in which a defendant involved in a criminal prosecution of first instance can file an appeal petition under the first Criminal Procedural Law (1979).

16. For a detailed description of *guanxi*, see Lucian Pye, *The Dynamics of Chinese Politics*, Cambridge, Massachusetts: Gunn & Hain, Publishers, Inc., 1981, P. 139.

17. For an explanation of how *guanxi* affects law enforcement, see, for example, Xiaoying Ma & Leonard Ortolano, Informal Rules of Behaviour Affecting Compliance, in: Ma & Ortolano, *Environmental Regulation in China: Insti-*

tutions, Enforcement, and Compliance, Lanham, Boulder New York, Oxford: Rowman & Littlefield Publishers, Inc.:2000, pp. 82-85.

18. For a definition of "face" and a description of how face-losing or saving behaviours affect law enforcement in China, see, *ibid.*, pp. 85-87.

19. It should be pointed out that the notion of "interest group" in the tightly knitted Chinese society might be different from that in democratic societies. The author borrows this concept in the sense that these "groups" can influence the party policy-making.

20. The role of interest groups in China's policy-making process has not attracted adequate attention as it should. For an analysis of interest groups in China, see He Qinglian, A Study of Interest Groups in the Current Chinese Society, *Shuwu* (Bookhouse), Vol. 3, 2000.

21. A recent example is that fearing the "subversive" information flow on the Internet, the Chinese government adopted new regulations, i.e. the Provisions for Information Service on the Internet, to limit foreign investment in the Internet service industry, despite the fact that the fledging industry has so far relied heavily on foreign venture capital and needs further support from foreign investment. The regulations make the Internet firm liable for site content and set out nine banned categories–including that which "harms state security, betrays national secrets, destroys national unity, hurts the good name and interests of the nation, destroys national religious policy, spreads rumours, damages social order or destroys social stability." See Reuters, China Lays down the Law on Internet, available at *International Herald Tribune*, 3 October 2000, p. 19.

22. Before 1994, in its annual review on the extension of China's MFN treatment, the US Congress had linked its trade policy with China's human rights records and other political issues. Even when the House of Representatives and the Senate consecutively passed the bill extending China's PNTR treatment, which will put an end to the practice of annual review, they still did not forget attaching to the bill provisions aimed at the monitoring of human rights development in China. On this, Sun Yuxi, Spokesman for Ministry of Foreign Affairs, commented: "This is a trade agreement between China and the United States and we think it is inappropriate to include in it items which have nothing to do with trade," quoted in Greg Torode, Landmark trade vote hailed, *South China Morning Post*, 21 September 2000, Internet Edition.

23. The United States and other WTO Members have made clear that the WTO will not be used as a political forum for both China and Taiwan to discuss the policy issues of One-China or Taiwan's independence.

24. It is observed that China has no tradition of judge-made law, although modern Chinese law has been a mixture of continental European model,

Anglo-American model and the Chinese traditional model (See Albert HY Chen, *An Introduction to the Legal System of the People's Republic of China*, Singapore, Malaysia, Hong Kong: Butterworths Asia, 1992, p. 22). Chinese law is basically composed of statutory provisions. From a legal point of view, these statutory provisions are the source of rules that are to be applied in economic and social life.

25. Murray Scot Tanner, Organizations and Politics in China's Post-Mao Law-Making System, in Pitman B. Potter (ed.): *Domestic Law Reforms in Post-Mao China*, M.E. Sharpe: Armonk, London, 1994, pp58-60, 65-71.

26. A typical example is the Enterprise Bankruptcy Law. This Law was promulgated on 2 December 1986 and came into force on 1 November 1988. Despite the fact that two thirds of all the 300,000 state-owned enterprises have run into difficulty and one thirds of them have reached the statutory line of bankruptcy, very few of them have gone bankrupt pursuant to the Law. (According to Li Shuguang, a bankruptcy expert, only some 16,000 enterprises—including private enterprises and collective enterprises and foreign investment enterprises—cases of bankruptcy were filed by mid 2001. See Li Shuguang, Bankruptcy Law in China: Lessons of the Past Twelve Years, *Harvard Asian Quarterly*, Winter/2001).

27. In theory or in the practice of countries with an established tradition of the rule of law, conflicting statutory provisions may be reconciled, e.g. by adjusting the meaning of competing provisions to achieve that result which will give effect to the purpose of those provisions while maintaining the unity of statutory scheme. However, that might prove to be a difficult or even impossible task in China due to an unskilful judiciary and/or interested legislators.

28. Notably the Ministry of Information Industry, which oversees telecom and the Internet, is particularly unwilling to open the telecommunication service market to foreign participation, although Minister Wu Jichuan is a liberal in rhetoric. According to the Far Eastern Economic Review, Wu moved to cancel foreign equity stakes in China's second telecom operator, Unicom, and in Chinese Internet content providers. See *Far Eastern Economic Review*, the Internet Edition, 25 November 1999.

29. For example, judicial independence means that judges handling a given case should be free from interference from other judges. In China, judges are not equal. Instead, they are fixed into a hierarchical bureaucracy. Every judge is made responsible for the head of a division that he belongs to, and the division is responsible to the Judicial Committee (*shenpan weiyuanhui*), which according to Article 11 of the Organizational Law of the People's Courts, is responsible for "summarizing judicial experience, discussing important and difficult cases and other questions relevant to judicial work." Similarly, pro-

fessionalism is also a problem with the Chinese judiciary. The Judges' Law requires judges to be graduates of tertiary educational institutions in law or in other subjects who have acquired specialized legal knowledge (Article 9 (6)). Moreover, the same article permits judges appointed before the coming into effect of the law who do not meet such standards to retain their posts by undergoing necessary training. As a matter of fact, most of judges are not university graduates. Many judges are former PLA officers. They learn law on the job and through such court-sponsored training programs as the "Spare Time Universities" (*yeyu daxue*) affiliated to High People's Courts or Intermediate People's Courts). Moreover, the presidents or vice presidents and other ranking court officials are normally transferred from military, Party or government posts.

30. For an analysis of the decentralising process in China, see Li Donglu, The Trend of Economic Decentralizing and its Impact on Foreign Policies (in Chinese), *Strategy and Management* (*Zhanlue yu guanli*), vol. 6, 1996, pp. 44-49.

31. According to a survey by the State Economic Restructuring Commission (SCER), which was directed toward local officials throughout the country, two thirds of the official responders stated that "for the sake of local interests, even if there exists constraints by the [central] policy, we will pursue the local interests irregardless of [policy]." See SCER, A Comprehensive Investigation Report of Local Officials in China (in Chinese), *Management World*, 1996, no. 2, p. 197.

    A typical example is as follows: In an effort to introduce competition in the grains distribution industry, which was traditionally reserved for state-owned grain companies, the Chinese government provided in a directive that companies shall be allowed to deal in the nation-wide distribution of grains as long as they meet such thresholds as license from the local grain administration. However, the national provision met with challenge in Hainan Province, which tried to protect the local grain distributing companies. In a joint notice, seven administrative departments under the provincial government required that grain providers out of the province further procure provincial approval before transporting grains into the province. Failure to meet the provincial requirement would be deemed as illegal trading of grains and thus invite severe punishment. See *Voice of China Monthly* (*Huasheng yuebao*), Vol. 5, 2000.

32. Evidence of this negative attitude towards Western-style international law can be found in an observation of Huan Xiang, the former Chairperson of the China International Law Society and senior diplomat: "Principles and rules of international law since Hugo Grotius's time, [in general] reflected the interests and demands of the bourgeoisie, the colonialists and in particular of the

imperialists. The big and strong powers have long been bullying the small and weak nations, sometimes even resorting to armed aggression. International law has often been used by the imperialists and hegemonists as a means to carry out aggression, oppression and exploitation and to further their reactionary foreign policies. Apologies for aggression and oppression can often be found in the writings on international law." See Huan Xiang, Strive to Build up New China's Science of International Law, in *Selected Articles from Chinese Yearbook of International Law*, Beijing: China Translation & Publ. Corp. 1983, p. 3.

33. Without exception, they stick to the notion of sovereignty, which is a keystone of customary international law. In this regard, it should be noted that the Chinese perspective of sovereignty is different from that of the Western countries.

   It has been a practice that China promotes its theory of Five Principles of Peaceful Existence on almost every international forum. The Five Principles, which are based on the notion of absolute sovereignty, include mutual-respect sovereignty and territorial integrity, mutual non-aggression, and mutual non-interference with internal affairs, equality and mutual benefits, and peaceful co-existence.

   China, sensitive about national sovereignty, has taken the position that "international agreement made without the participation and signature of China's representative will have no binding force whatsoever on China."

34. It is observed that from a practical standpoint, Chinese jurists accept the existence of general international law with uniform rules binding upon all countries. See Shao-chuan Leng, Arms Control, in Shao-chuan Leng et al, (ed.), *Law in Chinese Foreign Policy: Communist China & Selected Problems of International Law*, Dobbs Ferry, New York: Oceana Publications, Inc., 1972, p.243.

35. "Unequal treaties" is a term forged in the Chinese context and referred specifically to those treaties that were "imposed by foreign powers by use of force or coercion." See, for instance, Wang Xianshu (*ed.*), *International Law* (in Chinese), Beijing: the Press of China University of Political Science and Law, 1994, p. 367.

36. Most Chinese publicists agree that Article 38 of the Statute of the International Court of Justice can be interpreted as recognising customary law as one of the sources of international law (Article 38 of the Statute of the International Court of Justice: "1. The Court, whose function is to decide **in accordance with international law** such disputes as are submitted to it, shall apply...(b) international custom, as evidence of general practice accepted as law..." (Emphasis is added by the author.)

Nevertheless, some Chinese international lawyers tend to underestimate the momentum of customary international law vis-à-vis international treaties. See Wang Tieya, *Introduction to International Law (Guojifa Yinlun)*, Beijing: Peking University Press, 1998, p. But, for others, customary law is not self-evident and therefore subject to manipulation.

It is justified to assert that the doctrine of legal instrumentality also finds another expression in the current attitude of China towards general customary international law. As interpreted by Chinese diplomats, customary international law can be used to serve the foreign policy goals of China. In its international behaviour, China has shown no hesitation to use, whenever convenient, principles of international law to support its position or condemn the policies of others without being hampered by theoretical difficulties and inconsistencies. For example, China is impressively skilled in defending its positions and actions towards Taiwan in terms of sacred sovereign right and non-interference in internal affairs recognised by international law. In a recent protest against a bombing on the Chinese embassy in Belgrade, China accused the US-led NATO force of, among others, violating universally acknowledged diplomatic privileges and immunities.

37. For example, Article 142 (3) of the GPCL provides " International practice may be applied to matters for which neither the law of the People's Republic of China nor any international treaty concluded or acceded to by the People's Republic of China has any provisions." However, in view of China's long-standing viewpoint, it is arguable that the reference to "international practice" is not equivalent to customary rules of international law. As a matter of fact, the empirical evidence of judiciary practice shows that the Chinese courts apply, for example, rules like International Chamber of Commerce (ICC)'s standard commercial terms, e.g. Incoterms, as international practice in adjudicating cases involving foreign traders.

38. Given that such declarations may be made even unconditionally or on condition of reciprocity on the part of several or certain states, or for a certain time, this type of jurisdiction is called "optional compulsory jurisdiction" in the theory of international law. In 1946, the then Nationalist government of the Republic of China made such a declaration, but in 1972, soon after the People's Republic of China resumed the seat of China in the United Nations, the government of the PRC declared that it did not recognise the declaration of the Nationalist government.

39. See, Liang Xi, *International Law (Guoji fa)*, Wuhan: Wuhan University Press, 1993, p. 403.

40. For most Chinese publicists, individuals and companies can be directly entitled to certain rights and individuals can even be held guilty of crimes (for

example, war crimes) under international law, but they are not subjects of international law, because they are not in the same position as states to bear obligations under international law. See, for example, Liang Xi (ed.), *International Law (Guoji Fa)*, Wuhan: Wuhan University Press, 1993, pp.74-78.

41. The Chinese official attitude towards the status of private parties in international law and the immunity of sovereign states coincides with the traditional Chinese mentality. Traditionally, private parties are unwilling, if not discouraged, to challenge their government (See Wang Chengguang, *et al* (ed.), *Introduction to Chinese Law*, Hong Kong, Singapore: Sweet & Maxwell Asia, 1997, pp. 4-8.). As a matter of fact, even after the promulgation of APL in 1990, private parties still try to refrain from bringing the government to court. In a sense, in an administrative-dominant society, the government is not used to being challenged, let alone being challenged in international forum.

42. The New York Convention directly confers rights to a private party of a Contracting State to enforce an arbitral award in another Contracting State.

43. See the ICSID Convention. It provides that a Contracting State will be under an obligation to submit a particular dispute to conciliation or arbitration by ICSID if it gives consent in its agreement with the nationals of other Contracting States.

44. The Agreement, for example, provides that "China confirmed that, while it had limited its market access commitments in some sectors to permit foreigners to hold a minority equity interest, a minority shareholder can enforce, under China's laws, regulations and measures, rights in the investment." See the Last Paragraph of Section III (Protocol Commitments).

45. For example, see "China needs the WTO and the WTO needs China," *Economic News (Jingji ribao)*, 20 January 2000.

46. China's competition policy centres on the Anti-unfair Competition Law (1993) and the Regulations for Anti-dumping and the Regulations on Anti-subsidies (2001). The Anti-unfair Competition Law touches upon some of the competition issues, but fails to deal with monopoly. Presumably, the phenomenon is related to state monopoly in many industries.

47. The Organisation for Economic Co-operation and Development (OECD) has formulated an anti-corruption code, though not legally binding to nationals of its Members. The United States, which is also a member of the OECD, has enacted the Foreign Corrupt Practices Act.

48. Based on the amount of specific proposed investment, a proposal is finally submitted to authorities at corresponding level for approval, but the screening process normally involves lower-level authorities. For example, a proposed project of above US$30 million investment shall be finally examined and approved by the central authorities, but the authorities of the province where the investment is intended to be located is unexceptionally involved in the

screening process. Moreover, different government agencies—the department responsible for the administration of the industry to which the proposed investment belongs, the department of foreign trade and economic co-operation, the economic planning department, the department for industry and commerce, and the departments for environmental protection, fire fighting, etc, are involved in the screening process and many of them have the power to veto or defer the proposed investment. Furthermore, the authorities base their examining of the proposed investment project on varied, often vaguely worded and sometimes contradictory substantial requirements as well as procedural requirements. For an analysis of the screening regime, see Qingjiang Kong, Foreign Direct Investment Regime in China, 57 *Heidelberg Journal of International Law*, 4 (1997), p. 881.

49. Article 89 (1) of the Constitution (as amended in 1998).
50. Article 100 of the Constitution.
51. Article 90 of the Constitution.
52. Section 62 of the Interpretations on Certain Questions regarding the Administrative Procedure Law (SPR, 2000).
53. Resolution regarding the Strengthening of Legal Interpretation Work, promulgated by the 19th Session of the Standing Committee of the 5th National People's Congress on 10 June 1981.
54. Article 89 (9) of the Constitution. It is noteworthy that the Constitution differentiates between treaties and agreements. However, for the sake of convenience, the term "treaty" or "agreement" in this article is actually referred to as any international legal instrument unless otherwise indicated in the context. Cf., see above note 1.
55. Article 67 (14) of the Constitution provides that the NPC Standing Committee has the power to "decide on the ratification or abrogation of treaties and important agreements concluded with foreign states."
56. Article 7 of the Law of Procedures for Concluding Treaties provides that the following "treaties and agreements" need to be ratified by the NPC Standing Committee: (a) political treaties such as friendship and co-operation treaties and peace treaties; (b) treaties and agreements relating to territory and boundary-delimiting; (c) treaties and agreements on judicial assistance and extradition; (d) treaties and agreements that differ from the laws of the People's Republic of China; (e) treaties and agreements whose ratification is agreed on by Contracting Parties; (f) other treaties and agreements that require ratifying.
57. See Article 8 of the Law of Procedures for Concluding Treaties.
58. After heated debate and careful consideration, the Chinese government signed on the Covenant in 1997 and then referred it to the NPC Standing Committee for ratification in 1998. However, quite a few members of the NPC Standing

Committee then argued that time was not ripe for China to accord to its citizens rights as provided by the Covenant. Only after two years, did the same NPC Standing Committee agree to ratify it in February 2001 despite much opposition from its members.

59. The Court of First Instance of the European Communities holds the same view. See Opel Austria GmbH v. Council of the European Union, quoted from E. Lauterpacht et al (ed.), *International Law Reports*, Vol. 113, Cambridge: Cambridge University Press, 1999, p.297. For, specifically, the direct applicability of WTO Agreements, see Carlos D. Espósito, International Trade and National Legal Orders: The Problem of direct applicability of WTO Law, in: Paolo Mengazzi (ed.), *International Trade Law on the 50th Anniversary of the Multilateral Trade System*, Multa Paucis AG, 1999, pp.429-469.

60. Article 142 of the GPCL (1986). Also, see Article 238 of CPL, which reads "[w]here the provisions of international treaties which China has concluded or to which China is a party are different from those of this law, the former shall apply, except those clauses to which China has made reservation."

61. Li Peng, Chairman of the NPC Standing Committee, was reported to hold that the NPC should make feasibility studies on incorporating international agreements into national laws whose enactment falls exclusively within the scope of the NPC or its Standing Committee. Like in other countries, the State Council (executive branch of the Chinese government) assumes more and more powers that formerly belonged to the legislature (the NPC and its Standing Committee). Li's proposal might result from a consideration that the legislature should secure more power from the State Council. It would result in a positive effect on the implementation of the international agreements if it became a reality.

62. Article 7 of the Law of Procedures for Concluding Treaties.

63. According to Article 46 of the Vienna Convention, "[a] state may not invoke that fact that its consent to be bound by a treaty has been expressed in violation of its internal law regarding competence to conclude treaties invalidating its consent unless that violation was manifest and concerned a rule of its internal law of fundamental importance." As a contracting party, China is bound by the provision.

64. Early on 25 August 2000, 15 months before China's signing of the Accession Protocol, the NPC Standing Committee adopted the Decision on China's Accession to the WTO. The decision declared that the NPC Standing Committee was satisfied with the WTO negotiation up to that point and it "agrees that the State Council, in accordance with the afore-mentioned principles, conclude the WTO accession negotiations and designate its representative to sign the Accession Protocol on China's Accession to the World Trade Orga-

nization, thus completing the procedures on China's WTO accession subject to the ratification of the President of the country."

65. Provisions on the Implementation of the International Copyright Treaties (1992).

66. The Provisions on the Implementation of the Patent Co-operation Treaty in China (1993).

67. China acceded to the Vienna Convention on Diplomatic Relations (1961) in 1975.

68. Similarly, when the United Nations Convention on Contracts for the International Sale of Goods was ratified and became effective in 1988, the SPR in an internal directive ordered the courts at different levels to apply the convention directly in relevant cases. See SPR, Memorandum of the National Working Meeting on Adjudication of Economic Cases involving Foreign, Hong Kong or Macau Elements in Coastal Regions (12 June, 1989), Part III, Chapter 5 (entitled "Questions on Application of Laws").

69. In theory, direct application of international treaties by the court is different from private invocation.

70. The two cases can be found in Priscilla Leung Mei-fun (ed.), *China Law Report*, 1991, Vol. 3, Singapore, Malaysia, Hong Kong: Butterworths Asia, 1995, at pp. 740-744 and pp. 745-748.

71. According to a report by Xinhua News Agency on 4 March 2001, some 148 laws, regulations are being amended and some 571 to be repealed.

72. Article 8 of the Legislation Law.

73. Article 67 (7) of the Constitution.

74. Article 89 (4) of the Constitution provides that people's governments at all levels are under the leadership of the State Council, which has the power to determine the power of the administrative organs at the central and provincial levels. Hence, the State Council should be able to define the amending or repeal of rules by Ministries and by local people's governments, as well as amendment and repeal of administrative regulations by the State Council itself. Moreover, given that the local people's congress rules shall not contravene administrative regulations, the State Council should also be able to exercise control over the amending or repeal of the rules by local people's congresses.

75. No measures will be taken to conform with the international treaty before the inconsistency between the statutes and the international treaty comes to the attention of the authority possessing the power to amend the inconsistent provisions. Even if the authority has noticed the inconsistency, it is still unclear is how long it needs in order to take actions to remedy it. It is a worrysome fact that no Chinese law, including the Legislation Law, deals with this situation.

76. Reservations are generally not permitted under the WTO Agreements. The Agreement Establishing the World Trade Organization and the Agreement on Trade-related Aspects of Intellectual Property Rights (TRIPS) provide two examples. See, respectively, Article XVI (5) of the Agreement Establishing the World Trade Organization and Article 72 of the TRIPS Agreement. There are some provisions in some Multilateral Trade Agreements that allow developing countries to make reservations. However, from the negotiation process, it was found that China was not permitted to make reservations to those developing country provisions.

77. Article XXIV: 12 of the GATT (1994).

78. See the Understanding on the Interpretation of Article XXIV of the General Agreement on Tariffs and Trade 1994, Section 14.

79. Article 89 (4) of the Constitution.

80. Article 8 of the Legislation Law.

81. Article 67 (7) of the Constitution.

82. Article VI: 2(a) of the General Agreement on Trade in Services.

83. Article 41 (4) of the TRIPS Agreement.

84. Article 12 (2) of the APL provides that courts shall even not accept suits concerning regulations, decrees and orders by the administrative organs.

85. Article 12 (4) of the APL.

86. The Understanding on the Interpretation of Article XXIV of the General Agreement on Tariffs and Trade 1994 reiterates the obligation of Article XXIV: that each member "shall take such reasonable measures as may be available to it to ensure" observance of the provisions of WTO Agreements by regional and local governments and authorities within its territories. Article XVI (4) of the Agreement Establishing the World Trade Organisation is a similar provision.

87. John H. Jackson, *The World Trade Organisation: Constitution and Jurisprudence*, London: The Royal Institute of International Affairs, 1998, pp. 76-78.

88. Probably, the traditional preference for consultation and other amicable means for dispute settlement may find support in new context. A major power, with attractive market potential, presumably owns more bargaining power in diplomacy-negotiation-oriented processes of dispute settlement. A recent example is the dispute of garlic exports with Korea. The Korean government decided to impose a 300 percent punitive antidumping duty on garlic imported from China. China, which had recurred a huge deficit in relation to its trade with Korea, was angered by the failure of Korea to "give due and sympathetic consideration" to China's longstanding position of settling disputes through bilateral consultation, and responded by stopping imports from Korea of IT

products including mobile telephones, for which China is a real and prospective major market. In the subsequent consultation, China won this give-and-take game in that both withdrew their trade measures.

89. The DSU indeed leaves room for Members concerned to engage in consultation to settle their disputes. It, however, only requires parties mutually to "give sympathetic consideration to and afford adequate opportunity for consultation." See Article 4 (2) of the DSU.

90. The latter examples are the WTO Appellate Body decisions on the private counsel representation of Saint Lucia to the EU-Bananas Case and the Indonesia-Autos Case. See WT/DS27/AB/R and WT/DS54/R respectively. For private participation in the enforcement of WTO Agreements, see, for instance, Michael Laidhold, Private Party Access to the WTO: Do Recent Developments in International Trade Dispute Resolution Really Give Private Organisation a Voice in the WTO? *The Transnational Lawyer*, Vol. 12, 2 (1999), pp. 427-450; and Marco C. Bronckers, Private participation in the enforcement of WTO law: the new EC Trade Barriers Regulation, 33 *Common Market Law Review* (1996) 2, pp. 299-318.

91. Currently, procedural law rules are dispersed in varieties of laws, regulations and measures, including those specifically dealing with administrative consideration and administrative litigation, such as, the Administrative Considerations Law (NPC Standing Committee, 1 October 1999), the APL (NPC, enacted 1989, revised 1990), and other laws and regulations such as the Copyright Law (Article 50).

92. Foreign citizens share the same right as Chinese on the basis of reciprocity. Articles 67 of the APL provides that "[a] citizen, a legal person or any other organisations who suffers from damages because of infringement upon his or its lawful rights and interests by a specific administrative act of an administrative organ or the personnel of an administrative organ, shall have the right to claim compensation." Article 71 provides that "[f]oreign nationals, stateless persons and foreign organisations that are engaged in administrative suits in the People's Republic of China shall have the same litigation rights and obligations as citizens and organisations of the People's Republic of China."

93. Private party cannot challenge the non-conforming laws and regulations per se. See Article 12 (2) of the APL.

94. For instance, in the case of Jackson v. the People's Republic of China, China declared that it should be free from foreign jurisdiction based on the "internationally recognised principle of sovereign immunity." See *Chinese Yearbook of International Law* (in Chinese), 1983, Beijing: China Foreign Translation and Publication Company, 1993, pp. 31, 47-52.

95. For instance, see Article 90, Para. 2 of the Interpretations on Certain Questions regarding the Administrative Procedure Law (SPR, 2000).

Appendix

Table A.1 China's WTO Accession: Chronicles

21 April 1947	The Chinese Representative signed the Protocol On Provisional Application of the General Agreement on Tariffs and Trade
1 October 1949	The People's Republic of China was founded
6 March 1950	The "Nationalist Government" on Taiwan withdrawal was made to the Secretary General of the United Nations in the name of the "Republic of China". No Contracting Parties but Czechoslovakia challenged the legal force of the withdrawal. The withdrawal took effect on 5 May 1950
October 1971	The United Nations General Assembly passed Resolution 2758, which authorized the resumption of the People's Republic of China's membership in the United Nations. China did not show interest in applying for the GATT's contracting party
1981	China attended, as a non-voting delegate, the third Multi-Fibre Agreement (MFA) negotiation under the auspices of the Textile Committee under the GATT
May 1981	China became an observer of the Textile Committee
November 1982	China attended, for the first time, as an observer, the 38th Contracting Parties' Meeting of the GATT
January 1984	China signed the third MFA and became a full member of the Textile Committee
November 1984	China was allowed to attend, as an observer, the GATT Council and the meetings of its subordinate institutions. China has since then attended the GATT Contracting Parties' annual meeting.
April 1985	China became a member of the Informal Consultation Group of Developing Countries within the GATT
10 January 1986	The then Chinese leader expressed China's intention on the occasion of receiving the visiting Secretary-General of the GATT, Dunkel
10 July 1986	China informed Director-General of the GATT, formally submitting a request for the resumption of China's status as a GATT signatory (L/6017)

Table A.1   China's WTO Accession: Chronicles (*cont.*)

September 1986	China participated in the GATT's 8th round of negotiation, or the Uruguay Round Negotiation
March 1987	With Ambassador Pierre-Louis Girard as its Chairman, the Working Party, whose membership consists of all interested GATT contracting parties, was set up
15 April 1994	The Uruguay Round Negotiations concluded with the publication of the Marrakech Ministerial Statement in Morocco, China signed the Final Results of the Uruguay Round
1 January 1995	The WTO Agreement entered into force
July 1995	The first round negotiation for China's WTO accession kicked off
7 December 1995	China applied for accession to the Marrakesh Agreement Establishing the World Trade Organization; the existing Working Party on China's Status as a GATT 1947 Contracting Party was transformed into a WTO Accession Working Party
23 May 1997	The Working Party reached agreement on non-discriminatory treatment and judicial review
April 1999	During Premier Zhu Rongji's visit to the United States, the two sides concluded the Bilateral Agricultural Cooperation Agreement (ACA)
15 November 1999	China and the United States reached the Bilateral Agreement on Market Access relating to China's accession to the WTO
19 May 2000	China and the European Commission reached the Bilateral Agreement on Market Access relating to China's accession to the WTO
8 June 2001	China and the United States reached agreement on major outstanding issues concerning China's accession to the WTO in Shanghai, such as agricultural subsidies, annual farm imports from the U.S.
6 September 2001	China finished negotiation with the EU on remaining issues, primarily concerning insurance
13 September 2001	China concluded with Mexico the Bilateral Agreement on Market Access relating to China's accession to the WTO. This was the last of the 37 bilateral agreements

Table A.1 China's WTO Accession: Chronicles *(cont.)*

17 September 2001	The 18th meeting of the Working Party approved the draft Protocol for the Accession of China to the WTO
10 November 2001	The Ministerial Conference ratified by consensus the Report of Working Party, which contains the draft Accession Protocol
11 November 2001	China signed on the Protocol of Accession and submitted the Ratification of the Accession Protocol
20 November 2001	Mike Moore, Director-General of the WTO informed WTO Members of China's acceptance of the Accession Protocol

Index

Access
  Market access, 6-7, 16, 18, 28-34, 35,
    70-71, 159, 173, 237, 256, 295, 300,
    302, 307, 328
Accession, 3-51, 61-74, 76-78, 80, 82,
    85-86, 106-108, 117, 119, 121-122,
    126, 133-134, 140, 146-147, 158,
    160, 168-171, 173, 199, 207, 211,
    222, 230, 236-238, 240-242, 251,
    260-262, 269, 271, 279, 295-296,
    299-300, 302-303, 307-309, 318, 320,
    322, 327
Agreement
  Agreement on Basic
    Telecommunications Services
    (ABTS), 31, 235-236, 238-239, 260
  Agreement on Government
    Procurement (AGP), 184, 189
  Agreement on Trade-related
    Aspects of Investment Measures
    (TRIMS), 17
  Agreement on Trade-related
    Aspects of Intellectual Property
    Rights (TRIPS), 17
  Multilateral trade agreements, 122-
    123, 158
  Plurilateral trade agreements, 332
    (footnotes)
Anti-dumping, 11, 12, 49, 66-67, 76-77,
    80, 132, 134, 146

Anti-monopoly, 75, 167, 238
Appeal, 108, 125, 196, 272, 284
Appellate Body (AB), 100, 108, 125,
    142, 298, 329
Arbitration, 44, 305, 328
Asia-Pacific Economic Co-operation
    (APEC), 199

Balance of payment (BOPs), 64
Barrier(s)
  Non-tariff barriers, 9, 32-34, 80, 135
Basic telecommunications services
    (BTS), 234, 238
Bilateral
  Bilateral negotiation, 19, 28, 137

Compliance, 15, 49-50, 61, 64, 70, 74-77,
    82, 107-110, 142-144, 159, 171, 173,
    177, 213, 222, 255, 271, 298-301,
    320, 327, 329
Compensatory, 124
Concession(s), 4, 6, 17, 48, 125, 133-
    135, 137, 141-142, 160, 163-164,
    167, 263, 297, 309
Consensus
  Negative consensus, 124-125
Consultation, 5, 48, 69, 125-127, 135,
    138, 140, 142, 145-146, 195, 297
Constitution, 39-40, 104, 158, 311-314,
    316-318, 321, 324

Contracting party, 4-6, 13, 98-99, 296-297

Contractual joint venture(s) (CJV), 75, 81, 164-166, 168, 171, 175, 241, 320, 322

Copyright
On-line copyright, 207, 213

Council for Trade in Goods, 58 (footnotes)

Council for Trade-related Aspects of Intellectual Property Rights, 58 (footnotes)

Council for Trade in Services, 58 (footnotes)

Countervailing
Countervailing duty, 49

Customs
Customs valuation, 29, 66-67

Discrimination, 28, 63, 160

Dispute settlement
Dispute Settlement Body (DSB), 47, 124-127, 133, 142-144, 146-147, 297-299, 327
Dispute settlement mechanism, 12, 46, 51, 97, 100, 117, 123-128, 132-134, 138, 140, 142-145, 158, 298-299, 323, 327-328
Dispute settlement procedures, 124-125, 127, 142, 297, 330
Dispute Settlement Understanding (DSU), 124, 142-144, 297, 299, 327

Enforcement, 33, 37, 44, 46, 48-49, 70, 73, 77, 83, 85, 86, 100, 103-104, 107-108, 110, 135, 142, 159, 167, 170-171, 176, 198, 211, 221, 258, 262, 269-287, 295-330

Equity joint venture(s) (EJV), 75, 81, 160, 164-165, 175, 241, 320

European Commission, 136-137

European Union (EU), 7, 11, 19, 49, 78, 132-137, 141, 168, 213, 237, 241, 260

Foreign Direct Investment (FDI), 164

Foreign Exchange (Forex), 35-36, 61-64, 80-81, 84, 159, 164, 168-170, 175-176

Foreign Invested Enterprise (FIE), 63, 65, 75, 77, 81, 160-166, 168-176

General Agreement on Tariffs and Trade (GATT), 3-7, 9-10, 13-14, 17, 27, 34, 36, 64-66, 68, 98-99, 107-108, 159, 189, 296-297, 303-304, 308-309, 323, 330

General Agreement on Trade in Services (GATS), 71, 98, 108, 110, 158, 160, 170, 235-236, 238

Government procurement, 34, 37, 75, 183-200

Industrial policy, 33, 68, 163, 171, 242

Information technology (IT), 251, 262

Infringement, 70, 83, 85, 212, 215, 219, 221, 270-272, 275-283, 285-287

Intellectual Property Rights (IPRs), 28, 36-37, 40, 61, 65, 69, 70, 77, 81-84, 98, 159, 161, 209, 211-212, 218, 269-287, 300, 318, 326

Interconnection, 31, 235-236, 239-240, 260

International Centre for Settlement of Investment Disputes (ICSID), 144, 307, 328-329

International Monetary Fund (IMF), 9, 41-42, 64, 170

Internet
Internet regulation, 251-263
Internet Service Providers (ISP), 208, 216-217, 220-221, 253, 255-258, 261

Joint Venture(s)
  Contractual joint ventures (*see*
    under contractual)
  Equity joint venture(s) (*see* under
    equity)
Judicial independence, 79, 86, 101-102,
  106-107, 110, 171, 274
Judicial review, 17, 68, 73, 80, 83, 99,
  107-108, 110-111, 171, 187, 196,
  198, 274, 320, 325-326

Labour standards, 309
Legal culture, 301
License(s), 31, 33-34, 36, 66, 68, 75, 77-
  78, 163, 219, 220, 222, 234, 236, 238-
  239, 242, 254, 255

Memorandum of Understanding
  (MOU), 32-33, 40, 82, 278, 286, 300,
  318
Merger and Acquisition (M & A), 166
Ministry of Foreign Trade and
  Economic Cooperation
  (MOFTEC), 33, 35, 38, 67, 74, 77,
  122, 138-139, 160, 166, 174, 271
Most-favoured nation (MFN), 11-12,
  122, 160, 211, 237
Multilateral negotiation, 7, 296
Multilateral Trade Agreements, 122-
  123, 158

National People's Congress (NPC)
  National People's Congress
    Standing Committee (NPC
    Standing Committee), 7, 39, 41, 71,
    74-75, 104, 109, 161, 171, 186, 188,
    213, 233, 255, 275, 304, 311-315,
    317-321, 324
  National Treatment, 19, 31-32, 35, 72,
    108, 159-160, 173, 199, 211, 304,
    309-310

Open Door policy, 3, 7-9, 13-14, 37, 45-
  46, 295, 307

Panel
  Panel report(s), 124-125, 297
Patent, 36, 40, 75, 82, 136, 270, 272-278,
  300, 319-320
Performance requirements, 35-36, 159,
  169-170
Product-specific safeguards, 48-49, 146
Protocol
  Protocol on the Accession of the
    People's Republic of China
    (Accession Protocol), 7, 18-19, 28,
    36, 38, 47-49, 61, 64-66, 68-74, 80,
    82, 85, 107-108, 146-147, 158, 168-
    171, 260, 296, 318, 320, 322

Recommendations, 6, 47, 69, 125, 142,
  298
Rule of law, 43-45, 61, 71, 301, 306
Rule of man (Ren zhi), 43, 301
Rules of origin, 66-67

Safeguard(s)
  Product-specific safeguards, 48-49,
    146
  Safeguard measures, 48, 77, 139-140,
    254, 298
Sanitary and phytosanitary (SPS)
  Sanitary and phytosanitary
    measures, 68-69, 77, 81
Schedule(s), 6, 66, 70-71, 81, 159, 170,
  296, 309
Single package, 297
Sino-US Agreement, 12, 28-29, 34, 50,
  66, 74, 82, 162, 171, 236, 237, 306
Special Economic Zones (SEZs), 72,
  161, 163-164, 170, 173-174, 186,
  192, 312-313, 324

State-owned enterprise(s) (SOEs), 13,
    37-38, 62, 65, 81, 166, 190, 197, 198
Subsidies, 34, 49, 67-68, 76, 160
Supreme People's Court (SPC), 40-41,
    79-80, 85, 104, 213, 272-273, 276-
    278, 284, 313
Suspension, 125, 138

Taiwan Straits, 117, 123
Tariffs, 9, 28-29, 66, 68, 73, 80, 135, 138-
    140, 164, 171, 261
Technical barriers, 68, 77
Telecommunications
    Telecommunications services, 31,
        137, 163, 172-173, 234-235, 238-243,
        252, 254, 322
Terms of reference, 125
Textile(s), 12, 15, 28, 134-135, 141, 296
Tokyo Round, 189, 296-297
Trade Policy Review Mechanism
    (TPRM), 47
Trade Act of 1974, 12
Trademark(s), 75, 79, 82-83, 85, 110,
    270-272, 275, 277, 280-282, 284-285,
    300, 320
Trade Representative, 133
Trade-related Aspects of Intellectual
    Property Rights (TRIPS), 17, 269-
    270
Trade-related Aspects of Investment
    Measures (TRIMS), 36, 65, 68, 81,
    158
Transparency, 13-14, 19, 28, 34-35, 73,
    80, 84-85, 99, 101, 104, 170, 176,
    188, 194-195, 303-304
Treaty, treaties, 39-40, 74, 82, 100, 110,
    119, 133, 143, 161, 197, 207, 211-
    212, 218-220, 270, 295-296, 298,
    300-301, 303, 306-307, 314-319, 323-
    329

Unilateral, 11, 49, 135, 138, 141-143, 146,
    297, 298
Uruguay
    Uruguay Round, 5-6, 158, 189, 296

Value-added tax, 30, 164, 174
Value-added telecommunications
    services (VATS), 234, 237-238, 242

Wholly Foreign-Invested Enterprise(s)
    (WFIE), 75, 81, 162, 164-166, 168,
    171-172, 175-176
World Intellectual Property
    Organization (WIPO), 9, 207, 211,
    218-219, 222, 300
World Bank, 9, 41-42, 185
WTO
    WTO Agreement(s), 243, 298
    WTO Member(s), 7-10, 14-15, 46, 49,
        132, 146, 235-238